DATE DUE

THE ORGANIZATIONAL FRONTIERS SERIES

The Organizational Frontiers Series is sponsored by the Society for Industrial and Organizational Psychology (SIOP). Launched in 1983 to make scientific contributions to the field, the series has attempted to publish books that are on the cutting edge of theory, research, and theory-driven practice in industrial/organizational psychology and related organizational science disciplines.

Our overall objective is to inform and to stimulate research for SIOP members (students, practitioners, and researchers) and people in related disciplines, including the other subdisciplines of psychology, organizational behavior, human resource management, and labor and industrial relations. The volumes in the Organizational Frontiers Series have the following goals:

1. Focus on research and theory in organizational science, and the implications for practice
2. Inform readers of significant advances in theory and research in psychology and related disciplines that are relevant to our research and practice
3. Challenge the research and practice community to develop and adapt new ideas and to conduct research on these developments
4. Promote the use of scientific knowledge in the solution of public policy issues and increased organizational effectiveness

The volumes originated in the hope that they would facilitate continuous learning and a continuing research curiosity about organizational phenomena on the part of both scientists and practitioners.

Previous Frontiers Series volumes, all published by Jossey-Bass, include:

Personality and Work

Reconsidering the Role of Personality in Organizations

Murray R. Barrick

Ann Marie Ryan

Editors

Foreword by Neal Schmitt

JOSSEY-BASS
A Wiley Imprint
www.josseybass.com

Jossey-Bass books and products are available through most bookstores. To contact
Jossey-Bass directly call our Customer Care Department within the U.S. at 800-956-7739,
outside the U.S. at 317-572-3986 or fax 317-572-4002.

Jossey-Bass also publishes its books in a variety of electronic formats. Some content that
appears in print may not be available in electronic books.

Library of Congress Cataloging-in-Publication Data

Personality and work : reconsidering the role of personality in organizations /
Murray R. Barrick, Ann Marie Ryan, editors; foreword by Neil Schmitt.
     p.   cm.—(The organizational frontiers series)
Includes bibliographical references and index.
  ISBN 0-7879-6037-3 (alk. paper)
 1. Personality and occupation.   2. Job satisfaction.   3. Achievement
motivation.   4. Employees—Attitudes.   5. Corporate culture.
I. Barrick, Murray R.   II. Ryan, Ann Marie.   III. Series.
  BF698.9.03P47   2003
  158.7—dc21

                                2002155903

Printed in the United States of America
FIRST EDITION
HB Printing 10 9 8 7 6 5 4 3 2

Contents

Foreword

This is the nineteenth book in a series initiated by the Society for Industrial and Organizational Psychology in 1983 (SIOP) and published by Jossey-Bass. Originally published as the Frontiers Series, the SIOP Executive Committee voted in 2000 to change the name of the series to Organizational Frontiers Series in order to enhance the identity and visibility of the series. The purpose of the publication of series volumes in a general sense was to promote the scientific status of the field. Ray Katzell first edited the series, and Irwin Goldstein and Sheldon Zedeck followed him.

The editorial board chooses the topics of the volumes and the volume editors. The series editor and the editorial board then work with the volume editor in planning the volume and, occasionally, in suggesting and selecting chapter authors and content. During the writing of the volume, the series editor often works with the editor and the publisher to bring the manuscript to completion.

The success of the series is evident in the high number of sales (now over forty-five thousand). Volumes have received excellent reviews, and individual chapters as well as volumes have been cited frequently. A recent symposium at the SIOP annual meeting examined the impact of the series on research and theory in industrial/organizational (I/O) psychology. Although such influence is difficult to track and volumes have varied in intent and perceived centrality to the discipline, the conclusion of most participants was that the volumes have exerted a significant impact on research and theory in the field and are regarded as being representative of the best the field has to offer.

Another purpose of the series was to bring scientific research from other disciplines to bear on problems of interest to I/O psychologists. This volume, edited by Murray Barrick and Ann Marie Ryan, provides an in-depth examination of the role of personality in work behavior. Research on the nature of personality and the role of dispositional constructs in explaining a variety of work behavior exploded in the early 1990s. The renewed interest in this area began with the meta-analytic demonstration by Barrick and Mount (1991) that there are generalizable relationships between some personality constructs and work performance and the growing consensus among many personality researchers (Digman, 1990) that the myriad of personality measures and empirical studies on the structure of personality suggested that five major personality constructs represent the personality domain well. This book provides a review of some of this research and then goes well beyond a reexamination of these issues to explore the process by which personality exerts its influence on work outcomes. Also considered is a much wider array of work behavior (including contextual performance, counterproductive behavior, retaliatory behavior, retention, and learning) than simply performance of one's assigned work role. This book brings together basic personality researchers and those interested in applications of personality in the work context, one of the major goals of the series since its inception.

In Chapter One, Saucier and Goldberg provide a definition of personality, examine evidence on the structure of personality attributes, and raise issues about the adequacy of the Big Five model on several important criteria. Lucas and Diener next explore the evidence for, and the importance of, happiness variables (or satisfaction, to use a more common term in the I/O literature) as functional determinants of the choices people make and the behaviors in which they engage. They provide the quite reasonable, but rarely explored, hypothesis that the role of happiness in explaining worker behavior and productivity is dependent on the behaviors that are important and examined. Chapter Three, by Barrick, Mitchell, and Stewart, also reflects the theme that situational and motivational variables influence the relationship between personality and work behavior. Chapters Four (by Johnson), Five (by Weiss and Kurek), and Six (by Cullen and Sackett) explore in detail aspects of the process model of the personality-performance relationship. In Chapter Seven, Stewart makes a strong case that personality–work behavior relationships can be understood only by examining cross-level (individual, team, organization) effects.

Day and Kilduff consider similar issues in Chapter Eight and also point to the role of an individual's skill in monitoring and managing relationships in groups and organizations. In Chapter Nine, Ford and Oswald examine the evidence for and potential benefits of a consideration of dispositional determinants of learning and training performance, as well as the successful transfer of training to one's work situation. Chapter Ten by Ryan and Kristof-Brown considers the nature and importance of the fit between individuals and the organization in which they work. The last two chapters, by Hough and by Mount, Barrick, and Ryan, are consistent with the major message of this book: that models of personality-performance relationships must go well beyond the consideration of bivariate relationships. The challenge that these more complex models present for scientist and practitioner alike should provide an exciting and stimulating research venue for many years to come.

Our target audiences include graduate students in I/O psychology and organizational behavior, as well as doctoral-level researchers and practitioners who want to gain knowledge on the most up-to-date data and theory regarding the important role of personality in determining a variety of work behaviors as well as the reasons that these relationships exist (or do not exist) in various situations. Many of the topics and issues discussed in this book will be novel to many I/O psychologists and human resource practitioners. We have certainly read about personality, but there has not been a similar focus on understanding the mechanisms involved in personality-behavior relationships or the complex interplay of individual differences, situations, and outcomes. To the degree that this book fosters investigation of richer and more complex models of these relationships and stimulates interest among other I/O researchers and practitioners and a collaboration with researchers in other disciplines, it will advance our discipline and contribute to the goals of the Organizational Frontiers series.

The chapter authors deserve our gratitude for pursuing the goal of clearly communicating the nature, application, and implications of the theory and research described in this book. Production of a book such as this involves the hard work and cooperative effort of many individuals. The chapter authors and the editorial board played important roles in this endeavor. Because all royalties from the series volumes are used to help support SIOP financially, none of them received any remuneration. They deserve our appreciation for engaging in a difficult task for the sole purpose of furthering our understanding of organizational science.

We also express our sincere gratitude to Cedric Crocker, Julianna Gustafson, Matt Davis, and the entire staff at Jossey-Bass. Over many years and several volumes, they have provided support during the planning, development, and production of the series.

January 2003   Neal Schmitt
                                                        Michigan State University
                                                        Series Editor, 1998–2003

References

Barrick, M. R., & Mount, M. K. (1991). The Big Five personality dimensions in job performance: A meta-analysis. *Personnel Psychology, 44,* 1–26.

Digman, J. M. (1990). Personality structure: Emergence of the five factor model. *Annual Review of Psychology, 41,* 417–440.

Preface

The idea for this book is based on the notion that we all have personalities, and those personalities affect our behavior at work. Today, this proposition is widely accepted by psychologists, managers, and employees. For this reason, there is considerable interest in the field of industrial/organizational (I/O) psychology on the topic of personality and its influence at work. In fact, it is difficult to pick up a current research journal in human resources, organizational behavior, I/O psychology, or the general area of management without finding at least one article dealing with personality at work.

Such interest in noncognitive individual differences is a healthy sign that increased knowledge will be gained by bringing together a variety of theoretical perspectives for understanding personality in work settings. It is our belief that a thorough knowledge of personality as it affects organizational processes and outcomes requires addressing several important questions. First, what is personality, and how is it assessed? Second, how does personality affect various outcomes and behaviors? And third, what is the relationship between personality and behavior in specific work settings? For example, what is the role of personality in person-organization fit and person-job fit? What are the effects of personality in work teams?

In this book, some of the foremost scholars in the field address these questions. Across all chapters, the authors present theoretical perspectives, introduce models or frameworks, integrate and synthesize prior studies, and in myriad other ways make proposals that should stimulate future research and practice. We have been delighted with the contributions by the authors of these chapters. We particularly thank them for their thought-provoking work. We believe that these chapters will serve as influential research-oriented guides to the next wave of research on personality and work.

Acknowledgments

We express our sincere appreciation to all those who have contributed to the realization of this book. Most important, we thank the chapter authors. We were extraordinarily fortunate to have a number of highly influential researchers in the field with a wide range of expertise and interests willing to enlist in this effort. We were delighted with their contributions. We are also greatly indebted to Marcy Schaefer for her valuable assistance in preparing the manuscript for publication. We extend our thanks to Neal Schmitt, the Organizational Frontiers Series editor, and the entire Frontiers editorial board for comments and suggestions on our proposal for this book. Finally, we thank our families—Sarah, Courtney, and Jennifer; Brian, Marilyn, and Clare—for their continuing support and encouragement throughout this project.

January 2003   MURRAY R. BARRICK
                                                  Iowa City, Iowa

                                                  ANN MARIE RYAN
                                                  East Lansing, Michigan

The Contributors

Murray R. Barrick is the Stanley M. Howe Leadership Chair at the Tippie College of Business, University of Iowa. His research has been published in the *Journal of Applied Psychology, Personnel Psychology,* and *Organizational Behavior and Human Decision Processes,* among others. He was recognized by the Academy of Management with the Outstanding Published Paper Award in 1992 by the Scholarly Achievement Award Committee of the Personnel/Human Resources Division, and in 2001, he was the recipient of the Owens Scholarly Achievement Award. In 1997, he was elected a fellow of the Society of Industrial and Organizational Psychologists in the American Psychological Association. He also serves on the editorial boards of the *Journal of Applied Psychology* and *Personnel Psychology* and has served on the editorial board of the *Journal of Management.* He received his Ph.D. from the University of Akron in industrial/organizational psychology.

Ann Marie Ryan is a professor of industrial/organizational psychology at Michigan State University. Her research interests are in the areas of fairness and employment selection and recruitment procedures, and selection tools, and she has published widely in these areas. She is president of Division 14 of the American Psychological Association, the Society for Industrial and Organizational Psychology, and is editor of *Personnel Psychology.* She received her Ph.D. from the University of Illinois at Chicago.

Michael J. Cullen is completing his doctoral studies in industrial/organizational psychology at the University of Minnesota-Twin Cities. His interests are training, personality, and selection issues related to reducing counterproductivity in the workforce. He has coauthored a book chapter on integrity testing for the I/O volume of the *Comprehensive Handbook of Psychological Assessment* and has presented his research at annual conferences of the American Psychological Association and the Society for Industrial and Organizational Psychology. He obtained a B.A. from Princeton University and a J.D. from the University of Toronto Law School.

David V. Day is a professor of psychology at Penn State University and a fellow of the Society for Industrial and Organizational Psychology. His academic research interests are mainly in the areas of personality influences in organizations, as well as leadership and leadership development. He has published more than forty journal articles and book chapters, many pertaining to the topic of personality. He serves on the editorial board of the *Journal of Management* and is an associate editor of *Leadership Quarterly*. He received his Ph.D. in industrial/organizational psychology from the University of Akron.

Ed Diener is Alumni Professor of Psychology at the University of Illinois. He is past president of the International Society of Quality of Life Studies and the Society of Personality and Social Psychology (and Division 8 of the American Psychological Association) and editor of the *Journal of Personality and Social Psychology* and the *Journal of Happiness Studies*. He recently won the Distinguished Researcher Award from the International Society of Quality of Life Studies and a Distinguished Alumni Award from California State University at Fresno. He received his Ph.D. from the University of Washington in Seattle.

J. Kevin Ford is a professor of psychology at Michigan State University. His major research interests involve improving training effectiveness through efforts to advance our understanding of training needs assessment, design, evaluation, and transfer. He also concentrates on building continuous learning and improvement orientations within organizations. He has published widely and serves on the editorial board of *Human Performance*. He was the lead editor of the book *Improving Training Effectiveness in Work Organizations* and is coauthor with Irwin Goldstein on the fourth edition of *Training in Organizations*. He is a fellow of the American Psychological Association and the Society for Industrial and Organizational Psychology. He received his Ph.D. in psychology from Ohio State University.

Lewis R. Goldberg is a senior scientist at the Oregon Research Institute and an emeritus professor of psychology at the University of Oregon. He has been a Fulbright professor at the University of Nijmegen in the Netherlands and at Istanbul University in Turkey. He is a past president of the Society of Multivariate Experimental Psychology and has served on the editorial boards of the *Annual Review of Psychology* and over a dozen other psychological journals. His contributions to the scientific literature in personality and psychological assessment have been published widely. He received his Ph.D. from the University of Michigan.

Leaetta M. Hough, president of Dunnette Group, is an internationally recognized expert in the design and implementation of human resource management systems. She is also an expert in the development and use of personality inventories in work settings. Her work with personality variables during the 1980s was instrumental in reviving personality variables as respectable and highly useful individual difference variables for understanding and predicting behavior in the workplace. She is coeditor of the four-volume *Handbook of Industrial and Organizational Psychology* and senior author of the personnel selection chapter of the *Annual Review of Psychology* (2000) and the personality chapters in the *Comprehensive Handbook of Psychology* and *Handbook of Industrial, Work and Organizational Psychology*. She is a fellow of the American Psychological Society, the American Psychological Association, as well as its divisions 5 (Evaluation, Measurement, and Statistics) and 14 (Society for Industrial and Organizational Psychology). She received her Ph.D. from the University of Minnesota.

Jeff W. Johnson is a research scientist at Personnel Decisions Research Institutes, where he has directed and carried out many applied organizational research projects for government and private sector clients. He has conducted job and occupational analyses, designed assessment and personnel selection systems, designed performance evaluation systems, conducted validation studies, and assisted clients in the implementation of human resource systems.

His primary research interests are in the areas of personnel selection, performance measurement, research methods, and statistics. He has published in a variety of journals and is on the editorial board of *Personnel Psychology*. He received his Ph.D. in industrial/organizational psychology from the University of Minnesota.

Martin Kilduff is a professor of organizational behavior at Smeal College of Business Administration, Pennsylvania State University, University Park. His research focuses on how individuals help create the worlds that constrain and enable their behaviors. He is currently writing a book with Winpin Tsai on social networks and organizations and has published widely in journals. He received his Ph.D. in organizational behavior from Cornell University.

Amy Kristof-Brown is an assistant professor of management and organizations at the Henry B. Tippie College of Business, University of Iowa. She was recently appointed a Henry B. Tippie Research Fellow. Her research interests center around the compatibility or fit between individuals and their work environments, particularly as it influences the organizational selection process. She also investigates the role of applicant impression management on interview outcomes. She has published and presented several papers on these topics, including articles in *Journal of Applied Psychology, Personnel Psychology, Journal of Management, Journal of Vocational Behavior,* and *Human Resource Planning*. She received her Ph.D. in organizational behavior and human resource management from the University of Maryland.

Katherine E. Kurek is a doctoral student in industrial/organizational psychology at Purdue University and a research assistant at the Military Family Research Institute at Purdue. Her research interests include emotions in the workplace, job attitudes, and the influence of religion at work. She received her B.A. from Butler University, Indianapolis, Indiana.

Richard E. Lucas is an assistant professor in the Department of Psychology at Michigan State University. His research interests lie in the areas of personality and subjective well-being, and he has published a number of papers investigating these topics. Most recently, he has focused on examining the affective underpinnings of the extraversion personality dimension. He received his Ph.D. in personality psychology from the University of Illinois at Urbana-Champaign.

Terence R. Mitchell is Edward E. Carlson Professor of Business Administration and professor of psychology at the University of Washington. He has published over one hundred articles on the topics of decision making, leadership, motivation, and turnover. He is coauthor (with J. Larson) of *People in Organizations* and a joint author (with Phillip Birnbaum and William G. Scott) of *Organization Theory: A Structural and Behavioral Analysis*. Mitchell is a fellow of the American Psychological Association, the Society for Industrial/ Organizational Psychology (SIOP), and the American Academy of Management and received the SIOP Distinguished Scientific Contribution award in 1998. He received his Ph.D. from the University of Illinois.

Michael K. Mount is the Henry B. Tippie Professor of Human Resource Management in the Department of Management and Organizations at the University of Iowa. He has published numerous journal articles, book chapters, and convention papers on a variety of human resource management topics. His current research interests fall into two broad categories. The first examines the processes by which Five-Factor Model personality dimensions relate to job performance. The second examines the psychometric properties of multirater feedback ratings and how such ratings relate to organizational outcomes. He is a fellow in the Society for Industrial/Organizational Psychology and the American Psychological Association. He received his Ph.D. from Iowa State University in industrial/organizational psychology.

Frederick L. Oswald is an assistant professor in industrial/organizational psychology at Michigan State University. His research covers individual differences within ability, motivation, and personality domains as they relate to modeling and predicting performance criteria; methodology, particularly meta-analysis, with computer simulation work informing researchers and practitioners on how to interpret meta-analyses in organizational research; person-job fit applications in the context of the O*NET occupational database;

and Web-based testing in psychological research and personnel selection settings. He received his Ph.D. in psychology from the University of Minnesota.

Paul R. Sackett is a professor of psychology at the University of Minnesota. He has served as the editor of *Personnel Psychology*, president of the Society for Industrial and Organizational Psychology, cochair of the Joint Committee on the Standards for Educational and Psychological Testing, a member of the National Research Council's Board on Testing and Assessment, chair of American Psychological Association's Committee on Psychological Tests and Assessments and its Board of Scientific Affairs. His research interests revolve around psychological testing and assessment in workplace settings. He received his Ph.D. in industrial/organizational psychology from Ohio State University.

Gerard Saucier is associate professor in the Department of Psychology at the University of Oregon. He serves as associate editor of the *Journal of Research in Personality* and is on the editorial board of three other personality journals. He was the 1999 recipient of the Cattell Award for outstanding early career contributions from the Society of Multivariate Experimental Psychology. He has written extensively about issues related to personality measurement, the structure of personality attributes, and the representation of these attributes in language, and he carries out research on the structure of ideological beliefs and social attitudes. He received his Ph.D. from the University of Oregon.

Greg L. Stewart is an associate professor of management at the University of Iowa. His areas of expertise include organizational behavior and human resource management. He has published numerous articles related to organizational staffing, including an emphasis on understanding how employee personality traits affect performance. He also conducts research related to self-managing work teams and team leadership. His research articles have appeared in leading academic journals, including *Journal of Applied Psychology, Personnel Psychology, Academy of Management Journal, Organization Science,* and *Human Relations.* He earned his Ph.D. at Arizona State University.

Howard M. Weiss is professor of psychological sciences at Purdue University and codirector of the Military Family Research Institute at Purdue, an institute dedicated to conducting research on the relationships between quality of life and job satisfaction, retention, and work performance. His research interests focus on emotions in the workplace and job attitudes. His most recent publications are related to his theoretical framework, affective events theory. He received his Ph.D. in industrial/organizational psychology from New York University

Personality and Work

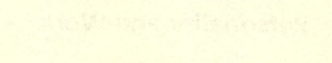

CHAPTER 1

The Structure of Personality Attributes

Gerard Saucier
Lewis R. Goldberg

In a classic early textbook, Allport (1937) reviewed definitions of the concept of personality. He called it "one of the most abstract words in our language" (p. 25) and discussed its broad connotations. Allport catalogued fifty distinct meanings—some from literary, theological, philosophical, juristic, and sociological traditions and others stressing external appearance or psychological constructs. The definition he proposed—"personality is the dynamic organization within the individual of those psychophysical systems that determine his unique adjustments to his environment" (p. 48)—was a synthesis of several psychological meanings of the concept.

Funder (2001) provided a more down-to-earth rendition: "an individual's characteristic patterns of thought, emotion, and behavior, together with the psychological mechanisms—hidden or not—behind those patterns" (p. 2). Few could argue that what Funder refers to is not personality; it is reasonably close to a consensual

Work on this chapter was supported by Grant MH-49227 from the National Institute of Mental Health, U.S. Public Health Service. For useful feedback on an earlier version of this chapter, we are grateful to Bob Altemeyer, Michael Ashton, Kimberley Barchard, Murray Barrick, Matthias Burisch, Roy D'Andrade, Ian J. Deary, Lisa Di Blas, David Funder, Richard Grucza, Gordon Hall, Robert Hogan, John A. Johnson, Boris Mlačić, Lawrence Pervin, Ralph Piedmont, Ann M. Ryan, Paul Slovic, and Harry Triandis.

view. It refers simultaneously to characteristics that are (1) ascribed to individuals, (2) stable over time, and (3) psychological in nature. Yet it also acknowledges that mechanisms explaining these traits may be difficult to isolate and measure.

Definitions make one's assumptions explicit, so how one defines personality is quite consequential: it affects how one selects variables when studying personality phenomena. What if one were to rely on some of the philosophical definitions of personality reviewed by Allport (1937), such as "the quality in every man which makes him worthwhile" (Adler, 1929, p. 8), "individuality which has become objective to itself" (Windelband, 1921, p. 281), or "selfhood" (Crutcher, 1931, p. 75)? With such definitions, one would hardly care to study the individual's actual behaviors at all.

But Allport's definition (1937) also highlights attributes that are seen as residing within the individual. Other ways of defining personality emphasize more external types of attributes, such as the role one assumes or the status one has achieved in society, one's external appearance (including personal attractiveness), and the reactions of others to the individual as a stimulus—that is, the person's social stimulus value (see MacKinnon, 1944). In work settings, of course, appearances are important. Moreover, Triandis (2001) suggests that in collectivist cultures, external factors are considered more important to personality than are the internal traits emphasized in individualist cultures.

Individual differences in externally defined attributes may be interwoven with individual differences in temperamental traits. Consider terms like *magnetic, charming, powerful,* and *likeable,* which seem to be partly internal and partly responses to the individual. Later in the chapter, we explore some structural models for personality that include such attributes.

Parsimony in Personality Models

Scale labels in personality inventories have a bewildering variety of constructs. And if one turns to single words potentially referring to personality attributes in modern languages, the situation becomes overwhelming. Allport and Odbert (1936), for example, catalogued nearly eighteen thousand words from *Webster's Second International Dictionary* referring to characteristics that might be used to distinguish one human being from another. In follow-up work, Norman (1967) judged that over thirty-five hundred of these terms refer to stable personality traits. Clearly, no single comprehensive model can capture all possible personality attributes. We must economize and reduce, seeking a more parsimonious summary of this vast domain of concepts.

In the field of biology, taxonomies have helped in organizing a huge number of species into a single framework indicating how each is related to the others. Correspondingly, in the field of personality, there has been a rising wave of interest in the search for a scientifically compelling taxonomy of the huge number of personality attributes. A taxonomy is a systematic division of phenomena into ordered groups or categories; in other words, it is a way of "chunking" things. A scientific taxonomy helps organize and integrate knowledge and research findings by providing a standard scientific nomenclature. Such a nomenclature facilitates communication among investigators and aids in the accumulation of empirical findings. Identifying a widely useful taxonomy of personality attributes is one of the most important goals of basic research in personality.

A central question in taxonomy construction concerns the procedures to be used to divide or group the phenomena under study. A variety of approaches might be employed, but the most useful is a class of statistical methods generically referred to as factor analysis. As Goldberg and Digman (1994) noted, factor analysis can be considered a variable-reduction procedure in which many variables are organized by a few factors that summarize the interrelations among the variables. These factors can be thought of as summary constructs, or as higher-level dimensions in a hierarchical model of the variables in the domain.

Anyone seeking to employ factor analysis must first make a crucial determination: which variables to include in the analysis. If some theory were available—one that was formulated clearly enough to specify the particular variables that should be measured—an investigator might rely on that theory for variable selection, as several investigators have proposed (Cloninger, 1987; Eysenck, 1991). This could lead to an advantageous linking of the taxonomic model with a scientific theory. Even failures to verify the model in empirical studies could lead to important advances in the development of the theory. However, the theory might omit some significant summary constructs that a more empirical approach might reveal.

Alternatively, one could take a strictly practical approach. One could build up a taxonomic model incrementally by developing successively more and more measures, each constructed to predict some important human outcome. This is the approach that Gough (1996) espoused in developing the California Psychological Inventory (CPI). Although Gough did not initially aspire to create a comprehensive taxonomy, analyses of the interrelations among the CPI scales eventually led him to develop some summary dimensions to encompass them. The measures developed by this practical approach typically have empirical strengths, but they are not theoretically organized and may omit important constructs that no one happened to think of investigating.

Yet another incremental approach to variable selection relies on an investigator's initial judgments of the most important variables to measure, later adding measures of other variables that empirically turn out to be relatively independent of those initially selected. Comrey (1988) used this approach to variable selection in the development of the Comrey Personality Scales, as did Tellegen (in press) in the development of his Multidimensional Personality Questionnaire (MPQ). If many investigators adopted this approach and they all ended up measuring the same constructs, those variables would have some privileged status in models of personality structure.

Unfortunately, this has not occurred. Despite the long tradition of packaging structural models into multiscale personality inventories, until recently there was little agreement among them on the most important variables of personality, and consequently none of them had become widely accepted as a comprehensive taxonomy of personality attributes. There are several reasons for this. First, research on each inventory has operated independent of that on other inventories, with little comparison or integration (Goldberg, in press). Second, inventories tend to become fixed in form at an early stage, with rare revisions to reflect new developments in theory or measurement; revisions may be scientifically desirable but problematic from a commercial standpoint (Goldberg, 1999). And perhaps most important, the rationale for variable selection in these inventories, although reasonable in one way or another, has not been particularly powerful.

The Basis for the Lexical Approach

Is there a more compelling rationale for personality variable selection? As has long been recognized (Allport, 1937; Cattell, 1943; Goldberg, 1981; Norman, 1963), some of the most basic personality attributes might be discovered from studying conceptions implicit in the use of the natural language. If a distinction is highly represented in the lexicon, it can be presumed to have practical importance. Personality concepts salient in the lexicon should not be left out of a taxonomy of personality attributes (Tellegen, 1993). That is, folk concepts of personality provide basic but not exhaustive (necessary but not sufficient) components for a science of personality attributes (Goldberg & Saucier, 1995).

This leads us to a key premise of the lexical approach to taxonomy construction: *the degree of representation of an attribute in language has some correspondence with the general importance of the attribute in real-world transactions.* Imagine an attribute for which there is, within one language, a dense cluster of loosely synonymous terms; such an attribute would certainly have a claim to importance, at least with respect to the language community within which it is so richly represented (Zipf, 1949). An attribute that is represented by multiple terms in a language will likely appear as a factor in multivariate analyses. Moreover, if the factor includes terms that are used with high frequency, the importance of the factor is underscored. Factors derived from studies of natural language personality descriptors in different languages provide a superb starting point for a taxonomy of personality attributes, particularly if widely diverse languages are studied. These factors are but a starting point because the lexicon could omit or underemphasize some scientifically important variables, and the meaning of single natural language terms can be vague, ambiguous, or context dependent (John, Angleitner, & Ostendorf, 1988). We can assume, however, that attributes richly represented in the lexicon are there for a reason.

Cross-cultural generalizability is a valuable criterion for adjudicating among competitor taxonomic structures. Psychology is the study of mind and behavior of humans in general, not just of humans in a narrow range of sociocultural settings. Structural models derived within one limited population, or a limited sample from that population, are prone to reflect the unique patternings found within that population or sample. Culture-specific patternings may be interesting in their own way, but models that transfer well across populations, and thus across languages and sociocultural settings, are more congruent with the scientific ideals of replicability and generalizability.

If we take cross-cultural generalizability as a criterion for a good taxonomic structure, we can apply this criterion in a lenient or a stringent way. The lenient way is to export a set of variables (most often, those represented in a single personality inventory) for use in other populations and then examine whether these pre-selected variables (after translation, if necessary) generate the same factor structure in each new language or culture. If the scales in a personality inventory generate similar factors across populations, one might argue that the structure is widely general-izable, as McCrae and Costa (1997) have done with respect to their revised NEO Personality Inventory (Costa & McCrae, 1992). However, this is not a very demanding test. It is not sufficient to show that when personality measures in a new language are made to conform to the procrustean specifications of one model, that model can be recovered. There may be a large number of possi-ble models that are equally exportable and maintain their factor structures across many populations.

A more challenging test of generalizability is to identify the most salient and important personality concepts within each lin-guistic and cultural context, derive an indigenous factor structure from those variables, and then examine the extent to which this new structure corresponds to any previously proposed models. A model that could meet this test in any language would have great psychological import; it could be considered far more ubiquitous and universal than a structure that simply met the less demanding imposed test (that is, showed a high degree of translatability).

The lexical approach involves such an indigenous research strategy. Analyses are carried out separately within each language, using a representative set of native language descriptors, rather than importing selections of variables from other languages (for example, English). The hope is that the findings from these lexi-cal studies will converge on a replicable pattern such that most lan-guages will reflect its imprint. An analogous, and possibly universal, pattern has been identified in studies of color words across lexi-cons (Kay & McDaniel, 1978), corresponding to the genetics and neurobiology of color perception.

What We Learn from Natural Language Personality Descriptions

The majority of lexical studies of personality descriptors have sought to test the most widely influential personality model of the past two decades: the Big Five factor structure (Goldberg, 1990, 1993b; John, 1990). The Big Five factors are customarily labeled Extraversion, Agreeableness, Conscientiousness, Emotional Stability (or its opposite, Neuroticism), and Intellect (or, in one inventory representation, Openness to Experience). There were signs of the Big Five structure in some studies from an earlier era (as detailed by Digman, 1990; Goldberg, 1993b; John, 1990), but its identification in studies of natural language descriptors in English (Goldberg, 1990) was decisive.

If we value cross-cultural generalizability, however, applicability to one language is not enough. As detailed in more lengthy reviews (Saucier & Goldberg, 2001; Saucier, Hampson, & Goldberg, 2000), lexical studies have yielded structures resembling the Big Five most consistently in languages originating in northern Europe, including German (Ostendorf, 1990) and Polish (Szarota, 1996), as well as English. Although a study in Turkish (Goldberg & Somer, 2000) also found a structure with much resemblance to the Big Five, studies of other non–Northern European languages (Church, Katigbak, & Reyes, 1998; Church, Reyes, Katigbak, & Grimm, 1997; Di Blas & Forzi, 1998; Szirmák & De Raad, 1994) have led to results that are less clearly supportive. And because a majority of studies have relied exclusively on self-report, the degree of generality of the Big Five in peer ratings is less certain than for self-ratings.

To this point, lexical studies have revealed a great deal about the relative robustness of the Big Five, as well as information about other less well-known candidate models, including some with fewer and some with more factors. We examine the most consistent findings from lexical studies to date by describing models with successively more factors.

What If We Allowed Ourselves Only One Factor?

Several lexical studies have reported evidence about factor solutions containing only one factor (Boies, Lee, Ashton, Pascal, & Nicol, 2001; Di Blas & Forzi, 1999; Goldberg & Somer, 2000;

Saucier, 1997). The findings from these studies have been quite consistent. The single factor contrasts a heterogeneous mix of desirable attributes at one pole with a mix of undesirable attributes at the other pole. This unrotated factor can be labeled Evaluation; it involves the contrast between socially desirable and socially undesirable personal qualities. We expect this one-factor structure to be the most replicable one across languages and cultures based on two principles: (1) the more terms that are associated with a factor, the more replicable should that factor be, and (2) because the first unrotated factor will have the most terms associated with it, it should be the most ubiquitous factor.

Findings of a single large evaluative factor are no doubt related to a classic finding in psychology. In judgments about the meanings of diverse objects in a wide array of cultural settings, a global evaluation factor (good versus bad) was typically found to be the single largest factor (Osgood, May, & Miron, 1975). Osgood hypothesized that the ubiquity of this evaluative factor was related to basic evolutionary principles: our forebears would not have survived if they had not become adapted at a very basic level to any signals of good versus bad objects or events—those leading to pleasure versus pain (for example, Can I eat it or will it eat me?).

Are Two Factors Better Than One?

Two-factor solutions from several lexical studies also suggest a consistent pattern: one factor includes attributes associated with positively valued dynamic qualities and individual ascendancy, whereas the other factor includes attributes associated with socialization, social propriety, solidarity, and community cohesion (Boies et al., 2001; Caprara, Barbanelli, & Zimbardo, 1997; Di Blas & Forzi, 1999; Digman, 1997; Goldberg & Somer, 2000; Hřebíčková, Ostendorf, Osecká, & Čermák, 1999; Paulhus & John, 1998; Saucier, 1997; Shweder, 1972; White, 1980). Such a factor structure resembles that embodied in the theoretical model of Bakan (1966), who labeled the two factors Agency and Communion. In addition, these two factors may be aligned with some of the other sets of dual personological constructs reviewed by Digman (1997) and by Paulhus and John (1998), including Hogan's (1983) distinction between "getting ahead" (Dynamism) and "getting along" (Social Propriety).

This constellation of two factors is also related to the three most ubiquitous dimensions of affective meaning, which include Potency (or Strength) and Activity in addition to Evaluation (Osgood et al., 1975). Whether this correspondence is due entirely to the imposition of universal tendencies in human cognition or to the natural structure of phenomena "out in the world" remains an open question. In judgments about human targets, Potency and Activity tend to merge into a single dimension that Osgood and his associates called Dynamism. Unpublished analyses with English-language adjectives indicate that the Big Two lexical factors are strongly related to the dimensions of affective meaning as indexed in pancultural bipolar scales applied in self-descriptions. The first unrotated lexical factor is strongly related to Evaluation (but independent of Potency and Activity), whereas the second unrotated lexical factor is related to Potency and Activity (but independent of Evaluation).

As is true of the Big One factor structure, no lexical study has presented evidence to contradict the view that this two-factor structure is ubiquitous across languages and cultures. If both the one- and two-factor structures eventually turn out to be universal, the latter has some advantage because two factors provide more information than one.

What Would Be a Big Three?

Findings from most lexical studies to date suggest the general rule that if three factors are extracted and rotated, these factors tend to be broad versions of Extraversion, Agreeableness, and Conscientiousness, the first three factors from the Big Five (Saucier & Goldberg, 2001). All lexical studies that have identified the Big Five in five-factor solutions and also report the character of the three-factor solution report this Big Three. Moreover, some studies that did not straightforwardly replicate the Big Five did replicate this lexical Big Three (Di Blas & Forzi, 1998, 1999; De Raad & Szirmák, 1994; Hahn, Lee, & Ashton, 1999), so it appears more robust than the Big Five. And the Big Three (like the one- and two-factor solutions already described) seem relatively unaffected by how wide versus narrow a variable selection one employs (Saucier, 1997).

However, at least two lexical studies have not replicated this Big Three in three-factor solutions, these being the studies in French

(Boies et al., 2001) and Filipino/Tagalog (A. T. Church, personal communication, Aug. 9, 1999). Thus, although it has been widely replicated, this Big Three may not be universal. Nonetheless, this three-factor lexical model does seem to be more general than a widely touted alternative: the Extraversion-Neuroticism-Psychoticism model of Eysenck (1991). The Eysenck model predicts the emergence of Neuroticism among the three largest factors and the collapse of Agreeableness and Conscientiousness into one "Psychoticism" factor (Goldberg & Rosolack, 1994).

Regularities at the Five-Factor Level

As we have noted, lexical studies in languages originating in northern Europe (including English) have been supportive of the Big Five, and so has a study in Turkish. But studies in Italian (De Raad, Di Blas, & Perugini, 1997) and Hungarian (Szirmák & De Raad, 1994) found no counterpart to the Intellect factor in five-factor solutions. Instead, there were two Agreeableness-related factors, one contrasting peacefulness with aggression and irritability and the other contrasting humaneness with greed and egotism (compare Deary, 1996). Extraction of additional factors was necessary to find a factor related to Intellect.

Several lexical studies have included a relatively broad selection of variables, each with terms that could be classified as referring to emotions and moods or as being unusually highly evaluative, and two of these studies included terms referring to physical appearance. Because none of these studies found the Big Five in a five-factor solution, it is clear that the appearance of the Big Five as the first five factors is contingent on some strictures in variable selection.

Lexical Seven-Factor Models

Although not finding the Big Five in five-factor solutions, studies with inclusive variable-selection criteria in English and Turkish did find Big Five–like factors in a seven-factor solution (Goldberg & Somer, 2000; Saucier, 1997; Tellegen & Waller, 1987). The two additional factors were Negative Valence (a factor emphasizing attributes with extremely low desirability and endorsement rates), found in all three studies, and either Positive Valence (a factor emphasizing vague positive attributes like Impressive and Outstanding and found in Tellegen & Waller, 1987) or Attractiveness (found in the other two studies).

Intriguingly, studies in two other languages with broad variable-selection criteria have led to an alternative seven-factor structure. The convergences between these studies occurred in spite of their many differences in methodology. Lexical studies in Filipino (Church et al., 1997, 1998) and Hebrew (Almagor, Tellegen, & Waller, 1995)—languages from widely separated language families and cultures—yielded a highly convergent seven-factor structure, although the similarity was obscured by discrepant labels. The English translations of marker adjectives for the Filipino and Hebrew factors have been shown to correspond in a one-to-one way (Saucier, 2002).

One of these new factors resembles the Negative Valence factor just described. Two of them resemble Big Five factors—Conscientiousness and Intellect. The other three Big Five factors—Extraversion, Agreeableness, and Emotional Stability—correlate substantially but in a complex way with the remaining four factors, which map an affective-interpersonal domain (compare Saucier, 1992). These four can be labeled Gregariousness (or Liveliness), Self-Assurance (or Mettle or Fortitude), Even Temper (Tolerant versus Temperamental), and Concern for Others (versus Egotism). Big Five Extraversion is related to Gregariousness and Self-Assurance, Emotional Stability to Self-Assurance and Even Temper, and Agreeableness to Even Temper and Concern for Others.

Similar factors have been obtained from lexical data in English (Saucier, 2002), and factors found in studies in Italian (Di Blas & Forzi, 1998) resemble the Multi-Language Seven. However, further replication tests are needed because few studies have used such inclusive variable-selection criteria. In any case, one would expect a model with more factors to have higher predictive validity, and there are some indications that this Multi-Language Seven model will outperform the Big Five in this regard (Saucier, 2002).

Implications and Limitations

In lexical studies, variable selection is taken out of the hands of the expert and entrusted to a more disinterested source (that is, a dictionary). Using this method, some consistencies in the structure of personality attributes become clear. We can discern a hierarchical structure, with very broad factors related to the affective meaning dimensions of Osgood et al. (1975) at the top of the hierarchy. At a slightly lower level of breadth are the Big Five or partially related alternatives that have been recovered in some languages. Although some investigators have claimed that factors like the Big Five are human universals (McCrae & Costa, 1997), this conclusion is certainly premature. Even at this early juncture, we can find studies of languages in which the Big Five do not seem to be the best model for representing the indigenous lexical structure. Clearly, tests of the Big Five against competitor structures are needed.

Moreover, there are some important limitations to the body of lexical studies carried out to date. More studies are needed in non-Western settings where the majority of the world's human population resides and with non-European languages. Lexical studies have focused almost entirely on those attributes represented in adjectives, although some attributes may be represented mainly as type nouns (Hick, Nerd, Slavedriver, Tease) or as attribute nouns (Integrity, Mettle); certainly more studies that include attributes represented in nonadjectival forms are needed. In addition, most lexical studies to date have relied exclusively on self-descriptions, a methodology whose use should be supplemented with descriptions by knowledgeable informants.

Another possible limitation of current lexical studies is that they have focused on the attributes of individuals, and few have examined the attributes of groups or organizations (Slaughter, Zickar, Highhouse, & Mohr, 2001). Given the long history of studies of organizational climate (Astin & Holland, 1961; Ellsworth & Maroney, 1972; Moos, 1972; Wolf, 1966), it would be extremely instructive to examine the structure of interorganizational differences using a comprehensive set of lexical stimuli. Is there something akin to the Big Five or other lexical structures when we study descriptions of groups rather than persons? Future research may provide an answer.

One might wonder why the factor structures found in lexical studies are so important, given that the currently dominant formats for personality assessment are inventories containing phrase- or sentence-length items. One huge advantage of lexical studies is that the personality-descriptive lexicon constitutes a far more bounded and finite population than the set of all possible questionnaire items, and therefore one can reasonably argue that a lexical variable selection (for example, the five hundred English adjectives of highest frequency of use; Saucier, 1997) is representative of that population. This makes it easier to arrive at defensible scientific generalizations about personality attributes.

As it happens, the structure of personality attributes as encoded in the scales included in current personality inventories may not differ markedly from that encoded in single person-descriptive terms. The higher-level factors from the Sixteen Personality Factor Inventory (16PF; Conn & Rieke, 1994) and the Revised NEO Personality Inventory (NEO-PI-R; Costa & McCrae, 1992) are variants of the Big Five. Six of the seven factors represented by the scales included in the Hogan Personality Inventory (HPI; Hogan & Hogan, 1995)—Sociability, Ambition, Adjustment, Likeability, Prudence, Intellectance, and School Success—have been shown to correspond fairly well to six of the Multi-Language Seven factors, with Negative Valence (and School Success) excluded (Saucier, 2002). Of course, future inventory scales need not be limited to the content found in lexical factors; lexical factors indicate necessary but not sufficient components for an adequate representation of personality attributes (Goldberg & Saucier, 1995). Lexical studies provide a superb initial grid for personality assessment, but they are not the entire enterprise.

Structural Models That Provide More Specific Constructs

Thus far, we have discussed only structures containing broad, orthogonal factors. We turn now to the more specific constructs that are agglomerated into these factors.

Some Advantages of Lower-Level Constructs

Hierarchical structural models, such as the consensual one that could emerge from lexical studies, are advantageously flexible. One can attain either great parsimony at the few-factor level or greater informativeness at levels with more factors. One can generate even more informativeness by subdividing the broader factors into more specific subcomponents (sometimes called facets).

However, it is possible that going to the facet level may require giving up some degree of cross-cultural replicability.

Broad factors have a number of limitations. They are composed of many variables, and this creates a degree of ambiguity. As Block (1995) and John (1990) have noted, investigators differ in the psychological meaning that they give to each of the Big Five factors (see Johnson & Ostendorf, 1993, for one plausible account of the reasons for this problem). For example, Extraversion can be thought of as a composite of Sociability, Assertiveness, and Positive Emotionality (as well as other related constructs), but some see Sociability as more central (Costa & McCrae, 1992), others see Assertiveness as more central (Goldberg, 1993b; Peabody, 1987), and still others see Positive Emotionality as more central (Watson & Clark, 1997). Although the factors are usually labeled with a single term, plumbing the psychological meaning of a broad factor like one of the Big Five is a cognitive task of considerable complexity. This is because a broad factor is not so much one thing as a collection of many things that have something in common. It is easy to ignore the diverse character of the variables contained within a broad factor. A better way to understand each factor might be to characterize its crucial subcomponents, which, although empirically interrelated, are conceptually distinct.

Indeed, identification of specific subcomponents can help to clarify the conceptualization of the broader factors (Briggs, 1989). Because broad factors blend together subcomponents that might be distinguished from one another, some of the finer features of personality description are lost when making only a few broad distinctions. Such finer features appear to reflect genetic sources of variation beyond those bearing on the broad-level factors (Jang, McCrae, Angleitner, Riemann, & Livesley, 1998). And a representation of personality structure that makes the finer features explicit potentially offers higher precision and accuracy (or "fidelity") in personality description. When categories are narrower, the exemplars for each are more similar, enhancing diagnostic value for specific instances (John, Hampson, & Goldberg, 1991). Broad-bandwidth constructs, on the other hand, sacrifice fidelity to gain efficiency.

A structural representation combining both broader and narrower constructs may be an optimal compromise. The broader-bandwidth level offers higher efficiency (parsimony), whereas the narrower level offers higher fidelity (predictive accuracy). More-over, to the extent that subcomponents are measured reliably, those measures afford valuable information about middle scorers on the broad dimensions, because middle scorers may score high on some subcomponents of a broad factor but low on others.

Perhaps the major benefit of measuring subcomponents per-tains to predictive validity. As diverse commentators (Goldberg, 1993a; Mershon & Gorsuch, 1988; Paunonen & Ashton, 2001) have pointed out, the amalgamation of measures into broad factors leads to a loss of specific variance, thus lowering the overall validity of the composite (for important potential exceptions, see Ones & Viswes-varan, 1996). Consequently, an investigator who seeks optimal pre-dictions should use as many specific sources of variance as statistical power, and thus sample size, will permit (Goldberg, 1993a).

The quest for high predictive accuracy leads to the develop-ment of measures at levels far more specific than the broad factors compared in lexical studies; such subcomponents are likely to pre-dict more powerfully than the single broad factor into which they are agglomerated. Even when more specific variables provide lit-tle predictive gain over the common factors, it can be useful to know which aspect of the common factor is responsible for the bulk of the correlation, thus providing more conceptual clarity.

How many hierarchical levels are needed? Eysenck (1991) de-scribed four for personality constructs. The lowest level includes iso-lated behaviors (talking with a stranger), and the second level includes recurring behaviors or habits (tending to talk to strangers). The third level involves clusters of interrelated habitual behaviors (sociability, liking to be with people), which one might think of as middle-level traits. The fourth level is composed of amalgamations of middle-level traits that form broad factors (such as Extraversion). Lexical studies suggest that this fourth level might itself be divided into two levels, including an even more highly abstract level such as is represented in composite factors like Evaluation, Social Propri-ety, and Dynamism. That is, one can blend the apparent primary personality factors to create a few higher-level combinations, as do some languages that combine the colors white, yellow, and red into a single word (translatable perhaps as "light/warm") and the col-ors black, blue, and green into another word ("dark/cool"); Kay and McDaniel (1978) call these composite colors.

Lexical studies comparing the lower-level subcomponents of broad factors are still in their infancy. Given the high similarity in the Big Five representations in the highly related English and German languages, Saucier and Ostendorf (1999) tested whether such similarity extends to the lower-level subcomponents as well. They found that although not all of the subcomponents from each language replicate perfectly, most of them did. Specifically, the replicated hierarchical subcomponents of the Big Five included four facets each for Extraversion, Agreeableness, and Conscientiousness and three each for Emotional Stability and Intellect.

Organizing the Subcomponents

There are two distinct ways of organizing the more specific subcomponents of the broad factors, called the horizontal and vertical approaches (Goldberg, 1993b), and any complete taxonomy of personality attributes must include both kinds of organizational features. The vertical aspect refers to the hierarchical relations among the variables (for example, Reliability is a more abstract and general concept than Punctuality), whereas the horizontal aspect refers to the degree of similarity among variables at the same hierarchical level (Wit involves aspects of both Intelligence and Humor).

The defining feature of horizontal models is that the relations among the variables are specified by the variables' locations in multidimensional space. When that space is limited to only two dimensions and the locations of the variables are projected to some uniform distance from the origin, the resulting structures are referred to as "circumplex" representations. The most famous example of such models is the Interpersonal Circle (Kiesler, 1983; Wiggins, 1979, 1980), which is based on variants of the Extraversion and Agreeableness factors in the Big Five model. Other examples of circumplex models include those that incorporate the first three of the Big Five factors (Di Blas & Forzi, 1999; Peabody & Goldberg, 1989; Stern, 1970); the affective-interpersonal factors based on Extraversion, Agreeableness, and Emotional Stability (Saucier, 1992); and two replicated nonevaluative factors (Saucier, Ostendorf, & Peabody, 2001).

A more comprehensive circumplex representation was proposed by Hofstee, De Raad, and Goldberg (1992). Dubbed the AB5C model, for Abridged Big Five-Dimensional Circumplex, this representation contains the ten bivariate planes formed from all pairs of the Big Five factors. In the AB5C model, each trait is assigned to the plane formed by the two factors with which it is most highly associated (for example, its two highest factor loadings). Variables that are located in close proximity in each plane are clustered together so as to form ninety clusters of interrelated traits. Because of the circular ordering of these clusters, they form forty-five bipolar dimensions. An inventory developed to measure these forty-five AB5C facets has been provided by Goldberg (1999).

At a less formal level, the scales in some personality inventories are ordered horizontally by the similarity among their scales; for example, the scales from the CPI are grouped on the profile sheet in such a way that adjacent scales are more highly associated with each other than are those located further away. Indeed, the locations of the scales on the profile sheets for most personality inventories are based on some degree of such horizontal ordering.

More recently, some inventory developers have used an explicitly hierarchical scheme for ordering their middle-level constructs. A few of these have been borrowed from lexical research on the Big Five factor structure. The most salient example of incorporating findings from lexical studies into inventory construction has been provided by Costa and McCrae (1992), who added the lexical Agreeableness and Conscientiousness factors to their original three-factor NEO inventory. The latest revision of their inventory has six subcomponents (called facets) associated with each of the five highest-level constructs (called domains), for a total of thirty scales.

Other multiscale personality inventories provide a wide range of organizational schemes for their middle-level personality constructs. For example, the sixteen scales of the 16PF are associated with five broad factors, and the eleven scales from the Multidimensional Personality Questionnaire (Tellegen, in press) are classified as facets of four factors. At the other extreme, the thirty-one scales from the Temperament and Character Inventory (TCI; Cloninger, Przybeck, Svrakic, & Wetzel, 1994) are organized as components of seven broad factors, as are the forty-four homogeneous item composites from the HPI. The CPI (Gough, 1996) has an open-ended number of middle-level constructs, since new ones can always be generated from the inventory's large item pool.

These middle-level facet systems appear to converge only partially; rarely are the same labels used for similar constructs. Because personality inventories are so widely employed, the high degree of divergence at the scale level, at least in terms of labels for the constructs, creates a scientific problem. Indeed, there is a virtual Tower of Babel with respect to the labels for middle-level constructs; every inventory developer seems to speak a different tongue. Although in numerous studies McCrae and Costa have studied the relations between the scales from various inventories and their own NEO-PI-R, they have concentrated on delineating joint broad factors, not on reconciling the competing sets of constructs found at the more specific level.

The degree of convergence between the lower-level models embodied in various personality inventories is not yet well understood, nor are the relations of these inventory-based models to those derived from lexical studies. More research is needed to develop an overarching structure linking the facet systems in various inventories and then linking these systems to lexical findings concerning the general structure of personality attributes. In addition, we should learn more about the degree to which these inventories might reference some useful personality characteristics that are not well captured in personality-descriptive lexicons.

For the industrial/organizational psychologist, the most important question concerns the comparative validity of each of the inventory and lexical models in predicting important human outcomes, especially those involved in the world of work. The manuals for many personality inventories include tables of correlations between its scale scores and various criterion indexes, but virtually all of the findings from different inventories are incommensurate. Test authors are not encouraged to conduct comparative validity studies, pitting their instrument against one or more others as predictors of the same set of criterion indexes. As a result, neither the science of personality assessment nor its applied practitioners have information about the comparative performance of the different instruments available in the marketplace. There is no Consumers Union for testing our tests.

One basic problem is that scientific goals may have become subjugated to commercial interests. To solve this problem, Goldberg (1999, in press) has recently developed a public domain venue for conducting comparative research, the International Personality Item Pool (IPIP). The IPIP is an international effort to develop and continually refine a set of broad-bandwidth personality inventories, all of whose items are freely available and whose scales can be used for scientific and commercial purposes. Although no one investigator alone has access to many diverse criterion settings, the international scientific community has such access, and the IPIP provides a venue for pooling their findings.

Because the IPIP is an open system for the accumulation of new personality measures, all we can provide here is a snapshot of its current status. Included at the IPIP Web site (http://ipip.ori.org/) are 280 personality scales, each developed from subsets of the 1,956 items now available in the pool. All of the IPIP items are in a common format, one that should elicit relatively faithful translations across diverse languages. The scales are intended to measure the constructs included in various lexical models, plus constructs similar to those included in each of six commercial personality inventories (NEO-PI-R, 16PF, CPI, HPI, MPQ, TCI) already mentioned in this chapter, in two other inventories—the revised Jackson Personality Inventory (Jackson, 1994) and the new Six Factor Personality Questionnaire (Jackson, Paunonen, & Tremblay, 2000)—and in eighteen other popular personality scales. (For further information about this ever expanding resource, see Goldberg, 1999, in press, and the IPIP Web site.)

There are many competing structural models of personality attributes at the middle hierarchical level. Indeed, it appears that the more specific is the level of constructs examined in these models, the more structural chaos is found, and the higher is the potential for confusion among researchers who are not committed to a single inventory. In some respects, this situation reflects a longstanding pattern in personality psychology: each expert has his or her own distinct personality theory, and each theory is accorded its own chapter in personality textbooks, with little empirical competition among the approaches. To employ a sports metaphor, we have bred a large number of racehorses, each having claims to superiority, but we have rarely bothered to pit them against one another in an actual race. It is time to conclude these preliminaries and get on with some meaningful competition. Comparative studies of structural models must now begin.

How Good Are Existing Structural Models?

Which is the best structural model of personality? In attempting to answer this question, we face severe limitations because relatively few studies have generated comparative evidence on the utility of multiple structural models. However, because most readers are familiar with the Big Five model, we can illustrate the potential application of relevant criteria with a brief discussion of how well the Big Five appears to satisfy them.

Many psychologists are interested in a structural model with a strong biological basis. It is relevant that all of the Big Five factors are moderately heritable. However, none is completely heritable, and none is strongly environmental with respect to shared family antecedents; we might find a competitor model (or variant of the Big Five) with more causal clarity at some point in the future. There is no clear evidence that the Big Five correspond to main lines of genetic or biological influence, but the same must be said for all other structural models at this time.

Reliability and validity are frequently referenced criteria for comparing models. The Big Five factors generally show impressive stability across time and agreement across observers, but we do not know if some competitor model might be better on these counts. Because they are factors based on lexical representation, the Big Five have substantial bandwidth and certainly represent socially important dimensions, although it is not clear that the Big Five captures all socially important dimensions. The Big Five does show impressive predictive validity, but models containing a wider range of individual differences would doubtless outperform the Big Five in this respect.

Generalizability across differing types of data and across cultural settings is a potentially important criterion. The Big Five has some generality across self- and peer-rating data (Goldberg, 1990,

1992), but it is not yet clear whether it is superior to potential competitor models in this regard. With respect to generalizability across cultures and languages, the Big Five appears adequate using the lenient criteria that we discussed earlier, but there may well be other models that meet stringent criteria even better. With respect to applicant samples in personnel selection, some have found the Big Five difficult to recover (Schmit & Ryan, 1993), and others have proposed models with more than five factors (Hough, 1994).

A more comprehensive model—one that covers the domain of important variables more thoroughly—will generally be preferred to a less comprehensive model. The Big Five may be adequately comprehensive if we use fairly narrow and conventional ways of defining what is a relevant personality variable and set a stringent threshold (a very low multiple correlation with the Big Five) for a variable to be judged "beyond the Big Five." But there are clearly dimensions of individual differences beyond the Big Five, particularly if we widen the taxonomy to include abilities, social attitudes, or appearance-related characteristics (Saucier & Goldberg, 1998). And given the indeterminate boundaries around the concept of personality, especially the ambiguity about whether externally defined attributes should be included, it makes sense to widen the taxonomy in this manner.

Many psychologists stress that a good structural model has a strong theoretical basis. The Big Five is often described as "merely" a descriptive taxonomy because it was empirically derived; there are other structural models that come packaged with more a priori theory, although the Big Five seems to be slowly accumulating theoretical perspectives post hoc (Wiggins, 1996).

In summary, the strongest performance of the Big Five seems to be on criteria like social importance, breadth, stability, cross-observer agreement, and generality across self- and peer-rating data. But the Big Five seems vulnerable to being bettered by another model on other criteria: causal clarity, correspondence to main lines of biological influence, predictive validity, generalizability across cultures and languages (by stringent criteria), association with theory, and comprehensiveness. However, we sorely lack comparative analyses involving multiple models with respect to all of these criteria. On the path to an optimal structural model for personality attributes, there is still much to learn.

Conclusion

We have seen important progress in discerning the structure of personality attributes. At the very broadest level (although too broad for some purposes), this structure appears to have much in common with Osgood's classic dimensions of affective meaning (1962), which were found in studies of the ways that diverse objects (not just persons) are judged and perceived. At a slightly less broad but more informative level are the well-known Big Five factors. The extent to which the Big Five is optimal at its level in the hierarchy is not fully determined. And at more specific levels, we find even less consensus about an optimal model for the classification and organization of personality attributes. Much remains unresolved, and therefore it is important to reflect on the range of criteria by which structural models can be compared—in other words, what makes a structural model good. Although the Big Five model seems to perform strongly on some criteria, on others it seems more vulnerable to being superseded eventually by alternative models. Future models may well be more comprehensive, more widely generalizable across languages and cultures, and associated with measures that are more highly predictive of a wide array of useful criteria.

References

Adler, M. F. (1929). Personality: How to develop it in the family, the school, and society. In *Essays in honor of John Dewey* (pp. 3–22). New York: Holt.

Allport, G. W. (1937). *Personality: A psychological interpretation.* New York: Holt.

Allport, G. W., & Odbert, H. S. (1936). Trait names: A psycho-lexical study. *Psychological Monographs, 47* (1, Whole No. 211).

Almagor, M., Tellegen, A., & Waller, N. (1995). The Big Seven model: A cross-cultural replication and further exploration of the basic dimensions of natural language of trait descriptors. *Journal of Personality and Social Psychology, 69,* 300–307.

Astin, A. W., & Holland, J. L. (1961). The Environmental Assessment Technique: A way to measure college environments. *Journal of Educational Psychology, 52,* 308–316.

Bakan, D. (1966). *The duality of human existence: Isolation and communion in Western man.* Boston: Beacon Press.

Block, J. (1995). A contrarian view of the five-factor approach to personality description. *Psychological Bulletin, 117,* 187–215.

Boies, K., Lee, K., Ashton, M. C., Pascal, S., & Nicol, A.A.M. (2001). The structure of the French personality lexicon. *European Journal of Personality, 15,* 277–295.

Briggs, S. R. (1989). The optimal level of measurement for personality constructs. In D. M. Buss & N. Cantor (Eds.), *Personality psychology: Recent trends and emerging directions* (pp. 246–260). New York: Springer.

Caprara, G. V., Barbanelli, C., & Zimbardo, P. G. (1997). Politicians' uniquely simple personalities. *Nature, 385,* 493.

Cattell, R. B. (1943). The description of personality: Basic traits resolved into clusters. *Journal of Abnormal and Social Psychology, 38,* 476–506.

Church, A. T., Katigbak, M. S., & Reyes, J.A.S. (1998). Further exploration of Filipino personality structure using the lexical approach: Do the Big Five or Big Seven dimensions emerge? *European Journal of Personality, 12,* 249–269.

Church, A. T., Reyes, J.A.S., Katigbak, M. S., & Grimm, S. D. (1997). Filipino personality structure and the Big Five model: A lexical approach. *Journal of Personality, 65,* 477–528.

Cloninger, C. R. (1987). A systematic method for clinical description and classification of personality traits. *Archives of General Psychiatry, 44,* 573–588.

Cloninger, C. R., Przybeck, T. R., Svrakic, D. M., & Wetzel, R. D. (1994). *The Temperament and Character Inventory (TCI): A guide to its development and use.* St. Louis, MO: Center for Psychobiology of Personality, Washington University.

Comrey, A. L. (1988). Factor-analytic methods of scale development in personality and clinical psychology. *Journal of Consulting and Clinical Psychology, 56,* 754–761.

Conn, S. R., & Rieke, M. L. (1994). *The 16PF Fifth Edition technical manual.* Champaign, IL: Institute for Personality and Ability Testing.

Costa, P. T., & McCrae, R. R. (1992). *Revised NEO Personality Inventory (NEO PI-R) and NEO Five-Factor Inventory (NEO-FFI) professional manual.* Odessa, FL: Psychological Assessment Resources.

Crutcher, R. (1931). *Personality and reason.* London: Favil.

Deary, I. J. (1996). A (latent) Big Five personality model in 1915? A reanalysis of Webb's data. *Journal of Personality and Social Psychology, 71,* 992–1005.

De Raad, B., Di Blas, L., & Perugini, M. (1997). Two independent Italian trait taxonomies: Comparisons with Italian and between Italian Germanic languages. *European Journal of Personality, 11,* 167–185.

De Raad, B., & Szirmák, Z. (1994). The search for the "Big Five" in a non-Indo-European language: The Hungarian trait structure and its relationship to the EPQ and the PTS. *European Review of Applied Psychology, 44,* 17–26.

Di Blas, L., & Forzi, M. (1998). An alternative taxonomic study of personality descriptors in the Italian language. *European Journal of Personality, 12,* 75–101.

Di Blas, L., & Forzi, M. (1999). Refining a descriptive structure of personality attributes in the Italian language: The abridged Big Three circumplex structure. *Journal of Personality and Social Psychology, 76,* 451–481.

Digman, J. M. (1990). Personality structure: Emergence of the Five-Factor Model. In M. R. Rosenzweig & L. W. Porter (Eds.), *Annual review of psychology* (Vol. 41, pp. 417–440). Palo Alto, CA: Annual Reviews.

Digman, J. M. (1997). Higher order factors of the Big Five. *Journal of Personality and Social Psychology, 73,* 1246–1256.

Ellsworth, R., & Maroney, R. (1972). Characteristics of psychiatric programs and their effects on patients' adjustment. *Journal of Consulting and Clinical Psychology, 39,* 436–447.

Eysenck, H. J. (1991). Dimensions of personality: 16, 5, or 3? Criteria for a taxonomic paradigm. *Personality and Individual Differences, 12,* 773–790.

Funder, D. C. (2001). *The personality puzzle* (2nd ed.). New York: Norton.

Goldberg, L. R. (1981). Language and individual differences: The search for universals in personality lexicons. In L. W. Wheeler (Ed.), *Review of personality and social psychology* (Vol. 2, pp. 141–165). Thousand Oaks, CA: Sage.

Goldberg, L. R. (1990). An alternative "Description of personality": The Big-Five factor structure. *Journal of Personality and Social Psychology, 59,* 1216–1229.

Goldberg, L. R. (1992). The development of markers for the Big-Five factor structure. *Psychological Assessment, 4,* 26–42.

Goldberg, L. R. (1993a). The structure of personality traits: Vertical and horizontal aspects. In D. C. Funder, R. D. Parke, C. Tomlinson-Keasey, & K. Widaman (Eds.), *Studying lives through time: Personality and development* (pp. 169–188). Washington, DC: American Psychological Association.

Goldberg, L. R. (1993b). The structure of phenotypic personality traits. *American Psychologist, 48,* 26–34.

Goldberg, L. R. (1999). A broad-bandwidth, public-domain, personality inventory measuring the lower-level facets of several five-factor models. In I. Mervielde, I. Deary, F. De Fruyt, & F. Ostendorf (Eds.), *Personality psychology in Europe* (Vol. 7, pp. 7–28). Tilburg, Netherlands: Tilburg University Press.

Goldberg, L. R. (in press). The comparative validity of adult personality inventories: Applications of a consumer-testing framework. In S. R. Briggs, J. M. Cheek, & E. M. Donahue (Eds.), *Handbook of adult personality inventories.* New York: Plenum.

Goldberg, L. R., & Digman, J. M. (1994). Revealing structure in the data: Principles of exploratory factor analysis. In S. Strack & M. Lorr (Eds.), *Differentiating normal and abnormal personality* (pp. 216–242). New York: Springer.

Goldberg, L. R., & Rosolack, T. K. (1994). The Big Five factor structure as an integrative framework: An empirical comparison with Eysenck's P-E-N model. In C. F. Halverson Jr., G. A. Kohnstamm, & R. P. Martin (Eds.), *The developing structure of temperament and personality from infancy to adulthood* (pp. 7–35). Mahwah, NJ: Erlbaum.

Goldberg, L. R., & Saucier, G. (1995). So what do you propose we use instead? A reply to Block. *Psychological Bulletin, 117,* 221–225.

Goldberg, L. R., & Somer, O. (2000). The hierarchical structure of common Turkish person-descriptive adjectives. *European Journal of Personality, 14,* 497–531.

Gough, H. G. (1996). *CPI manual* (3rd ed.). Palo Alto, CA: Consulting Psychologists Press.

Hahn, D. W., Lee, K., & Ashton, M. C. (1999). A factor analysis of the most frequently used Korean personality trait adjectives. *European Journal of Personality, 13,* 261–282.

Hofstee, W.K.B., De Raad, B., & Goldberg, L. R. (1992). Integration of the Big-Five and circumplex approaches to trait structure. *Journal of Personality and Social Psychology, 63,* 146–163.

Hogan, R. (1983). A socioanalytic theory of personality. In M. M. Page (Ed.), *Nebraska Symposium on Motivation* (pp. 336–355). Lincoln: University of Nebraska Press.

Hogan, R., & Hogan, J. (1995). *Hogan Personality Inventory manual* (2nd ed.). Tulsa, OK: Hogan Assessment Systems.

Hough, L. H. (1994). The "Big-Five" personality variables–construct confusion: Description versus prediction. *Human Performance, 5,* 139–155.

Hřebíčková, M., Ostendorf, F., Osecká, L., & Čermák, I. (1999). Taxonomy and structure of Czech personality-relevant verbs. In I. Mervielde, I. J. Deary, F. De Fruyt, & F. Ostendorf (Eds.), *Personality psychology in Europe* (Vol. 7, pp. 51–65). Tilburg, Netherlands: Tilburg University Press.

Jackson, D. N. (1994). *Jackson Personality Inventory–Revised manual* (2nd ed.). Port Huron, MI: Sigma Assessment Systems.

Jackson, D. N., Paunonen, S. V., & Tremblay, P. F. (2000). *Six Factor Personality Questionnaire manual.* Port Huron, MI: Sigma Assessment Systems.

Jang, K. L., McCrae, R. R., Angleitner, A., Riemann, R., & Livesley, W. J. (1998). Heritability of facet-level traits in a cross-cultural twin sample: Support for a hierarchical model of personality. *Journal of Personality and Social Psychology, 74,* 1556–1565.

John, O. P. (1990). The "Big Five" factor taxonomy: Dimensions of personality in the natural language and in questionnaires. In L. A. Pervin (Ed.), *Handbook of personality: Theory and research* (pp. 66–100). New York: Guilford Press.

John, O. P., Angleitner, A., & Ostendorf, F. (1988). The lexical approach to personality: A historical review of trait taxonomic research. *European Journal of Personality, 2,* 171–203.

John, O. P., Hampson, S. E., & Goldberg, L. R. (1991). The basic level in personality-trait hierarchies: Studies of trait use and accessibility in different contexts. *Journal of Personality and Social Psychology, 60,* 348–361.

Johnson, J. A., & Ostendorf, F. (1993). Clarification of the Five-Factor Model with the Abridged Big Five dimensional circumplex. *Journal of Personality and Social Psychology, 65,* 563–576.

Kay, P., & McDaniel, C. K. (1978). The linguistic significance of the meanings of basic color terms. *Language, 54,* 610–646.

Kiesler, D. J. (1983). The 1982 interpersonal circle: A taxonomy for complementarity in human transactions. *Psychological Review, 90,* 185–214.

MacKinnon, D. W. (1944). The structure of personality. In J. McV. Hunt (Ed.), *Personality and the behavior disorders* (Vol. 1, pp. 3–48). New York: Ronald Press.

McCrae, R. R., & Costa, P. T., Jr. (1997). Personality trait structure as a human universal. *American Psychologist, 52,* 509–516.

Mershon, B., & Gorsuch, R. L. (1988). Number of factors in the personality sphere: Does increase in factors increase predictability of real-life criteria? *Journal of Personality and Social Psychology, 55,* 675–680.

Moos, R. (1972). Assessment of the psychosocial environments of community-oriented psychiatric treatment programs. *Journal of Abnormal Psychology, 79,* 9–18.

Norman, W. T. (1963). Toward an adequate taxonomy of personality attributes: Replicated factor structure in peer nomination personality ratings. *Journal of Abnormal and Social Psychology, 66,* 574–583.

Norman, W. T. (1967). *2800 personality trait descriptors: Normative operating characteristics for a university population.* Ann Arbor: University of Michigan, Department of Psychology.

Ones, D. S., & Viswesvaran, C. (1996). Bandwidth-fidelity dilemma in personality measurement for personnel selection. *Journal of Organizational Behavior, 17,* 609–626.

Osgood, C. E. (1962). Studies on the generality of affective meaning systems. *American Psychologist, 17,* 10–28.

Osgood, C. E., May, W., & Miron, M. (1975). *Cross-cultural universals of affective meaning.* Urbana: University of Illinois Press.

Ostendorf, F. (1990). *Sprache und persönlichkeitsstruktur: Zur Validität des Fünf-Faktoren-Modells der Persönlichkeit* [Language and personality structure: Toward the validation of the Five-Factor Model of personality]. Regensberg, Germany: S. Roderer Verlag.

Paulhus, D. L., & John, O. P. (1998). Egoistic and moralistic biases in self-perception: The interplay of self-descriptive styles with basic traits and motives. *Journal of Personality, 66,* 1025–1060.

Paunonen, S. V., & Ashton, M. C. (2001). Big Five factors and facets and the prediction of behavior. *Journal of Personality and Social Psychology, 81,* 524–539.

Peabody, D. (1987). Selecting representative trait adjectives. *Journal of Personality and Social Psychology, 52,* 59–71.

Peabody, D., & Goldberg, L. R. (1989). Some determinants of factor structures from personality-trait descriptors. *Journal of Personality and Social Psychology, 57,* 552–567.

Saucier, G. (1992). Benchmarks: Integrating affective and interpersonal circles with the Big-Five personality factors. *Journal of Personality and Social Psychology, 62,* 1025–1035.

Saucier, G. (1997). Effects of variable selection on the factor structure of person descriptors. *Journal of Personality and Social Psychology, 73,* 1296–1312.

Saucier, G. (2002). *Multi-language structure of personality attributes: Development and test of an alternative to the Big Five.* Unpublished manuscript, University of Oregon.

Saucier, G., & Goldberg, L. R. (1998). What is beyond the Big Five? *Journal of Personality, 66,* 495–524.

Saucier, G., & Goldberg, L. R. (2001). Lexical studies of indigenous personality factors: Premises, products, and prospects. *Journal of Personality, 69,* 847–879.

Saucier, G., Hampson, S. E., & Goldberg, L. R. (2000). Cross-language studies of lexical personality factors. In S. E. Hampson (Ed.),

Advances in personality psychology (Vol. 1, pp. 1–36). East Sussex, England: Psychology Press.

Saucier, G., & Ostendorf, F. (1999). Hierarchical subcomponents of the Big Five personality factors: A cross-language replication. *Journal of Personality and Social Psychology, 76,* 613–627.

Saucier, G., Ostendorf, F., & Peabody, D. (2001). The non-evaluative circumplex of personality adjectives. *Journal of Personality, 69,* 537–582.

Schmit, M. J., & Ryan, A. M. (1993). The Big Five in personnel selection: Factor structure in applicant and non-applicant populations. *Journal of Applied Psychology, 78,* 966–974.

Shweder, R. A. (1972). *Semantic structure and personality assessment.* Unpublished doctoral dissertation, Harvard University.

Slaughter, J. E., Zickar, M. J., Highhouse, S., & Mohr, D. C. (2001). *Personality trait inferences about organizations: Development of a measure and assessment of construct validity.* Unpublished paper, Louisiana State University, Department of Psychology.

Stern, G. G. (1970). *People in context: Measuring person-environment congruence in education and industry.* New York: Wiley.

Szarota, P. (1996). Taxonomy of the Polish personality-descriptive adjectives of the highest frequency of use. *Polish Psychological Bulletin, 27,* 342–351.

Szirmák, Z., & De Raad, B. (1994). Taxonomy and structure of Hungarian personality traits. *European Journal of Personality, 8,* 95–118.

Tellegen, A. (1993). Folk concepts and psychological concepts of personality and personality disorder. *Psychological Inquiry, 4,* 122–130.

Tellegen, A. (in press). *MPQ (Multidimensional Personality Questionnaire): Manual for administration, scoring, and interpretation.* Minneapolis: University of Minnesota.

Tellegen, A., & Waller, N. G. (1987, Aug.). *Re-examining basic dimensions of natural language trait descriptors.* Paper presented at the Ninety-Fifth Annual Convention of the American Psychological Association, New York.

Triandis, H. C. (2001). Individualism-collectivism and personality. *Journal of Personality, 69,* 907–924.

Watson, D., & Clark, L. A. (1997). Measurement and mismeasurement of mood: Recurrent and emergent issues. *Journal of Personality Assessment, 68,* 267–296.

White, G. M. (1980). Conceptual universals in interpersonal language. *American Anthropologist, 82,* 759–781.

Wiggins, J. S. (1979). A psychological taxonomy of trait-descriptive terms: The interpersonal domain. *Journal of Personality and Social Psychology, 37,* 395–412.

Wiggins, J. S. (1980). Circumplex models of interpersonal behavior. In L. Wheeler (Ed.), *Review of personality and social psychology* (Vol. 1, pp. 265–294). Thousand Oaks, CA: Sage.

Wiggins, J. S. (Ed.). (1996). *The Five-Factor Model of personality: Theoretical perspectives.* New York: Guilford Press.

Windelband, W. (1921). *An introduction to philosophy* (J. McCabe, Trans.). New York: Holt.

Wolf, R. (1966). The measurement of environments. In A. Anastasi (Ed.), *Testing problems in perspective* (pp. 491–503). Washington, DC: American Council on Education.

Zipf, G. K. (1949). *Human behavior and the principle of least effort.* Reading, MA: Addison-Wesley.

CHAPTER 2

The Happy Worker

Hypotheses About the Role of Positive Affect in Worker Productivity

Richard E. Lucas
Ed Diener

The link between happiness and worker productivity has been called the Holy Grail of industrial psychology (Landy, 1989). Establishing that such a link exists would demonstrate the possibility of non-zero-sum interactions (R. Wright, 2000) between labor and management: an organization could increase productivity simply by increasing the happiness and satisfaction of its employees, and both organizations and employees would benefit. But the empirical evidence for the association between happiness and productivity has been as elusive as the relation itself is desirable. A series of qualitative and quantitative reviews (Brayfield & Crockett, 1955; Iaffaldano & Muchinsky, 1985; Vroom, 1964) showed that the association between happiness and productivity is trivial. These reviews have led some researchers to relegate the "notion of the happy-productive worker to the folklore of management—as an unsubstantiated claim of practitioners and the popular press" (Wright & Staw, 1999, p. 1).

In recent years, however, there has been a resurgence of interest in the happy worker; researchers have conducted more careful analyses of existing studies, developed new paradigms for testing the relation, and modified the original job satisfaction–productivity hypothesis. For example, Judge, Thoresen, Bono, and

Patton (2001) suggested that the meta-analysis of Iaffaldano and Muchinsky (1985), which found an average correlation of .17 between satisfaction and performance, underestimated the true correlation. In their updated meta-analysis, Judge et al. found a higher correlation of .30. Other researchers have suggested that positive affect and positive emotions (Baron, 1990; Cote, 1999; George & Brief, 1992; Staw & Barsade, 1993; Wright & Staw, 1999) are more likely than job satisfaction to make workers more productive.

In this chapter, we examine the assumptions underlying the happiness-productivity relation and propose hypotheses about the ways in which affect can lead to more or less productive workers depending on the tasks.

Definition of Happiness

Before we can determine whether happy workers are productive workers, we must clarify what we mean when we say that a worker is happy. Although the term *happiness* is easily understood by psychologists and laypeople alike, it is vague and can encompass a number of distinct constructs that result from different processes, have different correlates, and often have different effects. For this reason, we recommend that researchers who are interested in subjective feelings of well-being and happiness focus on one or more of four separable components of happiness at work (Diener, Suh, Lucas, & Smith, 1999). In this chapter, we use the terms *happiness* or *well-being* in general terms but refer to more specific constructs when discussing specific research findings and hypotheses.

The first two of these components, positive and negative affect, reflect a person's affective well-being. Positive affect refers to emotions and moods such as happiness, joy, excitement, and energy; negative affect refers to emotions and moods such as sadness, anxiety, fear, and anger. Although semantically these two clusters of emotion terms appear to reflect opposite poles of the same dimension, research has shown that positive and negative affect are at least separable (Diener & Emmons, 1984; Lucas, Diener, & Suh, 1996) and perhaps orthogonal (Watson, Clark, & Tellegen, 1988; but see Russell, 1980, for an opposing viewpoint). Furthermore, positive and negative affect have distinct patterns of correlations with personality traits (Costa & McCrae, 1980) and specific behaviors

(Clark & Watson, 1988). Therefore, it is necessary to measure and study positive and negative affect separately.

It is also important to note that the nature of affective constructs changes depending on the time frame in which they are measured. Researchers often distinguish between emotions, which are short-lived reactions to distinct events (Frijda, 1999), and moods, which are longer-lasting feelings that are not necessarily tied to a specific stimulus (Morris, 1999). In addition, research has shown stable individual differences in the tendency to experience positive and negative emotions and moods, and these affective dispositions are often captured when affect is measured over very long periods of time (Tellegen, 1985). We use the terms *emotions, moods,* and *affective dispositions* to refer to short-term reactions, long-lasting noncontingent feelings, and stable dispositions, respectively. We also recommend that organizational researchers explicitly state which component of affective experience they are trying to capture because the different components may have different implications for organizational outcomes (Ledford, 1999; Wright & Staw, 1999).

The third and fourth components of subjective well-being that are relevant to the happy-worker hypothesis reflect cognitive judgments of satisfaction with one's life and one's job. Cognitive judgments of life satisfaction reflect conscious evaluations of the conditions of one's life and are separable from (though related to) the amount of positive and negative affect that one experiences on a day-to-day basis (Lucas et al., 1996). Similarly, judgments of job satisfaction reflect conscious attitudes toward one's job (Judge et al., 2001). Although job satisfaction measures are influenced by the conditions that exist in one's job, they are also influenced by one's affective disposition and overall life satisfaction (Judge, Locke, & Durham, 1997). Therefore, researchers must be careful not to interpret job satisfaction measures as a proxy measure for the actual conditions of one's job. However, the moderate correlation between life satisfaction and job satisfaction does not preclude job satisfaction measures from providing unique information about an employee's attitudes toward his or her job, attitudes that may have distinct implications for productivity beyond the effects of life satisfaction or affective well-being.

It is also likely that there are additional traits and dispositions related to affective and cognitive well-being and with implications for productivity. For example, Judge and his colleagues (Judge, Erez, & Bono, 1998; Judge et al., 1997) argued that a set of self-concept personality variables (which they call core self-evaluations) is important for worker productivity. Specifically, they noted that self-esteem, generalized self-efficacy, locus of control, and neuroticism are important predictors of performance. Many of these variables are conceptually related to happiness and exhibit moderate to strong correlations with well-being measures (Lucas et al., 1996). Although there is conceptual overlap, these traits may affect performance and productivity through different mechanisms than do affect and satisfaction. For this reason, we restrict the focus of this chapter to affect and well-being and only occasionally discuss findings from this related literature.

Definition of Productivity

Subjective well-being research paints a complex picture of the happy worker. A single employee could simultaneously experience high levels of positive affect, average levels of negative affect, and low levels of job or life satisfaction, and each of these components of well-being could have distinct implications for productivity. Unfortunately, the complexities of research on the happy-productive worker do not end there. It is also clear that the outcome or criterion variable of interest, worker productivity, is multifaceted and complex. Productivity has been operationally defined in a variety of ways, ranging from objective measures including worker output, efficiency, turnover, and absenteeism, to more subjective measures, including supervisor ratings. Many of these different measures of productivity and performance do not correlate very highly (Meyer & Gupta, 1995). In addition, some researchers have suggested that happiness and satisfaction are more likely to affect organizational citizenship behaviors than direct measures of productivity and that these citizenship behaviors may have important positive implications for the organization (George & Brief, 1992).

As we shall see, different components of happiness and well-being are likely to influence these different forms of productivity in very different ways. In addition, certain forms of happiness may be related to certain types of halo effects, in which happy people are liked more and rated as being more productive even when there are no objective differences in productivity. Therefore, it will be necessary, when formulating and testing hypotheses, to state explicitly which form of productivity should be related to each component of well-being. Ideally, a variety of objective and subjective measures of productivity would be used to provide the most convincing tests of the happy worker hypothesis.

Mechanisms Underlying the Happy-Productive Worker Hypothesis

As Judge et al. (2001) pointed out in their review of the job satisfaction and productivity literature, early formulations of the happy-productive worker hypothesis were based on theories developed in the social psychological attitudes literature. These early formulations posited that job satisfaction is an attitude, attitudes lead to behavior, and therefore employees who have a positive attitude toward their job will engage in positive behaviors, which should result in higher productivity. In this version of the happy-productive worker hypothesis, happiness and satisfaction should result in higher productivity regardless of the nature of the tasks being performed.

Subsequent research has complicated this simple formulation. First, researchers discovered that job satisfaction measures tap more than just attitudes toward one's job. These measures also reflect temporary mood states and stable individual differences in affective predisposition and overall life satisfaction. In addition, researchers' understanding of moods and underlying affective dispositions has become increasingly sophisticated. Rather than seeing affect and satisfaction simply as reactions to the objective events and conditions that a person experiences, researchers who are examining subjective well-being have begun to realize that emotions and satisfaction can be functional and adaptive (Buss, 1991; Fredrickson, 1998). Furthermore, it seems likely that different forms of well-being have different functions, and thus different effects on life outcomes. With this increased complexity comes a need for more specific hypotheses about the effects of happiness on productivity. This specificity has only begun to be incorporated into organizational research.

Specific Effects of Happiness and Well-Being

We often think of satisfaction and emotions as the end result of a valenced event: when something pleasant happens, we feel satisfaction, happiness, and joy, and when something unpleasant happens, we experience dissatisfaction, anger, depression, or fear. In the work context, this means that employees will feel happy when work conditions are good and unhappy when work conditions are bad. Yet careful analysis of the nature of emotion suggests that emotions can play a much more complicated role in the way we approach the world and the specific actions we take in reaction to events. Frijda (1999), for example, views emotions as more than just a feeling of pleasure or pain combined with an appraisal of an object or event as good or bad. He argued that emotions have three additional components: *action readiness,* or the readiness for changes in behavior toward the environment, *autonomic arousal,* and *cognitive activity changes.* Although each of these components is elicited in reaction to some stimulus, they also prepare us to deal with the stimulus in a specific way. Fear and anger, for example, have distinct patterns of action readiness, autonomic arousal, and cognitive activity changes; we will act very differently toward an unpleasant stimulus depending on whether we feel fear or anger.

Interestingly, although many different negative emotions can be distinguished based on the unique pattern of these components, it appears that positive emotions are relatively undifferentiated and often do not have explicit action tendencies (Fredrickson, 1998). However, in her "Broaden and Build Model," Fredrickson held that most positive emotions can be described as promoting a tendency to increase and diversify one's resources in a general way. So although happiness may not lead to a specific action tendency in the same way that fear leads to a desire to flee, positive affect may lead to behaviors that serve to broaden and build one's social, material, and cognitive resources. Because the tendency to develop these resources has important implications for work behavior and because positive emotions comes closest to what we mean by happiness, we focus most of our discussion on the effects of positive affect on worker productivity.

In the next sections, we review the evidence for specific effects of happiness and well-being.

Social Relationships, Cooperation, and Helping Behavior

Perhaps the most robust finding in the study of subjective well-being is that affect and satisfaction are moderately to strongly correlated with a variety of social variables. For example, researchers have repeatedly shown that the personality trait of extraversion (which reflects the degree to which people enjoy and feel comfortable in social situations) is strongly correlated with subjective well-being. Lucas and Fujita (2000) showed that the meta-analytically derived average correlation between extraversion and positive affect is .37, that this correlation often rises to .80 when multiple measures of extraversion and pleasant affect are used to model the relation, and that the relation is not due to methodological artifacts such as response sets or item overlap in extraversion and pleasant affect scales. Lucas, Diener, Grob, Suh, and Shao (2000) showed that the relation is robust and consistent across a variety of cultures. Other researchers have shown that it is not just feelings of sociability that are related to well-being. Social activity itself is correlated with positive affect, both between persons and within persons over time (Clark & Watson, 1988; Lucas, 2000; Okun, Stock, Haring, & Witter, 1984).

One interpretation of these findings is that social activity and personality traits that promote social activity cause happiness and well-being. However, an equally plausible alternative—and one with an increasing amount of empirical support—is that positive affect actually causes people to engage in and enjoy social contact. For example, Isen (1970) and Cunningham (1988a) found that people who experienced a positive mood induction were more likely than those who did not to engage in social contact (including initiating conversation and disclosing personal information). Diener, Lyubomirsky, and King (2001) suggested at least three reasons that positive affect would foster positive interpersonal relationships. First, positive affect appears to make people like other people more (see, for example, Gouaux, 1971; Lyubomirsky & Tucker, 1998; Mayer, Mamberg, & Volanth, 1988), resulting in happy individuals' seeking out social contact and being more sensitive and attentive to those with whom they interact (Cunningham, 1988a; Isen, 1970). Second, people like happy people better than they like unhappy people (Diener & Fujita, 1995; Harker & Keltner, 2001; King & Napa, 1998), making it more likely that happy people will experience positive social relationships. Finally, the signs of happiness, laughter and smiling, indicate that one is friendly and open, and this signal invites others to become engaged.

In addition to this general tendency for happy people to be more socially engaged than unhappy people, a number of more specific effects of happiness lead to positive social interactions, and these effects have particularly important implications for happiness at work. For example, happy people appear to be more helpful and altruistic than unhappy people. This effect has been found in studies of dispositional affect as well as experimentally induced affect, and it has been found using a variety of techniques for manipulating mood and a variety of measures of helpfulness and altruism (see Diener et al., 2001, for a review). Carlson, Charlin, and Miller (1988) conducted a meta-analysis of studies examining the relation between positive mood and helping behavior and found evidence supporting four potential mechanisms underlying the relation. First, they suggested that a person who feels happy also feels efficacious and resource laden, and therefore is likely to share those resources with others. Second, they found evidence that helping behavior helps to prolong positive moods. Third, there was evidence that helping behavior is a by-product of other effects of pleasant moods, such as increased liking for others. And finally, they suggested that pleasant moods may cause people to feel a greater sense of interdependence and cooperation with others.

The suggestion of Carlson et al. (1988) that helping behaviors result from increased feelings of cooperation indicates that cooperation itself may be an additional benefit of pleasant affect. Carnevale and Isen (1986), for example, showed that people are more cooperative after experiencing a pleasant mood induction. Hertel, Neuhof, Theuer, and Kerr (2000) questioned the generalizability of this finding, however, and suggested that Carnevale and Isen's interpretation of participants' behavior as cooperative was incorrect. Hertel et al. argued that happy people are more likely to use heuristics to guide behavior (a possibility we discuss in more detail later in the chapter), and apparent cooperation may result from the use of a heuristic in which people simply respond in kind to interaction partners. According to Hertel et al., happy people are more likely to do what their partner is doing, and when their partner is acting cooperatively, the happy person will too. When the partner is acting uncooperatively, the happy person is likely to follow suit. Clearly, more research is needed to determine the effect of happiness on cooperative behavior. Happy people usually do tend to like other people and help other people more than do unhappy people. Thus, it would make sense that happy people are more cooperative as well. However, this may depend on the task they are performing and the specific behaviors of their interaction partners.

Implications for Work and Productivity

Happy workers experience greater social rewards than unhappy workers do. They are more likely than unhappy workers to like and be liked by their coworkers, and this greater liking may result in greater helping behavior from the happy worker and toward the happy worker. Thus, worker productivity could benefit from greater happiness in at least two types of jobs: (1) those in which pleasant social contact is a direct measure of job performance (for example, in customer service fields) and (2) those in which high levels of help and cooperation are required for successful performance.

There is some indirect support for each of these hypotheses. For example, Barrick and Mount (1991) found that extraversion (a trait that is moderately to strongly correlated with positive affect) is positively correlated with job performance in jobs that require social interaction, and Mount, Barrick, and Stewart (1998) found that extraversion was correlated with performance in jobs that required cooperation. In addition, organizational citizenship behaviors, which often have a social component, may be influenced by levels of positive affect (George & Brief, 1992; Organ, 1988), and these behaviors may have important implications for overall organizational effectiveness. In jobs with few social requirements, happiness may play less of a role.

The greater sociability of happy people may have drawbacks as well. In occupations that do not require social contact, the desire for social rewards may be a distraction. Too much "water-cooler talk" or other unnecessary social contact may result in lower productivity. In fact, Furnham and Miller (1997) found that although extraverted sales employees were more likely than introverted employees to be rated as high performers, young extraverts (who are likely to be dispositionally happy) were also absent most frequently. Furnham and Miller opined that this may be due to boredom and the fact that extraverts wanted to take days off to do activities that they found more exciting. At the team level, Barry and Stewart (1997) found that the percentage of extraverts within a team affected that team's performance. Although having some extraverts on a team was beneficial for performance (they argued that a mix of half extraverts and half introverts was ideal), too many extraverts was detrimental (perhaps because too many extraverts resulted in team members jockeying for control).

We must caution that the greater interpersonal attractiveness of happy people may lead to the perception that they are more productive when productivity is measured using supervisor ratings, a perception that may have real implications for the happy individual. For example, Burger and Caldwell (2000) found that job applicants high in positive affect were more likely to obtain follow-up interviews when seeking a job than were applicants who were low in positive affect. However, this perception may also be incorrect. Therefore, researchers who are interested in actual productivity must make sure to operationalize productivity in such a way that it cannot be influenced by likeability.

Energy and Activity

Research on the structure of positive affect suggests that feeling good is strongly associated with feeling energetic and active. In fact, Watson et al. (1988) argued that feelings of energy and activity define the positive affect dimension (Tellegen, 1985). In addition, correlational research shows that people who are high in positive affect tend to participate in more active behaviors. For example, after asking people to track their behaviors and emotions over time, Watson, Clark, McIntyre, and Hamaker (1992) found that people who were high in positive affectivity were more likely than those who were low in positive affectivity to engage in a variety of activities, including going to parties and museums and taking weekend trips. In addition, Csikszentmihalyi and Wong (1991) found that when students completed surveys multiple times during the day, the reports of positive affect were correlated with higher feelings of activity and greater participation in a variety of activities. There is even some experimental evidence that induced pleasant moods can lead to greater preference for active behaviors. Cunningham (1988b) found that students who had experienced a pleasant mood induction were more likely than those who did not experience the induction to express a preference for engaging in social and nonsocial active behaviors.

Implications for Work and Productivity

Although both correlational and experimental evidence demonstrates the link between happiness and activity, the precise mechanism underlying this relation has yet to be specified. Do happy people feel more energy than unhappy people in all types of activities, or do happy people seek out activities that are active and require energy? The answer to this question has important implications for the effect of worker happiness on productivity. If happiness makes people feel more active in general, there would be benefits in a wide variety of jobs. If happiness makes people seek out active occupations, then the benefits of happiness may be limited to these active jobs, and the happy worker may even be less productive in more sedate or less exciting occupations. Furthermore, the happy worker's desire for activity may lead to greater absenteeism because the worker is likely to seek more exciting activities (Furnham & Miller, 1997).

Self-Confidence, Motivation, and Approach Toward Goals

Recently, we argued that the facets of the extraversion personality trait are linked by their common association with positive affect (Lucas et al., 2000) and that investigators could begin to formulate hypotheses about the functions of positive affect by carefully examining these facets. The research we have already reviewed illustrates the usefulness of this approach: two cardinal features of extraversion, sociability and activity, have been shown to be related to and possibly outcomes of high positive affect. A third important characteristic of extraversion is the tendency to be self-confident and to have strong approach motivation (Depue & Collins, 1999). Diener and Fujita (1995), for example, noted that students with elevated dispositional positive affect were rated as being more self-confident and assertive by friends and family members than were people low in dispositional positive affect. Lucas et al. (1996) replicated this finding, showing that when self-esteem and subjective well-being variables were measured using a variety of methods of assessment (self-report, informant report, multiple forms), self-esteem was consistently correlated with life satisfaction, positive affect, and negative affect. Diener and Diener (1995) demonstrated that this correlation is significantly greater than zero in a variety of nations (though it was weaker and occasionally zero in collectivist cultures).

In addition, longitudinal and experimental studies show that this correlation is due, at least in part, to the effects of well-being on self-esteem. Headey and Veenhoven (1989), using a panel design, showed that there are mutual causal influences of life satisfaction on feelings of superiority and of feelings of superiority on life satisfaction. Sarason, Potter, and Sarason (1986) found that people who were asked to recall positive events from the past week (a positive mood induction) were more likely than those who did not recall these events to describe themselves in positive terms. Similarly, Wright and Mischel (1982) determined that induced positive mood caused respondents to report more favorable self-evaluations and more success on a laboratory task (in both retrospective assessments of success and expectancies for future success).

These positive self-perceptions are likely to lead to the setting of higher goals, increased approach motivation and approach behavior, and increased task persistence (see Carver & Scheier, 1990, for a more general discussion of the interrelations among affect, goals, and approach behaviors). Emmons (1986), for example, found that people high in positive affect were more likely than people low in positive affect to report having important goals in their lives, and experimental evidence (Baron, 1990; Hom & Arbuckle,

1988) shows that positive mood can have a causal effect on the goals that one sets. Positive affect also influences feelings of efficacy in specific tasks. Baron (1990) and Saavedra and Earley (1991) demonstrated that experimentally induced positive mood increases task-relevant feelings of self-efficacy. Thus, positive affect seems to have a wide-ranging effect on confidence, efficacy, and self-esteem.

Implications for Work and Productivity

The idea that happiness can lead to greater feelings of confidence along with increased motivation and persistence has been recognized as an important reason that happiness and productivity may be linked (George & Brief, 1992; Wright & Staw, 1999). If workers have greater self-confidence, set higher goals, and pursue those goals more persistently, it seems almost inevitable that they will be more productive, a hypothesis that was supported in the meta-analysis by Sadri and Robertson (1993) on the association between self-efficacy and performance. Yet these effects may depend on the extent to which the worker perceives his or her job as challenging. Self-confidence should affect performance only where competence is in question or in jobs where high levels of competence are required, and productivity in low-skill jobs may not benefit from workers' higher feelings of confidence.

Similarly, if employees do not perceive higher productivity as an important goal, no amount of happiness will make them approach this goal. Thus, some researchers have suggested that happiness may affect performance only when there is a clear link between performance and external rewards such as pay (see Judge et al., 2001, for a review; see Stewart, 1996, for a similar argument about the moderators of the extraversion-performance relationship). Providing rewards for performance presumably allows employees to see high performance as an important goal, and perhaps only in these circumstances will happiness affect productivity.

Another possibility is that the increased self-confidence associated with happiness may have negative consequences for productivity. In extreme forms, self-confidence may lead to arrogance, dominance, competition, and insubordination. Ironically, these potential negative effects of happiness are exactly opposite those examined in the section on social relationships, cooperation, and helping behavior. Is it possible that happiness can lead to feelings of sociability, helpfulness, and cooperation *and* to arrogance and insubordination? We do not believe (and have found no evidence) that happiness in any form is likely to lead to these more hostile forms of self-confidence. In fact, in experience sampling studies, we found that when people are feeling happy, they are likely to feel both more assertive *and* more affectionate (Lucas, 2000).

Organizational research may provide a useful test of these effects. Certain sales jobs, for example, require individuals to be sociable and friendly at the same time that they are trying to take advantage of the person to whom they are selling. Does positive affect make them appear more friendly at the same time that they are being more cunning (the appearance of helpfulness and cooperation), or does positive affect actually make sales associates more likely to give the buyer a better deal (actual helpfulness and cooperation)? Organizational settings can provide researchers with a unique opportunity to test these separable, and perhaps conflicting, effects of positive affect.

Health and Coping

In addition to the direct effects of happiness on work behavior, well-being may have additional indirect benefits for worker productivity and organizational efficiency. For example, researchers have shown that happy individuals have better health and coping outcomes than do unhappy individuals. Most of the research in this area has focused on the effects of negative affect and stress on health and immune functioning, and these studies often find that individuals with higher levels of stress and negative affect have poorer health outcomes (Salovey, Rothman, Detweiler, & Steward, 2000; Sapolsky, 1999). However, it is also possible that positive emotional and cognitive well-being may have similar effects or may at least moderate the effects of negative moods and stress. Correlational studies of mood and immune functioning over time (Stone, Cox, Valdimarsdottir, Jandorf, & Neale, 1987; Stone et al., 1994) and experimental studies of induced mood and immune functioning (Dillon, Minchoff, & Baker, 1986; Futterman, Kemeny, Shapiro, & Fahey, 1994) provide evidence that positive moods and immune functioning are linked.

The effect of positive emotions on health and immune functioning may be direct or be mediated by processes described in previous sections. For example, Sapolsky (1999) described the destructive effects that chronic stress has on the body and the immune system. He also noted that certain ways of responding to stress (including seeking social support, believing that one has control over the stressor, and having an optimistic view of one's situation) can moderate the harmful effects of stress. Notably, many of these moderators are strongly associated with happiness and well-being. Thus, although positive affect may not play a direct role in immune functioning, it may moderate the effects of negative affect on health outcomes (for a similar argument, see Danner, Snowdon, & Friesen, 2001). In addition, it appears that coping processes that are often linked with happiness may help individuals overcome the negative effects of stress. Scheier, Carver, and Bridges (2001) noted that subjective well-being and related variables (including dispositional optimism) are related to successful coping strategies like active engagement. Thus, happy individuals may be predisposed to cope more adaptively, allowing them to overcome the negative physical and mental health effects of stress.

Implications for Work and Productivity
Differences in health and coping can have significant and long-lasting effects on outcome variables. For one thing, positive affect may help employees to deal with stressors, and the ability to deal with stress may affect performance (see Spector, Dwyer, & Jex, 1988, for a discussion of the associations between stress and productivity). In addition, positive affect may have important indirect implications for employee productivity. Both Danner et al. (2001) and Ostir, Markides, Black, and Goodwin (2000) found evidence that positive emotionality predicted longevity (though Friedman, 1999, found opposite results, perhaps because happier participants were more likely to die from risky behaviors). It would be reasonable to assume, then, that happier workers would be less likely to miss work due to illness and may be less susceptible to the negative effects of stress. Cutting down on the number of illnesses would not only reduce absence, it could potentially decrease health care costs. Yet researchers must be careful to assess the impact of happiness and well-being very carefully. As the longevity literature shows, hap-

piness may have different effects on distinct reasons for absenteeism (see Kohler & Mathieu, 1993, for a discussion of the reasons for absenteeism). Happy workers may be less likely to miss work due to illness, but they may be more likely to miss work due to injuries from accidents or simply because they wanted to do something more exciting that day than go to work (Furnham & Miller, 1997). We should note, however, that Dalton and Mesch (1991) found that job satisfaction was related only to absence due to illness and not to absence due to other causes. Again, however, positive affect may function differently from job satisfaction, and thus we recommend that researchers go beyond simply examining outcome variables like absenteeism and try to incorporate additional measures that can explain exactly why happy workers are absent more or less frequently.

Creativity

Depending on the nature of the job in which a worker is engaged, creativity may be a powerful predictor of employee productivity. Individuals who can think of novel solutions to a problem or innovative strategies for accomplishing a task can greatly increase the productivity and efficiency of the organization where they work. Considerable evidence from laboratory studies shows that induced positive affect can lead to increased creativity. Isen and her colleagues have shown that inducing a pleasant mood leads to higher scores on the Remote Associates Test (which tests the associations one makes among three seemingly unrelated words; Estrada, Isen, & Young, 1994) and to more unusual responses in a word association task (Isen, Johnson, Mertz, & Robinson, 1985). Other researchers have shown that induced positive affect leads to the use of more creative strategies when estimating correlations (Sinclair & Mark, 1995), the listing of more unusual categories in a sorting task (Hirt, Melton, McDonald, & Harackiewicz, 1996; Murray, Sujan, Hirt, & Sujan, 1990), and the listing of more unusual exemplars of a category (Greene & Noice, 1988). Positive affective dispositions seem to have similar effects in laboratory tests of creativity: Cacha (1976) found that happy, relaxed, and bold children tended to score high in creativity.

When we move outside the laboratory, the evidence is slightly more complicated. A number of researchers have noted that creative artists often have bipolar disorder (Andreasen, 1987; Goodwin & Jamison, 1990; Richards, Kinney, Lunde, Benet, & Merzel, 1988) and that creative episodes often occur when the person is in a hypomanic (mildly manic) as opposed to depressive state (Richards, 1994; Richards & Kinney, 1990). This finding supports the notion that high positive affect is associated with creativity. But Feist (1998) noted that the personality traits that predicted creativity among artists were different from those that predicted creativity among scientists, and so creativity may be multidimensional and influenced by multiple factors. More research must be conducted before we can determine whether all types of creativity are related to and influenced by positive affect and feelings of well-being.

Implications for Work and Productivity

Fredrickson (1998) holds that happiness signals that one is safe and secure. This feeling may then prompt individuals to be playful and to try new things, a tendency that may result in novel solutions to problems and creative new ideas. However, creativity and playfulness may be adaptive only when workers have the freedom to play and when novel solutions are likely to increase performance. Certain tasks must be accomplished by following a precise set of guidelines, and the desire to try new things in these tasks may in fact result in decreased efficiency and perhaps even more mistakes. Thus, before researchers can determine whether the increased creativity that happy people exhibit will increase productivity, they must determine whether creative, playful approaches to a job will be helpful or detrimental to the overall functioning of their organization (for a similar interactional approach to understanding the associations between creativity and the traits of openness and conscientiousness, see George & Zhou, 2001).

Judgment and Decision Making

The literature on judgment and decision making presents a complicated picture of the cognitive processes that happy and unhappy individuals are likely to use. On the one hand, numerous studies show that happy individuals are less likely than neutral or sad individuals to evaluate the quality of arguments (Bless, Bohner, Schwarz, & Strack, 1990; Mackie & Worth, 1989) and are more likely to rely on stereotypes and preexisting judgments (Edwards & Weary, 1993; Meloy, 2000). These studies suggest that happy people are less careful and less analytical than unhappy people, which leads to more frequent errors and greater reliance on stereotypes and biases. On the other hand, in certain conditions (particularly when more personally relevant or more ecologically valid tasks are used), happy people have been shown to be more efficient in their cognitive processing. Baron (1990), for example, found that people who had experienced a positive mood induction were more likely than those who did not to use an efficient strategy in a clerical coding task, and Isen and Means (1983) showed that in a decision-making task, participants in a positive mood condition were more likely to ignore information that they had previously seen, resulting in a more efficient strategy. In addition, Bodenhausen, Kramer, and Süsser (1994) found that participants in a positive mood condition could overcome their stereotypes if they were told that they would be held accountable for their decisions.

Resolving the discrepancies in the literature has required emotion researchers to consider the function and effects of positive moods more carefully. Many emotion theorists now believe that positive moods are not tied to particular types of processing. Instead, moods may provide information about the conditions in the world around us, and it is that information that influences the choice of cognitive processing (Martin, Ward, Achee, & Wyer, 1993). Specifically, positive moods signify that things are going well, and therefore decisions can be made more quickly, less carefully, and with less concern about potential risks (Bless et al., 1996). As a result, people in positive moods will be likely to use heuristics to perform tasks. This results in more errors when attention to detail is required, but more efficient strategies when tasks are less difficult or more information needs to be synthesized.

Implications for Work and Productivity

The research on judgment and decision making illustrates that there are situations where a positive mood can lead to riskier decisions and less careful processing of available information. For jobs that require vigilance, caution, and careful consideration of all information, happy individuals may be less productive than less happy workers. Although happy individuals can sometimes overcome these deficits, it is unclear exactly when this occurs.

The increased vigilance of the unhappy worker does, however, have a trade-off: these workers may not be as efficient or as able to deal with complicated tasks as the happy individual. Happy workers may adopt more efficient processing strategies and more effective heuristics that allow them to accomplish complicated tasks very quickly, even if they are more likely to make errors. Thus, happy people may be able to engage in multitasking and other complicated tasks more effectively.

Job Characteristics That May Interact with Happiness

Based on current research on the functions of moods and emotions, we argue that any associations between happiness and productivity will not arise simply from an attitude-behavior link. In addition, although there are many general effects of well-being that may lead to slightly higher productivity, we do not expect many of these effects to be large. Instead, we believe that the most important effects of happiness and well-being on worker productivity are complex and varied, and most will interact with the nature of the tasks being performed. In this section, we speculate on the nature of job characteristics that could possibly interact with happiness to result in a more productive worker.

Social Contact

The most robust finding in the literature on the effects of happiness and well-being is that happy people enjoy, feel more confident in, and even attract social contact. This should make happy workers perform better in jobs that require social contact. Customer service jobs, sales jobs, and other occupations in which employees deal directly with customers and the general public will benefit from the happy worker's greater likeability and greater social competence. In addition, occupations that rely on teamwork and cooperation may benefit from employees with higher levels of positive affect. But because positive affect will likely increase employees' desire for social contact, greater positive affect may be detrimental in jobs where too much social contact is distracting and unproductive.

Interestingly, it may often be the case that for the same task, increased sociability may be both beneficial and detrimental at the same time. Happy sales employees probably benefit from increased likeability and greater sensitivity to the needs of their customers, but their greater feelings of helpfulness and sociability may also prevent them from making self-serving deals that are in the best interest of the organization. Similarly, happy technical support staff working for computer software or hardware companies may provide a more pleasant experience for customers seeking help, but these same workers may spend more time chatting, resulting in a less efficient process. In this case, two measures of employee productivity, customer satisfaction and amount of time spent per call, may conflict. It is unclear which measure will be affected more by differences in happiness, and therefore it is essential that researchers pay careful attention to the specific measures of productivity that are used, along with the specific mechanisms that lead to higher or lower productivity for the happy worker.

Negative Feedback and Failure

Happy workers are more likely to feel self-confident and persist in their efforts, even in the face of failure. Jobs vary in the extent to which individuals are likely to experience failure or receive negative feedback. For jobs where such feedback is frequent, happy workers may be more resilient and persistent than unhappy workers. For example, trial lawyers regularly face situations that have a clear winner and a clear loser. Lawyers who can persist in spite of the potential for failure and the actual experience of failure will be more likely to succeed in the future. Whenever jobs have the potential for frequent experience of failure or negative feedback, happy workers may have an advantage over unhappy ones. Where there is little of this feedback, happiness and self-confidence may have little benefit.

Structure

It is also likely that in highly structured and routinized jobs, affect is less likely to have effects on productivity. These jobs provide less opportunity for self-confidence, goal setting, and creativity to influence productivity because the procedures for accomplishing the job are strictly defined. Furthermore, in occupations where such structure and routine are required, increased positive affect may lead to greater playfulness, which can decrease productivity. Thus, we hypothesize that for more unstructured jobs such as chief executive officers and managers, affect can have an important impact on productivity. For highly prescripted jobs, affect should have less influence on performance. In support of this idea, Barrick and Mount (1993) found that extraversion was more strongly correlated with performance in jobs with greater autonomy.

Novelty and Complexity

For jobs that require novel responses, the happy worker may be able to synthesize information quickly and develop creative new strategies that can have a positive impact on productivity and performance. For complex and mentally challenging jobs, happy workers may be more likely to ignore irrelevant material and to use effective heuristics to simplify tasks. This should result in more efficient strategies and higher productivity. Less happy workers may be slower and more careful, resulting in an inability to make decisions and the use of overly cautious strategies.

Consequences of Errors

In some jobs, the cost of an occasional error is quite small; perhaps there are no important outcomes that result from the task or self-correcting mechanisms catch errors. In other jobs, however, errors are very costly, and constant vigilance is necessary. We hypothesize that happy people, who tend to be less vigilant than less happy people, may be at somewhat of a disadvantage when the costs of errors are quite high. Heart surgeons who must constantly monitor their actions and the conditions around them and mechanics checking jet engines for hairline cracks may be more careful in their activities when they have lower levels of positive affect. Thus, the consequences of errors and the potential for errors may interact with happiness in predicting worker productivity.

Conclusion

Positive affect, negative affect, life satisfaction, and job satisfaction are not simply attitudes about one's life and one's job. These components of happiness and well-being play a functional role in the choices that people make and the behaviors in which they engage. The research reviewed in this chapter shows that happy individuals are often more sociable, active, self-confident, healthier, more creative, and more likely to use quick and efficient strategies for processing information than are less happy individuals. Thus, happy individuals appear to have many advantages when interacting with the world. However, the specific impact that these differences will have on worker productivity likely depends on the nature of the worker's task. Happy workers may be more sociable, but whether this benefits productivity depends on the precise nature of their task. In addition, happy workers may be creative and efficient when performing complicated tasks, but this creativity and efficiency may come at the expense of caution and vigilance, which may result in costly errors. Thus, researchers interested in happy worker hypotheses must carefully examine the nature of the tasks in which workers will be engaged before making predictions about whether the hypothesis should hold.

Future research must determine whether selecting employees based on levels of happiness can increase productivity. Positive affect, negative affect, and life satisfaction are stable over time, and thus employers may want to match workers with tasks that are suitable for their dispositional level of happiness. However, much more research needs to be conducted on the specific interactions that occur before such selection procedures can be used confidently. Furthermore, even with the considerable stability in well-being levels, it is possible that programs to increase happiness may also be effective (Fordyce, 1977, 1983). If this is the case, research will be needed to determine whether selecting happy people or increasing overall levels of happiness provides the biggest boost to productivity.

In addition to suggesting some avenues for future research, we hope that we have been able to emphasize the importance of examining specific components of well-being, multiple objective and subjective indicators of productivity, and explicit mechanisms that can link the two. Evidence shows that different indicators of productivity may be uncorrelated (Meyer & Gupta, 1995) and may be differentially related to different forms of well-being. Furthermore, when researchers specify precise mechanisms linking specific components of happiness and specific forms of productivity, they can test each link in the chain from one construct to the other. This provides stronger evidence for the theories and prevents misinterpretation of the evidence. As studies of absenteeism and health have shown, happy workers may be more likely than unhappy workers to miss work due to illness but more likely than unhappy workers to miss work due to injuries or the desire to do something more fun. Therefore, studies that examine absenteeism without studying the reasons for it may not provide useful evidence about the processes underlying the happiness-absenteeism relation. Researchers who specify the precise mechanisms underlying the happy worker hypothesis in a specific context will be able to provide a stronger test of their theory.

The importance of the happy worker hypothesis may be increasing as the nature of work changes. Howard (1995) noted that as we have moved into a postindustrial information age, the focus of work has shifted from making products to managing and providing information. This shifting focus has resulted in increased numbers of service jobs, greater reliance on teamwork and the sharing of information, and higher involvement by workers. Many industries change quickly, and successful organizations adapt and provide novel products, services, and processes. These changes are transforming the nature of work in ways that have the potential to increase the influence of happiness and well-being on worker productivity. Therefore, the resurgence of interest in the happy worker hypothesis may be well timed to deal with the changing nature of work in the postindustrial information age.

References

Andreasen, N. C. (1987). Creativity and mental illness: Prevalence rates in writers and their first-degree relatives. *American Journal of Psychiatry, 144,* 1288–1292.

Baron, R. A. (1990). Environmentally induced positive affect: Its impact on self-efficacy, task performance, negotiation, and conflict. *Journal of Applied Social Psychology, 20,* 368–384.

Barrick, M. R., & Mount, M. K. (1991). The Big Five personality dimensions and job performance: A meta-analysis. *Personnel Psychology, 44,* 1–26.

Barrick, M. R., & Mount, M. K. (1993). Autonomy as a moderator of the relationships between the Big Five personality dimensions and job performance. *Journal of Applied Psychology, 78,* 111–118.

Barry, B., & Stewart, G. L. (1997). Composition, process, and performance in self-managed groups: The role of personality. *Journal of Applied Psychology, 82,* 62–78.

Bless, H., Bohner, G., Schwarz, N., & Strack, F. (1990). Mood and persuasion: A cognitive response analysis. *Personality and Social Psychology Bulletin, 16,* 331–345.

Bless, H., Clore, G. L., Schwarz, N., Golisano, V., Rabe, C., & Wolk, M. (1996). Mood and the use of scripts: Does a happy mood really lead to mindlessness? *Journal of Personality and Social Psychology, 71,* 665–679.

Bodenhausen, G. V., Kramer, G. P., & Süsser, K. (1994). Happiness and stereotypic thinking in social judgment. *Journal of Personality and Social Psychology, 66,* 621–632.

Brayfield, A. H., & Crockett, W. H. (1955). Employee attitudes and employee performance. *Psychological Bulletin, 52,* 396–424.

Burger, J. M., & Caldwell, D. F. (2000). Personality, social activities, job-search behavior and interview success: Distinguishing between PANAS trait positive affect and NEO extraversion. *Motivation and Emotion, 24,* 51–62.

Buss, D. M. (1991). Evolutionary personality psychology. *Annual Review of Psychology, 42,* 459–491.

Cacha, F. B. (1976). Figural creativity, personality, and peer nominations of pre-adolescents. *Gifted Child Quarterly, 20,* 187–195.

Carlson, M., Charlin, V., & Miller, N. (1988). Positive mood and helping behavior: A test of six hypotheses. *Journal of Personality and Social Psychology, 55,* 211–229.

Carnevale, P.J.D., & Isen, A. M. (1986). The influence of positive affect and visual access on the discovery of integrative solutions in bilateral negotiation. *Organizational Behavior and Human Decision Processes, 37,* 1–13.

Carver, C. S., & Scheier, M. F. (1990). Origins and functions of positive and negative affect: A control-process view. *Psychological Review, 97,* 19–35.

Clark, L. A., & Watson, D. (1988). Mood and the mundane: Relations between daily life events and self-reported mood. *Journal of Personality and Social Psychology, 54,* 296–308.

Costa, P. T., & McCrae, R. R. (1980). Influence of extraversion and neuroticism on subjective well-being: Happy and unhappy people. *Journal of Personality and Social Psychology, 38,* 668–678.

Cote, S. (1999). Affect and performance in organizational settings. *Current Directions in Psychological Science, 8,* 65–68.

Csikszentmihalyi, M., & Wong, M. M. (1991). The situational and personal correlates of happiness: A cross-national comparison. In F. Strack &

M. Argyle (Eds.), *Subjective well-being: An interdisciplinary perspective* (pp. 193–212). Elmsford, NY: Pergamon Press.

Cunningham, M. R. (1988a). Does happiness mean friendliness? Induced mood and heterosexual self-disclosure. *Personality and Social Psychology Bulletin, 14,* 283–297.

Cunningham, M. R. (1988b). What do you do when you're happy or blue? Mood, expectancies, and behavioral interest. *Motivation and Emotion, 12,* 309–331.

Dalton, D. R., & Mesch, D. J. (1991). On the extent and reduction of avoidable absenteeism: An assessment of absence policy provisions. *Journal of Applied Psychology, 79,* 67–76.

Danner, D. D., Snowdon, D. A., & Friesen, W. V. (2001). Positive emotions in early life and longevity: Findings from the nun study. *Journal of Personality Psychology, 80,* 804–813.

Depue, R. A., & Collins, P. F. (1999). Neurobiology of the structure of personality: Dopamine facilitation of incentive motivation and extraversion. *Behavioral and Brain Sciences, 22,* 491–569.

Diener, E., & Diener, M. (1995). Cross-cultural correlates of life satisfaction and self-esteem. *Journal of Personality and Social Psychology, 68,* 653–663.

Diener, E., & Emmons, R. A. (1984). The independence of positive and negative affect. *Journal of Personality and Social Psychology, 47,* 1105–1117.

Diener, E., & Fujita, F. (1995). Resources, personal strivings, and subjective well-being: A nomothetic and idiographic approach. *Journal of Personality and Social Psychology, 68,* 926–935.

Diener, E., Lyubomirsky, S., & King, L. A. (2001). *Is happiness a good thing? The benefits of long-term positive affect.* Manuscript in preparation, University of Illinois.

Diener, E., Suh, E. M., Lucas, R. E., & Smith, H. (1999). Subjective well-being: Thirty years of progress. *Psychological Bulletin, 125,* 276–102.

Dillon, K. M., Minchoff, B., & Baker, K. H. (1986). Positive emotional states and enhancement of the immune system. *International Journal of Psychiatry in Medicine, 15,* 13–18.

Edwards, J. A., & Weary, G. (1993). Depression and the impression formation continuum: Piecemeal processing despite the availability of category information. *Journal of Personality and Social Psychology, 64,* 636–645.

Emmons, R. A. (1986). Personal strivings: An approach to personality and subjective well-being. *Journal of Personality and Social Psychology, 51,* 1058–1068.

Estrada, C. A., Isen, A. M., & Young, M. J. (1994). Positive affect influences creative problem solving and reported source of practice satisfaction in physicians. *Motivation and Emotion, 18,* 285–299.

Feist, G. J. (1998). A meta-analysis of personality in scientific and artistic creativity. *Personality and Social Psychology Review, 2,* 290–309.

Fordyce, M. W. (1977). Development of a program to increase personal happiness. *Journal of Counseling Psychology, 24,* 318–355.

Fordyce, M. W. (1983). A program to increase happiness: Further studies. *Journal of Counseling Psychology, 30,* 483–498.

Fredrickson, B. L. (1998). What good are positive emotions? *Review of General Psychology, 2,* 300–319.

Friedman, H. S. (1999). Personality and longevity: Paradoxes. In J. M. Robine, B. Forette, C. Franceschi, & M. Allard (Eds.), *The paradoxes of longevity* (pp. 115–122). New York: Springer-Verlag.

Frijda, N. H. (1999). Emotions and hedonic experience. In D. Kahneman, E. Diener, & N. Schwarz (Eds.), *Well-being: The foundations of hedonic psychology* (pp. 190–210). New York: Russell Sage Foundation.

Furnham, A., & Miller, T. (1997). Personality, absenteeism and productivity. *Personality and Individual Differences, 23,* 705–707.

Futterman, A. D., Kemeny, M. E., Shapiro, D., & Fahey, J. L. (1994). Immunological and physiological changes associated with induced positive and negative mood. *Psychosomatic Medicine, 56,* 499–511.

George, J. M., & Brief, A. P. (1992). Feeling good—doing good: A conceptual analysis of the mood at work-organization spontaneity relationship. *Psychological Bulletin, 112,* 310–329.

George, J. M., & Zhou, J. (2001). When openness to experience and conscientiousness are related to creative behavior: An interactional approach. *Journal of Applied Psychology, 86,* 513–524.

Goodwin, F. K., & Jamison, K. R. (1990). *Manic-depressive illness.* New York: Oxford University Press.

Gouaux, C. (1971). Induced affective states and interpersonal attraction. *Journal of Personality and Social Psychology, 20,* 37–43.

Greene, T. R., & Noice, H. (1988). Influence of positive affect upon creative thinking and problem solving in children. *Psychological Reports, 63,* 895–898.

Harker, L., & Keltner, D. (2001). Expressions of positive emotions in women's college yearbook pictures and their relationship to personality and life outcomes across adulthood. *Journal of Personality and Social Psychology, 80,* 112–124.

Headey, B., & Veenhoven, R. (1989). Does happiness induce a rosy outlook? In R. Veenhoven (Ed.), *How harmful is happiness? Consequences of enjoying life or not* (pp. 106–127). Rotterdam, Netherlands: Universitaire Pers Rotterdam.

Hertel, G., Neuhof, J., Theuer, T., & Kerr, N. (2000). Mood effects on cooperation in small groups: Does positive mood simply lead to more cooperation? *Cognition and Emotion, 14,* 441–472.

Hirt, E. R., Melton, R. J., McDonald, H. E., & Harackiewicz, J. M. (1996). Processing goals, task interest, and the mood-performance relationship: A mediational analysis. *Journal of Personality and Social Psychology, 71,* 245–261.

Hom, H., & Arbuckle, B. (1988). Mood induction effects upon goal setting and performance in young children. *Motivation and Emotion, 12,* 113–122.

Howard, A. (1995). A framework for work change. In A. Howard (Ed.), *The changing nature of work* (pp. 3–44). San Francisco: Jossey-Bass.

Iaffaldano, M. T., & Muchinsky, P. M. (1985). Job satisfaction and job performance: A meta-analysis. *Psychological Bulletin, 97,* 251–273.

Isen, A. M. (1970). Success, failure, attention and reaction to others: The warm glow of success. *Journal of Personality and Social Psychology, 15,* 294–301.

Isen, A. M., Johnson, M. M., Mertz, E., & Robinson, G. F. (1985). The influence of positive affect on the unusualness of word associations. *Journal of Personality and Social Psychology, 48,* 1413–1426.

Isen, A. M., & Means, B. (1983). The influence of positive affect on decision-making strategy. *Social Cognition, 2,* 18–31.

Judge, T. A., Erez, A., & Bono, J. E. (1998). The power of being positive: The relation between positive self-concept and job performance. *Human Performance, 11,* 167–187.

Judge, T. A., Locke, E. A., & Durham, C. C. (1997). The dispositional causes of job satisfaction: A core evaluations approach. *Research in Organizational Behavior, 19,* 151–188.

Judge, T. A., Thoresen, C. J., Bono, J. E., & Patton, G. K. (2001). The job-satisfaction–job performance relationship: A qualitative and quantitative review. *Psychological Bulletin, 127,* 376–407.

King, L. A., & Napa, C. N. (1998). What makes a life good? *Journal of Personality and Social Psychology, 75,* 156–165.

Kohler, S. S., & Mathieu, J. J. (1993). Individual characteristics, work perceptions, and affective reactions influences on differentiated absence criteria. *Journal of Organizational Behavior, 14,* 515–530.

Landy, F. J. (1989). *Psychology of work behavior.* Pacific Grove, CA: Brooks/Cole.

Ledford, G. E., Jr. (1999). Happiness and productivity revisited. *Journal of Organizational Behavior, 20,* 25–30.

Lucas, R. E. (2000). *Pleasant affect and sociability: Towards a comprehensive model of extraverted feelings and behaviors.* Unpublished doctoral dissertation, University of Illinois.

Lucas, R. E., Diener, E., Grob, A., Suh, E. M., & Shao, L. (2000). Cross-cultural evidence for the fundamental features of extraversion. *Journal of Personality and Social Psychology, 79,* 452–468.

Lucas, R. E., Diener, E., & Suh, E. M. (1996). Discriminant validity of subjective well-being measures. *Journal of Personality and Social Psychology, 71,* 616–628.

Lucas, R. E., & Fujita, F. (2000). Factors influencing the relation between extraversion and pleasant affect. *Journal of Personality and Social Psychology, 79,* 1039–1056.

Lyubomirsky, S., & Tucker, K. L. (1998). Implications of individual differences in subjective happiness for perceiving, interpreting, and thinking about life events. *Motivation and Emotion, 22,* 155–186.

Mackie, D. M., & Worth, L. T. (1989). Processing deficits and the mediation of positive affect in persuasion. *Journal of Personality and Social Psychology, 57,* 27–40.

Martin, L. L., Ward, D. W., Achee, J. W., & Wyer, R. S. (1993). Mood as input: People have to interpret the motivational implications of their moods. *Journal of Personality and Social Psychology, 64,* 317–326.

Mayer, J. D., Mamberg, M. H., & Volanth, A. J. (1988). Cognitive domains of the mood system. *Journal of Personality 56,* 453–486.

Meloy, M. G. (2000). Mood-driven distortion of product information. *Journal of Consumer Research, 27,* 345–359.

Meyer, M., & Gupta, V. (1995). The performance paradox. In B. Staw & L. Cummings, (Eds.). *Research in organizational behavior* (Vol. 16, pp. 309–369). Greenwich, CT: JAI Press.

Morris, W. N. (1999). The mood system. In D. Kahneman, E. Diener, & N. Schwarz (Eds.), *Well-being: The foundations of hedonic psychology* (pp. 169–189). New York: Russell Sage Foundation.

Mount, M. K., Barrick, M. R., & Stewart, G. L. (1998). Personality predictors of performance in jobs involving interaction with others. *Human Performance, 11,* 145–166.

Murray, N., Sujan, H., Hirt, E. R., & Sujan, M. (1990). The influence of mood on categorization: A cognitive flexibility interpretation. *Journal of Personality and Social Psychology, 59,* 411–425.

Okun, M. A., Stock, W. A., Haring, M. J., & Witter, R. A. (1984). The social activity/subjective well-being relation: A quantitative synthesis. *Research on Aging, 6,* 45–65.

Organ, D. (1988). *Organizational citizenship behavior: The good soldier syndrome.* San Francisco: New Lexington Press.

Ostir, G. V., Markides, K. S., Black, S. A., & Goodwin, J. S. (2000). Emotional well-being predicts subsequent functional independence and survival. *Journal of the American Geriatrics Society, 48,* 473–478.

Richards, R. (1994). Creativity and bipolar mood swings: Why the association? In M. P. Shaw & M. A. Runco (Eds.), *Creativity and affect* (pp. 44–72). Norwood, NJ: Ablex.

Richards, R., & Kinney, D. K. (1990). Mood swings and creativity. *Creativity Research Journal, 3,* 202–217.

Richards, R., Kinney, D. K., Lunde, I., Benet, M., & Merzel, A. (1988). Creativity in manic-depressives, cyclothymes, their normal relatives, and control subjects. *Journal of Abnormal Psychology, 97,* 281–288.

Russell, J. A. (1980). A circumplex model of affect. *Journal of Personality and Social Psychology, 39,* 1161–1178.

Saavedra, R., & Earley, P. C. (1991). Choice of task and goal under conditions of general and specific affective inducement. *Motivation and Emotion, 15,* 45–65.

Sadri, G., & Robertson, I. T. (1993). Self-efficacy and work-related behavior: A review and meta-analysis. *Applied Psychology: An International Review, 42,* 139–152.

Salovey, P., Rothman, A. J., Detweiler, J. B., & Steward, W. T. (2000). Emotional states and physical health. *American Psychologist, 55,* 110–121.

Sapolsky, R. M. (1999). The physiology and pathophysiology of unhappiness. In D. Kahneman, E. Diener, & N. Schwarz (Eds.), *Well-being: The foundations of hedonic psychology* (pp. 453–469). New York: Russell Sage Foundation.

Sarason, I. G., Potter, E. H., & Sarason, B. R. (1986). Recording and recall of personal events: Effects on cognitions and behavior. *Journal of Personality and Social Psychology, 51,* 347–356.

Scheier, M. F., Carver, C. S., & Bridges, M. W. (2001). Optimism, pessimism, and psychological well-being. In E. C. Chang (Ed.), *Optimism and pessimism: Implications for theory, research, and practice* (pp. 189–216). Washington, DC: American Psychological Association.

Sinclair, R. C., & Mark, M. M. (1995). The effects of mood state on judgmental accuracy: Processing strategy as a mechanism. *Cognition and Emotion, 9,* 417–438.

Spector, P. E., Dwyer, D. J., & Jex, S. M. (1988). Relation of job stressors to affective, health, and performance outcomes: A comparison of multiple data sources. *Journal of Applied Psychology, 73,* 11–19.

Staw, B. M., & Barsade, S. G. (1993). Affect and managerial performance: A test of the sadder-but-wiser vs. happier-and-smarter hypotheses. *Administrative Science Quarterly, 38,* 304–331.

Stewart, G. L. (1996). Reward structure as a moderator of the relationship between extraversion and sales performance. *Journal of Applied Psychology, 81,* 619–627.

Stone, A. A., Cox, D. S., Valdimarsdottir, H., Jandorf, L., & Neale, J. M. (1987). Evidence that secretory IgA antibody is associated with daily mood. *Journal of Personality and Social Psychology, 52,* 988–993.

Stone, A. A., Neale, J. M., Cox, D. S., Napoli, A., Valdimarsdottir, H., & Kennedy-Moore, E. (1994). Daily events are associated with a secretory immune response to an oral antigen in men. *Health Psychology, 13,* 440–446.

Tellegen, A. (1985). Structures of mood and personality and their relevance to assessing anxiety, with an emphasis on self-report. In A. H. Tuma & J. D. Maser (Eds.), *Anxiety and the anxiety disorders* (pp. 681–706). Mahwah, NJ: Erlbaum.

Vroom, H. H. (1964). *Work and motivation.* New York: Wiley.

Watson, D., Clark, L. A., McIntyre, C. W., & Hamaker, S. (1992). Affect, personality, and social activity. *Journal of Personality and Social Psychology, 63,* 1011–1025.

Watson, D., Clark, L. A., & Tellegen, A. (1988). Development and validation of brief measures of positive and negative affect: The PANAS scales. *Journal of Personality and Social Psychology, 54,* 1063–1070.

Wright, J., & Mischel, W. (1982). Influence of affect on cognitive social learning person variables. *Journal of Personality and Social Psychology, 43,* 901–914.

Wright, R. (2000). *Nonzero: The logic of human destiny.* New York: Pantheon.

Wright, T. A., & Staw, B. M. (1999). Affect and favorable work outcomes: Two longitudinal tests of the happy-productive worker thesis. *Journal of Organizational Behavior, 20,* 1–23.

CHAPTER 3

Situational and Motivational Influences on Trait-Behavior Relationships

Murray R. Barrick
Terence R. Mitchell
Greg L. Stewart

Social cognitive theory suggests that a full understanding of human nature requires the study of three components: the person, the situation, and behavior (Bandura, 1986). A great deal of research in industrial/organizational psychology over the past hundred years has focused on the first component: the person. Considerable work has been invested in identifying which traits characterize an individual's personality and thereby make him or her different from other people. Today, a consensus has emerged that the second-order structure of personality consists of five (plus or minus two) major personality dimensions, known as the Big Five. In the past decade, a number of meta-analyses (Barrick & Mount, 1991; Hough, Eaton, Dunnette, Kamp, & McCloy, 1990; Hurtz & Donovan, 2000; Salgado, 1997) have shown that two of the five personality dimensions, Conscientiousness and Emotional Stability, predict performance outcomes in many, if not all, jobs, while the other three personality traits (Agreeableness, Extraversion, and Openness to Experience) are related to performance in some jobs or for specific criteria.

Less attention has been devoted to developing theory and research related to the influence of situations (Hattrup & Jackson, 1996; Murtha, Kanfer, & Ackerman, 1996; Peters & O'Connor, 1980; Stewart & Barrick, in press). Although there has been more discussion on these issues in the personality literature, there is a lack of theory related to the work context (Hattrup & Jackson, 1996). This is surprising given evidence that relationships between personality and performance are stronger when one accounts for the context a priori (Tett, Jackson, Rothstein, & Reddon, 1994). In short, meta-analytic true-score correlations between personality measures and performance tend to be significantly larger if researchers use their understanding of the job and organizational context (confirmatory versus exploratory analyses) to develop hypotheses about which personality traits are expected to be related to performance. Researchers thus seem capable of specifying which traits will be related to performance by accounting for situational demands (the job context). However, this approach provides no information about the process whereby the situation influences the relationship or about which aspects of the situation are crucial for moderating relationships with personality.

To advance research related to the situation, we need theory about how different settings influence relationships between personality and behavior. Although some work in the field of leadership has been done matching contexts and leader attributes (Fiedler, 1967), less work has been done in the field of motivation (Mitchell, 1997), which is particularly relevant for research on personality. We thus need to develop methods for conceptualizing the basic kinds of situations or, alternatively, identifying what variables are useful for comparing one situation with another. As a step toward this theoretical development, we focus on the distinction between competitive and cooperative situations. Although we agree that more dimensions will ultimately define work settings, these two have been shown to capture key differences in the social dynamics of work environments (Stewart & Barrick, in press).

The third component of the study of human nature involves behavior. Job analysts and others have devoted considerable effort to describing behavior at work (Harvey, 1991). In fact, Campbell (1991) argues that behavior is the only appropriate representation of performance in work contexts. However, there has not been enough theoretical and empirical work linking individual differences (cognitive abilities, personality traits, and interests) with job behavior constructs (delegating and coordinating, exchanging information, operating machines), particularly through well-grounded theories of motivation. According to social cognitive theory, an understanding of relationships between individual differences and job behavior requires an understanding of the cognitive processes that link them.

As Davis and Luthans (1980, p. 285) have pointed out, a main focus of social cognitive theory is "to investigate the mediating effects that covert cognitive processes have on an otherwise observable sequence of events." Cognition thus becomes the mediator that explains how situational factors and individual differences get translated into behavioral responses (Ajzen & Fishbein, 1980; Manz & Stewart, 1997). A major purpose of this chapter is to advance research focusing on work behavior by explicitly describing the cognitive processes that link personality traits to that behavior. These cognitive processes reflect cognitive-motivational work intentions, which reflect basic goals that people pursue at work. These intentions provide a goal-focused explanation of why certain personality traits are associated with high levels of work performance.

Figure 3.1 presents a social cognitive model that we will develop to describe how traits, situations, and cognitive-motivational work intentions relate to each other and thereby influence behavior. As shown, personality traits link to work intentions, which in turn influence performance. These relationships are moderated by situational demands associated with competitive and cooperative settings. To develop the model, we discuss the cognitive motivational work intentions through which personality affects behavior, specifically define and explore the mediating mechanisms of motivation on the personality-performance relationship, and then discuss the influence of situational demands and opportunities on these relationships.

How Do Distal Personality Traits Relate to Job Performance?

In the past decade, our understanding regarding the nature of relationships between personality traits and performance has been considerably enhanced by the study of specific personality con-

Figure 3.1. The Full Motivational Mediator Model.

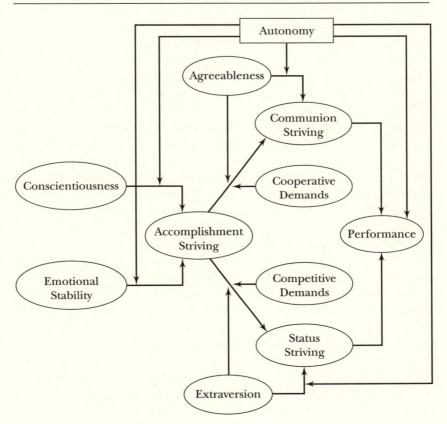

structs, typically based on the Five-Factor Model (FFM) of personality, and meta-analytic research. These studies reveal that two of the five personality traits, Conscientiousness and Emotional Stability, are universal predictors of overall job performance across nearly all jobs (Barrick, Mount, & Judge, 2001). In contrast, the other three traits (Extraversion, Agreeableness, and Openness to Experience) are contingent predictors of performance (Barrick et al., 2001). These traits relate to success in only a few jobs or with a few criteria. For example, Extraversion has been found to be related to performance in jobs with a large competitive social component (sales, managers). Agreeableness is a valid predictor of performance in jobs with cooperative demands or opportunities (use of work teams). Finally, Openness to Experience has not been found to relate to many outcomes of interest at work.

One explanation for the disappointing conclusions about Openness is that this trait is the least well understand personality construct in the FFM literature (Digman, 1990). Consequently, the weak relationships found to date may be attributable to an inadequately defined construct. Some researchers have even begun questioning the utility of this trait. However, recent evidence suggests that Openness to Experience may be related to creativity (George & Zhou, 2001). Such research may eventually help illustrate the validity of this construct. However, given the current ambiguity associated with Openness, it is not contained in our model.

Moving beyond our current understanding of the relationship between specific personality traits and overall performance requires an exploration of the mechanisms through which these personality traits influence performance. Today, most researchers assume that distal personality traits affect performance primarily through proximal motivational mediators (Barrick, Mount, & Strauss, 1993; Barrick, Stewart, & Piotrowski, 2002; Kanfer, 1991). Recent reviews of the motivation literature (Ambrose & Kulik, 1999; Mitchell & Daniels, 2002) point out that the construct currently dominating the motivational literature is goals (Austin & Vancouver, 1996). Goals, combined with efficacy and expectancy beliefs, have been integrated into an overarching self-regulatory, social cognitive approach to motivation that focuses on what the individual can do, wants to do, and will do in terms of future behavior and how such beliefs and aspirations affect current action.

The cognitive processes attributed to goal setting that are motivationally relevant are arousal, focusing attention, and establishing intentions. Establishing intentions includes the allocation of effort, persistence, and some sort of task strategy. Personality variables could probably influence most, if not all, of these factors. For example, goal discrepancies (distance to goal achievement) presumably cause arousal and direct attention. Thus, people who are focused on accomplishing task-oriented goals but are not accomplishing their interpersonal goals would be aroused and focused on this issue. They would allocate their attention on interpersonal activities that might close this gap and think about a plan (effort and persistence) to accomplish that end. It is these allocation and effort and persistence decisions that we describe as self-regulatory.

Regulatory goals can be organized hierarchically as well (Cropanzano, James, & Citera, 1992), ranging from abstract goal orientations or response styles (for example, motivational orientations toward achievement and affiliation) to midlevel goals, such as personal strivings and personal projects, to more concrete goals or specific performance goals complete with precise action plans. We believe that to predict relatively general performance measures, one should adopt relatively general midlevel goals. These goals are likely to reflect personal strivings (Emmons, 1989), which are formulated as specific means of attaining certain desired end states (to be one of the highest performers in the department, for example) at work. However, personal strivings are not so precise as to contain fully detailed plans and actions. They also are not so broad as to be unnecessarily vague and imprecise regarding future-directed plans. Rather, personal strivings represent broad, general intentions or motives that direct future courses of action at work. Although much research has gone into the higher-level motivational orientations (VandeWalle, 1999; Dweck, 1986) and specific task goals (Locke & Latham, 1990), less work in industrial/organizational psychology has gone into the midrange goals.

Sheldon, Elliot, Kim, and Kasser (2001) examined ten fundamental motives that people strive to fulfill through satisfying events or experiences. Across three different studies, they found that motives labeled as self-esteem, relatedness, autonomy, and competence were strongly related to an individual's most satisfying experiences. This suggests that people are motivated to achieve a sense of self-respect (self-esteem), meaningful contact with others (relatedness), enhanced perceived control (autonomy), and challenging work that demonstrates their own capabilities (competence). We believe that people incorporate these fundamental motives into their goals or personal strivings.

Two of these fundamental motives, striving for self-esteem and competence, should be related to goals or personal strivings associated with task achievement. Task-oriented employees have a strong desire to accomplish task-related goals as a means of expressing their competence and to build self-esteem (Stewart & Barrick, in press). We categorize the goals or personal strivings associated with task orientation as representing Accomplishment Striving.

Accomplishment Striving reflects an individual's intention to accomplish work tasks and is expected to be characterized by high task motivation. Behaviorally, Accomplishment Striving is likely to be expressed in a way that laypeople would call "work motivation"; these employees are likely to exert considerable task effort and maintain that effort over an extended period of time. We believe that Accomplishment Striving is cognitively represented and assessable as intentions. It differs from typical perceptions of motivation, however, as it relates to a generalized, individual difference measure representing intentions to exert effort and work hard. We believe it is likely caused by many determinants, including the person's personality traits and environmental features such as instructing the person to try harder, offering incentives to perform well, or making the task meaningful or difficult.

The results of Sheldon et al. (2001) also underscore that social interactions at work, or relatedness, is a fundamental motive. Researchers have identified two broad motivational intentions related to social interactions (Hogan & Shelton, 1998; Wiggins & Trapnell, 1996). The first dimension captures goals directed toward obtaining acceptance and intimacy in personal relationships. We label this personal striving Communion Striving. At work, Communion Striving would be expressed by actions associated with "getting along with others." The second dimension, called Status Striving, reflects goals directed toward obtaining power and dominance within a status hierarchy. At work, employees often achieve this by "getting ahead of others." We think of these two constructs as separate measures that comprehensively depict the social dynamics of the work setting. In some sense, this distinction is one between the vertical organizational structure (interacting with superiors and subordinates) and the horizontal structure (dealing with peers). One of the major goals of this chapter is to introduce the fundamental difference that emerges from these two personal strivings toward relatedness. In addition, this distinction is likely to have important effects at the organizational level, as well as the individual level, a topic to which we will return.

The Effect of Personal Strivings on Personality-Performance Relationships

The three motivational constructs of Accomplishment Striving, Communion Striving, and Status Striving allow us to relate individual differences in personality to performance on a variety of jobs. In this section, we relate the four relevant personality traits to the motivational constructs.

Conscientiousness and Emotional Stability are personality traits that are likely to be universal predictors of performance across a variety of jobs. To apply our motivational mediator model to the case of these two traits, we assume that both affect performance through work motivation, particularly motivation related to Accomplishment Striving. Conscientious people set goals, are more committed to those goals, and exert more effort (Barrick et al., 1993; Gellatly, 1996). Thus, they are more "motivated" at work and strive to achieve. In contrast, neurotic employees (low in Emotional Stability) have significantly reduced motivation at work. Emotionally unstable people do not see themselves as worthy, are less confident, are frequently distracted by worrying and become obsessed with details, and are more dissatisfied with themselves, their jobs, and lives. Thus, they are less motivated to accomplish tasks at work, and if they are "motivated" at all, it is to avoid failure at work. Based on this reasoning, we believe these two personality traits will relate to performance through on-task effort or Accomplishment Striving at work.

The effects for Conscientiousness and Emotional Stability on performance through Accomplishment Striving should exist across jobs. First, these personality traits have been found to be universal predictors of performance. Therefore, they would be expected to be valid predictors in all or nearly all jobs, which reduces (but does not eliminate) concerns about the effect of situational demands on these relationships. Second, Accomplishment Striving is a fundamental cognitive-motivational variable that affects behavior in all jobs; it is hard to conceive of a job where an employee's motivation to accomplish tasks will not affect performance. This may explain why Conscientiousness and Emotional Stability are universal predictors of performance. That is, if they are related to accomplishment striving, which in turn has universal applicability to work in all jobs, the expectation is that these two traits would be valid predictors in all, or nearly all, jobs.

Turning to the two interpersonal personality traits, Extraversion and Agreeableness are expected to affect job performance through our other two cognitive-motivational work intentions: Status Striving and Communion Striving. Lucas, Diener, Grob, Suh, and Shao (2000) demonstrate that the core features of Extraversion are energy, ascendance, and ambition. The primary essence of Extraversion is thus a sensitivity to obtaining rewards rather than sociability. In fact, they argue that sociability appears to be an important feature of Extraversion because it provides more opportunities to achieve status and rewards. Consequently, Extraversion will be related to Status Striving rather than Communion Striving. In contrast, the fundamental features of Agreeableness appear to be primarily related to affiliation and friendliness (Digman, 1990). Consequently, Agreeableness will be linked to personal strivings that contribute to Communion Striving and not to those related to Status Striving.

Confirmation for these relationships between personality and motivational strivings is found in a recent study by Barrick et al. (2002). In a study of 164 sales representatives, Barrick et al. demonstrated that Conscientiousness ($r = .39$) and Emotional Stability ($r = .15$) were significantly related to Accomplishment Striving. Extraversion was correlated with Status Striving ($r = .48$) and Agreeableness with Communion Striving ($r = .15$). Barrick et al. also examined the links among Accomplishment Striving, Communion Striving, and Status Striving. In accordance with the model presented in Figure 3.1, Accomplishment Striving and Status Striving were related to performance. Similarly, as expected, Communion Striving in this competitive sales setting, was not related to performance. Furthermore, as suggested in Figure 3.1, Status Striving mediated the relationship between Accomplishment Striving and performance. As we explain below, we expect similar mediation through Communion Striving in cooperative settings. People thus appear to be ultimately motivated to accomplish tasks in order to achieve either communion or status, depending on their traits and the situational context.

How Do Situational Demands Affect the Personality-Performance Link?

An undergraduate student noted, "I am extraverted with my friends but introverted when in a large lecture classroom." This statement, embodied by interactionists, indicates that a personality trait will be a significant predictor of behavior only in situations that are relevant to its expression and not so constrained as to disallow individual differences (Endler & Magnusson, 1976). To argue that situations do not matter implies that people will show powerful cross-situational consistency of responses. Yet to respond in exactly the same way across time and diverse situations would be maladaptive and is likely to result in many dysfunctional behaviors. Consequently, most researchers today recognize that to predict behavior with personality requires one to account for the situation (Kenrick & Funder, 1988). We believe personality will have its greatest effect on behavior when the situation is relevant to the trait's expression and is weak enough to allow the person to choose how to behave in that situation (Stewart & Barrick, in press).

Although work psychologists have examined how aspects of the immediate work situation affect variance in performance (the job analytic literature), no taxonomy has been developed that incorporates both situational and trait effects (Murtha et al., 1996) on motivational mediators. This unfortunate circumstance has long been recognized (Peters & O'Connor, 1980). Although there are many dimensions across which the work environment can be meaningfully categorized, here we focus on one broad aspect of situations: the social setting.

Cooperation and Competitive Demands

Research illustrates that although several dimensions of work design have been identified, an important component of many, if not all, theories of work design relates to how individuals contribute to the organization through social inputs. For example, a fundamental design feature of structural contingency theory recognizes the importance of interdependence among people in the organization, particularly the vertical (the authority system) and lateral relationships (the informal peer system). Similarly, at the organizational level, several dimensions of work design have been identified, but empirical research shows that many of them can be summarized by two parameters: (1) coordination or structuring of activities and (2) concentration of authority or interdependence among workers and managers (Pugh & Hickson, 1997). Thus, both individual- and organizational-level literatures on work design underscore the importance of determining how tasks are coordinated and controlled. These theories also assess the extent to which employees depend on each other for information, materials, and reciprocal inputs.

Ultimately, how the organization addresses the fundamental issues of coordination and control at work will have a substantive impact on the social dynamics of that work setting. One dimension along which the social aspects of work settings differ is how the firm structures the cooperative and competitive demands and opportunities in the organization. For example, an organization may design the job of marketing specialist so that employees work in a team that requires extensive interdependence to develop marketing campaigns. In another firm, the marketing specialist job may be designed to work independently of others. Furthermore, this organization may encourage multiple marketing specialists to vie for limited incentives or resources by making them available only to employees who have their marketing campaigns adopted by a customer. Thus, these two work settings will fundamentally differ in their cooperative and competitive social demands.

The importance of cooperative and competitive demands is supported by research that reveals that social aspects of work are psychologically meaningful to employees. How we see ourselves is substantially influenced by how we are defined in relation to others in the larger organization or society (Markus & Kitayama, 1991). Furthermore, Hogan (1996) argues that socioanalytic theory, which is based on an evolutionary perspective, identifies two critical social dimensions that people pursue. These dimensions address how individuals strive toward getting along with others (cooperation) and getting ahead of others (competition). People are thus predisposed to distinguish work settings according to the cooperative and competitive demands and opportunities of the situation. We propose that these distinctions will systematically affect the strength of the relationship between relevant personality traits and work performance.

Research from an ecological perspective of personality similarly suggests cooperation and competition as fundamental features of environments. Central to this perspective is the concept of affordances, which Gibson (1979) defines as the fundamental utilities or action possibilities that the physical or social environment offers. Baron and Boudreau (1987) extend this concept and argue that in social settings, the opportunity to engage in certain behaviors is dependent on the actions of others. In particular, cooperative and competitive behaviors require reciprocal, coordinated behavior from others. Specifically, Baron and Boudreau suggest that "helpfulness requires a helper and a recipient, competition requires a rival, and dominance requires a subordinate" (p. 1223). Traits are thus expressed when other people in the organizational environment afford (allow and encourage) their expression. In particular, environments tend to differ on the extent to which they afford demonstrations of competitive and cooperative behavior (Baron & Boudreau, 1987).

In accordance with the ecological notion of affordances, our focus on cooperative and competitive demands is driven in part by an observation that behavior in social settings corresponds to key individual differences. The two personality traits that appear to have the strongest influence on social behavior are Extraversion and Agreeableness (Graziano, Hair, & Finch, 1997; Lucas et al., 2000). The typical extravert craves excitement, is adventurous, and tends to be assertive and dominant, as well as sociable. Thus, the social behavior of highly extraverted individuals is characterized by demonstrations of dominance and competitiveness (Lucas et al., 2000). In contrast, agreeable people are helpful, trusting, and friendly; they are cooperative and work well with others. Highly agreeable employees prefer social situations that are characterized by cooperation, close relationships, and interpersonal harmony and acceptance.

The effects of cooperative and competitive situational differences on Extraversion and Agreeableness have been empirically demonstrated. In a meta-analysis, Mount, Barrick, and Stewart (1998) reported that Agreeableness was the most important personality predictor of performance in jobs involving interactions with others (ρ = .27, n = 1,491), particularly when those jobs involve interacting in teams (ρ = .35, n = 678). Results from Hough's meta-analysis (1992) support this; she found that Agreeableness correlated with measures of teamwork (r = .17). Agreeableness thus appears to be an important predictor of behavior in cooperative settings.

Barrick and Mount (1991) found Extraversion to be a valid predictor of performance in management and sales jobs, which have a high social component related to influencing or leading others (sales: ρ = .15, n = 2,316; management: ρ = .18, n = 11,335). Stewart (1996) also illustrated that Extraversion is quite sensitive to the situational influence of rewards. In this study, Extraversion was related to higher performance only on performance dimensions that were explicitly rewarded (new sales or customer relations). Empirical findings thus suggest that Extraversion is related to performance in situations where one can acquire and maintain status (that is, in competitive situations).

Autonomy

In addition to cooperative and competitive demands, the level of autonomy in the situation is likely to have a fundamental impact on the relationship between personality traits and performance. The nature of this effect is quite different from that attributed to the influence of cooperative or competitive social demands at work, however. In this case, autonomy relates to the extent to which the external environment constrains a person's freedom to behave in idiosyncratic ways (Barrick & Mount, 1993; Liu & Weiss, 2000). In strong situations, the organization exerts considerable pressure or demands to induce conformity. These controlling forces press the individual to behave in a specific way or exhibit a very narrow range of behaviors. In contrast, weak situations present few demands or presses to conform. In such settings, the individual determines which behaviors, if any, to undertake. The magnitude of the relationship between personality traits and behavior is thus greater in weak situations, or settings where people can perform their jobs in idiosyncratic ways.

A few studies demonstrate that personality is more useful in predicting behavior when autonomy is high than when it is low.

Data from 146 managers (Barrick & Mount, 1993) indicated that the predictive validity of two relevant personality predictors, Conscientiousness and Extraversion, was greater for managers in jobs high in autonomy compared with those in jobs low in autonomy. Lee, Ashford, and Bobko (1990) also found that the degree of autonomy a person has in his or her job moderated the relationships between Type A behavior and job performance, job satisfaction, and somatic complaints for employees from a variety of organizations. Based on these findings, we believe the degree of autonomy in the situation moderates the effects of all relevant personality predictors on performance.

The Role of Situational Factors

These situational effects are represented in the model (see Figure 3.1). First, the two interpersonal personality traits, Extraversion and Agreeableness, are expected to relate to behavior only when the relevant situational demands and opportunities are highly salient in the work setting. Specifically, Extraversion should relate to job performance only in settings that can be characterized as competitive work environments. In contrast, Agreeableness should predict performance behavior only when the work requires workers to cooperate. In a similar vein, Status Striving relates to performance only in competitive environments and Communion Striving only in cooperative settings.

The model also suggests that relevant personality traits have higher correlations with performance when the degree of autonomy in the job is high (a weak situation). Consequently, in jobs with high autonomy, the predictive validity of Extraversion should be higher if the job is competitive and the validity of Agreeableness should be higher for cooperative jobs. Furthermore, two personality traits, Conscientiousness and Emotional Stability, are expected to be valid predictors of performance in nearly all jobs. In settings where the situational pressures are weak (high autonomy), we expect the relationship between these traits and performance also to be higher than where autonomy is low. Thus, the level of autonomy in the job will moderate the relationship between Conscientiousness and Emotional Stability with performance in all or nearly all jobs, and either Extraversion or Agreeableness on performance depending on the degree of cooperative or competitive demands at work.

The Barrick et al. (2002) study is also suggestive about the importance of accounting for the cooperative and competitive demands salient in the situation. In this study, the job (telemarketing) was characterized as one high in competitive demands (with high sales pressure and contact with the customer limited to one brief telephone interaction), but low in cooperative demands (the sales representative works alone and is not dependent on others for performance). Given these situational factors, Barrick et al. expected Status Striving, but not Communion Striving, to be a relevant mediator of the personality-performance relationship. As expected, they found that Status Striving was related to performance ($r = .36$) and Communion Striving was not ($r = -.10$). More important, as predicted by the model in Figure 3.1, the major portion of the relationship between Extraversion and job performance was indirect through Status Striving (approximately 76 percent of the effect is mediated by Status Striving). Although Agreeableness was related to Communion Striving, neither Agreeableness nor Communion Striving was related to success in this sales job.

These results have important implications for the model. In essence, they show that relevant personality traits were related to job success through motivational mediators. Although this study was not able to contrast multiple situations (it did not include data from multiple jobs that differed in cooperative or competitive social demands), it did support the linkage expected for jobs with high competitive demands.

We realize that the model is silent regarding the effect that cooperative demands may have on competitive demands, and vice versa. In fact, Figure 3.1 implies that these situational demands are relatively independent. This is not our intent. Given our limited knowledge about the nature of these relationships, particularly at work, we believe that future research should strive to clarify the relationship among these competing demands (the need for teamwork, yet the need to be individually recognized and rewarded). For the time being, we anticipate that researchers will examine the relations among these variables in jobs that are clearly high in cooperative demands or competitive demands.

Future Research Directions

The model that we present here focuses on the processes through which traits influence performance. A major contention of the mediational portion of the model is that traits are expressed through broad goals, or personal strivings. Although this perspective is generally supported by theory and empirical research, there are some additional ways that goals and goal properties might mediate the personality-situation relationship with behavior. For example, Mitchell and Wood (1994) point out that some goals focus on process while others focus on outcomes. People high on Agreeableness may be more motivated by process goals, and people high on Conscientiousness may prefer outcome goals. In addition, research could test to see the consistency of goals preferred across different hierarchical levels. Individuals high on communion striving, for example, should also embrace values reflecting the importance of interpersonal harmony at the highest level and working in teams at a lower task-specific level. Similar type consistency would be expected for Status Striving and Accomplishment Striving. Examinations of such consistencies and goal preferences are clearly warranted and provide a potentially fruitful path for additional research.

Another major dimension of goal-setting research focuses on whether goals should be set by the self, assigned, or set participatively with one's boss. At least initially, we believe that personality factors might be related to preferences for these different strategies. For example, highly conscientious people might prosper with self-set goals, people high on Agreeableness might prefer the interpersonal process involved with participation, and emotionally stable people might prefer the concreteness and specificity of assigned goals. Thus, the goal construct and the goal-setting process also hold promise for further research on the mediating role between personality and behavior.

Sheldon and Elliot's self-concordance model (1999) provides some interesting thoughts for guiding future research. This model suggests that people are more likely to persist at and derive well-being from goals congruent with enduring interests and values. This perspective suggests that extraverted individuals are likely to work hardest in environments that afford competition, whereas agreeable individuals will work hardest in cooperative environments. However, Sheldon and Elliot also suggest that the attainment of self-concordant goals is key to individual well-being. Our model looks only at performance. Yet the self-concordance model suggests that agreeable individuals will derive satisfaction from working in cooperative environments, and extraverts will be happiest in competitive environments. Future models and research can likely benefit from directly examining the effects of personality not only on performance but also on employee satisfaction. More important, the model should be extended to other work behaviors, including withdrawal and counterproductive behavior.

The self-concordance model also suggests that competence, autonomy, and relatedness are primary mechanisms that ensure people will persist in goal-directed behavior. Our model is similar in its assertion that greater autonomy allows agreeable and extraverted people to pursue goals consistent with their trait preferences. The model is consistent with notions of relatedness in that it suggests that agreeable people prefer relating to others cooperatively, whereas extraverts prefer relating competitively. The model does not, however, specifically include a focus on competence. We believe that competence is likely to have important relationships with Conscientiousness, Emotional Stability, and Accomplishment Striving. For example, the relationship between Conscientiousness and Accomplishment Striving may be stronger if the person has high competence on the task, particularly if there is considerable autonomy in the job. We encourage future researchers to explore the nature of these relationships.

The model we present here highlights ways that situational characteristics affect the relationship between personality traits and job success. Our model emphasizes interpersonal contextual dimensions (competitive and cooperative demands) as critical situational variables that affect these relationships. Researchers should explore the role of other situational variables. For example, the emotional demands or emotional labor of the work context may be an important situational factor to consider. At an extreme, emotionally taxing work can result in burnout, which has been consistently linked with organizational consequences such as increased turnover, stronger intentions to leave, negative work attitudes, and reduced levels of performance (Brotheridge & Grandey, in press; Wright & Cropanzano, 1998). Personality traits like Emotional Stability and Extraversion are likely to be important predictors of burnout. Consequently, there may be value in assessing the emotional demands associated with various jobs on the personality—performance relationship. A taxonomy of emotional demands could focus on "emotional taxes" due to task demands (as with surgeons who face life-and-death decisions), interpersonal demands (such as sales representatives who have frequent interactions with challenging customers), and emotional control required by the job (for example, ambulance technicians who encounter emotionally demanding circumstances). With the development of a theoretically relevant taxonomy of emotional demands, we believe researchers could explore the effect these emotional factors have on the nature and magnitude of the relationship between specific personality traits and performance or affective outcomes.

Research on cognitive ability has illustrated that complexity of the job, as determined by job knowledge requirements, is an important determinant of the relationship between ability and performance (Hunter, 1986; Schmidt, Hunter, Outerbridge, & Trattner, 1986). Consequently, models of job performance must also include job complexity as an important situational variable. Is job complexity likely to be an important moderator for personality? We do not know. However, if it is, it may be because complexity is associated with greater discretion or autonomy, in addition to a need for more job-specific knowledge. Furthermore, if the job is too simple or too complex for the person's skills, it may have implications for motivation (not intrinsically motivating if too simple a job) or anxiety (if too difficult, it may increase the emotional labor of the job). Given this, research that extends our understanding of the role of job complexity on personality-performance relationships is important.

While these alternative perspectives suggest areas where our model will likely be refined, we believe that both our general model of the effects of person and situation variables on behavior and our specific model of how four personality traits relate to motivation and subsequently to performance can guide research. In the general model, we have proposed that at least two situational constructs (cooperative demands and competitive demands) are required to explain the relationship between the two interpersonal traits (Extraversion and Agreeableness) on performance. The influence of situational demands and opportunities relevant to these outcomes remains a relatively unexplored source of variance of potential importance to both researchers and practitioners alike. These frequently overlooked contextual factors are hypothesized to affect the level of observed performance, the relationship between personality and performance, and the personality-motivational-performance linkages. The limited empirical evidence available clearly justifies the need to explore the direct and interactive effects of situational demands as important determinants of these outcomes.

Conclusion

The model shown in Figure 3.1 is our interpretation of how specific distal personality traits, as well as situational factors, are related to important work behaviors on a day-to-day basis. This model emphasizes personal goals (strivings and projects) as the key proximal motivational variables through which our long-term dispositional tendencies are operationalized. Alternative theoretically relevant measures of motivation include expectancies and competency beliefs, affective variables, and subjective values and valences. We believe that focusing on cognitive-motivational goals captures much of the critical variance for the work motivation construct space relevant to these performance outcomes. Certainly, there is considerable support for the notion that cognitive processes (goals) are critical to understanding the relationship between person factors and job behaviors. Nevertheless, future research must address whether these goal-oriented variables adequately represent motivational effects.

Our model suggests that Accomplishment Striving is the engine through which the relevant social goals (either Status Striving or Communion Striving, depending on the situation) affect performance. The available data support this conjecture, but we still need direct comparisons of the effects of Accomplishment Strivings on either Status Striving and Communion Striving and, in turn, their effects on performance in a variety of work settings. This model also suggests that the explanation for the universal effects for Conscientiousness and Emotional Stability are due to their effects on Accomplishment Striving.

We have sought to show how person and situation factors are linked through motivational variables to predict a reasonably broad range of behavioral performance measures in various work contexts. Industrial/organizational psychologists have historically focused on the relationship between personality and performance. This chapter illustrates that we also need to account for situational determinants of behavior, as well as the mechanisms through which personality affects behavior. Pursuing this research will enable researchers to make progress on explaining both performance and affective work outcomes.

References

Ajzen, I., & Fishbein, M. (1980). *Understanding attitudes and predicting social behavior.* Upper Saddle River, NJ: Prentice Hall.

Ambrose, M. L., & Kulik, C. T. (1999). Old friends, new faces: Motivation research in the 1990s. *Journal of Management, 25,* 231–292.

Austin, J. T., & Vancouver, J. B. (1996). Goal constructs in psychology: Structure, process, and content. *Psychology Bulletin, 120,* 338–375.

Bandura, A. (1986). *Social foundations of thought and action: A social cognitive theory.* Upper Saddle River, NJ: Prentice Hall.

Baron, R. M., & Boudreau, L. A. (1987). An ecological perspective on integrating personality and social psychology. *Journal of Personality and Social Psychology, 53,* 1222–1228.

Barrick, M. R., & Mount, M. K. (1991). The Big Five personality dimensions and job performance: A meta-analysis. *Personnel Psychology, 44,* 1–26.

Barrick, M. R., & Mount, M. K. (1993). Autonomy as a moderator of the relationships between the Big Five personality dimensions and job performance. *Journal of Applied Psychology, 78,* 111–118.

Barrick, M. R., Mount, M. K., & Judge, T. A. (2001). The FFM personality dimensions and job performance: Meta-analysis of meta-analyses. *International Journal of Selection and Assessment, 9,* 9–30.

Barrick, M. R., Mount, M. K., & Strauss, J. P. (1993). Conscientiousness and performance of sales representatives: Test of the mediating effects of goal setting. *Journal of Applied Psychology, 78,* 715–722.

Barrick, M. R., Stewart, G. L., & Piotrowski, M. (2002). Personality and job performance: Test of the mediating effects of motivation among sales representatives. *Journal of Applied Psychology, 87,* 43–51.

Brotheridge, C. M., & Grandey, A. A. (in press). Emotional labor and burnout: Comparing two perspectives of "people work." *Journal of Vocational Behavior.*

Campbell, J. P. (1991). Modeling the performance prediction problem in industrial and organizational psychology. In M. D. Dunnette &

L. M. Hough (Eds.), *Handbook of industrial and organizational psychology* (pp. 687–732). Palo Alto, CA: Consulting Psychologists Press.

Cropanzano, R., James, K., & Citera, M. (1992). A goal hierarchy model of personality, motivation, and leadership. *Research in Organizational Behavior, 15,* 267–322.

Davis, T.R.V., & Luthans, F. (1980). A social learning approach to organizational behavior. *Academy of Management Review, 5,* 281–290.

Digman, J. M. (1990). Personality structure: Emergence of the Five-Factor Model. *Annual Review of Psychology, 41,* 417–440.

Dweck, C. S. (1986). Motivational processes affecting learning. *American Psychologist, 41,* 1040–1048.

Emmons, R. A. (1989). The personal strivings approach to personality. In L. A. Pervin (Ed.), *Goal concepts in personality and social psychology* (pp. 87–117). Mahwah, NJ: Erlbaum.

Endler, N. S., & Magnusson, D. (1976). *Interactional psychology and personality.* Washington, DC: Hemisphere.

Fiedler, F. E. (1967). *A theory of leadership effectiveness.* New York: McGraw-Hill.

Gellatly, I. R. (1996). Conscientiousness and task performance: Test of a cognitive process model. *Journal of Applied Psychology, 81,* 474–482.

George, J. M., & Zhou, J. (2001). When Openness to Experience and Conscientiousness are related to creative behavior: An interactional approach. *Journal of Applied Psychology, 86,* 513–524.

Gibson, J. J. (1979). *The ecological approach to visual perception.* Boston: Houghton Mifflin.

Graziano, W. G., Hair, E. C., & Finch, J. F. (1997). Competitiveness mediates the link between personality and group performance. *Journal of Personality and Social Psychology, 73,* 1394–1408.

Harvey, R. J. (1991). Job analysis. In M. D. Dunnette & L. M. Hough (Eds.), *Handbook of industrial and organizational psychology* (Vol. 2, pp. 71–164). Palo Alto, CA: Consulting Psychologists Press.

Hattrup, K., & Jackson, S. E. (1996). Learning about individual differences by taking situations seriously. In K. R. Murphy (Ed.), *Individual differences and behavior in organizations* (pp. 507–547). San Francisco: Jossey-Bass.

Hogan, R. (1996). A socioanalytic perspective on the Five-Factor Model. In J. S. Wiggins (Ed.), *The Five-Factor Model of personality* (pp. 163–179). New York: Guilford Press.

Hogan, R., & Shelton, D. (1998). A socioanalytic perspective on job performance. *Human Performance, 11,* 129–144.

Hough, L. M. (1992). The "Big Five" personality variables–construct confusion: Description versus prediction. *Human Performance, 5,* 139–155.

Hough, L. M., Eaton, N. K., Dunnette, M. D., Kamp, J. D., & McCloy, R. A. (1990). Criterion-related validities of personality constructs and the effect of response distortion on those validities. *Journal of Applied Psychology, 75,* 581–595.

Hunter, J. E. (1986). Cognitive ability, cognitive aptitudes, job knowledge, and job performance. *Journal of Vocational Behavior, 29,* 340–362.

Hurtz, G. M., & Donovan, J. J. (2000). Personality and job performance: The Big Five revisited. *Journal of Applied Psychology, 85,* 869–879.

Kanfer, R. (1991). Motivation theory and industrial and organizational psychology. In M. D. Dunnette & L. M. Hough (Eds.), *Handbook of industrial and organizational psychology* (pp. 75–170). Palo Alto, CA: Consulting Psychologists Press.

Kenrick, D. T., & Funder, D. C. (1988). Profiting from controversy: Lessons from the person-situation controversy. *American Psychologist, 43,* 23–34.

Lee, C., Ashford, S. J., & Boko, P. (1990). Interactive effects of "Type A" behavior and perceived control on worker performance, job satisfaction, and somatic complaints. *Academy of Management Journal, 33,* 870–881.

Liu, C., & Weiss, H. M. (2000). *Interactive effects of personality and situational strength on goal behaviors.* Working paper, Purdue University.

Locke, E. A., & Latham, G. P. (1990). *A theory of goal setting and task performance.* Upper Saddle River, NJ: Prentice Hall.

Lucas, R. E., Diener, E., Grob, A., Suh, E. M., & Shao, L. (2000). Cross-cultural evidence for the fundamental features of Extraversion. *Journal of Personality and Social Psychology, 79,* 452–468.

Manz, C. C., & Stewart, G. L. (1997). Attaining flexible stability by integrating total quality management and sociotechnical systems theory. *Organization Science, 8,* 59–70.

Markus, H. R., & Kitayama, S. (1991). Culture and self: Implications for cognition, emotion, and motivation. *Psychological Review, 98,* 224–253.

Mitchell, T. R. (1997). Matching motivational strategies with organizational contexts. *Research in Organizational Behavior, 19,* 57–149.

Mitchell, T. R., & Daniels, D. (2002). Motivation. In W. C. Borman, D. R. Ilgen, & R. J. Klimoski (Eds.), *Comprehensive handbook of psychology, Vol. 12: Industrial and organizational psychology.* New York: Wiley.

Mitchell, T. R., & Wood, R. E. (1994). Managerial goal setting. *Journal of Leadership Studies, 1,* 3–26.

Mount, M. K., Barrick, M. R., & Stewart, G. L. (1998). Five-Factor Model of personality and performance in jobs involving interpersonal interactions. *Human Performance, 11,* 145–165.

Murtha, T. C., Kanfer, R., & Ackerman, P. L. (1996). Toward an interactionist taxonomy of personality and situations: An integrative situational-dispositional representation of personality traits. *Journal of Personality and Social Psychology, 71,* 193–207.

Peters, L. H., & O'Connor, E. J. (1980). Situational constraints and work outcomes: The influences of a frequently overlooked construct. *Academy of Management Review, 5,* 391–397.

Pugh, D. S., & Hickson, D. J. (1997). *Writers on organizations* (5th ed.). Thousand Oaks, CA: Sage.

Salgado, J. F. (1997). The Five Factor Model of personality and job performance in the European community. *Journal of Applied Psychology, 82,* 30–43.

Schmidt, F. L., Hunter, J. E., Outerbridge, A. N., & Trattner, M. H. (1986). The economic impact of job selection methods on the size, productivity, and payroll costs of the federal workforce: An empirical demonstration. *Personnel Psychology, 39,* 1–29.

Sheldon, K. M., & Elliot, A. J. (1999). Goal striving, need-satisfaction, and longitudinal well-being: The Self-Concordance Model. *Journal of Personality and Social Psychology, 76,* 482–497.

Sheldon, K. M., Elliot, A. J., Kim, Y., & Kasser, T. (2001). What is satisfying about satisfying events? Testing 10 candidates' psychological needs. *Journal of Personality and Social Psychology, 80,* 325–339.

Stewart, G. L. (1996). Reward structure as a moderator of the relationship between Extraversion and sales performance. *Journal of Applied Psychology, 81,* 619–627.

Stewart, G. L., & Barrick, M. R. (in press). Lessons learned from the person-situation debate: A review and research agenda. In B. Smith & B. Schneider (Eds.), *Personality and organizations.* Mahwah, NJ: Erlbaum.

Tett, R. P., Jackson, D. N., Rothstein, M., & Reddon, J. R. (1994). Meta-analysis of personality–job performance relations: A reply to Ones, Mount, Barrick, and Hunter (1994). *Personnel Psychology, 47,* 147–156.

VandeWalle, D. (1999). *Goal orientation comes of age for adults: A literature review.* Paper presented at the Annual Meeting of the Academy of Management, Chicago.

Wiggins, J. S., & Trapnell, P. D. (1996). A dyadic-interactional perspective on the Five-Factor Model. In J. S. Wiggins (Ed.), *The Five-Factor Model of personality: Theoretical perspectives* (pp. 88–162). New York: Guilford Press.

Wright, T. A., & Cropanzano, R. (1998). Emotional exhaustion as a predictor of job performance and voluntary turnover. *Journal of Applied Psychology, 83,* 486–493.

CHAPTER 4

Toward a Better Understanding of the Relationship Between Personality and Individual Job Performance

Jeff W. Johnson

Researchers and practitioners in industrial and organizational (I/O) psychology have long been intrigued by the potential for measures of personality to describe, explain, and predict the behavior of individuals at work. Including personality variables in a selection system often has the effect of increasing its validity for predicting job performance, while simultaneously reducing adverse impact against protected groups (Hough, 2001). Although the usefulness of personality predictors is widely accepted today, academic I/O psychologists paid very little attention to personality measures from the mid-1960s to the mid-1980s (Schneider & Hough, 1995). This dearth of research is often attributed to an influential review of personality test validities by Guion and Gottier (1965), which concluded that research to that point had been so poorly done that personality measures should not be used to make employment decisions without clearer evidence of their validity. Other influences were the Civil Rights Act of 1964, which permitted the use of professionally developed ability tests but was not so explicit about personality inventories, and the emergence of Mischel's (1968) idea that behavior is determined more by situations than by traits (Guion, 1998).

In the late 1980s, the trait approach to personality was back in vogue, and the trait-versus-situation debate had produced a better understanding of how to predict behavior from traits. In early personality research, correlations were computed between all personality variables and all criteria. Most of these correlations were near zero, creating the impression that personality was generally unrelated to performance. We now better understand that the trait being investigated must be relevant to the criterion and that predictors and criteria should be conceptualized as constructs (Hough & Schneider, 1996). Personality research now involves the specification of a personality taxonomy, a job performance taxonomy, and hypothesized relationships between them. A meta-analysis by Tett, Jackson, and Rothstein (1991) found generally higher validities in studies that had a clearly stated hypothesis than in purely exploratory studies.

Meta-analyses of the criterion-related validity of personality variables have illustrated the benefit of using personality taxonomies as an organizing framework, revealing personality-performance relationships that had not been clear before (for example, Barrick & Mount, 1991; Hough, 1992; Hough, Eaton, Dunnette, Kamp, & McCloy, 1990). Barrick, Mount, and Judge (2001) conducted a second-order meta-analysis of all meta-analyses of the relationship between personality and performance conducted during the 1990s. Results were organized according to the Big Five dimensions of personality. Conscientiousness consistently predicted job performance across all criterion types and occupational groups and had the highest validity of all dimensions. Emotional Stability was the only other dimension to have nonzero true score correlations with overall work performance. Extraversion, Agreeableness, and Openness to Experience predicted some criterion types in some occupations. These results showed that the Big Five dimensions of personality are valid predictors of performance for at least some jobs and some criteria, although the magnitudes of the validities were relatively low.

Research has moved beyond the search for significant correlations between Big Five dimensions and general measures of job performance and is focused on understanding in greater depth the nature of personality and job performance, and how they are linked. This chapter focuses on two areas of research relevant to gaining this understanding. The first area is the development of a nomological net linking specific personality predictors to specific job performance criteria (Barrick et al., 2001; Hough & Furnham, 2002; Schneider, Hough, & Dunnette, 1996). Research has shown that lower-level facets of the same Big Five factor often have very different correlations with job performance criteria, revealing meaningful relationships that are masked if broader measures are used (Hough, 1992). Thus, linking specific predictor and criterion measures can result in increased correlations and better understanding of the relationship between personality and performance. The linking of these lower-level predictors and criteria requires taxonomies of specific personality and job performance constructs (Barrick et al., 2001). To that end, this chapter reviews the research on taxonomies of personality and individual job performance, and it proposes a taxonomy of job performance dimensions to be used in this type of linking research for forming hypotheses and cumulating results.

The second area of research is the development of models of the process by which personality influences job performance (Barrick et al., 2001; Schneider & Hough, 1995). This type of research has been in the form of searching for moderators of the relationship between personality and performance and searching for mediators of this relationship. The literature on moderators is extensive and is not reviewed in this chapter (interested readers should see Schneider & Hough, 1995; Chapter Three, this volume). This chapter focuses on reviewing the mediators linking personality and performance and integrating this research into a proposed model of the process by which personality influences job performance.

Personality Taxonomies

Two approaches to developing personality taxonomies are briefly reviewed here. The first approach is based on intercorrelations of personality dimensions; the second approach is based on correlations between personality dimensions and external criteria.

The Big Five and Its Facets

The Big Five (also known as the Five-Factor Model) has been ubiquitous in personality research, being robust and generalizable across rating sources, cultures, languages, and factor extraction and rotation methods (Hough & Furnham, 2002). The five factors are generally labeled Extraversion, Conscientiousness, Agreeableness, Emotional Stability, and Openness to Experience (Digman, 1990). Although the Big Five has advanced theory and practice as a useful framework for organizing and summarizing personality-performance relationships, it has been criticized for being insufficiently comprehensive and too heterogeneous (Block, 1995; Hough & Schneider, 1996; Paunonen & Jackson, 2000; Schneider & Hough, 1995). The number of lower-order facets of the Big Five is very open to debate, but Saucier and Ostendorf (1999) provided a good starting point by identifying eighteen subcomponents of the Big Five that were replicable across two languages:

Extraversion

Sociability

Unrestraint

Assertiveness

Activity-adventurousness

Agreeableness

Warmth-affection

Gentleness

Generosity

Modesty-humility

Conscientiousness

Orderliness

Decisiveness-consistency

Reliability, industriousness

Emotional Stability

Irritability

Security

Emotionality

Openness to Experience

Intellect

Imagination-creativity

Perceptiveness

Approaches for Maximizing Prediction

Rather than developing a personality taxonomy based on factor analysis of intercorrelations between scores on personality variables, Hough espouses a nomological–web clustering approach, in which taxons are based on similarities in patterns of relationships with variables outside the personality domain, such as job performance criteria (Hough & Ones, 2001; Hough & Furnham, 2002). Hough and Ones (2001) used this approach to propose a working taxonomy of personality variables, based on an extensive review of the literature. They called for other researchers to refine this taxonomy through theory and empirical evidence, creating more useful taxons that will lead to a better understanding of the relationships between personality and performance.

A related approach is the use of compound traits, which are combinations of basic personality traits that do not necessarily covary that are put together to maximize the prediction of a specific criterion construct (Hough & Schneider, 1996). Some examples of compound personality traits that have been found to be valid for predicting their intended criterion construct are integrity (Ones, Viswesvaran, & Schmidt, 1993), customer service orientation (Frei & McDaniel, 1998), employee reliability (Hogan & Hogan, 1989), and managerial potential (Gough, 1984). Hough and Ones (2001) suggested a number of other possible compound traits. The development of their working taxonomy will allow for the creation of compound traits to predict behavior for very specific or unique situations (Hough & Ones, 2001).

Models of Job Performance

Although there is little agreement on the appropriate personality taxonomy to use in researching personality-performance relationships, there have been concerted efforts on the part of recent researchers to organize personality variables into a taxonomy that makes sense. The same cannot be said for the criterion side. Most meta-analyses of personality-performance relationships have been limited to a hodgepodge of whatever criteria are available, and these criteria do not come close to representing the entire domain of individual job performance. This is a by-product of the decades of neglect suffered by the job performance construct. To realize Hough's (2001) vision of a matrix that links specific predictors to specific criteria, however, a taxonomy of job performance variables is just as important as a taxonomy on the predictor side. This section reviews recent models of job performance and integrates them into a proposed taxonomy to be used for personality research.

Performance Defined

This chapter focuses on individual job performance, which Campbell (1990; Campbell, McCloy, Oppler, & Sager, 1993) defined as behavior that is relevant to the goals of the organization and can be measured in terms of the level of the individual's contribution to those goals. Performance can be distinguished from effectiveness, which is some aggregate of the outcomes of performance that can be influenced to some extent by factors other than the individual's performance. Thus, this chapter includes only models of performance that are based on individual behaviors, not measures of effectiveness (such as dollar volume of sales). This chapter also does not include counterproductive or withdrawal behaviors, which are addressed in Chapter Six.

Campbell et al.'s (1993) model of performance consists of eight components, some or all of which should be adequate to describe all jobs in the U.S. economy:

- Job-specific task proficiency
- Non-job-specific task proficiency
- Written and oral communication proficiency

- Demonstrate effort
- Maintain personal discipline
- Facilitate peer and team performance
- Supervision/leadership
- Management/administration

This model is a useful starting point to which more specific dimensions can be added based on recent research on citizenship performance, adaptive performance, and managerial performance.

Citizenship Performance

Borman and Motowidlo (1993) proposed a model of performance with two components at the highest-level: task performance and contextual performance. Task performance consists of activities that (1) directly transform raw materials into the goods and services produced by the organization or (2) service and maintain the technical core by replenishing supplies, distributing products, and providing planning, coordination, supervising, and staff functions that allow for efficient functioning of the organization (Motowidlo, Borman, & Schmit, 1997). Contextual performance consists of activities that support the broader environment in which the technical core must function, including behaviors such as volunteering for tasks not formally part of the job, demonstrating effort, helping and cooperating with others, following organizational rules and procedures, and supporting organizational objectives (Borman & Motowidlo, 1993).

Contextual performance is similar in definition to Organ's (1988) organizational citizenship behavior (OCB), as well as other concepts such as prosocial organizational behavior (Brief & Motowidlo, 1986), extra-role behavior (Van Dyne, Cummings, & Parks, 1995), and organizational spontaneity (George & Jones, 1997). The primary difference between the definitions of OCB and contextual performance is that OCB was defined as extra-role, discretionary, and not formally recognized or rewarded by the organization. Organ (1997) recognized the lack of clarity this brought to the construct and refined the definition to make it more or less synonymous with contextual performance. Contextual performance, OCB, and related concepts are now often referred to as the same thing under the general label of citizenship performance (Borman & Penner, 2001; Coleman & Borman, 2000).

Confirmatory factor analyses have provided evidence for the distinction between task and citizenship performance (Conway, 1996; Johnson, 2001). Furthermore, research has shown that both task performance and citizenship performance are taken into consideration when supervisors evaluate others' performance (Conway, 1999; Johnson, 2001; Motowidlo & Van Scotter, 1994; Van Scotter & Motowidlo, 1996). Some research also shows that task performance is better predicted by ability and experience, and citizenship performance is better predicted by personality variables (Borman, Penner, Allen, & Motowidlo, 2001; Hurtz & Donovan, 2000).

The dimensionality of citizenship performance is muddled, with different authors offering different numbers of dimensions with different labels (Borman & Motowidlo, 1993; LePine, Erez, & Johnson, 2002; Organ, 1988; Podsakoff, MacKenzie, Paine, & Bachrach, 2000). In an attempt to clarify the latent structure of citizenship performance, Coleman and Borman (2000) identified twenty-seven citizenship performance behaviors based on all proposed models and discussions presented in the literature. The behaviors were sorted by forty-four I/O psychologists, and the similarity data were analyzed using factor analysis, multidimensional scaling, and cluster analysis. The authors rationally combined the results of the separate analyses into a single integrated model representing three categories of behavior. Borman, Buck et al. (2001) refined this taxonomy on the basis of a sort of approximately twenty-three hundred examples of citizenship performance taken from twenty-two studies, giving the categories the following labels and explanations:

Personal support: Behaviors benefiting individuals in the organization; includes helping, motivating, cooperating with, and showing consideration of others

Organizational support: Behaviors benefiting the organization; includes representing the organization favorably, showing loyalty, and complying with organizational rules and procedures

Conscientious initiative: Behaviors benefiting the job or task; includes persisting with extra effort to complete tasks, taking initiative, and engaging in self-development activities (Borman, Penner et al., 2001).

Motowidlo et al. (1997) suggested that behavior exemplifying conscientious initiative facilitates both the technical core and the broader work environment and should be considered an element of both task and citizenship performance. Johnson (2001) found that a factor model with conscientious initiative loading on both the task factor and the citizenship factor fit significantly better than models in which it loaded on just one or the other.

Adaptive Performance

Because of the increasingly dynamic nature of work environments, adaptive performance has recently received increased attention (Campbell, 1999; Hesketh & Neal, 1999; London & Mone, 1999; Pulakos, Arad, Donovan, & Plamondon, 2000). Adaptive performance is the proficiency with which a person alters his or her behavior to meet the demands of the environment, an event, or a new situation (Pulakos et al., 2000). Hesketh and Neal (1999) suggested that adaptive performance is a component of the performance domain that is separate from task and citizenship performance.

Pulakos et al. (2000) developed and found support for a taxonomy of adaptive performance consisting of eight dimensions. Johnson (2001) classified six of these dimensions as either task or citizenship performance. The other two dimensions are most similar to London and Mone's (1999) and Hesketh and Neal's (1999) conception of adaptive performance (self-managing learning experiences in anticipation of changing conditions, flexibility to cope with change). The dimension of learning work tasks, technologies, and procedures in response to changing conditions contains aspects of both task and citizenship performance. Learning new tasks, technologies, or procedures certainly influences task performance, and the aspect of seeking out learning opportunities in anticipation of changing conditions overlaps with the self-development component of conscientious initiative. The dimension of dealing with uncertain and unpredictable work situations is the only component of Pulakos et al.'s taxonomy that may well be distinct from task and citizenship performance. Elements of this dimension include taking action when necessary without having all the facts at hand; adjusting plans, actions, or priorities to deal with changing situations; and imposing structure to provide focus in dynamic situations.

Managerial Performance

A host of managerial performance taxonomies are available to expand on Campbell et al.'s (1993) supervision-leadership and management-administration components, two of which are exceedingly comprehensive. Borman and Brush (1993) found 187 dimensions of managerial performance from twenty-six published and unpublished studies. These dimensions were sorted into categories by twenty-five I/O psychologists, and factor analysis of a similarity matrix derived from these sortings yielded an eighteen-dimension structure. These dimensions are easily assigned to the task or citizenship performance categories or to one of Campbell et al.'s eight components (1993). Tett, Guterman, Bleier, and Murphy (2000) used a sorting method to develop a more specific managerial performance taxonomy of fifty-three competencies. They include a cross-reference of how their taxonomy fits with twelve other taxonomies, including that of Borman and Brush (1993).

An Integrated Model of Job Performance

The taxonomies reviewed in the previous section can be integrated into a single taxonomy that can be used to link specific personality constructs to specific performance constructs. The taxonomy is hierarchical but is not a latent variable model such as would be tested using factor analysis. Consistent with other conceptualizations of performance (for example, Motowidlo et al., 1997), this taxonomy is an aggregate model. The performance components at the higher levels are aggregate multidimensional constructs, or mathematical functions of the lower-order dimensions. This means that the dimensions assigned to the same higher-order dimension are not necessarily highly correlated with each other. For example, non-job-specific task proficiency refers to performance on tasks that may be performed in many jobs within an organization (for example, planning and organizing, making decisions, and using computers; Johnson, 2001). These tasks may have little in common with each other, but the aggregate of performance on all of these tasks represents a meaningful construct.

Table 4.1 contains the taxonomy, which has three components at the highest level: task performance, citizenship performance, and adaptive performance. At the next level, task performance is defined by five components from Campbell et al. (1993) and the aspects of conscientious initiative that are relevant to task performance. Supervision/leadership was renamed supervision because "leadership" is a less specific construct that is often an aggregate of task, citizenship, and adaptive performance (Leslie & Van Velsor, 1996). At the most specific level, each Level 2 dimension is defined by labels or descriptions from Pulakos et al. (2000), Borman and Brush (1993), and Campbell et al. (1993). Some dimensions are classified under more than one higher-order dimension. For example, physical adaptability could be job specific (as for a National Football League player) or non-job-specific (many jobs in the army). Job-specific task proficiency and non-job-specific task proficiency are very broad because of the multitude of task categories included under these umbrellas. Campbell et al. define job-specific task proficiency as the behaviors that distinguish the substantive content of one job from another (for example, designing architecture, driving a bus, directing air traffic). Non-job-specific tasks are those that are required across many jobs within an organization (for example, teach classes, use computers).

Citizenship performance includes Borman, Buck et al.'s (2001) three components, which are defined by additional descriptors from Borman, Buck et al., and dimensions from Campbell et al. (1993), Pulakos et al. (2000), and Borman and Brush (1993). Note that supervision is included as both a Level 2 dimension under task performance and a Level 3 dimension under personal support. This is because supervision is explicitly included in the definition of task performance as an element that services and maintains the technical core (Motowidlo et al., 1997), but some elements of supervision are clearly part of the definition of personal support (coaching, developing, and motivating others; Borman, Buck et al., 2001). "Demonstrate effort" is also included under both task and citizenship performance. "Handling work stress" is included under all higher-order dimensions of citizenship performance because it contains aspects from all three. Adaptive performance includes only the single Level 2 dimension of "Dealing with uncertain and unpredictable work situations," which is defined at Level 3 by Hesketh and Neal's (1999) "Demonstrating flexibility to cope with change" and further descriptors from Pulakos et al. (2000).

Table 4.1. An Integrated Model
of Job Performance Dimensions.

Level 1	Level 2	Level 3

Task Performance

Job-specific task proficiency[a]

Handling emergencies or crisis situations[b]

Physical adaptability[b] (see also non-job-specific task proficiency)

Technical proficiency[c]

Other job-specific task examples

Non-job-specific task proficiency[a]

Physical adaptability[b] (see also job-specific task proficiency)

Solving problems creatively[b]

Decision making/problem solving[c]

Other non-job-specific task examples

Written and oral communication proficiency[a]

Written communication proficiency

Oral communication proficiency

Management/administration[a]

Planning and organizing[c]

Administration and paperwork[c]

Coordinating resources[c]

Staffing[c]

Monitoring and controlling resources[c]

Supervision[a] (see also personal support)

Guiding, directing, and motivating subordinates and providing feedback[c]

Training, coaching, and developing subordinates[c]

Delegating[c]

Conscientious initiative[d] (see also citizenship performance)

Learning work tasks, technologies, and procedures[b]

Demonstrate effort[a] (similar to persisting to reach goals[c])

Citizenship performance

Conscientious initiative[d] (see also task performance)

Demonstrate effort[a] (similar to persisting to reach goals[c])

Table 4.1. An Integrated Model
of Job Performance Dimensions, Cont'd.

Level 1	Level 2	Level 3
		Handling work stress[b] (see also personal support and organizational support)
		Showing initiative[d]
		Engaging in self-development[d]
	Organizational support[d]	
		Maintain personal discipline[a]
		Handling work stress[b] (see also personal support and conscientious initiative)
		Representing the organization to customers and the public[c]
		Organizational commitment[c]
		Suggesting improvements[d]
	Personal support[d] (similar to facilitate peer and team performance[a])	
		Supervision[a] (see also task performance)
		Demonstrating interpersonal adaptability[b]
		Demonstrating cultural adaptability[b]
		Handling work stress[b] (see also organizational support and conscientious initiative)
		Maintaining good working relationships[c]
		Helping others[d]
		Cooperating[d]
		Showing consideration[d]
Adaptive performance		
	Dealing with uncertain and unpredictable work situations[b]	
		Demonstrating flexibility to cope with change[e]
		Taking action under uncertainty[b]
		Imposing structure to provide focus in dynamic situations[b]

[a]Campbell et al. (1993). [b]Pulakos et al. (2000). [c]Borman and Brush (1993). [d]Borman, Buck et al. (2001). [e]Hesketh and Neal (1999).

One could go to an even more specific level than Level 3 by including Tett et al.'s (2000) managerial competencies, many of which are relevant to all jobs. Level 3 is the most appropriate level for linking specific predictor constructs to specific performance constructs. Level 2 may be used for cumulating results across studies for meta-analyses, at least until sufficient data have been gathered to conduct meta-analyses at Level 3.

Task performance has generally not been predicted well by personality variables. In the U.S. Army's Project A, technical proficiency (job-specific task proficiency) and general soldiering proficiency (non-job-specific task proficiency) had very low correlations with all personality variables measured (Hough et al., 1990). Hough's (1992) meta-analysis found only intellectance to be related to technical proficiency. In a meta-analysis by Hurtz and Donovan (2000), the highest mean corrected correlations with criteria classified as task performance were .16 and .14 for Conscientiousness and Emotional Stability, respectively.

Hurtz and Donovan (2000) found personality to be a better predictor of citizenship performance. For job dedication (a combination of conscientious initiative and organizational support), mean corrected correlations were .20 for Conscientiousness and .14 for Emotional Stability. For interpersonal facilitation (personal support), mean corrected correlations were .18 for Conscientiousness, .17 for Emotional Stability, and .20 for Agreeableness. Organ and Ryan's (1995) meta-analysis showed Conscientiousness to correlate .30 with generalized compliance (part of organizational support) and .22 with altruism (part of personal support). Borman, Penner et al. (2001) updated this meta-analysis and found Conscientiousness, Agreeableness, positive affectivity, negative affectivity, and locus of control to have relatively high uncorrected mean correlations with a general citizenship performance composite (range of .13 to .24).

Several studies have investigated the relationship between personality variables and adaptability. In a study of over fifteen hundred managers, Conway (2000) found corrected correlations of .20 or greater between an adaptability performance dimension and the California Psychological Inventory (CPI) scales of responsibility, tolerance, achievement via independence, and intellectual efficiency. Mumford, Baughman, Threlfall, Uhlman, and Costanza

(1993) found that students low in evaluation apprehension, high in self-discipline, and high in creative achievement tended to perform better on an ill-defined task, which is an element of adaptive performance. LePine, Colquitt, and Erez (2000) found that Openness to Experience was positively related and dependability was negatively related to decision quality after the rules were unexpectedly changed on a decision-making task.

Theories of Individual Differences in Job Performance

According to Campbell (1990; Campbell et al., 1993), performance is a function of three determinants: declarative knowledge, procedural knowledge and skill, and motivation. Declarative knowledge represents factual knowledge about specific things, or knowing what to do. Procedural knowledge and skill is the degree to which one is able to perform a task. This is achieved when knowing what to do is combined with knowing how to do it. Campbell et al. define motivation as the combined effect of the choice to expend effort in a particular direction, the choice of the level of effort to expend, and the choice to persist at that level of effort. Performance on a job dimension is determined directly by some combination of these three determinants. The direct performance determinants are distinguished from indirect performance determinants, which can influence performance only by the direct determinants. Examples of indirect determinants provided by the organization include reward systems, training, and management practices. Personality is an example of an indirect determinant that the individual brings to the organization, along with abilities, interests, education, and experience.

This model has clear implications for the relationship between personality and performance on a particular performance dimension. Personality can influence performance only through its influence on declarative knowledge, procedural knowledge and skill, or motivation. This means that one way a personality variable may be related to performance on a dimension is if people higher on that variable tend to acquire more of the declarative or procedural knowledge necessary for performance on that dimension (McCloy, Campbell, & Cudeck, 1994). Many personality variables are likely most predictive of motivation. This is supported by Mc-Cloy et al. (1994), who found higher personality-performance correlations when performance was measured by ratings, which reflect all three performance determinants, than when performance was measured by job knowledge tests or work samples, which do not reflect motivation.

Research supports the notion of motivation as a mediator of the personality-performance relationship. Barrick, Mount, and Strauss (1993) found that the link between Conscientiousness and two measures of sales representative job performance (supervisor ratings and sales volume) was mediated by the motivational variables of goal setting and goal commitment. Gellatly (1996) found that performance expectancy and goal choice mediated the link between Conscientiousness and performance on an arithmetic task. Barrick, Stewart, and Piotrowski (2002) noted that the motivational variables of accomplishment striving and status striving mediated the relationship between Conscientiousness and job performance of sales representatives, and status striving mediated the relationship between Extraversion and job performance.

Campbell et al.'s (1993) model of performance determinants provides a general explanation of how individual differences in personality translate to individual differences in job performance on a particular dimension. Motowidlo et al. (1997) expanded this model to explain why personality should be a better predictor of contextual performance dimensions than of task performance dimensions. They split declarative knowledge and procedural knowledge and skill into task knowledge and skill and contextual knowledge and skill. Task knowledge is knowledge of facts, principles, and procedures relevant to the core technical functions of the organization, and task skill is skill in performing necessary actions to complete tasks. Contextual knowledge is knowledge of facts, principles, and procedures relevant to maintaining the organizational environment in which the technical core must function (such as knowing how to cooperate with others and how to present a favorable image of the organization), and contextual skill is skill in performing actions known to be effective in situations calling for contextual performance. Task knowledge and skill are determined primarily by cognitive ability, which is supported by ample research (Borman, White, & Dorsey, 1995; Hunter, 1983;

Lance & Bennett, 2000). Motowidlo et al. suggest that personality should be the primary determinant of contextual knowledge and skill, because people possessing personality characteristics consistent with a particular element of contextual knowledge or skill should be more likely to notice the relative effectiveness of certain patterns of behavior in relevant situations, and thus more likely to master that knowledge or skill.

The Motowidlo et al. (1997) model is further distinguished from the Campbell et al. (1993) model by replacing motivation with task and contextual work habits. Work habits are patterns of behavior that people learn over time that can facilitate or interfere with job performance. They include characteristic motivational responses such as choices for the amount, intensity, and duration of effort to expend; tendencies to approach or avoid certain situations; procrastination; or persistence in the face of adversity. They also include characteristic responses that are not necessarily motivational in nature. Motowidlo et al. give an example of a sales representative who has been trained in the best way to deal with an angry customer and has shown the ability to do so, but occasionally reverts to pretraining habits of reacting with hostility. Task work habits are characteristic responses to situations that interfere with or facilitate the completion of tasks. Contextual work habits are characteristic responses that interfere with or facilitate performance in contextual work situations. Motowidlo et al. suggested that task habits are predicted by both cognitive ability and certain personality variables (such as Conscientiousness), and contextual habits are predicted primarily by certain other personality variables (such as Agreeableness and Extraversion). Because personality variables are expected to influence more determinants on the contextual side of the model and ability variables are expected to influence more determinants on the task side of the model, personality should be more related to contextual performance and ability should be more related to task performance.

Some studies have attempted to test the mediating aspects of the Motowidlo et al. (1997) model. Schmit, Motowidlo, Degroot, Cross, and Kiker (1996) investigated the mediating role of contextual knowledge in the personality–contextual performance relationship in a sample of sales associates. In this study, the personality measures assessed Extraversion, Agreeableness, and

Conscientiousness. The contextual knowledge measure was a situational interview designed to assess the participants' knowledge of appropriate customer service behaviors, and the job performance measure was supervisor ratings of the participants' customer service–related job performance. Schmit et al. found that contextual knowledge mediated the personality-contextual job performance relationship in the case of Extraversion. These results are somewhat difficult to interpret because customer service is probably a combination of task and contextual performance.

Schneider and Johnson (2001) used a situational judgment test as a measure of contextual knowledge for the dimensions of personal support and conscientious initiative. Predictors were agreeableness, achievement, dependability, and cognitive ability. Criteria were supervisor ratings of personal support, conscientious initiative, and customer service performance. The contextual knowledge mediation hypothesis was tested separately for each construct, and support was mixed. Conscientious initiative knowledge did not mediate the relationship between achievement and conscientious initiative performance. When testing the relationship between agreeableness and personal support performance, a model in which personal support knowledge mediated the relationship fit equally as well as a model in which there was no mediation. For customer service, the mediation effect was found for achievement but not for dependability or agreeableness.

Schneider and Johnson (2003) tested a more complete version of the Motowidlo et al. (1997) model in a sample of employees in customer contact positions in a large company. The criteria were supervisor ratings of customer service task performance, conscientious initiative, and personal support. Task and contextual knowledge were measured with a situational judgment test. The indirect determinants were cognitive ability, agreeableness, and achievement. The Motowidlo et al. model was not supported; there were no mediation effects of task or contextual knowledge. Support was found for an alternative model that involved two changes from the original model. First, a direct path was added from achievement to task knowledge, because people higher on achievement should tend to acquire more task-relevant knowledge. The second change was to make conscientious initiative a mediating variable between achievement and the dimensions of personal support and task performance. A measure of conscientious initiative may be more a measure of motivation than one of performance. Because demonstrating effort necessarily precedes any type of performance and is related to both task and contextual performance, conscientious initiative was expected to influence both personal support and task performance directly. In this model, task knowledge mediated the relationship between ability and task performance and the relationship between achievement and task performance. Personal support knowledge did not mediate the relationship between agreeableness and personal support, and conscientious initiative knowledge did not mediate the relationship between achievement and conscientious initiative. Conscientious initiative did mediate the relationships between achievement and the dimensions of personal support and task performance.

Expanding the Motivation Construct

The models of Campbell et al. (1993) and Motowidlo et al. (1997) differ in how they conceptualize motivation. Campbell et al. use a cognitive choice model of motivation, in which the choice to perform leads directly to behavior. There is no explicit provision for motivational processes that may be used to overcome difficulties in the accomplishment of the intention to perform. Campbell et al. do say that the investigator's favorite model of motivation can be inserted into that component of their theory, so the theory does allow for a conceptualization of motivation that is more complex than the three choices they specify. Because motivation is such an important mediating variable between personality and job performance, it is necessary to describe that aspect of the model more completely to provide a true understanding of the nature of this relationship.

Motowidlo et al. (1997) replaced the motivation component with work habits, which they defined as stylistic ways that people handle different kinds of situations that occur on the job, learned as their basic tendencies (personality traits) interact with their environments over time. Habits are an important component to include in a model of performance determinants because they may interfere with performance despite motivation to perform in a certain way. Rather than replacing the motivation component, however, work habits should be included in addition to motivation. Although Motowidlo et al. included choices for how much effort to exert and for how long as examples of characteristic motivational responses under work habits, this appears to exclude motivational choices that go against one's habitual tendencies. For example, a person's characteristic tendency may be to exert as little effort as possible, but he or she may choose to go against that tendency in response to a new bonus structure that rewards productivity.

Habits influence behavior despite intentions to behave otherwise because they require very little attention. To implement an intention that goes against habitual tendencies and other intentions competing for one's attention, one must engage self-regulatory or volitional mechanisms. Self-regulation refers to the higher-level cognitive processes that guide the allocation of attention, time, and effort across activities directed toward attaining a goal (Kanfer, 1990) and protect an intention from being replaced by a competing action tendency before the intended action is completed (Kuhl, 1985). This is a critical component of motivation that is missing from the models of Campbell et al. (1993) and Motowidlo et al. (1997).

Some theories integrate cognitive choice and self-regulatory aspects of motivation (Heckhausen & Kuhl, 1985). The importance of this integrative perspective for the purposes of this chapter is that different dispositional variables are proposed to influence motivation at different stages, providing a framework for more systematic investigation of how personality affects motivation and job performance (Kanfer, 1990). Mitchell and Daniels (2002) distinguished between proactive and on-line cognitive processes. Proactive cognitive processes occur before a task is begun and reflect cognitions about expectations for achieving a goal or the value of outcomes resulting from achieving a goal. During this phase, people determine what course of action to take, resulting in the formation of an intention. Mitchell and Daniels include expectancy, self-efficacy, and goal setting in the proactive category of motivation theories. On-line cognitive processes occur while the person is working on a task and are characterized by self-regulatory processes that are necessary to maintain goal-directed action. This phase refers to the process of implementing an intention to achieve a goal. Control theory, action theory, and self-regulation are on-line theories of motivation (Mitchell & Daniels, 2002).

A third component of motivation that can be influenced by personality is psychological motives. Motive-based theories focus on the influence on behavior of one or more psychological motives (for example, altruism, personal development, competence), recognizing that people may have very different purposes for exhibiting the same behavior (Borman & Penner, 2001). The types of motives that are likely to be influenced by personality are values, interests, preferences (Dawis, 1991), and attitudes (Penner, Midili, & Kegelmeyer, 1997). Motives are expected to influence proactive cognitive processes directly (Kanfer, 1992). The following sections review how personality has been shown to be related to each component of motivation.

Motives

One type of motive that has been extensively studied is job attitudes. Job attitudes tend to be more strongly related to OCB than are personality variables (Podsakoff et al., 2000), leading Organ and Ryan (1995) to conclude that the relationship between personality and OCB is probably mediated by attitudes such as job satisfaction, organizational commitment, and fairness perceptions. Many studies have shown relationships between personality variables and job attitudes (for example, Judge & Bono, 2001; Judge, Higgins, Thoresen, & Barrick, 1999).

Rioux and Penner (2001) developed a scale to measure motives for engaging in OCB and identified three motives through factor analysis: prosocial values, organizational concern, and impression management. They administered this scale and other measures to a sample of city government employees and obtained self-, peer-, and supervisor ratings on five aspects of OCB. For peer ratings, the prosocial values motive was significantly related to the altruism and civic virtue dimensions of OCB, and the organizational concern motive was significantly related to civic virtue. These two motives also accounted for significant unique variance in these dimensions beyond that accounted for by measures of personality, perceived organizational justice, and positive mood. Two personality variables from the Prosocial Personality Battery (Penner, Fritzsche, Craiger, & Freifeld, 1995) were included in this study. Other-oriented empathy correlated .46 with prosocial values and .27 with organizational concern. Helpfulness correlated .31 with prosocial values. Other correlations were very small. These results indicate that certain motives for engaging in citizenship performance contribute uniquely to the prediction of citizenship performance and can be predicted by personality variables.

Barrick et al. (2002) developed a measure of three psychological motives: accomplishment striving, status striving, and communion striving (that is, getting along with others). Although they referred to these variables as intentions or goals, the variables better fit the definition of motives because of their lack of specificity (these motives would lead an individual to choose a specific goal). The authors found that Conscientiousness and Extraversion were related to both accomplishment striving and status striving, Emotional Stability was related to status striving, and Agreeableness was related to communion striving. These motives mediated the relationship between the personality variables and a measure of sales representative job performance.

Chan and Drasgow (2001) developed a measure of motivation to lead, which fits in the motive component of motivation because it is defined as an individual difference construct that influences decisions to participate in leadership activities and intensity of effort. Each Big Five personality variable was found to be a significant predictor of at least one of the three factors of motivation to lead.

Proactive Cognitive Processes

Judge and Ilies (2002) conducted a meta-analysis of the relationship between the Big Five and the proactive motivation constructs of expectancy motivation, self-efficacy, and goal setting. Studies measuring expectancy generally asked respondents to indicate the extent to which exerting effort in a particular direction would result in a specific outcome. Neuroticism and Conscientiousness were most highly correlated with expectancy motivation. Neuroticism and Extraversion were most strongly related to self-efficacy, with Conscientiousness and Openness to Experience also displaying nonzero correlations.

The goal-setting variables measured in studies included in Judge and Ilies (2002) generally measured goal content (choices of goal level or goal difficulty). All the Big Five traits had nonzero relationships with goal content, with Neuroticism, Agreeableness, and

Conscientiousness showing the strongest relationships. Less research has examined personality correlates of goal commitment. Hollenbeck and Klein (1987) suggested need for achievement, Type A personality, self-esteem, and locus of control as indirect determinants of goal commitment. Partial support for this model was provided by Hollenbeck, Williams, and Klein (1989), who found that commitment to difficult goals was stronger when individuals were high in need for achievement and had an internal locus of control. In other studies, need for achievement (Kernan & Lord, 1988) and Conscientiousness (Barrick et al., 1993) were positively related to goal commitment.

On-Line Cognitive Processes

Kuhl's (1985) action control theory focuses on the translation of an intention to an action through self-regulatory processes. According to action control theory, self-regulatory skill is partially determined by an individual's action or state orientation. More action-oriented individuals are better able to devote their attention to the current goal. More state-oriented individuals tend to ruminate on alternative goals or emotional states, reducing the cognitive resources available for striving for the current goal. Diefendorff, Hall, Lord, and Strean (2000) evaluated the construct validity of a revised version of a measure of action-state orientation, the Action Control Scale (Kuhl, 1994). This scale measures three dimensions of action-state orientation: preoccupation (the degree to which individuals detach from thoughts about interfering goals), hesitation (the difficulty in initiating goal-directed action), and volatility (the degree to which individuals become distracted when working on a task). These dimensions were regressed on measures of the Big Five. Emotional Stability contributed significantly to the prediction of all three dimensions, and dependability (Conscientiousness) and Extraversion contributed significantly to the prediction of the hesitation dimension. The action control subscales contributed significant variance beyond the Big Five to the prediction of supervisor ratings of task performance and several OCB dimensions in a sample of employed students.

Kanfer and Heggestad (1997) proposed a taxonomy of motivational traits and skills. Motivational skills were defined as individual differences in self-regulatory patterns of activity during the goal-striving stage. They focused on two self-regulatory strategies proposed by Kuhl (1985): emotion control and motivation control. Emotion control facilitates task performance by protecting attention and effort from distracting emotional states (for example, depression). Motivation control increases the strength of a current intention by selectively processing information that supports it. They focused on the trait constructs of achievement and anxiety based on the strength of research evidence supporting them. Achievement is characterized by the two distinct aspects of mastery (the desire to master a task for personal excellence) and competitive excellence (the desire to rival and surpass others). Anxiety is characterized by the constructs of general anxiety (neuroticism or emotional stability), fear of failure (tendency to avoid goals or situations that might lead to failure), and test anxiety (anxiety restricted to testing situations). Individual differences in traits are proposed to influence motivational skill development through the differential opportunities with which they are likely to be associated. For example, high-achievement individuals are more likely to put themselves in challenging situations, giving them more opportunity to develop motivational skills.

Proposed Model of the Relationship Between Personality and Individual Performance

A proposed model of pathways by which individual differences in a personality variable influence individual performance on a given performance component is presented in Figure 4.1. This model is compatible with those of Campbell et al. (1993) and Motowidlo et al. (1997) and adds elements to both. Consistent with Campbell et al., performance on any particular job performance component is a function of declarative knowledge, procedural knowledge and skill, and motivation. One difference is the expanded conceptualization of motivation. Another is the addition of a fourth determinant, work habits, in recognition of the possibility that job-relevant behavior can occur automatically despite motivation to behave otherwise. Work habits also influence performance indirectly by influencing the need for and choice of self-regulatory strategies. For simplicity, the only indirect determinants included are personality variables and ability variables. This model could be expanded to

Figure 4.1. A Proposed General Model of the Relationship Between Personality and Job Performance.

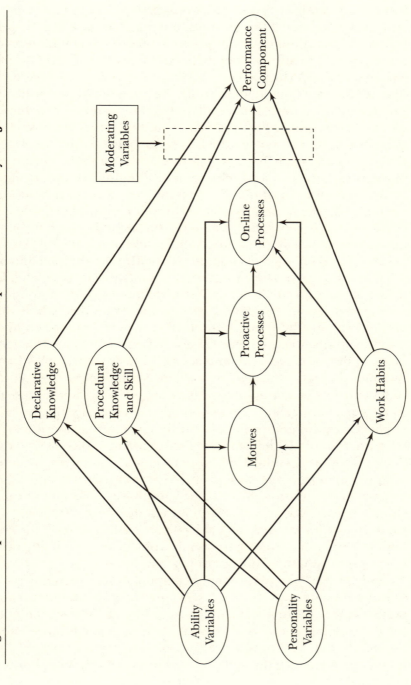

include other classes of individual (for example, experience, interests) or organizational (for example, training, rewards) indirect performance determinants. The relative strength of each path from one construct to another depends on the predictor variables included and the performance component that is the criterion, even for performance components within the same broad performance category (task, citizenship, or adaptive). For example, if achievement were used to predict the demonstrating effort dimension of citizenship performance, the strongest path would likely go through motivation because motivation is highly relevant to demonstrating effort and achievement is highly relevant to each component of motivation. If sociability were used to predict the maintaining good working relationships dimension of citizenship performance, however, the stronger paths would likely go through declarative knowledge and procedural knowledge and skill. This is because social knowledge and skill are highly relevant to maintaining good working relationships, they are likely to be predicted by sociability, and sociability is not as strong a predictor of motivation.

Figures 4.2 and 4.3 contain illustrative examples of how this model explains the prediction of specific performance components from specific predictor variables. Both figures include cognitive ability, achievement, and sociability as potential predictor variables. In Figure 4.2, the performance component is technical proficiency. Cognitive ability is the dominant predictor because of its influence on technical job knowledge, technical skill, and task habits. Cognitive ability may also influence motivation, primarily because it should be related to self-efficacy and choice of goal difficulty (Phillips & Gully, 1997). Achievement should also predict unique variance in technical proficiency, primarily through its influence on motivation, but also because high-achievement individuals tend to acquire more job knowledge necessary for good performance and to develop habits that are effective for achieving high performance. Sociability should contribute little if anything to the prediction of technical proficiency.

In Figure 4.3, the performance component is maintaining good working relationships. In this case, cognitive ability would predict performance only to the extent that cognitive ability contributes to the determination that one kind of social response is more effective than another (Motowidlo et al., 1997). Achievement would also predict performance through its influence on motivation, but this

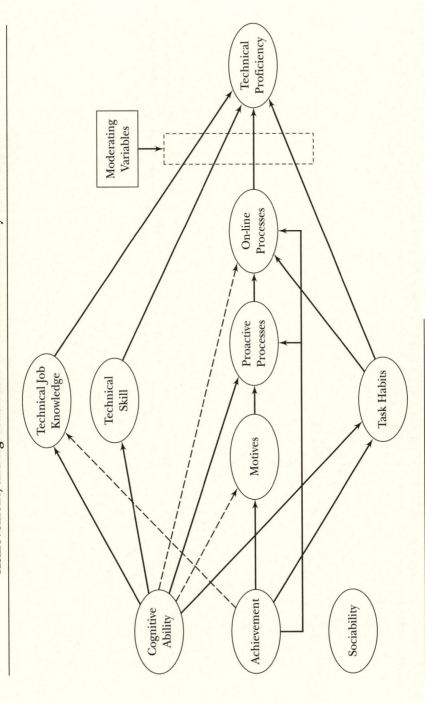

Figure 4.2. Hypothesized Relationships Linking Cognitive Ability, Achievement, and Agreeableness to Technical Proficiency Performance.

Note: The dotted lines represent relatively weaker relationships.

Figure 4.3. Hypothesized Relationships Linking Cognitive Ability, Achievement, and Agreeableness to Maintaining Good Working Relationships Performance.

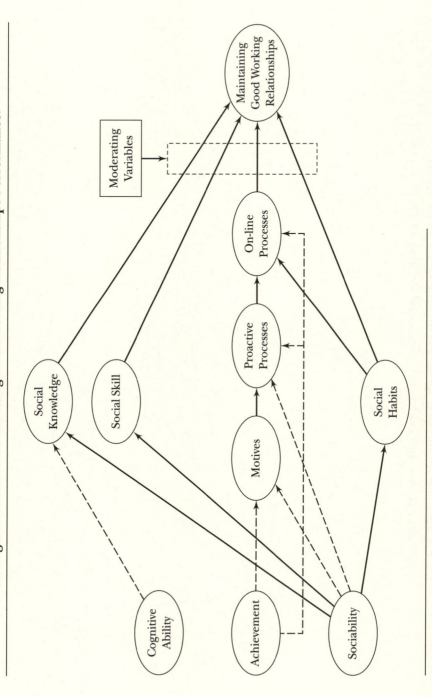

Note: The dotted lines represent relatively weaker relationships.

influence should be less than what would be expected for technical proficiency. The dominant predictor in this case would be sociability, which should directly influence social knowledge, social skill, social habits, and some aspects of motivation (for example, prosocial motives, self-efficacy, goal commitment).

It is important to keep in mind the numerous potential moderators that can influence the extent to which personality predicts performance. Examples of moderator variables are situational strength (Beaty, Cleveland, & Murphy, 2001), occupation (Barrick et al., 2001), time on job (Helmreich, Sawin, & Carsrud, 1986), and autonomy (Gellatly & Irving, 2001). Some studies have found an interaction between personality and ability in predicting performance (Wright, Kacmar, McMahan, & Deleeuw, 1995), although most recent studies have shown no interaction (Mount, Barrick, & Strauss, 1999; Sackett, Gruys, & Ellingson, 1998). Multiple personality traits may also interact to influence performance. For example, Witt, Burke, Barrick, and Mount (2002) found a significant interaction between Conscientiousness and Agreeableness in five samples of employees in occupations characterized by cooperative interactions with others.

The purpose of this model is to identify the constructs through which personality variables work to influence performance on specific performance dimensions. It can be used to choose appropriate personality predictors for a given criterion construct. The strength of the relationship between the predictor and the criterion depends on (1) the number of direct determinants of the criterion to which the predictor is related, (2) the strength of the relationship between the predictor and each direct determinant, (3) the strength of the relationship between each direct determinant and the criterion, and (4) the presence of relevant moderators. Ability variables should be most predictive for task performance dimensions because of their strong relationships with task knowledge, task skill, and task habits and the strong relationships between these direct determinants and task performance. Personality variables should also contribute, but to a lesser degree because of their strong relationships with motivation but weaker relationships with task knowledge, task skill, and task habits. Personality variables should be most predictive when predicting citizenship performance because of their strong relationships with motivation and citizenship knowledge, skill, and habits. Ability variables should be predictive to a lesser extent because of their weaker associations with these constructs. Personality variables are probably most predictive of adaptive performance because of the importance of self-regulatory skills when quickly adjusting to a new situation. Ability variables should also be strongly related because of the importance of skills such as problem solving.

An immediate need for research with this model is the mediating effect of citizenship knowledge and skill. So far, support for this effect has been mixed at best. In addition, we have very little idea at this time how the aspect of performance being studied influences the predictors of motivation. For example, certain personality variables are likely to be highly related to motives, expectancies, self-efficacy, goal content, and goal commitment when the criterion is a dimension of citizenship performance, but they have no relationship to these constructs when the criterion is a dimension of task performance.

Conclusion

This chapter has reviewed and advanced research in two areas relevant to understanding the link between personality and individual job performance. The first area is identifying relationships between specific personality predictors and specific job performance criteria. According to Hough (2001; Hough & Ones, 2001), an important goal for personality researchers is the development of a nomological net of personality-performance relationships for use in building predictor equations for specific situations. The taxonomy of performance dimensions proposed in this chapter is a step in this direction. This taxonomy includes task performance, citizenship performance, and adaptive performance at the highest level, with a second and third level of more specific dimensions. To advance our state of knowledge most efficiently, primary studies must be conducted relating specific personality variables to these performance dimensions, and meta-analyses must summarize this research at more specific levels than the Big Five and overall task and citizenship performance. This performance taxonomy should also be refined by identifying other important performance dimensions that are not adequately represented in the taxonomy.

The second area of research is investigating the mediating variables through which personality influences job performance. The

Campbell et al. (1993) and Motowidlo et al. (1997) models were combined, revised, and expanded to more completely explain the process by which individual differences in personality traits lead to individual differences in specific dimensions of performance. This model can be used to guide research linking specific personality variables to specific performance dimensions by helping to identify theoretically relevant predictors for different criteria. In this model, the construct of motivation was expanded to highlight how different personality variables influence different components. Self-regulation is the primary component that previous models were missing. This construct is very important because it is strongly related to personality; helps explain how people with similar knowledge, ability, goals, and desire to perform differ in their level of performance; and helps explain how people overcome their habits to perform in accordance with their goals. Further research relating specific personality variables to specific motivation components will be valuable in expanding this model and furthering our understanding of the personality-performance link.

References

Barrick, M. R., & Mount, M. K. (1991). The Big Five personality dimensions and job performance: A meta-analysis. *Personnel Psychology, 44,* 1–26.

Barrick, M. R., Mount, M. K., & Judge, T. A. (2001). Personality and performance at the beginning of the new millennium: What do we know and where do we go next? *International Journal of Selection and Assessment, 9,* 9–30.

Barrick, M. R., Mount, M. K., & Strauss, J. R. (1993). Conscientiousness and performance of sales representatives: Test of the mediating effects of goal setting. *Journal of Applied Psychology, 78,* 715–722.

Barrick, M. R., Stewart, G. L., & Piotrowski, M. (2002). Personality and job performance: Test of the mediating effects of motivation among sales representatives. *Journal of Applied Psychology, 87,* 43–51.

Beaty, J. C., Cleveland, J. N., & Murphy, K. R. (2001). The relation between personality and contextual performance in "strong" versus "weak" situations. *Human Performance, 14,* 125–148.

Block, J. (1995). A contrarian view of the Five-Factor approach to personality description. *Psychological Bulletin, 117,* 187–215.

Borman, W. C., & Brush, D. H. (1993). More progress toward a taxonomy of managerial performance requirements. *Human Performance, 6,* 1–21.

Borman, W. C., Buck, D. E., Hanson, M. A., Motowidlo, S. J., Stark, S., & Drasgow, F. (2001). An examination of the comparative reliability, validity, and accuracy of performance ratings made using computerized adaptive rating scales. *Journal of Applied Psychology, 86,* 965–973.

Borman, W. C., & Motowidlo, S. J. (1993). Expanding the criterion domain to include elements of contextual performance. In N. Schmitt & W. C. Borman (Eds.), *Personnel selection in organizations* (pp. 71–98). San Francisco: Jossey-Bass.

Borman, W. C., & Penner, L. A. (2001). Citizenship performance: Its nature, antecedents, and motives. In B. W. Roberts & R. T. Hogan (Eds.), *The intersection of personality and industrial/organizational psychology* (pp. 45–61). Washington, DC: American Psychological Association.

Borman, W. C., Penner, L. A., Allen, T. D., & Motowidlo, S. J. (2001). Personality predictors of citizenship performance. *International Journal of Selection and Assessment, 9,* 52–69.

Borman, W. C., White, L. A., & Dorsey, D. W. (1995). Effects of ratee task performance and interpersonal factors on supervisor and peer performance ratings. *Journal of Applied Psychology, 80,* 168–177.

Brief, A. P., & Motowidlo, S. J. (1986). Prosocial organizational behaviors. *Academy of Management Review, 11,* 710–725.

Campbell, J. P. (1990). Modeling the performance prediction problem in industrial and organizational psychology. In M. D. Dunnette & L. M. Hough (Eds.), *Handbook of industrial and organizational psychology* (2nd ed., Vol. 1, pp. 687–732). Palo Alto, CA: Consulting Psychologists Press.

Campbell, J. P. (1999). The definition and measurement of performance in the new age. In D. R. Ilgen & E. D. Pulakos (Eds.), *The changing nature of performance: Implications for staffing, motivation, and development* (pp. 399–429). San Francisco: Jossey-Bass.

Campbell, J. P., McCloy, R. A., Oppler, S. H., & Sager, C. E. (1993). A theory of performance. In N. Schmitt & W. C. Borman (Eds.), *Personnel selection in organizations* (pp. 35–70). San Francisco: Jossey-Bass.

Chan, K., & Drasgow, F. (2001). Toward a theory of individual differences and leadership: Understanding the motivation to lead. *Journal of Applied Psychology, 86,* 481–498.

Coleman, V. I., & Borman, W. C. (2000). Investigating the underlying structure of the citizenship performance domain. *Human Resource Management Review, 10,* 25–44.

Conway, J. M. (1996). Additional construct validity evidence for the task/contextual performance distinction. *Human Performance, 9,* 309–329.

Conway, J. M. (1999). Distinguishing contextual performance from task performance for managerial jobs. *Journal of Applied Psychology, 84,* 3–13.

Conway, J. M. (2000). Managerial performance development constructs and personality correlates. *Human Performance, 13,* 23–46.

Dawis, R. V. (1991). Vocational interests, values, and preferences. In M. D. Dunnette & L. M. Hough (Eds.), *Handbook of industrial and organizational psychology* (2nd ed., Vol. 2, pp. 833–871). Palo Alto, CA: Consulting Psychologists Press.

Diefendorff, J. M., Hall, R. J., Lord, R. G., & Strean, M. L. (2000). Action-state orientation: Construct validity of a revised measure and its relationship to work-related variables. *Journal of Applied Psychology, 85,* 250–263.

Digman, J. M. (1990). Personality structure: Emergence of the Five-Factor Model. *Annual Review of Psychology, 41,* 417–440.

Frei, R. L., & McDaniel, M. A. (1998). Validity of customer service measures in personnel selection: A review of criterion and construct evidence. *Human Performance, 11,* 1–27.

Gellatly, I. R. (1996). Conscientiousness and task performance: Test of a cognitive process model. *Journal of Applied Psychology, 81,* 474–482.

Gellatly, I. R., & Irving, P. G. (2001). Personality, autonomy, and contextual performance of managers. *Human Performance, 14,* 231–245.

George, J. M., & Jones, G. R. (1997). Organizational spontaneity in context. *Human Performance, 10,* 153–170.

Gough, H. G. (1984). A managerial potential scale for the California Psychological Inventory. *Journal of Applied Psychology, 69,* 233–240.

Guion, R. M. (1998). *Assessment, measurement, and prediction for personnel decisions.* Mahwah, NJ: Erlbaum.

Guion, R. M., & Gottier, R. F. (1965). Validity of personality measures in personnel selection. *Personnel Psychology, 18,* 135–164.

Heckhausen, H., & Kuhl, J. (1985). From wishes to action: The dead ends and short cuts on the long way to action. In M. Frese & J. Sabini (Eds.), *Goal directed behavior: The concept of action in psychology* (pp. 134–160). Mahwah, NJ: Erlbaum.

Helmreich, R. L., Sawin, L. L., & Carsrud, A. L. (1986). The honeymoon effect in job performance: Temporal increases in the predictive power of achievement motivation. *Journal of Applied Psychology, 71,* 185–188.

Hesketh, B., & Neal, A. (1999). Technology and performance. In D. R. Ilgen & E. D. Pulakos (Eds.), *The changing nature of performance: Implications for staffing, motivation, and development* (pp. 21–55). San Francisco: Jossey-Bass.

Hogan, J., & Hogan, R. (1989). How to measure employee reliability. *Journal of Applied Psychology, 74,* 273–279.

Hollenbeck, J. R., & Klein, H. J. (1987). Goal commitment and the goal-setting process: Problems, prospects, and proposals for future research. *Journal of Applied Psychology, 72,* 212–220.

Hollenbeck, J. R., Williams, C. R., & Klein, H. J. (1989). An empirical examination of the antecedents of commitment to difficult goals. *Journal of Applied Psychology, 74,* 18–23.

Hough, L. M. (1992). The "Big Five" personality variables–construct confusion: Description versus prediction. *Human Performance, 5,* 139–155.

Hough, L. M. (2001). I/Owes its advances to personality. In B. W. Roberts & R. T. Hogan (Eds.), *The intersection of personality and industrial/ organizational psychology* (pp. 19–44). Washington, DC: American Psychological Association.

Hough, L. M., Eaton, N. K., Dunnette, M. D., Kamp, J. D., & McCloy, R. A. (1990). Criterion-related validities of personality constructs and the effect of response distortion on those validities. *Journal of Applied Psychology, 75,* 581–595.

Hough, L. M., & Furnham, A. (2002). Importance and use of personality variables in work settings. In W. Borman, D. Ilgen, & R. Klimoski (Eds.), *Comprehensive handbook of psychology, Vol. 12: Industrial and organizational psychology.* New York: Wiley.

Hough, L. M., & Ones, D. S. (2001). The structure, measurement, validity, and use of personality variables in industrial, work, and organizational psychology. In N. R. Anderson, D. S. Ones, H. K. Sinangil, & C. Viswesvaran (Eds.), *Handbook of work psychology* (pp. 233–277). Thousand Oaks, CA: Sage.

Hough, L. M., & Schneider, R. J. (1996). Personality traits, taxonomies, and applications in organizations. In K. R. Murphy (Ed.), *Individual differences and behavior in organizations* (pp. 31–88). San Francisco: Jossey-Bass.

Hunter, J. E. (1983). A causal analysis of cognitive ability, job knowledge, job performance, and supervisor ratings. In F. Landy, S. Zedeck, & J. Cleveland (Eds.), *Performance measurement and theory* (pp. 257–266). Mahwah, NJ: Erlbaum.

Hurtz, G. M., & Donovan, J. J. (2000). Personality and job performance: The Big Five revisited. *Journal of Applied Psychology, 85,* 869–879.

Johnson, J. W. (2001). The relative importance of task and contextual performance dimensions to supervisor judgments of overall performance. *Journal of Applied Psychology, 86,* 984–996.

Judge, T. A., & Bono, J. E. (2001). Relationship of core self-evaluation traits—self-esteem, generalized self-efficacy, locus of control, and emotional stability—with job satisfaction and job performance: A meta-analysis. *Journal of Applied Psychology, 86,* 80–92.

Judge, T. A., Higgins, C. A., Thoresen, C. J., & Barrick, M. R. (1999). The Big Five personality traits, general mental ability, and career success across the life span. *Personnel Psychology, 52,* 621–652.

Judge, T. A., & Ilies, R. (2002). Relationship of personality to performance motivation: A meta-analytic review. *Journal of Applied Psychology, 87,* 797–807.

Kanfer, R. (1990). Motivation theory and industrial and organizational psychology. In M. D. Dunnette & L. M. Hough (Eds.), *Handbook of industrial and organizational psychology* (2nd ed., Vol. 1, pp. 75–170). Palo Alto, CA: Consulting Psychologists Press.

Kanfer, R. (1992). Work motivation: New directions in theory and research. In C. L. Cooper & I. T. Robertson (Eds.), *International review of industrial and organizational psychology* (pp. 1–42). New York: Wiley.

Kanfer, R., & Heggestad, E. D. (1997). Motivational traits and skills: A person-centered approach to work motivation. *Research in Organizational Behavior, 19,* 1–56.

Kernan, M. C., & Lord, R. G. (1988). Effects of participative vs. assigned goals and feedback in a multitrial task. *Motivation and Emotion, 12,* 75–86.

Kuhl, J. (1985). Volitional mediators of cognition-behavior consistency: Self-regulatory processes and action vs. state orientation. In J. Kuhl & J. Beckmann (Eds.), *Action control: From cognition to behavior* (pp. 101–128). New York: Springer-Verlag.

Kuhl, J. (1994). Action versus state orientation: Psychometric properties of the action control scale (ACS-90). In J. Kuhl & J. Beckmann (Eds.), *Volition and personality: Action versus state orientation* (pp. 47–59). Seattle: Hogrefe & Huber.

Lance, C. E., & Bennett, W. (2000). Replication and extension of models of supervisory job performance ratings. *Human Performance, 13,* 139–158.

LePine, J. A., Colquitt, J. A., & Erez, A. (2000). Adaptability to changing task contexts: Effects of general cognitive ability, conscientiousness, and openness to experience. *Personnel Psychology, 53,* 563–593.

LePine, J. A., Erez, A., & Johnson, D. E. (2002). The nature and dimensionality of organizational citizenship behavior: A critical review and meta-analysis. *Journal of Applied Psychology, 87,* 52–65.

Leslie, J. B., & Van Velsor, E. (1996). *A look at derailment today: North America and Europe.* Greensboro, NC: Center for Creative Leadership.

London, M., & Mone, E. M. (1999). Continuous learning. In D. R. Ilgen & E. D. Pulakos (Eds.), *The changing nature of performance: Implications for staffing, motivation, and development* (pp. 119–153). San Francisco: Jossey-Bass.

McCloy, R. A., Campbell, J. P., & Cudeck, R. (1994). A confirmatory test of a model of performance determinants. *Journal of Applied Psychology, 79,* 493–505.

Mischel, W. (1968). *Personality and assessment.* New York: Wiley.

Mitchell, T. R., & Daniels, D. (2002). Motivation. In W. Borman, D. Ilgen, & R. Klimoski (Eds.), *Comprehensive handbook of psychology, Vol. 12: Industrial and organizational psychology.* New York: Wiley.

Motowidlo, S. J., Borman, W. C., & Schmit, M. J. (1997). A theory of individual differences in task and contextual performance. *Human Performance, 10,* 71–83.

Motowidlo, S. J., & Van Scotter, J. R. (1994). Evidence that task performance should be distinguished from contextual performance. *Journal of Applied Psychology, 79,* 475–480.

Mount, M. K., Barrick, M. R., & Strauss, J. P. (1999). The joint relationship of conscientiousness and ability with performance: Test of the interaction hypothesis. *Journal of Management, 25,* 707–721.

Mumford, M. D., Baughman, W. A., Threlfall, K. V., Uhlman, C. E., & Costanza, D. P. (1993). Personality, adaptability, and performance: Performance on well-defined and ill-defined problem-solving tasks. *Human Performance, 6,* 241–285.

Ones, D. S., Viswesvaran, C., & Schmidt, F. L. (1993). Comprehensive meta-analysis of integrity test validities: Findings and implications for personnel selection and theories of job performance. *Journal of Applied Psychology, 78,* 679–703.

Organ, D. W. (1988). *Organizational citizenship behavior: The good soldier syndrome.* San Francisco: New Lexington Press.

Organ, D. W. (1997). Organizational citizenship behavior: It's construct clean-up time. *Human Performance, 10,* 85–97.

Organ, D. W., & Ryan, K. (1995). A meta-analytic review of attitudinal and dispositional predictors of organizational citizenship behavior. *Personnel Psychology, 48,* 775–802.

Paunonen, S. V., & Jackson, D. N. (2000). What is beyond the Big Five? Plenty! *Journal of Personality, 68,* 821–835.

Penner, L. A., Fritzsche, B. A., Craiger, J. P., & Freifeld, T. R. (1995). Measuring the prosocial personality. In J. Butcher & C. D. Spielberger (Eds.), *Advances in personality assessment* (Vol. 10, pp. 147–163). Mahwah, NJ: Erlbaum.

Penner, L. A., Midili, A. R., & Kegelmeyer, J. (1997). Beyond job attitudes: A personality and social psychology perspective on the causes of organizational citizenship behavior. *Human Performance, 10*, 111–131.

Phillips, J. M., & Gully, S. M. (1997). Role of goal orientation, ability, need for achievement, and locus of control in the self-efficacy and goal-setting process. *Journal of Applied Psychology, 82*, 792–802.

Podsakoff, P. M., MacKenzie, S. B., Paine, J. B., & Bachrach, D. G. (2000). Organizational citizenship behaviors: A critical review of the theoretical and empirical literature and suggestions for future research. *Journal of Management, 26*, 513–563.

Pulakos, E. D., Arad, S., Donovan, M. A., & Plamondon, K. E. (2000). Adaptability in the workplace: Development of a taxonomy of adaptive performance. *Journal of Applied Psychology, 85*, 612–624.

Rioux, S. M., & Penner, L. A. (2001). The causes of organizational citizenship behavior: A motivational analysis. *Journal of Applied Psychology, 86*, 1306–1314.

Sackett, P. R., Gruys, M. L., & Ellingson, J. E. (1998). Ability-personality interactions when predicting job performance. *Journal of Applied Psychology, 83*, 545–556.

Saucier, G., & Ostendorf, F. (1999). Hierarchical subcomponents of the Big Five personality factors: A cross-language replication. *Journal of Personality and Social Psychology, 76*, 613–627.

Schmit, M. J., Motowidlo, S. J., Degroot, T., Cross, T., & Kiker, D. S. (1996, Apr.). Explaining the relationship between personality and job performance. In J. M. Collins (Chair), *Personality predictors of job performance: Controversial issues.* Symposium conducted at the Eleventh Annual Conference of the Society for Industrial and Organizational Psychology, San Diego, CA.

Schneider, R. J., & Hough, L. M. (1995). Personality and industrial/organizational psychology. In C. L. Cooper & I. T. Robertson (Eds.), *International review of industrial and organizational psychology* (pp. 75–129). New York: Wiley.

Schneider, R. J., Hough, L. M., & Dunnette, M. D. (1996). Broadsided by broad traits: How to sink science in five dimensions or less. *Journal of Organizational Behavior, 17*, 639–655.

Schneider, R. J., & Johnson, J. W. (2001, Apr.). *The mediating role of contextual knowledge in predicting contextual performance.* Poster presented at the Sixteenth Annual Conference of the Society for Industrial and Organizational Psychology, San Diego, CA.

Schneider, R. J., & Johnson, J. W. (2003). *Testing a theory of task and citizenship performance: Negative findings and proposed modifications.* Manuscript submitted for publication.

Tett, R. P., Guterman, H. A., Bleier, A., & Murphy, P. J. (2000). Development and content validation of a "hyperdimensional" taxonomy of managerial competence. *Human Performance, 13,* 205–251.

Tett, R. P., Jackson, D. N., & Rothstein, M. (1991). Personality measures as predictors of job performance: A meta-analytic review. *Personnel Psychology, 44,* 703–742.

Van Dyne, L., Cummings, L. L., & Parks, J. M. (1995). Extra role behaviors: In pursuit of construct and definitional clarity (a bridge over muddied waters). In L. L. Cummings & B. M. Staw (Eds.), *Research in organizational behavior* (Vol. 17, pp. 215–285). Greenwich, CT: JAI Press.

Van Scotter, J. R., & Motowidlo, S. J. (1996). Interpersonal facilitation and job dedication as separate facets of contextual performance. *Journal of Applied Psychology, 81,* 525–531.

Witt, L. A., Burke, L. A., Barrick, M. R., & Mount, M. K. (2002). The interactive effects of Conscientiousness and Agreeableness on job performance. *Journal of Applied Psychology, 87,* 164–169.

Wright, P. M., Kacmar, K. M., McMahan, G. C., & Deleeuw, K. (1995). $P = f(M + A)$: Cognitive ability as a moderator of the relationship between personality and job performance. *Journal of Management, 21,* 1129–1139.

CHAPTER 5

Dispositional Influences on Affective Experiences at Work

Howard M. Weiss
Katherine E. Kurek

Personality constructs enter into the explanatory systems of every variable of interest to industrial/organizational psychology (I/O). Affect is clearly no exception, and in this chapter, we provide some general thoughts on how personality-affect connections can be understood and studied. We have not attempted to review the I/O literature on the relations of personality constructs with affect constructs. Readers interested in that review might look to Staw (in press). Nor have we tried to make precise predictions about specific personality constructs, beyond relevant clarifying illustrations. Instead, we focus on some broad issues concerning how that relationship can be productively conceptualized. We believe the time is right to think seriously about the study of personality and affective reactions and think that analysis will be advanced by a more process-oriented discussion of affect. In effect, we are playing to our strengths as affect researchers and hope that the more knowledgeable personality researchers who comprise the readers of this volume will bring that knowledge to bear on the conceptual and process issues we address.

If we are to have a useful discussion of the relationship between personality and affect, we have to make clear that affect and personality are very different kinds of constructs and that the differences are so fundamental that simple examinations of relationships between the two, as is often seen in the literature, can be misleading and misdirected.

Affect is a state, and the fundamental characteristic of state constructs is change. If we can envision a continuous stream of experience, we can also envision particular moments in that stream when change occurs, when people move from one state to another. Such states can vary in length. Pain from touching a hot surface can last moments. Anger or guilt can last for hours. Marriage is a state that for some can last for decades, for others weeks. Nonetheless, and regardless of the time frame, states are time-bound constructs.

By this characterization, affect is a state. Researchers make the distinction between two forms of affect: moods and discrete emotions. Moods are generally considered to be more diffuse affective states, lacking a defining object, and disconnected from particular objects or circumstances. Discrete emotions are affective states that are connected to objects or circumstances. They are about something. The difference can be seen in the language of moods and discrete emotions. "I'm feeling angry with my boss" and "I'm feeling guilty about missing my son's soccer game" are statements in the language of emotion. "I'm feeling down" and "I'm feeling kind of perky" are statements in the language of mood.

Both moods and emotions are state variables, characterized by beginnings and endings. Affective states, when compared to other kinds of state variables, are generally of relatively short duration. For example, moods might last for a few minutes, as is often the case in the laboratory, to a few hours. The experience of anger or guilt might follow the same sort of time frame.

Figures 5.1, 5.2, and 5.3 illustrate the momentary variability of affect. In each of the cases illustrated in these figures, data were collected by using ecological momentary assessment (Stone, Shiffman, & DeVries, 1999) to capture momentary affective states among workers. Participants were signaled at random points through the day and asked to indicate their current mood states (pleasant versus unpleasant and aroused versus unaroused). These immediate mood states were collected over two- or three-week periods.

These charts are useful but rather limited in their description of true affective experience as it plays out over time. By dropping

Figure 5.1. One Manager's Emotional States over Ten Days.

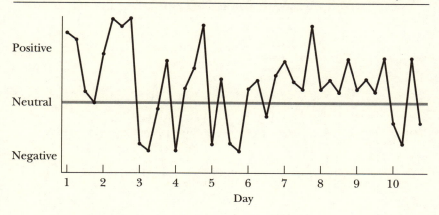

Figure 5.2. Another Manager's Emotional States over Ten Days.

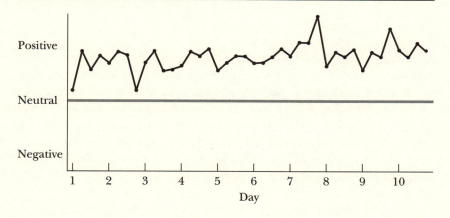

Figure 5.3. A Graduate Student's Emotional States over Fifteen Days, with Some Corresponding Events.

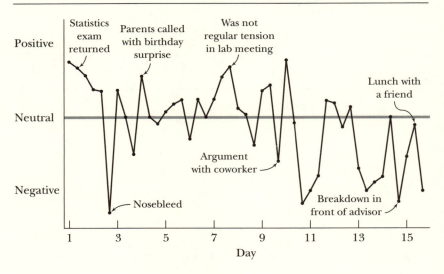

in at random points during the day, we are unable to capture the holistic, episodic nature of any particular affective experience. We miss its beginning and its end, and thereby miss the meaning and coherence of the experience itself. In addition, by assessing only the positive or negative nature of the affective state, we miss the discrete emotional experience. Moods may be well captured by dimensional reductions, but discrete emotions are not. In these kinds of data, we fail to discriminate among these different kinds of experiences.

Nonetheless, these data can help us make a few points about affective states. Simple observation of these data illustrates the momentary and transient nature of affective states. They also show that individual affective experiences examined over time have distinctive patterns and that various parameters can be used to describe these patterns. For example, observers can see that individuals appear to vary in their average levels of positive and negative affect. They also vary in the variability of affect itself, the intensity of peaks and valleys, and the time span for movement from one state to another. Not observable but still present are distinct cycles to affective states, cycles whose frequencies or periods vary from one person to another. Affective experiences are state constructs that vary in direction, intensity, subjective experience, and length of time.

What kind of construct is personality? Let us first say that for this discussion, we will be talking of personality in trait or disposition terms. We recognize that there are personality researchers who find this framework limiting (see Pervin, 1994, and accompanying commentaries as examples), but it is clear that in the I/O literature generally and in the work affect literature in particular, the trait concept overwhelmingly predominates. So what kind of construct is a personality trait? Of most importance for us is that it is an attribute of a person that has no built-in time frame, no "on and off" element. We will not get into the issue of whether it can change or whether it is largely inherited, only that it is distinguished from state variables. State variables, by definition, come and go. Trait variables, by definition, do not.

Immediately, we see a disconnect. By asking the general question of the relationship between affect and personality, we are inquiring how a state like construct, characterized by its variability, can be explained by a trait construct defined by its stability. This is no small problem. Yet we also believe that solutions are available.

However, before we discuss what we think are appropriate solutions, it will be useful to provide an overview of the nature of I/O research on dispositions and affect. This will tell us how researchers have dealt with the disconnect and also what they have not done but could do.

Organizational Research on Affect and Personality

Our examination of the existing research in the I/O literature seeks not to review specific findings but rather to identify certain key themes in the way the research has been conducted.

To identify the body of I/O research on personality and affect, we conducted a literature search where we entered key search words such as *emotions, affect, mood,* and specific emotion words (for example, *anger*) into the PsycINFO database. An enormous list was generated, but only terms related to work or organizations are included in our overview.

We believe that the literature can be characterized by four major observations that are relevant to the objectives of this chapter:

1. In the literature on personality and affect in work settings, affective experiences are frequently studied not as affect itself but as related constructs, such as job satisfaction and psychological strain.
2. Studies of personality and affective reactions in organizational settings have primarily involved the examination of aggregate affective constructs as dependent variables.
3. The general format for studying affect-related experiences involves cross-sectional questionnaire studies that are unable to capture the affect process as it unfolds over time.
4. Affective experiences and personality variables create a murky pool in which there is no clear distinction between a stable characteristic and an experience in progress.

Our first point is that many organizational studies on personality and affect have examined such things as job satisfaction (Bluen, Barling, & Burns, 1990; Fisher, 2000; Hart, 1999; Judge, Locke, & Durham, 1997; Porac, Ferris, & Fedor, 1983), psychological strain (Chen & Spector, 1991; Jex & Bliese, 1999; Saks & Ashforth, 2000), and burnout (Wright & Cropanzano, 1998; Zellars & Perrewe, 2001); fewer have looked at emotions or moods at work. Although these regularly studied phenomena are potentially influenced by affective experiences and are related conceptually, they are not the same as actual affective experiences (Weiss, 2002a). Job satisfaction is a good example.

Job satisfaction is an attitude, not an affective state. As an attitude, it is best conceptualized as an evaluation of one's job, influenced in part by affective events that have occurred at work (Weiss, 2002b; Weiss & Cropanzano, 1996) and, as a source of error, the mood one is in at the time of making the evaluation (Brief, Butcher, & Roberson, 1995). In addition, most measures of job satisfaction have a large cognitive component (Brief & Roberson, 1989). The studies reviewed often used highly cognitive measures, such as the Minnesota Satisfaction Questionnaire (Hart, 1999; Smith & Tziner, 1998; Watson & Slack, 1993) and the Job Descriptive Index (Glynn, 1998; Judge & Hulin, 1993; Levin & Stokes, 1989). In addition, job satisfaction, unlike affective experiences, is a fairly stable construct. Although results generally show moderate relations between affective personality constructs and job satisfaction, these results, weak or strong, tell us very little about personality and true affective reactions.

Psychological strain as an outcome of exposure to job stressors has many operationalizations, including job satisfaction, frustration, anxiety, depression, burnout, and physical health problems. Some of these may be considered emotional reactions, but, interestingly, even so are generally measured over a period of time (say, in the past month). For example, Chen and Spector (1991) asked participants "how they generally felt at work during the past 30 days," but they called this a "state" measure of anger. The same type of measure has been used with anxiety (Jex & Gudanowski, 1992; Jex & Spector, 1996; Spector, Chen, & O'Connell, 2000).

Our second conclusion relates to the first point. Overwhelmingly, when more clearly affective constructs have been studied, aggregate measures have been used as the dependent variable. Sometimes measures of relatively stable constructs like satisfaction are used; sometimes people are asked to aggregate their momentary experiences subjectively over a particular time period (for example, "How have you typically felt over the last month?"); sometimes researchers aggregate momentary data mechanically. The Job Affect Scale (Brief, Burke, George, Robinson, & Webster, 1988) used in several studies (George, 1990; Saavedra & Kwun, 2000) asks for the respondent's mood for the past week rather than at the moment the person is responding to the items. Stokes and Levin (1990) related their new negative affectivity scale to experienced positive and negative affect over a one-week period. Other studies have used one-day measures, assessing the respondents' judgments of their average moods over the course of a day (Bohle & Tilley, 1993). Although these studies have found relationships between personality constructs and individual differences in average affect, this paradigm is not able to explain the within-person changes in affect, which we have noted is a large portion of the total variance in emotional states.

There are some notable exceptions in the literature that ask for emotional states at a specific point in time as they are occurring (Weiss, Nicholas, & Daus, 1999; Wofford, Goodwin, & Daly, 1999). However, even here, the momentary data are often aggregated before analysis. Wofford et al. (1999) asked for recollections of emotions felt in specific situations, such as "on last being with their supervisor" or "on last returning home from work." The responses for five different situations were then averaged to obtain an affect score to be assessed in relation to various personality variables.

Our third observation is that the use of one-time surveys has been the overwhelming format of choice for those studying personality and affective experiences. Studies are often conducted in a cross-sectional, one-time assessment of all variables of interest (George, 1990; Saavedra & Kwun, 2000). Some studies have used longitudinal designs (Portello & Long, 2001; Spector & O'Connell, 1994) but are still assessing the affective constructs at one, or maybe two, points in time. For example, Spector and O'Connell (1994) gathered information on personality at time 1 and then twelve to fifteen months later assessed the level of job strain that participants experienced. It should be noted that the majority of the studies that fall under this category were aimed at studying things that we have concluded are not affect but related constructs such as job satisfaction and psychological strain.

Other techniques (such as diary or experiential sampling methods) have been used more rarely, but in a higher percentage, in studies specifically interested in affective experiences as the dependent variable (Bohle & Tilley, 1993; Portello & Long, 2001; Shiu, 1998). These formats are better able to capture the affective process. However, the same problem of aggregation persists with some of these methods. Despite the attempt to measure a momentary phenomenon, when looking at personality, many diary studies average the momentary data (see Weiss et al., 1999, as an example) or ask for the respondent's feelings or mood for that day (Buunk & Verhoeven, 1991). This masks any qualitative changes that have occurred throughout the day. Some studies, however, have used an experiential sampling technique to assess the pattern of emotions by asking the participants about their current emotional states at several points in time, resulting in a profile of the participant's emotional states over the time of the study and looking at personality correlates with the patterns. Research employing this format (Weiss et al., 1999) has required innovative methods of comparing the stable personality construct to varying emotional responses. One such technique uses the statistical estimates of the distribution parameters, such as the standard deviation of reported emotions (Kurek, Le, & Weiss, 2001), as dependent variables. Other studies have used multilevel modeling techniques to assess the variability within and between people in cross-level analyses using these types of data (see Portello & Long, 2001, as an example). Studies employing these more intense data collection formats have been few in number and still fail to capture the full emotion episode.

Our fourth conclusion about this literature is that there is no clear distinction between affective experience and personality. The averaging of moods and emotions across time dispositionalizes affect, creating, in effect, alternative measures of personality. Personality is generally defined as a consistent pattern of behaviors across time. When someone engages in many specific instances of behavior or attitude across time, this is described as personality, whereas any particular behavior at one point in time would not be labeled in this manner. Someone who is negative over many points in time will be labeled a pessimist, but being pessimistic once does not constitute a pessimist. The point here is that the longer the time frame is in which we are assessing any particular behavior, the more dispositionalized it becomes, and therefore the closer it comes to a measure of personality than of a situationally specific construct such as affect.

In our review of the literature, it occurred to us that there is a hazy line between the dispositional measures, such as positive and negative affectivity, and the time-bound affect measures. We typically measure one's personality or disposition as the individual's typical response. For example, the Positive Affectivity and Negative Affectivity Scales (Watson, Clark, & Tellegen, 1988) ask for the extent to which the respondents "typically" experience a list of twenty emotions. However, when we are trying to predict a time-bound behavior such as affect using an aggregate measure, we are essentially measuring the same construct as those that capture "typical" experiences.

In sum, as a result of examining the literature as a whole, it becomes clear how I/O researchers have dealt with the problem of using a time-free construct like personality to explain a time-bound construct like affect states. Essentially, they have dispositionalized affect itself. They have done this in one of two ways. One way has been to examine constructs that are traitlike in terms of time frame and to call them affect constructs. This is the satisfaction paradigm. The other way has been to aggregate the momentary experiences either by asking people to provide judgments about their typical or general affective states or to create such summaries mechanically from momentary data. The latter approach loses the within-person variability, which is essential to understanding affective experiences over time, as we have seen. The former approach also loses such dynamic data and suffers from the biases inherent in these recollective judgments. Neither approach pays much attention to the nature of affect processes.

Process Approaches for Linking Personality to Dynamic Outcomes

Going back to our original figures and looking at the patterns of affect over time, we can see that the mean level of affect is not the only parameter that can be used in examining differences in these patterns. For example, the standard deviation of those experiences over time can be predicted from personality variables that capture differences in affective responsivity. Weiss et al. (1999) showed that Larsen and Diener's affective intensity measure (1987) predicted individual differences in affective variability. Weiss et al. (1999) and others have also looked at individual differences in the extent to which regular cycles exist in individual affect patterns. Such cycles may also have personality correlates.

Although examination of the various parameters besides mean levels is an important undertaking, it still focuses on using personality to explain between-person differences in affective states. Yet the within-person component of affective variability is what jumps out at any person who is studying affective experiences over time. People can feel angry in the morning and happy in the afternoon. They can and do move from state to state throughout the course of a day. Personality focused on between-person variance is limited in what it can accomplish. Yet our dilemma with within-person variance is that we are asked to predict and explain variable responses in the individual using stable characteristics of that person. Such an activity is inherently inconsistent. This is not to say that stable characteristics are not relevant to affect processes. However, if we are to go beyond predicting affective aggregates, using stable characteristics to explain affective experiences as they are experienced, that is, varying over time, we must focus on personality constructs that interact with varying environmental events. We must focus on reactivity constructs, not tendencies to display certain levels of affect across situations, and study these reactivity constructs as they interact with changing events. We will discuss here various constructs that predict differences in the way people respond to stimuli. We will also say that a search for these constructs must begin with an examination of the processes that generate emotional states at particular times.

The 1990s saw a resurgence of interest in trait theories of personality, in both I/O and other areas of psychology, stimulated by research done within the Big Five approach. This reinvigoration of trait psychology was followed by a reinvigoration of critiques of dispositional personality generally (Mischel & Shoda, 1995, 1998; Pervin, 1994) and the Big Five in particular (Block, 1995). We do not revisit these issues here. However, we believe the position that Mischel and Shoda described is of great relevance for reconciling the conceptual disconnect we have been referring to.

Mischel and Shoda (1995, 1998) have described what they see as two traditions in personality psychology. One, the behavioral disposition tradition, has sought to create personality constructs that operationalize consistencies in behaviors over time. These dispositions or traits predispose people to behave in a certain way across time and situations. Mischel and Shoda argue that researchers within this tradition acknowledge that cross-situational consistency is generally low but not zero. They then focus on that part of the total variance that represents the stability component and seek to explain individual differences in this portion of the variance. In so doing, they treat the within-person variance, which can be quite substantial, as error. Clearly, this is the approach that best characterizes current I/O research on personality and affect. The alternative approach, the mediational process approach, treats the within-person variance as real and to be explained, not thrown away. This approach argues that the role of personality is not to be found by dispositionalizing the behavioral (or affective) expression but rather to search for personality contributions in the mediating processes that are appropriate for the variable in question. Analyses driven by this tradition respect the within-person variability across situations but seek to find coherence in these dynamic outcome patterns—coherence driven by characteristics of individuals' processing systems, values, goals, and others that interact with the situation.

It should be clear by now that our position is very much consistent with the mediational tradition described by Mischel and Shoda (1995, 1998). Examining the dispositional or stable component of affective states by correlating personality traits with mean levels of affect aggregated over time or with self-reports of typical affect seems to miss the point of studying affect. "Dispositionalizing" affect removes the essential features of the construct, simply for the purpose of generating associations with other known individual dispositions. Intraindividual variability, the essential characteristic of affective states, is treated as error variance, to be removed in the search for dispositional explanation.

Are we therefore arguing against a role for personality in affective processes? Clearly we are not. Instead, we are suggesting that the place to find personality effects is in the mediating processes of affect generation. Here we are taking the position of Mischel and Shoda (1995, 1998). Instead of looking for stability in the expression of moods and emotions, we are suggesting that we look for the multiple ways in which personality enters into the causal chain of emotion generation and emotion consequences. Because that chain is defined by the way individuals interact with and understand environmental events and conditions, the position easily accommodates the consistent aspects of human personality with the changing nature of emotional states. We believe that the reconciliation between changing affect states and stable characteristics of individuals is to be found by examining how those stable characteristics influence the various elements of the mediational processes by which events influence affective reactions and affective reactions influence behaviors, attitudes, and cognitive processes of relevance to work settings. We discuss possible influences of personality after a brief discussion of the emotion-generating process.

A General Discussion of Affect Processes

Our discussion of affect generation processes is intentionally global and overly general. Researchers on emotions have not settled on one perspective for understanding how emotions are elicited (Weiss, 2002a). Researchers on moods have hardly addressed the issue at all. Our discussion in this and the next section follows the general outline of a cognitive appraisal approach. Researchers preferring another perspective may therefore disagree with the particulars of these discussions. We believe that they will not disagree with the general message, however.

Emotions are elicited by events. Although most emotion theories use these events as the starting point for emotion generation, the events we experience are not entirely externally caused or random. We make decisions that expose us to certain events. Although there are certainly events that are beyond our control, we create our own environments in which we have a greater tendency to experience certain types of events. Some events are thrust on us. Others are partly our own creation. Still, emotions are reactions to events.

Not all events culminate in emotional responses. Cognitive appraisal theorists argue that events are appraised or evaluated along a number of dimensions, and these appraisals are the proximal cause of emotional responses (Smith & Kirby, 2001). These appraisal theories generally posit two types of appraisals in emotion generation. Primary appraisal is usually seen as an assessment of "concern relevance." Is this thing that has happened of relevance to my goals (proximal or distal) and values? As a result of the first appraisal process, both the valence and intensity of the emotion are determined (Lazarus, 1991). If it is of relevance and beneficial for one's goals and well-being, the valence of the emotion will be positive. If it hinders attainment of one's goals, the emotion will be negative. The more important the goal is, the more intense the emotion is. As Weiss and Cropanzano (1996) noted, people will be focusing on different aspects of their goal hierarchies at any particular time. This focus will influence the judgments made regarding the relevance and importance of the event to one's goals. An event that helps an individual achieve an important goal will produce a strong, positive emotion.

Whereas primary appraisal determines the valence and intensity of the emotion experienced, secondary appraisal determines the particular discrete emotion experienced. Although different theorists propose different appraisal dimensions, all of them agree that the event is evaluated in relation to several attributes (such as causal attribution, coping potential, and stability of the event), and the pattern of attributions results in the elicitation of the particular emotion. (See Smith and Ellsworth, 1985, or Lazarus, 1991, for a more thorough discussion of this process.)

Although we have emphasized the discrete, transient nature of emotional states, Frijda (1993) has discussed the concept of "emotion episode," that is, emotional reactions extended over time. In these emotion episodes, people experience a dynamic flow of emotional reactions over an extended time. Sometimes these discrete emotions are different emotions, but all cohere around a single underlying theme (a company layoff, for example). The emotion episode is characterized by a heightened arousal and attention with the same underlying theme as the instigating event. During this time, people are trying to deal with the emotions, and their behaviors are controlled by the emotion. To understand the affective process fully, we must recognize the characteristics of these emotional episodes. For example, it is the peak and end of the emotional experience that appear to be remembered when looking back on an event (Fredrickson, 2000).

Emotion processes do not stop with emotion elicitation. Moods and discrete emotions have behavioral consequences that are of great relevance to organizational functioning. Mood states bias judgments and decisions. They influence helping behaviors. They change the nature of cognitive processing (Weiss, 2002a). Discrete emotions are accompanied by particular behavioral tendencies and also have processing implications (Tagney, 1999). In addition, emotion and mood regulation processes accompany affective states as people try to manage their emotions, sustaining positive experiences and coping with negative ones. These regulatory processes generally put demands on cognitive resources. They influence attentional processes that have an impact on task performance and involve particular and individualized strategies.

To simplify the explanation (perhaps overly so), the affect process starts with the appraisal of emotion-relevant events and ends with a variety of emotion-caused responses. Intervening are a host of mediational processes. At any point along the way, personality may make a difference.

Connecting Dispositions to the Emotion Process

The emotion processes just discussed suggest that there are several places in which dispositions may influence emotional experiences and their consequences (see Figure 5.4). The environment that one creates, the appraisal processes, the emotional episodes, and the behavioral and attitudinal reactions that one has when emotions are experienced can all be influenced in different ways.

Consistent with a general process approach we are advocating, Larsen (2000c; Larsen, Diener, & Lucas, 2002) has proposed a simple stimulus-organism-response (S-O-R) model for understanding the role of personality dispositions in emotion processes. Larsen argues that dispositions may influence the S-O link in terms of processes related to stimulus sensitivity. He then suggests that dispositions may influence the O-R link by connecting with processes related to emotional response regulation. Larsen et al. (2002) present a full discussion of dispositional influences on both links. Our discussion is very much in keeping with Larsen's model, with issues of cognitive appraisal added to the process elements.

Figure 5.4. Some Possible Personality Influences on the Emotion-Generating Process.

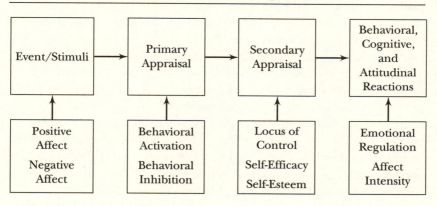

The observation that affective states are generally reactions to specific events suggests that the first place to look for a connection between personality and affect is in the experience of and reaction to events. In this regard, two links are particularly relevant. First, aspects of personality may influence events themselves. Second, and perhaps more important, aspects of personality may influence reactivity to events.

Personality may actually influence the events we experience, or, more precisely, the behavioral manifestations of personality traits may influence the nature of these events. For example, people who present a generally positive demeanor may be more likely to have positive things happen to them. Other people like them and enjoy being around them. Conversely, negative affective expressions may elicit negative events.

In support of this idea, Magnus, Diener, Fujita, and Pavot (1993) examined the relationships between extraversion and neuroticism, on the one hand, and self-reports of "objective" or verifiable positive and negative life events, on the other. Verifiable events were examined in order to reduce the effect of personality on the interpretation of more subjective occurrences. The data were collected in two waves. In the first wave, respondents completed the NEO Personality Inventory (NEO-PI; Costa & McCrae, 1985). In the second wave, four years later, respondents reported on the frequency of the occurrence of various positive and negative objective life events. Extraversion significantly predicted the frequency of positive but not negative events over the next four years. Neuroticism significantly predicted the frequency of negative but not positive events over the next four years. Similarly, van Os, Park, and Jones (2001) showed that childhood assessments of neuroticism could predict the occurrence of stressful life events among a cohort of adults in their late thirties and early forties.

Research on personality and the occurrence of affect-generating life events has been confined to studying affective personality dimensions like neuroticism and extraversion. This is the result of trying to discover mediational processes to explain the often found correlations between these affective traits and general assessments of emotional well-being. However, the relationship between personality and affect-generating events need not be limited to those personality dimensions thought to be affective in nature. For example, conscientiousness is known to (modestly) predict performance (Barrick & Mount, 1991). If performance feedback, both external and internal, can have affective consequences, then conscientiousness may enter into an affect generation process. Specifically, those who are more conscientious do a good job and receive positive feedback, which leads to positive emotional reactions (pride); those who are less conscientious do not do such a good job, resulting in negative feedback and negative emotional reactions (dejection).

Reactivity to similar events can vary among individuals, and this variability can be related to personality differences. Weiss et al. (1999) showed that intraindividual variability in self-reports of mood over a three-week period could be predicted by individual differences in Larsen and Diener's Affect Intensity Measure (AIM; 1987), and Kurek et al. (2001) replicated this finding in their sample of graduate students. These studies replicate in the workplace numerous other studies conducted by Larsen and his colleagues on various nonwork samples. Larsen and Diener consider the AIM a measure of affective reactivity to events, both positive and negative. In support of this interpretation, Larsen, Diener, and Emmons (1986) showed that AIM differences in a student sample predicted the strength of emotional responses to a constant set of emotional events among these students. Although more recent research has questioned the factorial purity of the AIM (Bryant, Yarnold, & Grim, 1996), Larsen's research does illustrate stable individual differences in reactivity to emotional events.

Frequently found relationships between trait extraversion and neuroticism and aggregate mood states can also be explained by differential reactivity to positive and negative events. In a series of studies, Larsen and colleagues (Larsen & Ketelaar, 1989, 1991; Rusting & Larsen, 1999; Zelenski & Larsen, 1999) have shown that extraversion predicts responsivity to positive but not negative mood inductions, and neuroticism predicts responsivity to negative but not positive mood inductions.

An alternate personality structure, one coming from investigations into the physiology of affective reactions, also supports the logic of individual differences in reactivity to affective events. Gray (1987) proposed two physiological systems, one reacting to positive stimuli and the other negative stimuli. These behavioral approach and behavioral inhibition systems are thought to integrate motivational, emotional, and personality findings. Much research has been conducted under this framework. Carver and White (1994) have created a paper-and-pencil measure (the Behavioral Inhibition and Behavioral Activation Scales, BIS/BAS) of individual differences in the reactivity of the two systems. Davidson (1995) and Sutton and Davidson (1997) have good summaries of the nature of the systems and a brief history of the research that has been conducted.

Davidson (1995) describes the anatomical location of the two systems. He suggests that individual differences in the cortical activity in different areas of the brain are related to the emotional reactivity to positive and negative stimuli. The frontal or anterior areas of the right hemisphere are responsible for withdrawal responses, and the anterior areas of the left hemisphere are responsible for approach behavior. Sensitivity to positive and negative stimuli is thought to produce affective reactions and, in turn, behavioral approach and avoidance behaviors (Davidson, 1995).

Exposure to positive and negative stimuli seems to produce the predicted effects on cortical activity in the appropriate areas. Davidson (1995) has shown that the relative cortical activity is an individual difference that predicts the intensity of reactions to positive and negative stimuli. These cortical activity asymmetries are more highly related to paper-and-pencil measures of the BIS and BAS, such as Carver and White's BIS/BAS (1994), than they are with measures of positive and negative affectivity. The underlying systems are systems of reactivity, not stable affect differences.

Gable, Reis, and Eliott (2000) examined daily experience of positive and negative events and daily reports of positive and negative affect. Consistent with expectations, they found in two studies that individual differences in levels of the BIS (using Carver and White's BIS/BAS measure) moderated the relationship between daily experience of negative events and daily reports of negative affect. Inconsistent with expectations, however, in neither study was a moderating effect of differences in behavioral activation on the relationship between positive events and positive affect found.

Cognitive appraisal theory and research suggests that discrete emotional experiences are the result of a primary appraisal process and a secondary appraisal process. Primary appraisal involves assessment of goal relevance and determines the direction and amplitude of emotional response. Secondary appraisal involves assessments of such things as responsibility, coping potential, and modifiability and determines the particular discrete emotions experienced. If these appraisals are integral to the emotion-generation process, then individual differences in appraisal tendencies might also be a place to look for a connection between stable characteristics of individuals and emotional reactions.

Interestingly, as Griner and Smith (2000) have pointed out, although an essential element of appraisal theory is to show how different people can construe the same situation in different ways, clearly implicating the importance of individual differences in values, needs, and appraisal tendencies, almost all research on appraisals has asked about the appraisals directly, ignoring the question of the source of the appraisals. Griner and Smith have begun to rectify that situation by showing that individual differences in affiliation motive can influence the judgment of affiliative importance in emotion-eliciting circumstances.

All appraisal researchers suggest that goal structures provide the standards on which events are evaluated in primary appraisal processes (Smith & Kirby, 2001). As such, individual differences in these goal structures can influence affect-generation processes. Different types of goals or goal structures can lead people to interpret the same event as personally relevant or not personally relevant. Some people tend to focus on things that they "ought" to do to avoid negative consequences, while others focus on things they "want" to do to improve themselves (Higgins, 1998). The differences between these broad goals have an impact on the resultant emotions that are experienced (Brockner & Higgins, 2001; Higgins, 1998). Goal structures may even change the valence of whether the event is helping one attain one's goal or hindering it. A person with a focus on learning a task (rather than performing better than others) may see a failure as a challenge (that is, something positive) rather than a failure or hindrance to his or her goal. These interpretations lead to very different emotional reactions. Dweck and her colleagues (Dweck & Leggett, 1988; Grant & Dweck, 1999) have come to the conclusion that such goal tendencies are consistent across time and can therefore be viewed as precursors to personality traits.

Primary appraisal is thought to be followed by secondary appraisal in the generation of discrete emotions. Different theorists have proposed different appraisal dimensions, and so it is difficult to generate particular dispositional components that would be universally accepted as relevant to secondary appraisal. Nonetheless, enough commonalities exist to suggest avenues for exploration. Many appraisal theorists discuss the importance of the assessment of personal accountability. External attribution for events can lead to non-self-focused emotions like anger. Personal attribution can lead to self-focused emotions like guilt. Individual differences in locus of control (that is, the tendencies to judge events as self or externally caused) will therefore influence the particular emotions generated by particular events and outcomes.

Many theorists also discuss the role of changeablity of the state, particularly with regard to negative states (Smith & Kirby, 2001). Clearly, dispositions such as self-esteem or self-efficacy are likely to be relevant to such judgments and therefore to the differential elicitation of discrete emotions. In a related fashion, studies have shown that learned helplessness attributional style (Abramson, Seligman, & Teasdale, 1978), a personality trait characterized by a belief in an inability to change one's situation, is associated with depression (Yee, Edmondson, Santoro, Begg, & Hunter, 1996).

Overall, while much has been done on the appraisal dimensions that generate discrete emotions, less research has been done on appraisal templates, that is, stable differences in appraisal tendencies. Certainly, individual personality dimensions developed in other contexts can and have been shown to be relevant to emotional appraisal. However, more coherent attempts to tie dispositions to the full nature of emotional appraisal are infrequently encountered but would be very useful.

Emotion processes do not stop with emotion generation. Emotions elicit cognitive, attitudinal, and behavioral responses of relevance to work behavior (see Brief & Weiss, 2002, for a current review), and individual differences in personality are likely to touch on these processes as well. In recent years, a great deal of attention has been paid to processes of emotion regulation. Gross (1999) published an important paper on emotion regulation, and Larsen (2000b) had a lead article in *Psychological Inquiry* on mood regulation. In the organizational literature, Pugh (2002) has published a good general discussion of individual and group emotion-regulation processes. To refer back to Larsen's general model

(2000a) of individual differences in emotion processes, these are discussions of the output side. All of these discussions of emotion regulation mention the role of personality in regulatory processes, but in most of the chapters, the personality discussion is somewhat isolated and not well integrated with the basic processes.

Nonetheless, certain traits are clearly relevant and worth discussing. Pugh (2002), summarizes the work on emotional expressivity (Friedman, Prince, Riggio, & DiMatteo, 1980; Gross & John, 1998) and its relevance to regulatory processes. Emotional expressivity refers to individual differences in the extent to which people overtly express their emotions. Pugh suggests that emotional expressivity acts as an "output filter" between emotional experiences and their expression and that this filter is relatively stable. Its relevance for understanding emotion-generated behavioral outcomes in organizations is discussed by Pugh.

Emotions are known to disrupt ongoing activities and interfere with performance tasks, partly through the interference effects of rumination and intrusive thought. Numerous discussions of emotions, cognitive interference, and rumination have been published in the past few years (see Sarason, Pierce, & Sarason, 1996, and Martin & Tesser, 1996). All indicate the importance of cognitive interference for understanding the performance consequences of emotions. In this area, Sarason and his colleagues have developed a measure of individual differences in the tendency to engage in interfering thoughts during task performance, the Thought Occurrence Questionnaire (Sarason, Sarason, Keefe, Hayes, & Shearon, 1986). This disposition appears to be a prime candidate for understanding differences in the work performance consequences of emotional states. Finally, both Larsen (2000b) and Parkinson and Totterdell (1999) have recently offered classification schemes for affect-regulation strategies. Larsen has suggested that such schemes readily lend themselves to dispositional analyses of regulatory processes.

Affective states influence judgments and behaviors in ways other than through the by-products of regulatory processes. Both discrete emotions, and particularly mood states, bias memory and judgments and influence the depth of cognitive processing (Weiss, 2002a). Gohm and Clore (2000) have presented an analysis of the role that personality plays in the link between mood states and these information processing outcomes that is totally consistent with the process logic we have been arguing for. They first lay out the stages linking immediate mood states with judgments and processing outcomes. Working from the "affect as information" approach, they propose the key stages of reaction, attention (to affective states or reactions), and attribution (for affective states or reactions). They then propose a classification of individual difference measures relevant to these stages and organize relevant existing trait measures into their classificatory scheme. The program has the virtue of tying personality directly to process and the added advantage of using personality moderator predictions as a way of testing the validity of process.

Conclusion

This chapter was intended to offer thoughts on studying the relationship between personality and affect. The overabundance of studies correlating various personality traits with dispositionalized operations of affect attests more to the simplicity of thinking about this relationship than to the utility of conducting such studies. This body of research tells us much less than we need to know about affect and personality.

The primary source of difficulty is the disconnect between the stable (by definition) nature of personality traits and the transient, time-bound nature of affective states. Affect states, as states, change over time, and the changing nature of these states makes explanation by way of stable dispositions difficult, but not impossible.

The answer to the conceptual disconnect, however, is not found in remaking state variables into trait variables. Correlations may be found between personality and aggregated mood or job satisfaction, but such correlations do little to help us understand the role of dispositions in explaining true affective experiences. Rather, we argue that the role of personality can be found by first taking a thorough look at the complex chain of processes that link events to emotional reactions and emotional reactions to behavioral, cognitive, and attitudinal outcomes. This examination will find that personality constructs of many different types have various roles to play all along the mediational path.

There are wrong turns to be taken here as well. We believe that one risk is the arbitrary creation of dispositionalized elements of the process. So, for example, Larsen et al. (2002) look at the mediational processes (good) but then suggest that researchers should examine individual differences in these processes. We agree that there are likely to be individual differences in these mediational processes, but we also believe that full, productive analysis will link these differences to existing and well-accepted personality constructs (positive affectivity, negative affectivity, self-efficacy, affect intensity, and others), not create new measures of individual differences in mediational constructs (the "tendency to see events as personally relevant"). Tying together existing constructs with mediational processes brings more information to the analysis, information gleaned from the nomological network of the already existing variables. Dispositionalizing process does not do this to the same extent.

The other risk is the generation of a laundry list of disconnected personality findings, a natural outcome of the complexity of emotion processes. We understand this risk but at this point choose to accept it. Emotion processes are complex. Consequent dispositional contributions are also going to be complex. For the time being, this is the price to be paid for careful study of dispositional-process links.

Our final comment goes beyond issues of affect. Many outcomes of interest to I/O psychologists vary substantially over time. Dispositional explanations of these variables tend to focus on the same sort of aggregations characteristic of the research on affect. As with affect, the within-person variance goes unmodeled and is treated as error. Personality has a role in explaining the dynamic nature of these outcomes, but as we suggest, that role will be defined by appropriate connections to mediational processes.

References

Abramson, L. Y., Seligman, M. E., & Teasdale, J. D. (1978). Learned helplessness in humans: Critique and reformulation. *Journal of Abnormal Psychology, 87,* 49–74.

Barrick, M. R., & Mount, M. K. (1991). The Big Five personality dimensions and job performance: A meta-analysis. *Personnel Psychology, 44,* 1–26.

Block, J. (1995). A contrarian view of the five-factor approach to personality description. *Psychological Bulletin, 117,* 187–215.

Bluen, S. D., Barling, J., & Burns, W. (1990). Predicting sales performance, job satisfaction, and depression by using the Achievement Strivings and Impatience-Irritability dimensions of Type A behavior. *Journal of Applied Psychology, 75,* 212–216.

Bohle, P., & Tilley, A. J. (1993). Predicting mood change on night shift. *Ergonomics, 36,* 125–133.

Brief, A. P., Burke, M. J., George, J. M., Robinson, B. S., & Webster, J. (1988). Should negative affectivity remain an unmeasured variable in the study of job stress? *Journal of Applied Psychology, 73,* 193–198.

Brief, A. P., Butcher, A. H., & Roberson, L. (1995). Cookies, disposition, and job attitudes: The effects of positive mood-inducing events and negative affectivity on job satisfaction in a field experiment. *Organizational Behavior and Human Decision Processes, 62,* 55–62.

Brief, A. P., & Roberson, L. (1989). Job attitude organization: An exploratory study. *Journal of Applied Social Psychology, 19,* 717–727.

Brief, A. P., & Weiss, H. M. (2002). Organizational behavior: Affect in the workplace. *Annual Review of Psychology, 53,* 279–307.

Brockner, J., & Higgins, E. T. (2001). Regulatory focus theory: Implications for the study of emotions at work. *Organizational Behavior and Human Decision Processes, 86,* 35–66.

Bryant, F. B., Yarnold, P. R., & Grim, L. G. (1996). Towards a measurement model of the Affect Intensity Measure: A three-factor model. *Journal of Research in Personality, 30,* 223–247.

Buunk, B. P., & Verhoeven, K. (1991). Companionship and support at work: A microanalysis of the stress-reducing feature of social interaction. *Basic and Applied Social Psychology, 12,* 243–258.

Carver, C. S., & White, T. L. (1994). Behavioral inhibition, behavioral activation, and affective responses to impending reward and punishment: The BIS/BAS Scales. *Journal of Personality and Social Psychology, 67,* 319–333.

Chen, P. Y., & Spector, P. E. (1991). Negative affectivity as the underlying cause of correlations between stressors and strains. *Journal of Applied Psychology, 76,* 398–407.

Costa, P. T., & McCrae, R. R. (1985). *The NEO Personality Inventory manual.* Odessa, FL: Psychological Assessment Resources.

Davidson, R. J. (1995). Cerebral asymmetry, emotion and affective style. In R. J. Davidson & K. Hugdahl (Eds.), *Brain asymmetry* (pp. 361–387). Cambridge, MA: MIT Press.

Dweck, C. S., & Leggett, E. L. (1988). A social-cognitive approach to motivation and personality. *Psychological Review, 95,* 256–273.

Fisher, C. D. (2000). Mood and emotions while working: Missing pieces of job satisfaction? *Journal of Organizational Behavior, 21,* 185–202.

Fredrickson, B. L. (2000). Extracting meaning from past affective experiences: The importance of peaks, ends, and specific emotions. *Cognition and Emotion, 14,* 577–606.

Friedman, H. S., Prince, L. M., Riggio, R. E., & DiMatteo, M. R. (1980). Understanding and assessing nonverbal expressiveness: The Affective Communication Test. *Journal of Personality and Social Psychology, 39,* 333–351.

Frijda, N. H. (1993). Moods, emotion episodes, and emotions. In M. Lewis & J. M. Haviland-Jones (Eds.), *Handbook of emotions* (pp. 381–404). New York: Guilford Press.

Gable, S. L., Reis, H. T., & Eliott, A. J. (2000). Behavioral activation and inhibition in everyday life. *Journal of Personality and Social Psychology, 78,* 1135–1149.

George, J. M. (1990). Personality, affect, and behavior in groups. *Journal of Applied Psychology, 75,* 107–116.

Glynn, M. A. (1998). Situational and dispositional determinants of managers' satisfaction. *Journal of Business and Psychology, 13,* 193–209.

Gohm, C. L., & Clore, G. L. (2000). Individual differences in emotional experience: Mapping available scales to processes. *Personality and Social Psychology Bulletin, 26,* 679–697.

Grant, H., & Dweck, C. S. (1999). A goal analysis of personality and personality coherence. In D. Cervone & Y. Shoda (Eds.), *The coherence of personality: Social-cognitive bases of consistency, variability, and organization* (pp. 345–371). New York: Guilford Press.

Gray, J. A. (1987). *The psychology of fear and stress* (2nd ed.). Cambridge: Cambridge University Press.

Griner, L. A., & Smith, C. A. (2000). Contributions of motivational orientation to appraisal and emotion. *Personality and Social Psychology Bulletin, 26,* 727–740.

Gross, J. J. (1999). Emotion regulation: Past, present, future. *Cognition and Emotion, 13,* 551–573.

Gross, J. J., & John, O. P. (1998). Mapping the domain of expressivity: Multimethod evidence for a hierarchical model. *Journal of Personality and Social Psychology, 74,* 170–191.

Hart, P. M. (1999). Predicting employee life satisfaction: A coherent model of personality, work and nonwork experiences, and domain satisfactions. *Journal of Applied Psychology, 84,* 564–584.

Higgins, E. T. (1998). Promotion and prevention: Regulatory focus as a motivational principle. In M. P. Zanna (Ed.), *Advances in experimental social psychology* (Vol. 30, pp. 1–46). Orlando, FL: Academic Press.

Jex, S. M., & Bliese, P. D. (1999). Efficacy beliefs as a moderator of the impact of work-related stressors: A multilevel study. *Journal of Applied Psychology, 84,* 349–361.

Jex, S. M., & Gudanowski, D. M. (1992). Efficacy beliefs and work stress: An exploratory study. *Journal of Organizational Behavior, 13,* 509–517.

Jex, S. M., & Spector, P. E. (1996). The impact of negative affectivity on stressor-strain relations: A replication and extension. *Work and Stress, 10,* 36–45.

Judge, T. A., & Hulin, C. L. (1993). Job satisfaction as a reflection of dis-position: A multiple source causal analysis. *Organizational Behavior and Human Decision Processes, 56,* 388–421.

Judge, T. A., Locke, E. A., & Durham, C. C. (1997). The dispositional causes of job satisfaction: A core evaluations approach. *Research in Organizational Behavior, 19,* 151–188.

Kurek, K. E., Le, B., & Weiss, H. M. (2001). Studying affective climates using Web-based experiential sampling methods. In H. Weiss (Chair), *Experience sampling methods (ESM) in organizational research.* Symposium conducted at the Sixteenth Annual Conference of the Society for Industrial and Organizational Psychology, San Diego, CA.

Larsen, R. J. (2000a). Emotion and personality: Introduction to the spe-cial symposium. *Personality and Social Psychology Bulletin, 26,* 651–654.

Larsen, R. J. (2000b). Toward a science of mood regulation. *Psychological Inquiry, 11,* 129–141.

Larsen, R. J. (2000c). Maintaining hedonic balance: Reply to commen-taries. *Psychological Inquiry, 11,* 218–225.

Larsen, R. J., & Diener, E. (1987). Affect intensity as an individual differ-ence characteristic: A review. *Journal of Research in Personality, 21,* 1–39.

Larsen, R. J., Diener, E., & Emmons, R. A. (1986). Affect intensity and re-actions to daily life events. *Journal of Personality and Social Psychology, 51,* 803–814.

Larsen, R. J., Diener, E., & Lucas, R. E. (2002). Emotion: Models, mea-sures, and individual differences. In R. G. Lord, R. J. Klimoski, & R. Kanfer (Eds.), *Emotions in the workplace: Understanding the structure and role of emotions in organizational behavior* (pp. 64–106). San Fran-cisco: Jossey-Bass.

Larsen, R. J., & Ketelaar, T. (1989). Extraversion, neuroticism and sus-ceptibility to positive and negative mood induction procedures. *Per-sonality and Individual Differences, 10,* 1221–1228.

Larsen, R. J., & Ketelaar, T. (1991). Personality and susceptibility to posi-tive and negative emotional states. *Journal of Personality and Social Psychology, 61,* 132–140.

Lazarus, R. S. (1991). *Emotion and adaptation.* New York: Oxford Univer-sity Press.

Levin, I., & Stokes, J. P. (1989). Dispositional approach to job satisfaction: Role of negative affectivity. *Journal of Applied Psychology, 74,* 754–758.

Magnus, K., Diener, E., Fujita, F., & Pavot, W. (1993). Extraversion and neuroticism as predictors of objective life events: A longitudinal analysis. *Journal of Personality and Social Psychology, 65,* 1046–1053.

Martin, L. L., & Tesser, A. (1996). Some ruminative thoughts. In R. S. Wyer Jr. (Ed.), *Ruminative thoughts: Advances in social cognition* (Vol. 9, pp. 1–47). Mahwah, NJ: Erlbaum.

Mischel, W., & Shoda, Y. (1995). A cognitive-affective system theory of personality: Reconceptualizing situations, dispositions, dynamics, and invariance in personality structure. *Psychological Review, 102,* 246–268.

Mischel, W., & Shoda, Y. (1998). Reconciling processing dynamics and personality dispositions. *Annual Review of Psychology, 49,* 229–258.

Parkinson, B., & Totterdell, P. (1999). Classifying affect-regulation strategies. *Cognition and Emotion, 13,* 277–303.

Pervin, L. A. (1994). A critical analysis of current trait theory. *Psychological Inquiry, 5,* 103–113.

Porac, J. F., Ferris, G. R., & Fedor, D. B. (1983). Causal attributions, affect, and expectations for a day's work performance. *Academy of Management Journal, 26,* 285–296.

Portello, J. Y., & Long, B. C. (2001). Appraisals and coping with workplace interpersonal stress: A model for women managers. *Journal of Counseling Psychology, 48,* 144–156.

Pugh, S. D. (2002). Emotional regulation in individuals and dyads: Causes, costs, and consequences. In R. G. Lord, R. J. Klimoski, & R. Kanfer (Eds.), *Emotions in the workplace: Understanding the structure and role of emotions in organizational behavior* (pp. 147–182). San Francisco: Jossey-Bass.

Rusting, C. L., & Larsen, R. J. (1999). Clarifying Gray's theory of personality: A response to Pickering, Corr, and Gray. *Personality and Individual Differences, 26,* 367–372.

Saavedra, R., & Kwun, S. K. (2000). Affective states in job characteristics theory. *Journal of Organizational Behavior, 21,* 131–146.

Saks, A. M., & Ashforth, B. E. (2000). The role of dispositions, entry stressors, and behavioral plasticity theory in predicting newcomers' adjustment to work. *Journal of Organizational Behavior, 21,* 43–62.

Sarason, I. G., Pierce, G. R., & Sarason, B. R. (1996). Domains of cognitive interference. In I. G. Sarason, G. R. Pierce, & B. R. Sarason (Eds.), *Cognitive interference: Theories, methods, and findings* (pp. 139–152). Mahwah, NJ: Erlbaum.

Sarason, I. G., Sarason, B. R., Keefe, D. E., Hayes, B. E., & Shearon, E. N. (1986). Cognitive interference: Situational determinants and trait-like characteristics. *Journal of Personality and Social Psychology, 51,* 215–226.

Shiu, A. T. (1998). The significance of sense of coherence for the perceptions of task characteristics and stress during interruptions amongst a sample of public health nurses in Hong Kong: Implications for nursing management. *Public Health Nursing, 15,* 273–280.

Smith, C. A., & Ellsworth, P. C. (1985). Patterns of cognitive appraisal in emotion. *Journal of Personality and Social Psychology, 48,* 813–838.

Smith, C. A., & Kirby, L. D. (2001). Affect and cognitive appraisal processes. In J. P. Forgas (Ed.), *Handbook of affect and social cognition* (pp. 75–92). Mahwah, NJ: Erlbaum.

Smith, D., & Tziner, A. (1998). Moderating effects of affective disposition and social support on the relationship between person-environment fit and strain. *Psychological Reports, 82,* 963–983.

Spector, P. E., Chen, P. Y., & O'Connell, B. J. (2000). A longitudinal study of relations between job stressors and job strains while controlling for prior negative affectivity and strains. *Journal of Applied Psychology, 85,* 211–218.

Spector, P. E., & O'Connell, B. J. (1994). The contribution of personality traits, negative affectivity, locus of control, and Type A to the subsequent reports of job stressors and job strains. *Journal of Occupational and Organizational Psychology, 67,* 1–12.

Staw, B. M. (in press). The dispositional approach to job attitudes: An empirical and conceptual review. In B. Schneider & B. Smith (Eds.), *Personality and organization.* Mahwah, NJ: Erlbaum.

Stokes, J. P., & Levin, I. M. (1990). The development and validation of a measure of negative affectivity. *Journal of Social Behavior and Personality, 5,* 173–186.

Stone, A. A., Shiffman, S. S., & DeVries, M. W. (1999). Ecological momentary assessment. In D. Kahneman, E. Diener, & N. Schwarz (Eds.), *Well-being: The foundations of hedonic psychology* (pp. 26–39). New York: Russell Sage Foundation.

Sutton, S. K., & Davidson, R. J. (1997). Prefrontal brain asymmetry: A biological substrate of the behavioral approach and inhibition systems. *Psychological Science, 8,* 204–210.

Tagney, J. P. (1999). The self-conscious emotions: Shame, guilt, embarrassment, and pride. In T. Dalgleish & M. J. Power (Eds.), *Handbook of cognition and emotion.* New York: Wiley.

van Os, J., Park, S.B.G., & Jones, P. B. (2001). Neuroticism, life events and mental health: Evidence for person-environment correlation. *British Journal of Psychiatry, 178,* s72–s77.

Watson, D., Clark, L. A., & Tellegen, A. (1988). Development and validation of brief measures of positive and negative affect: The PANAS scales. *Journal of Personality and Social Psychology, 54,* 1063–1070.

Watson, D., & Slack, A. K. (1993). General factors of affective temperament and their relation to job satisfaction over time. *Organizational Behavior and Human Decision Processes, 54,* 181–202.

Weiss, H. M. (2002a). Conceptual and empirical foundations for the study of affect at work. In R. G. Lord, R. J. Klimoski, & R. Kanfer (Eds.), *Emotions in the workplace: Understanding the structure and role of emotions in organizational behavior* (pp. 20–63). San Francisco: Jossey-Bass.

Weiss, H. M. (2002b). Deconstructing job satisfaction. Separating evaluations, beliefs and affective experiences. *Human Resource Management Review, 12,* 173–194.

Weiss, H. M., & Cropanzano, R. (1996). Affective events theory: A theoretical discussion of the structure, causes, and consequences of affective experiences at work. *Research in Organizational Behavior, 18,* 1–74.

Weiss, H. M., Nicholas, J. P., & Daus, C. S. (1999). An examination of the joint effects of affective experiences and job beliefs on job satisfaction and variations in affective experiences over time. *Organizational Behavior and Human Decision Processes, 78,* 1–24.

Wofford, J. C., Goodwin, V. L., & Daly, P. S. (1999). Cognitive-affective stress propensity: A field study. *Journal of Organizational Behavior, 20,* 687–707.

Wright, T. A., & Cropanzano, R. (1998). Emotional exhaustion as a predictor of job performance and voluntary turnover. *Journal of Applied Psychology, 83,* 486–493.

Yee, P. L., Edmondson, B., Santoro, K. E., Begg, A. E., & Hunter, C. D. (1996). Cognitive effects of life stress and learned helplessness. *Anxiety, Stress and Coping: An International Journal, 9,* 301–319.

Zelenski, J. M., & Larsen, R. J. (1999). Susceptibility to affect: A comparison of three personality taxonomies. *Journal of Personality, 67,* 761–791.

Zellars, K. L., & Perrewe, P. L. (2001). Affective personality and the content of emotional social support: Coping in organizations. *Journal of Applied Psychology, 86,* 459–467.

CHAPTER 6

Personality and Counterproductive Workplace Behavior

Michael J. Cullen
Paul R. Sackett

Despite overwhelming evidence that personality traits are useful predictors of counterproductive workplace behaviors (CWBs), little progress has been made in describing the processes underlying the observed empirical linkage between personality and CWBs. In brief, we lack an understanding of why personality traits should be predictive of counterproductive behavior. A sound theoretical understanding of the basis for our empirical findings is necessary not only to make sense of these results in the aggregate, but also to guide future research in profitable directions. In this chapter, we aim to chart a tentative course for researchers interested in exploring more deeply the relationships between personality and CWBs.

Foundation Understandings

This chapter rests on an understanding of what counterproductive work behavior is and documentation that personality traits are useful predictors of CWBs.

Defining Counterproductive Work Behavior

Counterproductive workplace behavior at the most general level refers to any intentional behavior on the part of an organization member viewed by the organization as contrary to its legitimate interests (Sackett & DeVore, 2001). We distinguish counterproductive behavior from counterproductivity, viewing the latter as the tangible outcomes of counterproductive behavior. We view counterproductive behavior as a facet of job performance and performance as reflecting behaviors rather than outcomes. For example, in a given time period, violation of safety procedures (behaviors) may not result in any injuries (outcomes), thus illustrating the distinction between counterproductive behavior and counterproductivity.

This definition of CWB takes the perspective of the organization. Thus, a behavior can be performed by many employees in an organization (for example, a setting where taking sick leave when not actually sick has become widespread), and hence the behavior is not deviant in the norm-violation sense; nevertheless, the organization may view the behavior as contrary to its legitimate interests.

CWBs encompass a broad number of categories of behaviors. Gruys (2000) sorted behaviors in the literature into eleven categories:

- Theft and related behavior
- Destruction of property
- Misuse of information (reveal confidential information; falsify records)
- Misuse of time and resources (waste time, alter time card, conduct personal business during work time)
- Unsafe behavior
- Poor attendance
- Poor-quality work (intentionally slow or sloppy work)
- Alcohol use
- Drug use
- Inappropriate verbal actions (argue with customers; verbally harass coworkers)
- Inappropriate physical actions (physically attack coworkers; physical sexual advances toward coworker)

This list is presented to give a sense of the range of behaviors in this domain rather than as an exhaustive compilation.

An important issue is the need for an understanding of the covariance structure of CWBs. There has been a tendency to treat each form of CWB as discrete, resulting in separate literatures on behavior categories such as theft, drug and alcohol use, absenteeism, and unsafe behaviors. Sackett and DeVore (2001) reviewed literature on the interrelationships among CWBs. Self-report, other-report, and direct judgments of likelihood of co-occurrence support the notion of positive interrelationships among CWBs. Self-report data indicated positive correlations in the range of .30 between individual counterproductive behaviors but higher correlations of about .50 between composites of related behaviors, a finding replicated with data using supervisor ratings. It also appears reasonable to think in terms of an overall CWB construct, as grand composites across broad ranges of CWBs exhibit internal consistency reliabilities in the .80s and .90s. Sackett and DeVore suggest a hierarchical model, with a general CWB factor at the top; a series of group factors, such as the organizational deviance and interpersonal deviance factors identified by Bennett and Robinson (2000), below this general factor; and specific behavior domains, such as theft, absence, safety, and drug and alcohol use below these group factors. Researchers and practitioners may focus at different levels of this hierarchy for different applications. In many personnel selection settings, organizations are interested in identifying prospective employees who will not engage in the broad range of CWBs, and thus may focus on the broad CWB construct. In contrast, an intervention may be sought that will deal effectively with a single specific problem behavior (for example, widespread violation of safety procedures).

Another important issue is the relationship between CWBs and the domains of organizational citizenship behaviors (OCBs) and contextual performance. One perspective, articulated by Bennett and Stamper (2001), views these as positive (OCB) and negative (CWB) discretionary behavior and hypothesizes that they reflect opposite ends of an overall continuum of discretionary behavior. Empirical evidence does suggest that these two domains are related, though methodology appears to have a strong influence on study findings. Sackett and DeVore (2001) report a correlation of about −.60 between supervisor ratings of the two domains, based on the results of a meta-analysis and two large-scale individual studies. In contrast, much smaller correlations are found with self-reports of behavior in the two domains. Laczo

(2002) reports $r = -.17$ between the two domains; Miles, Borman, Spector, and Fox (2002) report $r = -.11$; and Kelloway, Loughlin, Barling, and Nault (2002) report $r = -.20$. Perhaps most telling in resolving the issue of viewing OCBs and CWBs as one or two dimensions is emerging evidence of different correlates of the two domains. For example, Miles et al. report that a measure of negative affectivity correlates .35 with CWB and .12 with OCB. Thus, although the OCB and CWB domains are not unrelated, we view them as two meaningfully distinct domains.

Personality as a Predictor of CWBs

As summarized by Sackett and DeVore (2001), the results of countless individual studies and at least three meta-analyses have established that personality traits are useful predictors of a wide variety of CWBs. Meta-analytic evidence from the integrity testing literature, the Big Five literature, and the literature on the prediction of military performance all make clear that some personality dimensions show consistent relationships to CWBs. The strongest findings are for the dimension of Conscientiousness. First, integrity tests showed sizable relationships (mean observed $r = .27$ and .20 for two different types of integrity tests) with CWBs, and research on the constructs underlying integrity tests showed that Conscientiousness was the single largest source of variance in integrity tests, followed by Agreeableness and Emotional Stability (Ones, Viswesvaran, & Schmidt, 1993). Second, Hough (1992) separated the Big Five Conscientiousness dimension into dependability and achievement subfacets and reported similar relationships with CWB criteria (mean observed $r = .19$ and .24 for achievement and dependability). Third, the military's Project A similarly separated dependability and achievement and reported comparable findings (mean observed $r = .18$ and .30 for achievement and dependability; McHenry, Hough, Toquam, Hanson, & Ashworth, 1990). These conclusions were based on well over one hundred studies of several hundred thousand individuals. Thus, among the Big Five personality dimensions, Conscientiousness is the strongest predictor of a broad class of CWBs. There is also general support for the hypothesis that Emotional Stability and Agreeableness are predictive of broad categories of CWBs.

At a more molecular level, various studies have demonstrated the utility of these three Big Five traits and their lower-order facets in predicting a variety of more specific CWBs. For instance, researchers have demonstrated the utility of one or more of these traits as predictors of absenteeism (Judge, Martocchio, & Thoresen, 1997), turnover (Barrick & Mount, 1996), delinquency (Hough, 1992), workplace violence (Ones & Viswesvaran, 2001), substance abuse (Schmidt, Viswesvaran, & Ones, 1997), property damage (Ones & Viswesvaran, 1998), and a broad array of violent and nonviolent criminal behaviors (Collins & Schmidt, 1993; Eysenck & Gudjonsson, 1988).

Why Do Personality Traits Predict CWBs?

A basic premise of this chapter is that there are many ways in which personality traits may influence the occurrence of CWBs. In order to organize the hypothesized lines of causal influence, it is useful to draw a distinction between what we will term initiated CWBs and reactive CWBs. Initiated CWBs are, as the label implies, initiated by the individual to satisfy some need or motive. Individuals may initiate a counterproductive behavior (for example, steal from the organization) to satisfy a motive such as pleasure, greed, thrill seeking, risk taking, or attention seeking. Reactive CWBs, in contrast, are engaged in by the individual in response to some actual or perceived organizational event. In these cases, the behavior is engaged in to satisfy a motive such as retaliation, revenge, release, or escape.

Several observations about this distinction are in order. First, any type of CWB could be initiated in some settings and reactive in others. One individual may steal to satisfy a need for risk taking, while another may steal in retaliation for perceived mistreatment by a supervisor. Thus, it is not the case that types of CWBs can be categorized as initiated or reactive. Second, any given CWB may be engaged in to satisfy multiple motives. Two individuals may both be seeking an outlet to react to perceived injustice but differ in risk-taking propensity; the one high in risk-taking propensity may choose theft as the means of retaliation, while the one low in risk-taking propensity may choose to extend work breaks.

This distinction between initiated and reactive CWBs is reflected in Figure 6.1, which is the organizing device for this chapter. As Figure 6.1 indicates, one manner in which personality traits

Figure 6.1. Model of Linkages Between Personality and Counterproductive Work Behaviors.

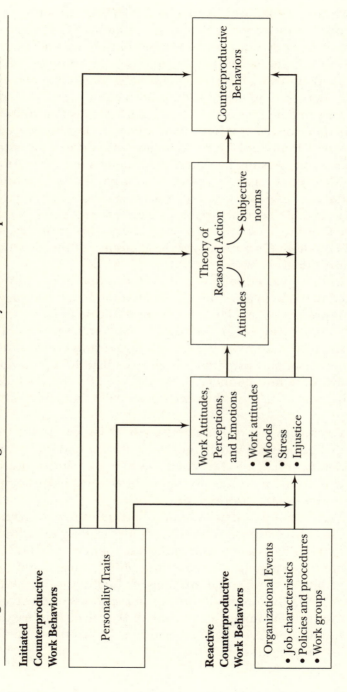

may influence the occurrence of CWBs is by initiating those behaviors. We hypothesize that as an initiator of CWBs, personality traits exert both a direct line of causal influence and a more indirect line of influence by helping to shape the attitudes held toward the CWBs and a set of perceptual variables including perceived job stress, perceived injustice and dissatisfaction.

A second manner in which personality traits may influence the occurrence of CWBs is by moderating relationships between organizational events and CWBs. As Figure 6.1 indicates, we hypothesize that specific personality traits moderate two sets of relationships. The first is the relationship between organizational features (job characteristics, work group characteristics, or company policies) and a set of perceptual variables including perceived job stress, perceived injustice, or dissatisfaction. The second is the relationship between those perceptual variables and the counterproductive behaviors themselves.

In this chapter, we point to evidence that personality may be linked to CWBs in all of these ways. We do not mean to suggest that a comprehensive explanatory model of these linkages is possible at this stage. Indeed, any attempt to explain the processes linking personality and CWBs is part of a larger and continuing effort within personality psychology itself to explain how personality and behavior are interconnected. In sum, we offer here a model that posits five mechanisms by which personality can affect CWBs:

1. Personality as a direct determinant of CWBs. We will posit limited instances in which individuals are "hard-wired" by biological and neurochemical mechanisms to engage in counterproductive behavior (impulsive behavior that bypasses cognitive assessment of appropriateness).
2. Personality as a determinant of attitudes toward counterproductive behaviors, with such attitudes leading to various CWBs.
3. Personality as a determinant of a set of perceptual variables including workplace satisfaction, moods, stress, and injustice, with these perceptual variables leading to various CWBs.
4. Personality as a moderator of perceptions of environmental events (personality leads some to perceive as unjust organizational events seen as just by others), with those perceptions leading to various CWBs.

5. Personality as a moderator of cognitive, affective, and emotional reactions to perceived environmental events (personality leads to different behavioral reactions to injustice).

We explore each of these possibilities in the five sections that follow.

Personality as a Direct Determinant of Counterproductive Behavior

One reason personality traits may influence the occurrence of counterproductive behaviors is that they reflect internal biological states that predispose us toward certain relatively stable patterns of behavior in general. The idea that personality traits may reflect biological states has a long history in the field of personality psychology. Allport (1937) conjectured that traits reflect neuropsychic systems with motivational properties. Murray (1938) viewed needs as "psycho-chemical" forces, and Eysenck (1990) attempted to link his three-factor theory of traits—Extraversion, Neuroticism, and Psychoticism—to individual differences in nervous system functioning and formation (Winter & Barenbaum, 1999). More recently, McCrae and Costa (1999) have defined traits as deep, unobservable psychological entities that are biological in origin.

Recent empirical evidence is strongly supportive of the thesis that personality traits are reflections of events taking place at the molecular level. In particular, by examining the neurotransmitters that govern the transmission of nerve impulses and their linkages to human behavior, researchers are beginning to identify the biological states associated with our personality traits.

To date, the most progress has been made in relation to the traits of Extraversion and Impulsivity, which as a trait essentially reflects a state of high Extraversion, low Conscientiousness, and low Agreeableness (Digman, 1997; Eysenck, 1997). There is emerging consensus that the neurotransmitter dopamine influences the expression of either extraverted-type behaviors or impulsive behaviors, or both. Disagreement remains, however, about whether the line of neurobiological influence lies more properly with Extraversion or Impulsivity specifically. One group of researchers contends that dopamine production directly influences extraverted-type behavior only (Depue & Collins, 1999), while another group contends that dopamine production influences behaviors more closely aligned with aggressive or impulsive-sensation-seeking behaviors (Gray, 1991; Cloninger, Svrakic, & Przybeck, 1993; Zuckerman, Kuhlman, Thornquist, & Kiers, 1991).

The fact that so much of the research linking biology to personality has centered on the trait of Impulsivity makes it especially important, for the purposes of this chapter, to understand the biological theory of personality. Apart from its links to counterproductive behaviors through its relationship to the higher-order factors of Conscientiousness and Agreeableness, Impulsivity is predictive of many counterproductive behaviors in its own right. For instance, Impulsivity has been found to be a moderately good predictor of alcohol, marijuana, cigarette, and psychedelic drug use (Watson & Clark, 1993), juvenile delinquency (Robins, John, Caspi, Moffitt, & Stouthamer-Loeber, 1996), verbal slurs, and coercive actions (Baumeister, Heatherton, & Tice, 1994; Hynan & Grush, 1986).

The fact that dopamine or other neurotransmitters influence the occurrence of a certain set of behaviors does not normally mean that our behavior is determined solely by those neurotransmitters. Whether we succumb to the influence of any biological state may simply depend on whether we choose to be guided by their influence. For instance, although various biological systems may tell us we are hungry and increase the odds of our eating, in most cases we are able to resist these impulses by making a conscious decision not to eat. In similar fashion, although high dopamine levels may be associated with a tendency to engage in impulsive behaviors at work, such as substance abuse, in most cases we are able to resist these impulses by making a conscious decision not to use these substances.

Although we are usually able to resist the influence of biological states through choice behavior, this may not always be the case. For instance, if neurotransmitter levels are extreme enough, they may induce personality disorders or psychopathological states. The neurotransmitter serotonin provides a case in point. Extremely low levels of serotonin are known to produce very aggressive behavior and are often associated with psychopathy, murder, and suicide (Zuckerman, 1995). Such cases call into question whether an individual has much choice whether to engage in the behaviors associated with a particular neurotransmitter.

In such cases, a given personality trait, as a reflection of an underlying biological state, should have a direct effect on behavior because its influence is for the most part unmediated by any choice behavior on the part of the individual coworkers. Although personality traits can be considered direct determinants of counterproductive behaviors in these extreme cases, we hypothesize that these occasions will be somewhat rare. In most cases, we expect personality traits to exert their influence on counterproductive behaviors indirectly, through their effect on either our attitudes toward various counterproductive behaviors or general workplace attitudes or moods. Indeed, when individuals possess extreme levels of a neurotransmitter that regulates a given personality trait, the population under consideration may no longer be a "normal" population of adults. For instance, many of these individuals may satisfy the clinical criteria for a particular personality disorder. Individuals who are very high on neuroticism may satisfy many of the diagnostic criteria for borderline personality disorder, including vulnerability, anxiety, and depression. Similarly, individuals who are very high on the Conscientiousness dimension may satisfy many of the criteria for obsessive personality disorder, such as a preoccupation with order and perfectionism (Widiger, Verheul, & van den Brink, 1999).

Research into the links between biology and personality is in its infancy. The important point for the purpose of this chapter is that in an as yet undetermined number of cases, counterproductive behaviors at work may in fact be manifestations of clinical disorders that have their origins in biological systems. The extent to which this is true has not yet been adequately addressed.

Personality as a Determinant of Attitudes Toward CWBs

Personality traits may exert their influence on counterproductive behaviors indirectly by influencing our attitudes toward those behaviors. For instance, the trait of Agreeableness may produce an unfavorable attitude toward aggressive acts, which may in turn make it unlikely that an individual will engage in violent acts in the workplace. A body of evidence in fact links personality traits to the attitudes we hold toward certain behaviors and our attitudes toward those behaviors to whether we choose to engage in them.

The Theory of Reasoned Action

Attitudes are a summary evaluative judgment of a psychological object. The judgment is usually couched in dimensions such as good-bad, pleasant-unpleasant or likeable-unlikable (Ajzen, 2001; Eagly & Chaiken, 1993). We focus here on Fishbein and Ajzen's theory of reasoned action (1975), which is currently the most widely endorsed theory of attitude formation (Ajzen, 2001). According to the theory, our attitudes toward a behavior are the product of two things: our beliefs about the consequences of engaging in a given behavior and our evaluation of the desirability of the consequences of that behavior. These two elements are multiplied to obtain an individual's overall attitude toward a behavior.

According to the theory of reasoned action, behavioral intention is normally the best predictor of how a person will behave, and behavioral intentions are a weighted additive function of a person's attitude toward the behavior (A) and his or her subjective norms (SN) about what others think he or she should do. The subjective norm element is composed of a normative belief about whether relevant individuals or groups think the individual should or should not perform the behavior and the individual's motivation to comply with that individual or group.

The theory of reasoned action has been successfully used to predict the behavioral intention to commit a number of behaviors, including having an abortion, smoking marijuana, and choosing among political candidates (Beck & Ajzen, 1991). On rarer occasions, the theory has been applied to socially undesirable behaviors, such as lying, cheating, and shoplifting (Beck & Ajzen, 1991).

More recently, in his theory of planned behavior, Ajzen (1991) has argued that behavior is a function of both behavioral intention and perceived behavioral control, which refers to people's perception of the ease or difficulty of performing a given behavior. While we acknowledge that there may be instances where perceived behavioral control can influence the occurrence of a CWB (theft or destruction of property), these instances would seem to be rare. For the vast majority of CWBs (unsafe behavior, poor attendance, poor-quality work, drug use, alcohol use), we would expect most people to be confident they can perform these behaviors. Thus, for the purposes of this chapter, we focus on the attitudinal and subjective norm components articulated in the original theory of reasoned action.

Personality and the Theory of Reasoned Action

The fact that behavioral intention to engage in a counterproductive behavior is a function of attitudes toward that behavior and subjective norms concerning that behavior suggests four possible paths through which personality can influence the occurrence of CWBs. Specifically, personality can influence either of the belief components associated with our attitude toward a given counterproductive behavior (that is, beliefs about the consequences of the behavior or beliefs about the desirability of those consequences), or either of the subjective norm components related to that behavior (beliefs about what relevant others believe one should do and motivation to comply with that norm).

Beliefs About the Consequences of CWBs

There would appear to be a wide range of potential perceived consequences of engaging in CWBs. We posit that two key consequences are detection and sanction. For example, if I steal from the organization, will I be detected, and, subsequently, if detected, will there be sanctions? Other consequences are possible as well, such as effects on self-image and effects on how one is viewed by others.

Of interest, then, is the question on whether personality variables are related to these beliefs. It is interesting to note that item formats explicitly dealing with these perceptions are a part of some integrity tests. For example, a public domain instrument developed by Ryan and Sackett (1987) contains the agree-disagree item, "A person could steal company merchandise for 10 years without being caught." The established link between Conscientiousness, Agreeableness, and Emotional Stability and integrity test score suggests that personality traits are linked to beliefs about the likelihood that certain CWBs are detected. There appears to be little systematic research on the relationship between personality variables and various perceived consequences of CWBs. However, one personality trait that may affect this perception is self-monitoring (Snyder, 1987). High and low self-monitors differ in the importance they accord to making a good impression. Individuals high in self-monitoring care about what other people think of them, and they may adjust their behavior to enhance others' perception of them. Because they are less concerned with public perceptions of their behavior, low self-monitors may not perceive any personal consequences for committing a CWB. In contrast, high self-monitors may perceive that there are very important negative social consequences to such behavior and thus be less likely to commit CWBs.

Covey, Saladin, and Killen (1989) demonstrated that high self-monitors will not increase their rate of cheating when given incentives, whereas low self-monitors will do so. Beliefs about the potential social embarrassment of getting caught may be enough to dissuade the high self-monitor from engaging in high-risk cheating.

Beliefs About the Desirability of the Consequences of CWBs

Let us consider next how personality traits might be related to our beliefs about the desirability of outcomes arising from CWBs. As an example, we consider how a particular personality trait, achievement striving, might influence our attitude toward the counterproductive behavior of production deviance, that is, not working diligently on the job.

One mechanism through which the trait of achievement striving could affect judgments about the desirability of the consequences of not working hard is cognitive dissonance theory (Festinger, 1957). According to dissonance theory, individuals are motivated to maintain a logical consistency surrounding the items of knowledge, information, or beliefs that relate to them or their surroundings. When important beliefs are not consistent with each other, dissonance theory predicts that an individual will experience a state of psychological discomfort and attempt to ease that discomfort by making the beliefs consonant with each other.

How do these insights apply to our example? Individuals who are low on achievement striving think of themselves, and are thought of by others, as unambitious, unindustrious, and unenterprising (Costa & McCrae, 1992). Accordingly, these individuals hold the important self-belief that they lack ambition. Assume they also hold the belief that production deviance will have negative consequences for them. These two beliefs are not consonant with each other. The unambitious individual knows that his lack of ambition is likely to lead to a lack of effort at work—and thus, possibly, production deviance—but also believes that this lack of effort will be bad for him. Accordingly, holding these joint beliefs should create a state of psychological discomfort. Dissonance theory predicts that this individual should be motivated to reduce the discomfort by changing his behavior or modifying one of these beliefs. One possible dissonance-reducing strategy is to change his behavior at work by exerting more effort. In this case, production deviance will not occur, and dissonance will be eliminated. However, individuals really lacking in ambition may find it difficult to exert the necessary effort to avoid engaging in production deviance. For this reason, this individual may choose to reduce dissonance by changing his belief about the desirability of the consequences of production deviance. For example, he may decide that the consequences of lack of ambition, and specifically production deviance, are not so undesirable after all.

If this manner of thinking rings true for the individual low on achievement striving, then the attitude toward production deviance should be enhanced for this individual. Holding the subjective norm component constant, this enhanced attitude toward production deviance should increase the likelihood that an individual low in achievement striving will engage in production deviance.

Beliefs About the Existence of Norms About CWBs

Beliefs about norms may be specific to the current work situation or more general. According to the theory of reasoned action, a given CWB will be more likely to be performed, all else equal, if a person believes that the behavior is widespread. This in and of itself is straightforward; the question of interest is individual differences in such beliefs. Departures from a "correct" perception of, say, the proportion of employees who steal may occur as a result of multiple mechanisms, including selective observation and selective recall.

It is worth noting that normative beliefs about CWBs, and about counterproductive behaviors outside the workplace, are a commonly used item format in overt integrity tests. The Ryan and Sackett (1987) integrity instrument contains agree-disagree items such as, "Most of my friends have taken a little money or merchandise from their employer," "Just about everyone has shoplifted something," and "Most people cheat on their income tax." A factor analysis of one widely used integrity test, the London House Personnel Selection Inventory, identifies a normative beliefs factor as one of four factors underlying overall test scores (Harris & Sackett, 1987). Given that such items contribute substantially to integrity test scores and given the relationship between integrity test scores and Conscientiousness, Agreeableness, and Emotional Stability, it is likely that there is indeed a link between personality and normative beliefs about CWBs.

Motivation to Comply with Perceived Norms About CWBs

Personality traits can also affect the subjective norm component of the behavioral intention equation by influencing our motivation to comply with workplace norms. In our view, the two traits likely to affect motivation to comply with workplace norms are the "dutifulness" facet of Conscientiousness and the "compliance" facet of Agreeableness. Individuals who are dutiful are characterized by a tendency to adhere strictly to their ethical principles and fulfill their moral obligations (Costa & McCrae, 1992). As such, they are likely to be motivated to comply with the normative behavioral standards that have been set in the workplace. In contrast, individuals who are not dutiful do not take these obligations very seriously and may thereby be less likely to care whether they are obeying workplace norms. In a similar vein, individuals low on compliance are characterized by a tendency to be aggressive and a preference to compete rather than cooperate (Costa & McCrae, 1992). Such individuals may simply not be motivated, by virtue of their low levels of compliance, to observe the wishes of those in charge of the workplace.

If the traits of dutifulness and compliance do affect motivation to comply with workplace norms, then these traits directly affect the subjective norm component of the behavioral intention equation. Specifically, these traits weaken the subjective norm component. Thus, holding attitude toward showing up late constant, low levels of compliance and dutifulness should increase the likelihood an individual will engage in a given counterproductive behavior.

Personality as a Determinant of Moods and Work Attitudes

As Figure 6.1 illustrates, we hypothesize that personality traits indirectly influence the occurrence of counterproductive behaviors by shaping attitudes toward CWBs, as discussed in the previous section, and by shaping workplace emotions, work attitudes, and perceptions of the work environment. Here we refer to attitudes toward work, in contrast with the previous focus on attitudes toward CWBs. In the discussion that follows, we examine the influence of personality traits on workplace moods and job attitudes specifically as representative features of the set of work attitudes, perceptions, and emotions in Figure 6.1.

Personality and Mood

To understand how personality traits can affect the occurrence of CWBs through mood states, it is important to review the manner in which these traits are linked to mood states generally. We discuss this from the standpoint of the Three-Factor Model of personality introduced by Tellegen (1985).

Tellegen (1985) identifies three orthogonal personality dimensions: Extraversion/Positive Emotionality (E/PE), Neuroticism/Negative Emotionality (N/NE), and Disinhibition/Constraint (DvC). For the purposes of this section, the N/NE and E/PE factors are the most relevant factors. N/NE refers to the extent to which an individual perceives the world as threatening, problematic, and distressing, and E/PE concerns an individual's willingness to engage the environment (Clark & Watson, 1999). Abundant evidence links these two factors to the Big Five factors. Essentially, E/PE and N/NE dimensions represent the Extraversion and Neuroticism dimensions from the Big Five (McCrae & Costa, 1985; Watson, Clark, & Harkness, 1994).

An important feature of Tellegen's conception (1985) of E/PE and N/NE—and one that distinguishes it from the Big Five conception of Extraversion and Neuroticism—is that different affective states are at the core of the E/PE and N/NE dimensions. For instance, despite transitory shifts in mood, those high in N/NE generally experience the world as distressing and frequently experience feelings of guilt, sadness, anger, and contempt. In contrast, individuals high on the E/PE dimension generally feel joyful, interested, attentive, excited, and enthusiastic.

Research is now considering the extent to which E/PE and N/NE, and the emotions and moods they engender, relate to workplace behaviors. Although few studies have specifically studied the relationship between PE and CWBs, some have demonstrated that high PE is positively related to positive moods at work and that such positive moods are related to a variety of helping behaviors classified as organizational citizenship behaviors (George, 1991). From a theoretical perspective, positive moods are theorized to be linked to helping behaviors because these moods facilitate perceiving people in a positive light and induce people to be attracted to others (George & Brief, 1992).

Just as there are good reasons for hypothesizing that individuals high on E/PE will engage in helping behaviors, there are good reasons for hypothesizing that individuals low on E/PE may engage in a variety of CWBs. Individuals who are low in E/PE often experience moods such as sluggishness and drowsiness (Watson & Tellegen, 1985). It seems reasonable to hypothesize that those who are often sluggish and drowsy will lack the energy and enthusiasm required to make the effort to show up for work on time and tackle jobs with the energy required to do them well. They may therefore be likely to engage in CWBs such as absenteeism, production deviance, and misallocation of time-related resources. In line with this hypothesis, George (1989) found that positive moods at work were significantly negatively correlated with absence.

There are also good reasons for hypothesizing that individuals high on N/NE will engage in an assortment of CWBs. Individuals high on this dimension are prone to experience feelings of sadness, anger, and contempt. One might reasonably expect these feelings to be linked to both aggressive and passive counterproductive behaviors. To date, however, very little research has explored the linkages among negative affect, mood at work, and the behavioral consequences of these feelings. Some studies have investigated the relationship between negative affect and withdrawal behaviors, but results are somewhat inconsistent. For instance, Cropanzano, James, and Konovsky (1993) found that negative affect was associated with turnover intentions, but George (1989) did not. In light of the strong theoretical reasons for believing that negative affect should be related to many of the counterproductive behaviors listed in Figure 6.1, we encourage researchers to explore those linkages more fully.

Personality and Job Satisfaction

One of the most frequently studied work attitudes is job satisfaction, often defined as an affective reaction to one's job (Fisher, 2000) or a pleasurable or emotional state resulting from an appraisal of one's job (Locke, 1969). Theoretically, there are a number of reasons that personality should be predictive of job satisfaction. Perhaps the most straightforward explanation is that our natural resting state of E/PE or N/NE may affect our affective judgments about the world in which we work. For instance, individuals who are higher on the E/PE dimension may be more inclined to make a positive summary evaluation of the work environment. In contrast, individuals high on N/NE may be more inclined to make a negative summary evaluation of the work environment.

Mood induction experiments provide some support for this proposition, especially with respect to negative affect. For instance, individuals with higher negative affect are more susceptible to a negative mood induction than those low in negative affect (Larsen & Ketelaar, 1991) and more resistant to a positive mood induction (Brief, Butcher, & Roberson, 1995). Thus, individuals high on N/NE may have a predisposition to focus on what is negative in the work environment and ignore what is positive. A recent meta-analysis by Connolly and Viswesvaran (2000) confirms that negative and positive affect are strongly related to job satisfaction. They found that the sample-size weighted corrected mean correlations of job satisfaction with positive and negative affect were, respectively, .49 and −.33. As we will explore more fully, the link between job satisfaction and various CWBs is well established. In particular, job satisfaction is negatively related to turnover (Carsten & Spector, 1987) and absenteeism (Hackett, 1989).

In closing this section, we note that Figure 6.1 posits that the attitudinal and normative components of the theory of reasoned action both mediate and moderate the linkage between our set of work attitudes, perceptions, and emotions and CWBs. We have already sought to explain the manner in which personality traits affect the attitudinal and normative components of the theory of reasoned action and will not duplicate that process in respect of the set of work attitudes, perceptual variables, and emotional variables in Figure 6.1. We simply point out that there are a variety of means through which the attitudinal and normative components might mediate the relationship among work attitudes, workplace perceptions, emotions, and CWBs. For a simple example of mediation, perceptions of workplace injustice may adversely affect the motivation of an individual to comply with the wishes of others, thus decreasing the value of the subjective norm component of the behavioral intention equation and, consequently, increasing the likelihood that an individual will engage in a CWB. For an example of moderation, the presence of a workplace security camera would be expected to increase the perceived negative consequences of engaging in a CWB. In this manner, it should foster negative attitudes toward CWBs, thus reducing the behavioral intention to engage in them. The altered behavioral intention should affect the relationship between perceptions of injustice and the probability that perception will be translated into a CWB.

Personality as a Moderator of the Relationship Between Organizational Features and Satisfaction, Perceived Injustice, and Stress

Our discussion to this point has focused on the role personality traits may play in initiating counterproductive behaviors. We now turn to a set of processes wherein organizational events and features trigger the occurrence of unwanted behaviors. Because counterproductive behaviors occur in this process as a reaction to organizational events, we classify these types of behaviors as reactive CWBs.

We hypothesize that organizational events influence reactive CWBs indirectly by influencing employees' perceptions of job stress, job satisfaction, and justice, which in turn influence the occurrence of the counterproductive behaviors. For the purposes of this chapter, we interpret the phrase *organizational events* very broadly to include job characteristics, work group characteristics, and company policies and practices.

Personality traits are hypothesized to operate as moderators at two points. First, they are hypothesized to moderate the relationship between the organizational events and employee perceptions of stress, justice, and dissatisfaction. Second, they are hypothesized to moderate the relationship between these perceptions and the occurrence of the CWBs. This section foucses on the relationship between events and perceptions and then on the relationship between perceptions and CWBs.

Organizational Events and Perceptual Variables

One of the most widely investigated relationships among the organizational and perceptual variables in Figure 6.1 is the relationship between job characteristics and job satisfaction. Originally, Hackman and Oldham's job characteristics model (1976) hypothesized that five core task dimensions—task identity, task variety, autonomy, task significance, and feedback—would be linked to a number of psychological states, such as job satisfaction, and subsequent organizational events, such as absence and turnover. Research has indeed established that the attributes that Hackman and Oldman named are useful predictors of job satisfaction (Agho, Mueller, & Price, 1993; Ambrose & Kulik, 1999). Researchers have also investigated the relationship between job characteristics and perceived job stress. Workload, fluctuations in the amount of work demanded at different times, and the amount of control or discretion an individual has over the work process have all been linked to perceived job stress (Bromet, Dew, Parkinson, & Schulberg, 1988; Perrewe & Ganster, 1989; Spector, 1986; Tetrick & LaRocco, 1987).

Company policies and procedures have been linked to both job satisfaction and perceptions of injustice. For instance, both organizational constraints (O'Connor, Peters, Rudolph, & Pooyan, 1982) and work schedules have been linked to lower job satisfaction (Ralston, 1989). Organizational justice studies are concerned with investigating the perceived fairness of procedures and outcomes in organizations. As such, it is usually divided into two categories: procedural justice, which is concerned with the perceived fairness of the procedures used to determine organizational outcomes, and distributive justice, which is concerned with perceptions of the fairness of the outcomes themselves. Perceptions of injustice are by definition caused by workplace policies and procedures. Research examining which types of policies and procedures can give rise to perceptions of injustice has burgeoned in recent years and includes procedures relating to selection and staffing, performance appraisal, compensation, and layoffs (Gilliland & Chan, 2001).

Personality as a Moderator of the Organizational Event–Perception Relationship

We hypothesize that one significant moderator of the relationship between the stated organizational events and perceptual variables is neuroticism, or negative affect. Specifically, we hypothesize that individuals high on negative affect will be more likely to perceive organizational events as stressful, unjust, or unsatisfying than will individuals who are low on negative affect. Such individuals are predisposed to respond negatively to perceptual stimuli.

Some research does demonstrate that individuals high on negative affect interpret ambiguous stimuli in a threatening manner and may therefore see crises where others do not (Costa & McCrae, 1990; Watson & Clark, 1984). One particularly intriguing line of research in support of this position comes from mood-induction experiments, which have found that individuals higher in negative affect are more susceptible to a negative mood induction than individuals with low negative affect (Levin & Stokes, 1989) and more resistant to a positive mood induction (Brief et al., 1995). Parkes (1990) found that negative affect moderated the relationship between work demands and well-being, such that individuals high on negative affect perceived their work environment as being more stressful than individuals low on negative affect. Similarly, Moyle (1995) found that negative affect moderated the relationship between control over the work environment, time constraints, and symptoms of stress. These relationships are supportive of the hypothesis that negative affect moderates the relationship between organizational events and perceptions of stress, injustice, and dissatisfaction. However, research into these relationships is only in the initial stages, and further research is encouraged.

The above discussion focuses on neuroticism and negative affect as personality dimensions for which we can offer broad hypotheses. It is also worth noting that in specific circumstances, one could posit relationships between many other personality dimensions and perceptions of satisfaction, stress, and injustice. A company policy restricting socializing among employees at work may influence these perceptions among extraverts but not introverts. A change in job design adding public speaking to work requirements may be stressful for introverts but not extraverts. A change in work rules setting higher performance standards may be stressful to highly conscientious workers concerned about meeting the standard, but not to less conscientious workers not concerned about meeting the standard. As these examples illustrate, such effects are specific to the situation in question. One would not posit, for example, Extraversion as a generalizable moderator of the job-characteristics–satisfaction relationship.

Personality as a Moderator of the Relationship Between Satisfaction, Perceived Injustice, and Stress and CWBs

Here, we explore the possibility that there are individual differences in the relationship between dissatisfaction, perceived injustice, and stress and engaging in various CWBs. There are two separate issues here: whether dissatisfaction, injustice, and stress lead to engaging in CWBs, and if so, which CWB is exhibited.

Satisfaction, Perceived Injustice, Stress, and CWBs

Research has linked satisfaction, perceived injustice, and stress to CWBs. The relationship between job satisfaction and employee turnover has been the focus of much of this research. In particular, many structural models have been created to explain the relationship between job satisfaction and turnover (Bannister & Griffeth, 1986; Dalessio, Silverman, & Schuck, 1986; Hom, Griffeth, & Sellaro, 1984; Mobley, Horner, & Hollingsworth, 1978). Other meta-analyses have found significant relationships between overall job satisfaction and absenteeism (Hackett, 1989).

Perceptions of injustice are also related to theft (Greenberg, 1993; Skarlicki & Folger, 1997), retaliatory behaviors (Skarlicki, Folger, & Tesluk, 1999), organizational withdrawal, and other CWBs. In a recent meta-analysis, Colquitt, Conlon, Wesson, Porter, and Ng (2001) reported that the estimated population correlation between procedural justice and withdrawal, after correcting for sampling error and unreliability, was −.36 for procedural justice and −.41 for distributive justice.

Finally, perceptions of workplace stress often result in CWBs. In the face of a perceived environmental stressor, individuals must somehow cope. CWBs such as withdrawal from work or substance abuse may be the chosen ways of coping. Perceived work stress has been linked to withdrawal (Leiter & Robichaud, 1997), turnover intention (Jamal, 1990), and sabotage (Storms & Spector, 1987).

Personality Traits as Moderators

In the previous section, we asserted that specific personality traits moderate the relationship between the organizational events and perceptions of satisfaction, injustice, and stress. That discussion examined whether people perceive organizational events as stressful, unjust, or unsatisfying. By asserting that personality traits moderate the relationship between the perceptual variables and counterproductive behaviors, as we do here, we are asserting that personality influences how we react to stress, job dissatisfaction, and feelings of injustice, assuming we do experience those feelings.

As indicated in Figure 6.1, we are not positing that personality traits operate independent of cognition in moderating the linkage among stress, job dissatisfaction, feelings of injustice, and CWBs. Instead, we hypothesize that the moderating effect of personality traits on these relationships is mediated by the attitudinal and subjective norm components of the theory of reasoned action. Having already explained how personality traits might affect the attitudinal and normative components of the theory of reasoned action, we focus here on a consideration of which personality traits are likely to moderate the relationship between perceptions of workplace dissatisfaction, stress, and injustice and CWBs.

We hypothesize that the chief moderators of the relationship between the perceptual variables and CWBs are Impulsivity, Extraversion, and Conscientiousness and that individuals higher on Impulsivity, lower on Extraversion, and lower on Conscientiousness will be more likely to react to those perceptions by engaging in CWBs than individuals at the opposite ends of those dimensions.

Many studies have examined the relationship between personality traits and coping with stress. Most of the research in this regard has been conducted in relation to neuroticism, or negative affect, and many studies find that negative affect is associated with avoidance-based coping, distancing oneself, hostile reactions, and detachment rather than problem-focused coping and support seeking (Bolger, 1990; Costa & McCrae, 1989; Folkman & Lazarus, 1985; Smith, Pope, Rhodewalt, & Poulton, 1989). Other studies find that pessimism, a trait often associated with negative affect, is a moderator of the stress-outcome relationship (Carver & Scheier, 1999). Optimists tend to cope by using more problem-focused coping strategies, whereas pessimists tend to cope by disengaging from goals. In general, these studies support the contention that neuroticism represents a vulnerability factor that predisposes an individual to react negatively toward stressors (Spielberger, Gorsuch, & Lushene, 1970). They are also consistent with the view of neuroticism reflected in personality inventories themselves, which often explicitly contain items directed to the issue of stress reactivity (for example, "I sometimes get too upset by minor setbacks"; Watson & Hubbard, 1996).

In terms of implications for CWBs, this research suggests that individuals high in negative affect may respond to stressful work environments (and potentially to job dissatisfaction and injustice as well) by engaging in retaliatory work behaviors and reducing effort on work-related tasks. Support for these hypotheses comes from a study by Skarlicki et al. (1999), who found that the relationship between perceptions of injustice and retaliatory behaviors by employees had the strongest effect on individuals low in Agreeableness and high on negative affect, and Strutton and Lumpkin (1992), who found that pessimists react to work stress by increasing the number of non-work-related behaviors, such as sleeping, eating, or drinking.

The question of which CWBs the high-negative-affect individual will perpetrate in response to feelings of stress or dissatisfaction may depend somewhat on the level of specificity at which one measures the broader construct of neuroticism. According to Costa and McCrae (1992), neuroticism is characterized by the six facets of anxiety, angry hostility, depression, self-consciousness, impulsiveness, and vulnerability. One can readily imagine that individuals high on the depression facet specifically may react to perceptions of stress, injustice, and dissatisfaction very differently from individuals who are high on the angry hostility component. In the former case, we would hypothesize that reactions to the perceptual variables might manifest themselves in more withdrawal types of behaviors, such as absenteeism or production deviance, whereas in the latter case, the reactions might include more aggressive behaviors, such as theft or inappropriate verbal or physical actions.

Individuals who are high on Extraversion are often described as friendly, sociable, warm, and outgoing (Costa & McCrae, 1992). What will the reactions of these people be to organizational dissatisfaction, stress, or perceptions of injustice? Although little research bears on this question, it seems reasonable to take our cue from the stress-response literature. In general, research has demonstrated that extraverted individuals use more problem-based coping strategies in reaction to stressful events than introverts do (McCrae & Costa, 1986; Vollrath, Banholzer, Caviezel, Fischli, & Jungo, 1994). Highly extraverted individuals also tend to seek out more social support in reaction to stressful events than introverts do and to be more restrained in their reaction to stress (McCrae & Costa, 1986). As many commentators have noted, these responses are not altogether unexpected. Because individuals high on Extraversion, or positive emotionality, are prone to feeling joyful, attentive, and enthusiastic, we would expect them to look for positive ways of dealing with perceptions of stress, dissatisfaction, and injustice. Two of these methods are to seek out support from others and look for realistic solutions to problems. Thus, unless the social support received is in the form of suggestions for retaliatory behavior against the company, we would not expect extraverts to engage in many counterproductive behaviors in response to these perceptions.

Individuals who are conscientious are dutiful, orderly, self-disciplined, competent, and achievement striving and are described by words such as thorough, organized, industrious, efficient and enterprising (Costa & McCrae, 1992). Little research bears on the issue of Conscientiousness as a moderator of the relationship between stress, dissatisfaction, and justice and CWBs. However, the stress-response literature once again suggests a reasonable hypothesis. In general, this literature suggests that in response to stressful life events, conscientious individuals engage in more active planning, less maladaptive coping, and more support-seeking behavior than do nonconscientious individuals (Jelinek & Morf, 1995; Vollrath et al., 1994; Vollrath, Torgersen, & Alnaes, 1995; Watson & Hubbard, 1996). These findings suggest that conscientious individuals will seek out more constructive ways to deal with stress, dissatisfaction, and injustice than will nonconscientious individuals, resulting in fewer counterproductive behaviors.

Conclusion

We have sought to trace the multiple processes through which personality may influence the occurrence of counterproductive behaviors. Our central thesis has been that there are many ways in which personality traits may exert their causal influence in relation to these behaviors. In particular, we have argued that personality traits may exert their causal influence by initiating, both directly and indirectly, the occurrence of counterproductive behaviors and by moderating the relationship between organizational events and perceptions of job satisfaction, stress, and injustice and these perceptions and counterproductive behaviors.

As we mentioned at the outset, this chapter is part of an ongoing effort within personality psychology to understand the causal paths between personality and behavior generally. As such, the chapter is necessarily preliminary, provisional, and incomplete. It is our hope that we have sparked the interest of researchers interested in the linkages between personality and counterproductive behaviors and provided direction for future research in this area.

References

Agho, A. O., Mueller, C. W., & Price, J. L. (1993). Determinants of employee job satisfaction: An empirical test of a causal model. *Human Relations, 46,* 1007–1027.

Ajzen, I. (1991). Theory of planned behavior. *Organizational Behavior and Human Decision Processes, 50,* 179–211.

Ajzen, I. (2001). Nature and operation of attitudes. *Annual Review of Psychology, 52,* 27–58.

Allport, G. W. (1937). *Personality: A psychological interpretation.* New York: Holt.

Ambrose, M. L., & Kulik, C. T. (1999). Old friends, new faces: Motivation research in the 1990s. *Journal of Management, 25,* 231–292.

Bannister, B. D., & Griffeth, R. W. (1986). Applying a causal analytic framework to the Mobley, Horner, and Hollingsworth (1978) turnover model: A useful reexamination. *Journal of Management, 12,* 433–443.

Barrick, M. R., & Mount, M. K. (1996). Effects of impression management and self-deception on the predictive validity of personality constructs. *Journal of Applied Psychology, 81,* 261–272.

Baumeister, R. F., Heatherton, T. F., & Tice, D. M. (1994). *Losing control: How and why people fail at self-regulation.* Orlando, FL: Academic Press.

Beck, L., & Ajzen, I. (1991). Predicting dishonest actions using the theory of planned behavior. *Journal of Research in Personality, 25,* 285–301.

Bennett, R. J., & Robinson, S. L. (2000). Development of a measure of workplace deviance. *Journal of Applied Psychology, 85,* 349–360.

Bennett, R. J., & Stamper, C. L. (2001). *Corporate citizenship and deviancy: A study of discretionary work behavior.* Manuscript submitted for publication.

Bolger, N. (1990). Coping as a personality process: A prospective study. *Journal of Personality and Social Psychology, 59,* 525–537.

Brief, A. P., Butcher, A. H., & Roberson, L. (1995). Cookies, disposition and job attitudes: The effects of positive mood inducing events and negative affectivity on job satisfaction in a field experiment. *Organizational Behavior and Human Decision Processes, 62,* 55–62.

Bromet, E. J., Dew, M. A., Parkinson, D. K., & Schulberg, H. C. (1988). Predictive effects of occupational and marital stress on the mental health of a male workforce. *Journal of Organizational Behavior, 9,* 1–13.

Carsten, J. M., & Spector, P. E. (1987). Unemployment, job satisfaction and employee turnover: A meta-analytic test of the Muchinsky model. *Journal of Applied Psychology, 72,* 199–212.

Carver, C. S., & Scheier, M. F. (1999). Stress, coping, and self-regulatory processes. In L. A. Pervin & O. P. John (Eds.), *Handbook of personality: Theory and research* (2nd ed., pp. 553–575). New York: Guilford Press.

Clark, L. A., & Watson, D. (1999). Temperament: A new paradigm for trait psychology. In L. A. Pervin & O. P. John (Eds.), *Handbook of personality: Theory and research* (pp. 399–423). New York: Guilford Press.

Cloninger, C. R., Svrakic, D. M., & Przybeck, T. R. (1993). A psychobiological model of temperament and character. *Archives of General Psychiatry, 50,* 975–990.

Collins, J. M., & Schmidt, F. L. (1993). Personality, integrity, and white collar crime: A construct validity study. *Personnel Psychology, 46,* 295–311.

Colquitt, J. A., Conlon, D. E., Wesson, M. J., Porter, C. O., & Ng, K. Y. (2001). Justice at the millennium: A meta-analytic review of 25 years of organizational justice research. *Journal of Applied Psychology, 86,* 425–445.

Connolly, J. J., & Viswesvaran, C. (2000). The role of affectivity in job satisfaction: A meta-analysis. *Personality and Individual Differences, 29,* 265–281.

Costa, P. T., & McCrae, R. R. (1989). Personality, stress and coping: Some lessons from a decade of research. In K. S. Markides & C. L. Cooper (Eds.), *Aging, stress, social support and health* (pp. 267–283). New York: Wiley.

Costa, P.T.J., & McCrae, R. R. (1990). Personality: Another "hidden factor" in stress research. *Psychological Inquiry, 1,* 22–24.

Costa, P.T.J., & McCrae, R. R. (1992). *The revised NEO Personality Inventory manual.* Odessa, FL: Psychological Assessment Resources.

Covey, M. K., Saladin, S., & Killen, P. J. (1989). Self-monitoring, surveillance, and incentive effects on cheating. *Journal of Social Psychology, 129,* 673–679.

Cropanzano, R., James, K., & Konovsky, M. A. (1993). Dispositional affectivity as a predictor of work attitudes and job performance. *Journal of Organizational Behavior, 14,* 595–606.

Dalessio, A., Silverman, W. H., & Schuck, J. R. (1986). Paths to turnover: A re-analysis and review of existing data on the Mobley, Horner, and Hollingsworth turnover model. *Human Relations, 39,* 245–263.

Depue, R. A., & Collins, P. F. (1999). Neurobiology of the structure of personality: Dopamine, facilitation of incentive motivation, and extraversion. *Behavioral Brain Sciences, 22,* 491–517.

Digman, J. M. (1997). Higher-order factors of the Big Five. *Journal of Personality and Social Psychology, 73,* 1246–1256.

Eagly, A. H., & Chaiken, S. (1993). *The psychology of attitudes.* Fort Worth, TX: Harcourt Brace.

Eysenck, H. J. (1990). Biological dimensions of personality. In L. Pervin (Ed.), *Handbook of personality: Theory and research* (pp. 244–276). New York: Guilford Press.

Eysenck, H. J. (1997). Personality and experimental psychology: The unification of psychology and the possibility of a paradigm. *Journal of Personality and Social Psychology, 73,* 1224–1237.

Eysenck, H. J., & Gudjonsson, G. H. (1988). *The causes and cures of criminality.* New York: Plenum Press.

Festinger, L. (1957). *A theory of cognitive dissonance.* New York: Harper-Collins.

Fishbein, M., & Ajzen, I. (1975). *Belief, attitude, intention, and behavior: An introduction to theory and research.* Reading, MA: Addison-Wesley.

Fisher, C. D. (2000). Mood and emotions while working: Missing pieces of job satisfaction? *Journal of Organizational Behavior, 21,* 185–202.

Folkman, S., & Lazarus, R. S. (1985). If it changes it must be a process: Study of emotion and coping during three stages of a college examination. *Journal of Personality and Social Psychology, 48,* 150–170.

George, J. M. (1989). Mood and absence. *Journal of Applied Psychology, 74,* 317–324.

George, J. M. (1991). State or trait: Effects of positive mood on prosocial behaviors at work. *Journal of Applied Psychology, 76,* 299–307.

George, J. M., & Brief, A. P. (1992). Feeling good—doing good: A conceptual analysis of the mood at work–organizational spontaneity relationship. *Psychological Bulletin, 112,* 310–329.

Gilliland, S. W., & Chan, D. (2001). Justice in organizations: Theory, methods and applications. In N. Anderson, D. S. Ones, H. K. Sinangil, & C. Viswesvaran (Eds.), *Handbook of industrial, work and organizational psychology* (Vol. 2, pp. 143–165). Thousand Oaks, CA: Sage.

Gray, J. A. (1991). Neural systems, emotion and personality. In J. Madden (Ed.), *Neurobiology of learning, emotion and affect* (pp. 273–306). New York: Raven Press.

Greenberg, J. (1993). Stealing in the name of justice. *Organizational Behavior and Human Decision Processes, 54,* 81–103.

Gruys, M. L. (2000). *The dimensionality of deviant employee behavior in the workplace.* Unpublished doctoral dissertation, University of Minnesota.

Hackett, R. D. (1989). Work attitudes and employee absenteeism: A synthesis of the literature. *Journal of Occupational Psychology, 62,* 235–248.

Hackman, J. R., & Oldham, G. R. (1976). Motivation through the design of work: Test of a theory. *Organizational Behavior and Human Performance, 16,* 250–279.

Harris, M. M., & Sackett, P. R. (1987). A factor analysis and item response theory analysis of an employee honesty test. *Journal of Business and Psychology, 2,* 122–135.

Hom, P. W., Griffeth, R. W., & Sellaro, C. L. (1984). The validity of Mobley's (1977) model of employee turnover. *Organizational Behavior and Human Decision Processes, 34,* 141–174.

Hough, L. M. (1992). The "Big Five" personality variables–construct confusion: Description versus prediction. *Human Performance, 5,* 139–155.

Hynan, D. J., & Grush, J. E. (1986). Effects of impulsivity, depression, provocation, and time on aggressive behavior. *Journal of Research in Personality, 20,* 158–171.

Jamal, M. (1990). Relationship of job stress and Type-A behavior to employees' job satisfaction, organizational commitment, psychosomatic health problems, and turnover motivation. *Human Relations, 43,* 727–738.

Jelinek, J., & Morf, M. E. (1995). Accounting for variance shared by measures of personality and stress-related variables: A canonical correlation analysis. *Psychological Reports, 76,* 959–962.

Judge, T. A., Martocchio, J. J., & Thoresen, C. J. (1997). Five-Factor Model of personality and employee absence. *Journal of Applied Psychology, 82,* 745–755.

Kelloway, E. K., Loughlin, C., Barling, J., & Nault, A. (2002). Self-reported counterproductive behaviors and organizational citizenship behaviors: Separate but related construct. *International Journal of Selection and Assessment, 10,* 138–146.

Laczo, R. (2002). *An examination of the dimensionality of non-task performance.* Unpublished doctoral dissertation, University of Minnesota.

Larsen, R. J., & Ketelaar, T. (1991). Personality and susceptibility to positive and negative emotional states. *Journal of Personality and Social Psychology, 61,* 132–140.

Leiter, M. P., & Robichaud, L. (1997). Relationships of occupational hazards with burnout: An assessment of measures and models. *Journal of Occupational Health Psychology, 2,* 35–44.

Levin, I., & Stokes, J. P. (1989). Dispositional approach to job satisfaction: Role of negative affectivity. *Journal of Applied Psychology, 74,* 752–778.

Locke, E. A. (1969). What is job satisfaction? *Organizational Behavior and Human Decision Processes, 4,* 309–336.

McCrae, R. R., & Costa, P. T. (1985). Comparison of EPI and psychoticism scales with measures of the Five-Factor theory of personality. *Personality and Individual Differences, 6,* 587–597.

McCrae, R. R., & Costa, P. T. (1986). Personality, coping, and coping effectiveness in an adult sample. *Journal of Personality, 54,* 385–405.

McCrae, R. R., & Costa, P. T., Jr. (1999). A Five-Factor theory of personality. In L. A. Pervin & O. P. John (Eds.), *Handbook of personality: Theory and research* (2nd ed., pp. 139–153). New York: Guilford Press.

McHenry, J. J., Hough, L. M., Toquam, J. L., Hanson, M. A., & Ashworth, S. (1990). Project A validity results: The relationship between predictor and criterion domains. *Personnel Psychology, 43,* 335–354.

Miles, D. E., Borman, W. E., Spector, P. E., & Fox, S. (2002). Building an integrative model of extra work behaviors: A comparison of counterproductive work behavior and organizational citizenship behavior. *International Journal of Selection and Assessment, 10,* 46–52.

Mobley, W. H., Horner, S. O., & Hollingsworth, A. T. (1978). An evaluation of precursors of hospital employee turnover. *Journal of Applied Psychology, 63,* 408–414.

Moyle, P. (1995). The role of negative affectivity in the stress process: Tests of alternative models. *Journal of Organizational Behavior, 16,* 647–668.

Murray, H. A. (1938). *Explorations in personality.* New York: Oxford University Press.

O'Connor, E. J., Peters, L. H., Rudolph, C. J., & Pooyan, A. (1982). Situational constraints and employee affective reactions: A partial field replication. *Group and Organizational Studies, 7,* 418–428.

Ones, D. S., & Viswesvaran, C. (1998). Integrity testing in organizations. In R. W. Griffin & A. O'Leary-Kelly (Eds.), *Dysfunctional behavior in organizations: Violent and deviant behavior* (pp. 243–276). Greenwich, CT: JAI Press.

Ones, D. S., & Viswesvaran, C. (2001). Integrity tests and other criterion-focused occupational personality scales (COPS) used in personnel selection. *International Journal of Selection and Assessment, 9,* 31–39.

Ones, D. S., Viswesvaran, C., & Schmidt, F. L. (1993). Comprehensive meta-analysis of integrity test validities: Findings and implications for personnel selection and theories of job performance. *Journal of Applied Psychology, 78,* 679–703.

Parkes, K. R. (1990). Coping, negative affectivity, and the work environment: Additive and interactive predictors of mental health. *Journal of Applied Psychology, 75,* 399–409.

Perrewe, P. L., & Ganster, D. C. (1989). The impact of job demands and behavioral control on experienced job stress. *Journal of Organizational Behavior, 10,* 213–229.

Ralston, D. A. (1989). The benefits of flextime: Real or imagined? *Journal of Organizational Behavior, 10,* 369–373.

Robins, R. W., John, O. P., Caspi, A., Moffitt, T. E., & Stouthamer-Loeber, M. (1996). Resilient, overcontrolled, and undercontrolled boys: Three replicable personality types. *Journal of Personality and Social Psychology, 70,* 157–171.

Ryan, A. M., & Sackett, P. R. (1987). Pre-employment honesty testing: Fakeability, reactions of test takers, and company image. *Journal of Business and Psychology, 1,* 248–256.

Sackett, P. R., & DeVore, C. J. (2001). Counterproductive behaviors at work. In N. Anderson, D. Ones, H. Sinangil, & C. Viswesvaran

(Eds.), *International handbook of work psychology* (pp. 145–164). Thousand Oaks, CA: Sage.

Schmidt, F. L., Viswesvaran, V., & Ones, D. S. (1997). Validity of integrity tests for predicting drug and alcohol abuse: A meta-analysis. *National Institute on Drug Abuse Research Monograph, 170,* 69–95.

Skarlicki, D. P., & Folger, R. (1997). Retaliation in the workplace: The roles of distributive, procedural, and interactional justice. *Journal of Applied Psychology, 82,* 434–443.

Skarlicki, D. P., Folger, R., & Tesluk, P. (1999). Personality as a moderator in the relationship between fairness and retaliation. *Academy of Management Journal, 42,* 100–108.

Smith, T. W., Pope, M. K., Rhodewalt, F., & Poulton, J. L. (1989). Optimism, neuroticism, coping, and symptom reports: An alternative interpretation of the Life Orientation Test. *Journal of Personality and Social Psychology, 56,* 640–648.

Snyder, M. (1987). *Public appearances/private realities.* New York: Freeman.

Spector, P. E. (1986). Perceived control by employees: A meta-analysis of studies concerning autonomy and participation at work. *Human Relations, 39,* 1005–1016.

Spielberger, C. D., Gorsuch, R. L., & Lushene, R. E. (1970). *Manual for the state-trait anxiety inventory.* Palo Alto, CA: Consulting Psychologists Press.

Storms, P. L., & Spector, P. E. (1987). Relationships of organizational frustration with reported behavioural reactions: The moderating effect of locus of control. *Journal of Occupational Psychology, 60,* 227–234.

Strutton, D., & Lumpkin, J. (1992). Relationship between optimism and coping strategies in the work environment. *Psychology Reports, 71,* 1179–1186.

Tellegen, A. (1985). Structures of mood and personality and their relevance to assessing anxiety, with an emphasis on self-report. In A. H. Tuma & J. D. Maser (Eds.), *Anxiety and the anxiety disorders* (pp. 681–706). Mahwah, NJ: Erlbaum.

Tetrick, L. E., & LaRocco, J. M. (1987). Understanding, prediction, and control as moderators of the relationships between perceived stress, satisfaction, and psychological well-being. *Journal of Applied Psychology, 72,* 538–543.

Vollrath, M., Banholzer, E., Caviezel, C., Fischli, C., & Jungo, D. (1994). Coping as a mediator or moderator of personality in mental health? In B. De Raad, W.K.B. Hofstee, & G.L.M. VanHeck (Eds.), *Personality psychology in Europe* (Vol. 5, pp. 262–273). Tilburg: Tilburg University Press.

Vollrath, M., Torgersen, S., & Alnaes, R. (1995). Personality as long-term predictor of coping. *Personality and Individual Differences, 18,* 117–125.

Watson, D., & Clark, L. A. (1984). Negative affectivity: The disposition to experience aversive emotional states. *Psychological Bulletin, 96,* 465–490.

Watson, D., & Clark, L. A. (1993). Behavioral disinhibition versus constraint: A dispositional perspective. In D. M. Wegner & J. W. Pennebaker (Eds.), *Handbook of mental control* (pp. 506–527). Upper Saddle River, NJ: Prentice Hall.

Watson, D., Clark, L. A., & Harkness, A. R. (1994). Structures of personality and their relevance to psychopathology. *Journal of Abnormal Psychology, 103,* 18–31.

Watson, D., & Hubbard, B. (1996). Adaptational style and dispositional structure: Coping in the context of the Five-Factor Model. *Journal of Personality, 64,* 737–774.

Watson, D., & Tellegen, A. (1985). Toward a consensual structure of mood. *Psychological Bulletin, 98,* 219–235.

Widiger, T. A., Verheul, R., & van den Brink, W. (1999). Personality and psychopathology. In L. A. Pervin & O. John (Eds.), *Handbook of personality: Theory and research* (2nd ed., pp. 347–366). New York: Guilford Press.

Winter, D. G., & Barenbaum, N. B. (1999). History of modern personality theory and research. In L. A. Pervin & O. P. John (Eds.), *Handbook of personality: Theory and research* (2nd ed., pp. 3–27). New York: Guilford Press.

Zuckerman, M. (1995). Good and bad humors: Biochemical bases of personality and its disorders. *Psychological Science, 6,* 325–332.

Zuckerman, M., Kuhlman, D. M., Thornquist, M., & Kiers, H. (1991). Five (or three) robust questionnaire scale factors of personality without culture. *Personality and Individual Differences, 12,* 929–941.

CHAPTER 7

Toward an Understanding of the Multilevel Role of Personality in Teams

Greg L. Stewart

Work organizations have increasingly adopted team structures; a recent survey suggests that as many as half of the Fortune 500 use teams in some part of their operation (Devine, Clayton, Philips, Dunford, & Melner, 1999). Although small group researchers have studied teams for decades, industrial/organizational (I/O) psychologists have only recently begun to examine how teams alter human resource practices.

One area of emerging research focuses on the role of personality in team contexts. This research originates from two perspectives. One examines how team settings create an environment that influences relationships between individual personality traits and individual performance (Mount, Barrick, & Stewart, 1998). The other examines how individual traits aggregate to form team-level personality, which in turn affects team and organizational performance (for example, Barrick, Stewart, Neubert, & Mount, 1998; Barry & Stewart, 1997). Personality can thus be studied in team settings at both the individual and team levels of analysis. In this chapter, I review research related to both levels, illustrate areas where additional research is needed, and develop a multilevel perspective of personality in teams.

Individual-Level Relationships in Teams

Research that focuses on relationships between individual traits and individual performance in team settings is an extension of existing personality research. Grounded in an interactionist perspective (Snyder & Ickes, 1985), these analyses suggest that teams create a setting requiring increased cooperation, thereby altering the impact of certain traits on individual performance (see Chapter Three, this volume). Team structure thus creates organization and team-level factors that influence individual-level personality relationships.

Research Findings

A meta-analysis by Mount et al. (1998) examined relationships between Five-Factor Model (FFM) traits and overall job performance in a team environment. We found Agreeableness to have the strongest relationship (ρ = .33), followed by Emotional Stability (ρ = .27), Extraversion (ρ = .22), Conscientiousness (ρ = .21), and Openness to Experience (ρ = .16). We also examined relationships with a more specific performance criterion of how well the team members interacted with others. The results were similar: the strongest relationship was for Agreeableness (ρ = .35), followed by Emotional Stability (ρ = .25), Conscientiousness (ρ = .17), Extraversion (ρ = .16), and Openness to Experience (ρ = .07). Neuman and Wright (1999) found Agreeableness and Conscientiousness to predict peer ratings of individual performance beyond job-specific skills and general cognitive ability. Agreeableness thus appears to be a particularly important predictor of individual performance in team settings, which is somewhat counter to findings in settings that do not involve extensive teamwork (Barrick, Mount, & Judge, 2001). The impact of Emotional Stability and Extraversion on individual performance also appears to be magnified in some team settings.

Why are some traits linked more strongly to performance in team settings? Barry and Stewart (1997) found social inputs to mediate the relationship between Extraversion and peer ratings from teammates. Stewart, Fulmer, and Barrick (2002) also explored this question by examining relationships between FFM traits and team member roles. Agreeable team members contributed to team success by filling social roles. Conscientious team members filled critical task roles. Agreeable and conscientious team members were also more accurate in their self-perceptions of social and task roles, respectively. Team members high on Emotional Stability were similarly found to be more accurate in their self-perceptions of both social and task roles. These results suggest that similar to other settings, Conscientiousness is linked to individual performance primarily through behavior that represents task contributions. Unique to team settings, Agreeableness is linked to performance primarily because of the social demands. The relatively stronger relationship for Emotional Stability may also stem from greater awareness of how an individual member contributes to the team.

One effect of organizing workers into teams thus appears to be an increased emphasis on social inputs, and thereby on associated traits such as Agreeableness and sometimes Extraversion. Selecting team members with desirable personality traits may thus be helpful for improving individual performance in team settings. However, as we will see, this improvement in individual performance does not always translate into an improvement in team performance.

Directions for Future Research

Alternative theoretical perspectives provide some interesting ideas for future research. One is the notion that in a team setting, an individual's environment is predominantly composed of other team members. An interesting question is whether the traits of a team member influence the behavior of other team members. Evidence that this occurs is found in theory developed by LePine and Van Dyne (2001). In their model, team member responses to a low performer depend on attributions. A team member low in Conscientiousness evokes an internal attribution of high controllability. Teammates see the low-conscientious person as able but unwilling to perform at a higher level and thus respond with behavior aimed at providing either encouragement and motivation or rejection in the form of criticism. In contrast, a highly conscientious team member who is not performing well evokes either external attributions or peer behavior directed toward training. The conscientiousness of team members thus influences the behavior of their teammates.

LePine and Van Dyne (2001) also suggest that a very agreeable team member may evoke feelings of empathy in teammates, increasing the likelihood that they will direct their efforts toward training behavior.

Other traits have not generally been examined in terms of their influence on teammates. For instance, the inclusion of a highly extraverted team member is likely to alter the entire setting because extraverts compete with others and create a less cooperative environment (Barrick, Stewart, & Piotrowski, 2002). It also seems possible that an emotionally unstable individual can change the environment, creating an environment of mistrust and anxiety. Such an effect of creating mistrust can be particularly harmful because team trust has been identified as an important factor for eliminating dysfunctional conflict in teams (Simons & Peterson, 2000). Studying the impact of a team member's traits through the impact on other team members thus appears to be an area where future research is likely to be enlightening. Indeed, an understanding of the dynamic interplay among team members is likely to provide substantial insight into how personality traits have unique effects in team settings.

Another theoretical perspective that can provide insight concerns the effects of situational strength and autonomy. Some settings provide strong situations where behavior is mostly a function of environment rather than traits. Other settings provide very weak situations where the influence of traits is relatively strong in comparison to the environment (Kenrick & Funder, 1988). The best established moderator in individual settings is perhaps autonomy. Barrick and Mount (1993) found stronger trait-behavior relationships for settings with high autonomy. A common feature of teams is increased autonomy, suggesting that trait-behavior relationships should generally be enhanced in team settings. The autonomy created by teams needs closer examination before drawing this conclusion.

Higher autonomy at the team level does not necessarily translate to higher autonomy at the individual level. Barker (1993) studied manufacturing teams that were collectively given high levels of team autonomy, which they used to create norms and rules that tightly controlled individual behavior. Autonomy at the team level should therefore not be assumed to equal autonomy at the individual level. The introduction of empowered teams into an organization may thus either increase or decrease individual-level relationships between personality and behavior, depending on the extent to which autonomy filters to the individual level of analysis. Group-level features of teams such as autonomy, cohesion, hierarchical control, norms, and conflict may thus moderate relationships between traits and behavior. Future research that looks at how these group-level characteristics moderate individual-level personality relationships should be fruitful.

An alternative perspective also suggests that situational strength may have a unique effect in team settings. Maslach, Santee, and Wade (1987) manipulated the perception of peer opinion in small groups. Participants in their study were assessed to determine how the relationship between their traits and behavior was affected by consistency of peer opinions. In one scenario, a strong situation was created by participants' being led to believe that their peers were in agreement about a topic. In the other scenario, a weak situation was created by participants' being led to believe that their peers held a split opinion. The linkage between the participants' traits and behavior was strongest when the peer opinion was unanimous. This finding led Maslach et al. (1987, p. 102) to conclude that "strong situations may make self-presentational concerns very salient, particularly when the situation that is strong is social and interpersonal in nature (such as social norms or the demands made by other people). Under such circumstances, a person's traits and self-concept may be more directly involved in the attempt to behave in more self-expressive or self-enhancing ways; consequently, the link between personality and behavior should be strong, not weak."

The findings of Maslach et al. (1987) suggest that teams may create the very type of social setting where a strong situation created by peers actually results in closer linkage between traits and behavior. A person's desire to retain and enhance his or her self-concept and individual identity may result in that individual's behaving consistently with his or her traits because of the strong peer pressure to do otherwise. Given that the effect operates in social and interpersonal settings, it is most likely to occur in teams, thereby creating a strong situation whereby traits have a stronger link to behavior. Future research should thus look at how consistency among the traits and behaviors of teammates creates a strong situation and thereby influences relationships between an individual's traits and behavior.

Research at the individual level of analysis thus highlights the potential uniqueness of team settings. Interpersonal traits, particularly Agreeableness, are better predictors of performance than they are in individually oriented settings. Much of this effect likely occurs through the interplay of team member traits, whereby the traits of one's teammates influence relationships between one's traits and behavior. Only limited research has been done in this area, but several theoretical perspectives suggest that future research may be a key to unlocking a better understanding of personality in team settings.

From a practice perspective, research suggests that traits can be useful predictors of individual performance. Similar to non-team settings, Conscientiousness and Emotional Stability are helpful facilitators of task-oriented performance dimensions. In contrast to many individual performance settings, Agreeableness is a critical predictor of social inputs. These social inputs improve not only team viability but also the likelihood of synergistic actions that ultimately improve individual task performance. Nevertheless, personality traits should be used cautiously as performance predictors in team settings, because the traits that lead to improved performance for an individual may have a negative influence on the inputs of others and thereby harm collective performance. Specific examples of such an effect, along with guidelines for practice, will be described below in relation to a cross-level discussion of personality.

Team-Level Personality

Applying the concept of personality to teams risks anthropomorphism, which occurs when things not human are ascribed human characteristics. Although such application can often be dangerously superficial, Kozlowski and Klein (2000) point out that a process of emergence can occur whereby individual phenomena aggregate to form collective phenomena. The key to effective cross-level application is to clearly describe the nature of the construct at the new level and how the phenomena are linked across levels.

Can Teams Have Personality?

Personality at the individual level is defined as a person's social reputation or the structures, dynamics, processes, and propensity inside a person (Hogan, 1991). Extending this definition to the team level of analysis suggests that teams can have personality to the extent that they have regularities in behavior that are perceived consistently by outside observers and internal dynamics and processes that influence their actions. Teams have observable regularities in both behavior and internal processes, suggesting that the construct of personality may indeed be useful at the team level of analysis.

A key difference from individual-level research is that the trait should be descriptive of the group as a whole rather than of individuals who comprise the team. At the individual level, the dimensions on which people vary are captured in lexical approaches, which assume that "those individual differences that are most significant in the daily transactions of persons with each other will eventually become encoded into their language" (Goldberg, 1981, p. 142). The question is the extent to which descriptors at the individual level have application to daily transactions at the team level. Kets de Vries and Miller (1986) did some initial work in this area by describing how organizations develop pathological tendencies that are similar to individual-level pathologies such as depression and compulsion. Although this approach is insightful, a lexical focus on the descriptive concepts encoded into language can potentially provide greater insight into the daily activities of teams.

Lexical classification of normal personality at the individual level has converged on the FFM. Factor analysis of trait descriptions across languages and cultures suggests that trait descriptors can ultimately be grouped into five broad categories (Barrick & Mount, 1991; Digman, 1990). The FFM classifications are Agreeableness (friendliness, generosity, cooperative), Conscientiousness (efficient, organized, thorough), Extraversion (sociable, outgoing, ascendant), Emotional Stability (relaxed, optimistic, unfearful), and Openness to Experience (unconventional, imaginative, adventurous). An important question is thus how well team regularities can be grouped into the FFM classifications.

Although no empirical research compares lexical descriptions of teams with descriptions of individuals, a number of studies and case descriptions adopt language that is highly similar to FFM dimensions. Bettenhausen and Murnighan (1991) created cooperative and competitive bargaining teams. These teams differed substantially on Agreeableness, with some being described as argumentative and stubborn and others as trusting and straightforward. Davis-Sacks (1990) studied a credit analysis team of federal employees. Although individuals were described as conscientious, the team did not meet its major deadline and was described with terms like *careless* and *unreliable,* which are negative markers of Conscientiousness. Barker (1993) examined manufacturing teams that could be classified as low in Emotional Stability. Over time, the teams developed a sense of sadness and fear. Consistent with low Emotional Stability, they expressed feelings of vulnerability and self-consciousness. Cohen and Denison's study of flight teams (1990) contrasted an extraverted team with an introverted one. The extraverted team constantly chatted with flight passengers, enjoyed receiving attention, and competed hard to excel at customer service. The introverted team was less hurried and less enthusiastic. Although the individual team members were somewhat outgoing, the team as a whole adopted a relatively detached approach to social interaction. Saavedra (1990) reported differences that are representative of Openness to Experience. One beer sales team followed standard operating procedures and did not look for alternative methods of accomplishing tasks. Another team constantly altered procedures and approached tasks in unconventional ways.

Based on common descriptors of teams, the FFM appears to be at least somewhat adaptable for describing important traits at the team level of analysis. Yet the extent to which FFM trait descriptors are capable of capturing the full range of team regularities and trends is unknown. This is an area where additional research is needed. Nevertheless, because the FFM is based on studies that have incorporated as many as eighteen thousand descriptors (Allport & Odbert, 1936; Goldberg, 1981), it seems quite possible that it may have adequate breadth to summarize important team traits. Even if additional research discovers that the FFM is not as useful for describing teams as individuals, existing evidence does support the idea that teams develop both behavioral regularities and internal processes. The concept of personality at the team level does appear to be meaningful and may even present an alternative to the ubiquitous input-process-output model that permeates teams research. Indeed, the notion of personality at the team level may provide a mechanism for describing and integrating both internal and external characteristics and interactions.

How Do Traits Form at the Team Level?

A theoretical perspective for answering the question of where team traits come from can be found in individual-level trait theory. Research has found individual traits to be the result of two forces: genetics and environment (Plomin & Daniels, 1987). This analogy suggests the need to identify both nature and nurture effects at the team level.

The nurture analogue at the team level is relatively easy: a team's external influences should influence the team similarly to how an individual's surroundings influence that person. To date, most of the research related to external influences on team trait development has focused on the tasks that a team performs. Because genes are the raw material of individuals, a useful analogue to a gene is the individual. This analogue cannot, however, be directly applied to the team level, because teams can change their members but people cannot to date change their genes. Nevertheless, thinking of members as genes does provide some potential insight into how team personality forms and cross-level relationships between the concept of personality at individual and team levels.

Because individuals at the team level are analogous to genes at the individual level, theoretical models of the process through which genes combine to influence an individual's traits can be helpful for understanding how individual characteristics combine to form a team's traits. Specific gene combinations are referred to as genotypes. The expressed trait is referred to as a phenotype. A genotype thus represents the actual genes that a person possesses, and the phenotype is the trait that others observe. Applying genetic concepts to the team level suggests that the genotype is defined by a summary of the characteristics of the individuals. The phenotype is more difficult to describe and depends on the process through which individual-level characteristics combine to create a team-level trait.

At the individual level, genes combine through three different effects (Rowe, 1994). First, dominance takes place when the presence or absence of a specific gene combination determines the manifestation of the trait. For teams, this effect suggests that the team-level trait (phenotype) is dependent on the inclusion, or exclusion, of at least one member who possesses (or does not possess) the individual characteristic. Second, an additive process occurs when gene combinations representing high trait expressions substitute linearly for gene combinations associated with lower trait expressions. Applied to the team level, this additive effect suggests that a team-level trait (phenotype) is determined by the extent to which team members in aggregate possess that trait. Finally, epistasis occurs when the combination of genes related to a particular trait depends on the genes related to a different trait. At the team level, epistasis may be exhibited when the manner in which individual team member traits combine to create a certain team-level trait depends on some other characteristic of the team. For instance, if a team has one member high on openness and one low on openness, the team-level openness trait may depend on the extent to which the two team members are extraverted.

The application of these gene effects is similar to methods already adopted to capture team-level personality. Taking more of a nurture perspective to personality formation, Barrick et al. (1998) used Steiner's taxonomy of tasks (1972) as a basis for choosing a method to aggregate individual traits into team-level constructs. We suggested that trait formation is an averaging process when teams engage in additive tasks, making the mean of the individual trait scores an appropriate form of aggregation. The desirable personality traits of each member form a collective resource pool. For compensatory tasks, where outcomes are the product of an averaging of diverse inputs, team traits are dependent on the distribution of individual traits. The variance of the individual trait measure is thus a useful form of aggregation. Conjunctive tasks require inputs from each member of a group, suggesting that the inclusion of an individual with a low score on a desirable trait may adversely affect team performance. The lowest individual trait score can thus be used as an indicator of the team-level trait. In contrast, high performance on disjunctive tasks requires only a single team member to excel, suggesting that the highest individual trait score may be representative of the team trait.

The dominance effect from genetics and the maximum and minimum methods from task type both suggest that a team's traits are often dependent on the individual traits of a single team member. The additive process of gene combination and the notion of additive tasks are alternative perspectives that lead to the same approach of using the mean of individual trait scores as the team's trait score. The epistasis effect for gene combination suggests that individual traits may somehow interact to form a team trait, and the notion of compensatory tasks suggests that in some settings, the distribution of individual traits is critical for understanding the team trait.

These forms of aggregation are similar to processes that Kozlowski and Klein (2000) described. They suggest that a lower-level phenomenon (individual personality) emerges into a higher-level phenomenon (team personality) through composition, a linear combination similar to an additive effect, or compilation, which represents nonlinear interactive combination similar to dominance and epistasis. The three methods can also be viewed from Chan's typology (1998) as process models of composition in that the team-level parameter is an analogue of parameters at the lower level. The additive process does, however, operate the same as Chan's additive model, in that it is simply a summation of individual characteristics. Combining the genetic perspective with multilevel theories thus suggests that individual characteristics aggregate to the team level in several ways.

Research Findings

Similar to research at the individual level, Agreeableness has been found to be a critical trait at the team level. Barrick et al. (1998) found mean and minimum levels of Agreeableness to correlate with team performance. We also found four operationalizations (mean, minimum, maximum, variance) to correspond with increased social cohesion and decreased team conflict. Neuman and Wright (1999) similarly found the lowest individual score for Agreeableness to correspond with team-level interpersonal skills, as well as team-level measures of accuracy and work completion. As predicted by a dominance effect, the inclusion of a single individual either very high or very low on Agreeableness seems to have a large impact on collective cooperativeness, and thereby the performance of the team. In accordance with the additive notion of combining individuals and the additive nature of tasks, average levels of Agreeableness also appear to correspond with higher team performance. Teams composed of agreeable members thus seem to have higher performance because they cooperate more and work together better.

Barrick et al. (1998) also found Extraversion, regardless of the method of operationalization (mean, variance, minimum, maximum), to correspond with higher levels of social cohesion. All methods of operationalization for Extraversion, except variance, also corresponded with reduced team conflict. However, only the Extraversion minimum score corresponded with team performance, with the inclusion of one very introverted person harming performance. Barry and Stewart (1997), using the proportion of individuals high on Extraversion as a variance indicator, found teams consisting of approximately half extraverts to have the highest performance. Extraversion does appear to translate into differences in cohesion and conflict, which is supportive of the notion that this individual-level trait translates into a team-level trait. Moreover, Extraversion appears to aggregate in both a dominant and an additive manner.

Agreeableness and Extraversion thus represent two interpersonal traits that have important team-level effects. This is not surprising given that interpersonal traits can be exhibited only in the presence of other people. Kenrick and Funder (1988) concluded that the presence of even a single individual with very desirable or very undesirable interpersonal traits can influence relationships within an entire group. In accordance with this observation, interpersonal traits appear to combine at least somewhat in a dominant fashion, whereby one individual strongly influences the team trait. The overall trait for the team is thus quite dependent on the interpersonal traits of individual team members, particularly if those individual traits are extreme.

Given that conscientiousness generally relates to performance across tasks and roles, it seems reasonable to predict that team-level conscientiousness will form in an additive fashion. This is supported by Barrick et al. (1998), who found the mean level of Conscientiousness to correlate with team performance. However, the evidence also supports a dominance effect for Conscientiousness. Neuman and Wright (1999) found the inclusion of a single team member low on Conscientiousness to harm measures of team accuracy and work completion. Conscientiousness is thus likely to aggregate by both additive and dominance effects, with the team's tasks potentially playing an important role. Tasks that are not highly interdependent and allow team members to compensate for the shortcomings of individuals should result in more of an additive effect.

Emotional Stability at the team level also seems to operate with additive and dominant effects. Barrick et al. (1998) found that the mean and minimum levels of Emotional Stability relate to a variety of team process measures, including cohesion, conflict, flexibility, communication, and workload sharing. The inclusion of even a single member low on Emotional Stability thus seems to have a harmful impact on the internal dynamics of a team.

Future Research

The primary method of assessing team personality is thus to measure and aggregate individual-level measures. In essence, each of the current approaches suggests that team-level personality can be assessed through measuring and statistically combining individual-level traits. This approach can be justified theoretically. However, little effort has been directed toward assessing whether team traits can be reliably assessed with measures targeted specifically at team-level perceptions. Can available individual-level trait measures be adapted to measure traits at the team level of analysis reliably? If team traits change with tasks, are team-level traits stable enough to label as personality? One method of assessing this is to ask team members and observers to provide measures of regularities and patterns for the collective group. In essence, this is what Chan (1998) refers to as a referent-shift consensus composition model, where individuals provide data but the target of their response is the team as a whole rather than an individual. Future research should compare this cross-level approach to measurement with currently adopted measures that aggregate individual-level traits. Such comparisons will likely shed light on relationships between individual and team-level traits.

An aspect of the gene combination analogy that has not been explored is epistasis. Do traits interact with each other? One possibility is that individual traits interact to influence team-level traits. This seems most possible when there are status differences in the team: people with higher status have stronger influences on groups (Berger, Webster, Ridgeway, & Rosenholtz, 1986). Extraverted people also tend to be aggressive and seek dominance over others (Stewart & Barrick, in press). The other individual traits of the extravert may thus have a greater influence on the team trait. For instance, an individual who is high on both Extraversion and Openness to Experience may influence the team toward developing openness. In contrast, an individual-level combination of Openness and low Extraversion may not be influential. Research related to such interactions, particularly with Extraversion in team settings, is needed and should provide additional insight into the process of team trait formation.

With the exception of perspectives that assess a team's tasks, little work has been done to understand the influence of environmental factors on team personality development. Perhaps the best-developed insights into the effect of environment on team personality are in the area of team norms, defined as "informal rules that groups adopt to regulate and regularize group members' behavior" (Feldman, 1984, p. 47). This definition is very similar to the concept of personality. In fact, a lexical approach to team personality in many ways provides a framework for labeling various norms. Feldman (1984) suggests that norms develop in four ways: members carry over behavior from past situations, team members and leaders make explicit statements, critical events occur, and primacy effects make early patterns difficult to alter. The first two are likely captured by the notion of individual traits. Previous experiences influence individual traits, and statements are manifestations of those traits. However, critical events and primacy suggest that events that occur in the team's life span can have an impact on the traits that the team develops. Similar to personality at the individual level (Wrightsman, 1994), these norms may develop fairly early and become somewhat resistant to change.

One interesting external influence that may create norms, and thereby team-level personality, is the amount of autonomy given to a team as a whole. Consistent with research at the individual level (Barrick & Mount, 1993), it seems possible that individual traits will have more influence on a team trait when the team as a collective group has high autonomy. Teams with low autonomy are not likely to develop consistent traits, but teams with high autonomy should develop unique norms, and thus traits, that represent combinations of individual traits. For instance, the dominance effect for the interpersonal trait of Agreeableness is likely stronger when team autonomy allows norms consistent with a very disagreeable member's having great latitude in choosing his or her behavior, thereby influencing others.

Another potentially important external influence is leadership. Linking back to the work of psychodynamic scholars such as Freud, personality development is shown to be strongly influenced by authority figures. The relationship that a team experiences with its leader early in its development phases may influence its team-level traits. For instance, a leader who makes statements that encourage exploration and creativity may develop norms that increase team Openness to Experience (Feldman, 1984). A leader who intermittently gives and takes away team autonomy may create norms that result in an emotionally unstable team (Stewart & Manz, 1995). Such influences may be particularly strong soon after the team is formed, before strong tendencies and patterns of interaction have developed.

Stage theories of individual trait development may also inform team-level research. Erikson (1963) proposed that personality development occurs at stages across the life span. Other researchers (Levinson, 1986) have suggested that a particularly important stage occurs at about midlife, when environmental influences can have a relatively stronger influence. This perspective is supported for teams by Gersick's model of punctuated equilibrium (1989). Her findings suggest that a team's characteristics are developed early in its life span, but then undergo radical change near the temporal midpoint of its existence. Team designers and leaders can thus time their interventions to occur near a team's temporal midpoint in order to maximize the likelihood of altering norms that influence patterns of behavior and interaction.

Research related to the team level of analysis is thus rather limited. The research that exists supports the notion that individual traits can combine to influence a team trait in an additive or a dominant effect. Although researchers have not yet looked at how different individual traits may interact to form a team-level trait, the epistasis effect suggests that future work in this area should be quite informative. A great deal of additional work also needs to be done to assess the impact of environment. As research evolves, we will be better able to develop theory that explains how individual traits combine with team environmental factors to influence team trait development.

From a practice perspective, research suggests that team-level traits do have an impact on team performance. One method of influencing these traits is careful selection of team members. The inclusion of a single team member who is very low on Agreeableness, Conscientiousness, or Emotional Stability can potentially harm the performance of the entire team. The desirability of Extraversion for any individual also appears to depend on the levels of Extraversion for other team members. These effects suggest that the importance of selecting employees with desirable traits may be even more critical in team settings than in settings that rely primarily on individual performance. This is because of the potential dominance effect of an individual trait on the team trait, whereby the trait of one individual has a large impact on performance at the team level. The utility of personality traits as performance predictors, particularly Agreeableness, is thus likely to be severely underestimated by studies that measure individual but not team performance.

A Multilevel Perspective

Kozlowski and Klein (2000) provide a useful framework for summarizing the multilevel effects of personality in teams. They suggest that cross-level models, which describe relationships between different constructs at different levels of analysis, tend to take three forms:

- A direct effects model, which occurs when a construct at one level (individual personality) is hypothesized to directly influence a construct at another level (team-level personality)

- A moderator model, which exists when a construct at one level (team cohesion) is hypothesized to influence the relationship between two constructs at a different level (individual traits and individual performance)
- A frog pond model, which occurs when the effect of a construct at one level (an individual trait) is dependent on the relative standing of that construct in a higher-order construct (team personality as expressed by an overall mean)

Several of the multilevel effects of personality in team settings can be summarized by looking at them in terms of this framework.

Direct Effects

The influence of individual-level personality on team-level personality represents a cross-level direct effect. This effect is best seen as a mixed determinant model because the individual-level traits are expected to interact with team- and organization-level constructs to influence team-level personality. Nevertheless, the traits of individuals are expected to have a direct effect on the team-level trait.

Conscientiousness and Emotional Stability should operate in teams much as they do at the individual level: more is better. Of increased interest across levels are the interpersonal traits. Because individual Agreeableness and Extraversion appear to influence the team traits in a dominant fashion, one individual can have a substantial influence on team traits. These traits thus take on increased importance in team settings, primarily because of the direct influence on team-level constructs.

The direct effects model thus highlights the influence of individual traits on team traits and thereby on team performance. Most important, this model highlights the importance of caution when determining the process by which individual-level traits aggregate to influence the individual trait. Because some traits aggregate in a dominant fashion, they will take on increased importance in team settings. For instance, a full understanding of the utility of Agreeableness as a selection predictor requires cross-level research that examines its impact not only on individual performance but also on team-level performance. Research related to Extraversion also clearly illustrates the need for careful analysis before assuming that an increase in performance at the individual level translates into an increase in performance at the team level. An important cross-level conclusion is thus that organizations need to think of team-level effects when they make individual selection decisions. In many cases, the impact on collective performance is likely to go well beyond what might be determined through measuring only individual performance.

Moderator Effects

The influence of the team setting on relationships between individual traits and individual performance represents a moderator model. The team setting, which can be viewed as either a team or an organization-level construct, creates a setting that magnifies the importance of cooperative social relationships. Agreeable people have a natural tendency to cooperate with others, making agreeableness an important predictor of individual performance in team settings. The higher-level construct of team-based organizational structure thus moderates the relationship between individual-level agreeableness and individual performance.

Another interesting moderator effect appears to occur when team structure moderates the relationship between one individual's traits and another person's individual behavior. Based on the work of LePine and Van Dyne (2001), team members adjust their behavior dependent on how they perceive the traits of their teammates. Because this effect is predicted only in an interdependent team setting, the higher-order construct of team structure again moderates the relationship between two individual-level variables. Various theoretical perspectives also suggest that team-level constructs such as cohesion and conflict may influence relationships between traits and individual behavior.

Perhaps the key lesson learned from the moderator perspective is that the higher-level construct of teams has the potential to alter individual-level relationships. Most of our research in the field of industrial/organizational psychology has focused on performance in individually oriented settings, suggesting that we need to revisit many of our currently held assumptions. Although the focus of this chapter has been on personality, these assumptions are associated with several core ideas of human resource management such as job analysis, selection, and compensation. How can job analysis inform and guide organizations that assign relatively large pieces of work to groups rather than individuals? Is cognitive ability as valuable a performance predictor in settings where a high-ability member interacts and potentially compensates for lower-ability teammates? Does compensation that provides individual incentives harm contributions toward a collective goal? In each of these cases, it seems possible that the higher-order construct of team structure calls into question some of the basic findings of research conducted in individual performance settings, suggesting the need for additional cross-level research.

Frog Pond Effects

The least researched models are frog pond models. In these models, the effect of an individual's traits is dependent on the configuration of the individual traits of others. For instance, the conscientiousness of an individual team member may affect team-level conscientiousness only if other team members are relatively very low on conscientiousness. The one study that looked at traits in this fashion was by Barry and Stewart (1997). We found that the proportion of extraverts to be linked to team performance. This frog pond perspective assessed how the relationships among an individual-level construct related to team-level outcomes such as cohesion and performance.

Additional frog pond models have the potential to provide great insight. They can even be combined with direct effects and moderator models. For instance, it seems possible that from a direct-effects perspective, the influence of any individual trait on the team trait may be influenced by how different a particular individual is from the other members of the team. From a moderator-effects perspective, the relationship between an individual's traits and the behavior of others may be influenced by how different that person is from others in the group. Indeed, frog pond models in the realm of personality appear to be an important area of research that has not yet been fully pursued.

Conclusion

An understanding of personality in teams requires a true multilevel perspective that incorporates various cross-level effects. At one level, the team setting magnifies the importance of certain interpersonal traits, particularly Agreeableness. These traits lead to both higher individual-level performance and a direct influence on team-level characteristics. One way of viewing these characteristics is to think of teams in trait terms. Adapting the individual-level framework of the FFM to the team level of analysis suggests that our understanding can advance as we see teams in terms of their Agreeableness, Conscientiousness, Emotional Stability, Extraversion, and Openness to Experience. These team-level effects can then be assessed in terms of their influence on and interaction with other team-level factors.

Personality does appear to be an important construct in teams, but it can be understood only from a multilevel perspective. This perspective is required because teams represent a group-level phenomenon that interacts with the individual-level perspective prevalent in most personality research. Future research and practice will advance as researchers and practitioners take into account these cross-level relationships and seek understanding across both individual and group levels of analysis. Indeed, this multilevel perspective appears to be one of the most critical areas for future research in the field of personality.

References

Allport, G. W., & Odbert, H. S. (1936). Trait-names: A psycho-lexical study. *Psychological Monographs, 47* (Whole No. 211).

Barker, J. R. (1993). Tightening the iron cage: Concertive control in self-managing teams. *Administrative Science Quarterly, 38,* 408–437.

Barrick, M. R., & Mount, M. K. (1991). The Big Five personality dimensions and job performance: A meta-analysis. *Personnel Psychology, 44,* 1–26.

Barrick, M. R., & Mount, M. K. (1993). Autonomy as a moderator of the relationships between the Big Five personality dimensions and job performance. *Journal of Applied Psychology, 78,* 111–118.

Barrick, M. R., Mount, M. K., & Judge, T. A. (2001). The FFM personality dimensions and performance: A meta analysis of meta-analyses. *International Journal of Selection and Assessment, 9,* 9–30.

Barrick, M. R., Stewart, G. L., Neubert, M. J., & Mount, M. K. (1998). Relating member ability and personality to work-team processes and team effectiveness. *Journal of Applied Psychology, 83,* 377–391.

Barrick, M. R., Stewart, G. L., & Piotrowski, M. (2002). Personality and sales performance: Test of the mediating effects of motivation. *Journal of Applied Psychology, 87,* 43–51.

Barry, B., & Stewart, G. L. (1997). Composition, process, and performance in self-managed groups: The role of personality. *Journal of Applied Psychology, 82,* 62–78.

Berger, J., Webster, M., Jr., Ridgeway, C., & Rosenholtz, S. J. (1986). Status cues, expectations, and behavior. In E. J. Lawler (Ed.), *Advances in group processes* (Vol. 3, pp. 1–22). Greenwich, CT: JAI Press.

Bettenhausen, K. L., & Murnighan, J. K. (1991). The development of an intragroup norm and the effects of interpersonal and structural challenges. *Administrative Science Quarterly, 36,* 20–35.

Chan, D. (1998). Functional relations among constructs in the same content domain at different levels of analysis: A typology of composition models. *Journal of Applied Psychology, 83,* 234–246.

Cohen, S. G., & Denison, D. R. (1990). Flight attendant teams. In J. R. Hackman (Ed.), *Groups that work (and those that don't): Creating conditions for effective teamwork* (pp. 382–397). San Francisco: Jossey-Bass.

Davis-Sacks, M. L. (1990). Credit analysis team. In J. R. Hackman (Ed.), *Groups that work (and those that don't): Creating conditions for effective teamwork* (pp. 126–145). San Francisco: Jossey-Bass.

Devine, D. J., Clayton, L. D., Philips, J. L., Dunford, B. B., & Melner, S. B. (1999). Teams in organizations: Prevalence, characteristics, and effectiveness. *Small Group Research, 30,* 678–711.

Digman, J. M. (1990). Personality structure: Emergence of the Five-Factor Model. *Annual Review of Psychology, 41,* 417–440.

Erikson, E. H. (1963). *Childhood and society* (2nd ed.). New York: Norton.

Feldman, D. C. (1984). The development and enforcement of group norms. *Academy of Management Review, 9,* 47–53.

Gersick, C.J.G. (1989). Making time: Predictable transitions in task groups. *Academy of Management Journal, 32,* 274–309.

Goldberg, L. R. (1981). Language and individual differences: The search for universals in personality lexicons. In L. Wheeler (Ed.), *Review of personality and social psychology* (Vol. 2, pp. 141–166). Thousand Oaks, CA: Sage.

Hogan, R. T. (1991). Personality and personality measurement. In M. D. Dunnette & L. M. Hough (Eds.), *Handbook of industrial and organizational psychology* (Vol. 1, pp. 873–919). Palo Alto, CA: Consulting Psychologists.

Kenrick, D. T., & Funder, D. C. (1988). Profiting from controversy: Lessons from the person-situation controversy. *American Psychologist, 43,* 23–34.

Kets de Vries, M.F.R., & Miller, D. (1986). Personality, culture, and organization. *Academy of Management Review, 11,* 266–279.

Kozlowski, S.W.J., & Klein, K. J. (2000). A multilevel approach to theory and research in organizations: Contextual, temporal, and emergent processes. In K. J. Klein & S.W.J. Kozlowski (Eds.), *Multilevel theory, research, and methods in organizations: Foundations, extensions, and new directions* (pp. 3–90). San Francisco: Jossey-Bass.

LePine, J. A., & Van Dyne, L. (2001). Peer responses to low performers: An attributional model of helping in the context of groups. *Academy of Management Review, 26,* 67–84.

Levinson, D. J. (1986). A conception of adult development. *American Psychologist, 41,* 3–13.

Maslach, C., Santee, R. T., & Wade, C. (1987). Individuation, gender role, and dissent: Personality mediators of situational forces. *Journal of Personality and Social Psychology, 53,* 1088–1093.

Mount, M. K., Barrick, M. R., & Stewart, G. L. (1998). Five-Factor Model of personality and performance in jobs involving interpersonal interactions. *Human Performance, 11,* 145–165.

Neuman, G. A., & Wright, J. (1999). Team effectiveness: Beyond skills and cognitive ability. *Journal of Applied Psychology, 84,* 376–389.

Plomin, R., & Daniels, D. (1987). Why are children in the same family so different from one another? *Behavioral and Brain Sciences, 10,* 1–60.

Rowe, D. C. (1994). *The limits of family influence: Genes, experience and behavior.* New York: Guilford Press.

Saavedra, R. (1990). Beer sales and delivery teams. In J. R. Hackman (Ed.), *Groups that work (and those that don't): Creating conditions for effective teamwork* (pp. 361–381). San Francisco: Jossey-Bass.

Simons, T. L., & Peterson, R. S. (2000). Task conflict and relationship conflict in top management teams: The pivotal role of intragroup trust. *Journal of Applied Psychology, 85,* 102–111.

Snyder, M., & Ickes, W. (1985). Personality and social behavior. In G. Lindsey & E. Ironstone (Eds.), *Handbook of social psychology* (3rd ed., Vol. 2, pp. 993–947). Reading, MA: Addison-Wesley.

Steiner, I. D. (1972). *Group process and productivity.* Orlando, FL: Academic Press.

Stewart, G. L., & Barrick, M. R. (in press). Lessons learned from the person-situation debate: A review and research agenda. In B. Smith & B. Schneider (Eds.), *Personality and organizations.* Mahwah, NJ: Erlbaum.

Stewart, G. L., Fulmer, I. S., & Barrick, M. R. (2002). *Linking team personality to roles and self-perceptions in teams.* Unpublished manuscript.

Stewart, G. L., & Manz, C. C. (1995). Leadership for self-managing work teams: A typology and integrative model. *Human Relations, 48,* 747–770.

Wrightsman, L. S. (1994). *Adult personality and development: Theories and concepts.* Thousand Oaks, CA: Sage.

CHAPTER 8

Self-Monitoring Personality and Work Relationships
Individual Differences in Social Networks

David V. Day
Martin Kilduff

Relationships form the core of any organization. Creating and maintaining effective work relationships allows for task coordination, information flow, and other work processes necessary for accomplishing the goals and objectives of an organization. Management, in particular, is a relationship-based discipline. According to Gabarro (1987), "The importance of interpersonal relationships as an aspect of management is documented in study after study of managerial behavior, regardless of national culture or type of management job" (p. 172).

Relationships are also important for individual success. An emerging literature demonstrates the role that social capital plays in individual job performance, leadership, and career success. Social capital is created when relations between people are formed that help facilitate instrumental organizational action (Coleman, 1990). Social capital is a key to individual success because it provides access to critical information and other social resources (Seibert, Kraimer, & Liden, 2001). There are also individual differences in the quantity and quality of relationships that form the basis of social capital.

Our purpose is to examine the theory and research pertaining to individual differences in personality that shape the development and maintenance of the kinds of network structures that allow more (or less) access to vital social resources. We also consider the configuration of these relationships, the influence of individual personality on network configurations in organizations, and the structural constraints imposed on certain network configurations.

Historically, relationships tend to be viewed as mainly dyadic in nature (Graen & Scandura, 1987). A broader perspective, however, considers that every relationship constitutes a system. Specifically, relationships are open systems that are nested in a larger social environment (Reis, Collins, & Berscheid, 2000). These systems are simultaneously evolving and influencing each other over time. For example, two people in a romantic relationship are connected to many other people in the larger social environment, but only some of these other people are likely to have accurate perceptions of, or the ability to exercise influence on, the state and fate of the couple's relationship (Agnew, Loving, & Drigotas, 2001). The nature of the dyadic relationship may change significantly as the dyad's embeddedness in the larger social network changes. For example, the extent to which a married couple maintains traditional versus egalitarian spousal roles may depend not just on the views held by the couple but also on the extent to which the pre-marriage network ties of the husband and wife (to friends and female relatives, respectively) are maintained (Bott, 1957).

Relationships vary in terms of strength, reciprocity, and type. Relationship quality is an important but overlooked aspect of the social resources available in a network (Krackhardt, 1999). In particular, some working relationships stabilize at a relatively superficial level of exchange, others at rather deep levels of mutuality (Gabarro, 1987). Personality influences both the content and the structure of social networks in work settings, one relationship at a time. Our focus is on one particular set of dispositional motives shown to be relevant for understanding how individuals shape their social worlds: those associated with the construct of self-monitoring personality (Snyder, 1974, 1987).

Why do people form and maintain relationships? The answers to this purportedly obvious question are not so simple. There are multiple possible motives for every relationship that is formed, sustained, or broken. According to social exchange theory (Blau, 1974; Thibaut & Kelley, 1959), relationships are built as a way of obtaining something of value from another person—a means to an end—in exchange for something offered to the other party. Research on the affiliation motive has shown that people prefer to affiliate with similar others, especially when they face uncertainty (Schachter, 1959). The social comparison motive proposes that affiliation choices are particularly important in situations where there is no objective standard against which to compare abilities, opinions, or behaviors (Festinger, 1954). Relationships are also used for purposes of status enhancement and self-validation (Gangestad & Snyder, 2000)—essentially, of presenting the self in the best possible light according to personal values.

Answering the deeper question of what people want from relationships is a way of understanding why they are formed. It is a way of understanding motive. In considering the motives of individuals, it is apparent that individual differences at least partially guide what is desired from relationships. People do not all want the same thing from their relationships, and their desires are shaped by various individual motives.

Self-Monitoring Personality

In addition to guiding individual thinking and behavior, motives are shaped by dispositional factors such as personality. One particular personality construct with demonstrated relevance (validity) in organizational contexts is self-monitoring (Day, Schleicher, Unckless, & Hiller, 2002; Snyder & Copeland, 1989). An underlying assumption of the self-monitoring construct is that people differ in the extent that they monitor (observe, regulate, and control) the public appearance of self they display in social settings and in creating and managing their interpersonal relationships (Snyder, 1974, 1987). Interesting and somewhat unique aspects of self-monitoring as a personality construct are the emphases on the conceptualization and representation of self in social situations and two separate, distinct, and independent self-monitoring orientations (Gangestad & Snyder, 1985). High self-monitors tend to be pragmatic in presenting themselves in interpersonal situations in that they regulate their behavior to promote situationally appropriate interaction outcomes.

Low self-monitors are more likely to adopt a principled interpersonal orientation in which there is a high correspondence between their attitudes, beliefs, and values (that is, their genuine selves) and their social behavior.

Previous research has shown that self-monitoring has good discriminant validity with other personality constructs. As Snyder (1987) noted, "The list of other measures with which self-monitoring is *not* meaningfully correlated is a long one" (p. 27). This list includes constructs such as locus of control, field dependence, self-esteem, social desirability, neuroticism, trait anxiety, and intelligence. A recent meta-analysis of the relationships between self-monitoring and the Big Five personality factors also indicates generally good discriminant validity (Schleicher & Day, 2002). The sample weighted correlations between self-monitoring and Agreeableness ($r = .04$), Conscientiousness ($r = -.02$), and Neuroticism ($r = -.01$) all indicate construct independence (there were insufficient study numbers to examine Openness to Experience). As would be expected, however, there was a moderately large overall correlation with Extraversion ($r = .37$). This is expected because Extraversion is one of the subscales of the Self-Monitoring Scale (the others being acting and other-directedness). Nonetheless, self-monitoring has been shown to be a conceptually distinct and meaningful construct apart from its subscales (Gangestad & Snyder, 2000).

Another interesting aspect of the historical development of the self-monitoring construct is that the scientific study of self-monitoring personality and social behavior has progressed through a sequence of increasingly more complex research strategies (Snyder & Ickes, 1985). The early-adopted dispositional strategy assumed that consistencies in social behavior could be understood in terms of relatively enduring dispositional characteristics associated with self-monitoring. In general, this approach worked to identify categories of people who demonstrated those dispositional and behavioral characteristics of interest and provided a psychometrically sound measure of those categories (the Self-Monitoring Scale). The interactional strategy that followed assumed that the noted variation in social behavior was due to the interaction of dispositional and situational factors. Empirically, this general strategy sought to identify moderator variables that illuminated those conditions in which self-monitoring personality predicted (or did not predict) behavior. The most complex situational strategy seeks to understand the reciprocal influences of situations and personality on social behavior, with a focus on understanding how high and low self-monitors choose and influence their situations. These choices regarding settings and situations are thought to reflect important aspects of personal identity, such as representations of self, beliefs, attitudes, values, and traits (Snyder, 1987). The current state of self-monitoring research, which differentiates it from the focus of most other personality research, especially in industrial/organizational psychology, is focused on this third strategy. It assumes that the situations in which people find themselves are due in large part to their individual choices. In particular, we address the theory and research that pertains to the respective choices that high and low self-monitors make regarding their relationships with others in organizations.

A recent review and synthesis of the literature on self-monitoring proposes that the relationships constructed by high self-monitors may derive from a status enhancement motive, whereas relationships constructed by low self-monitors may derive from a self-validation motive (Gangestad & Snyder, 2000). Relationships to high self-monitors are, in part, a means for impression and image management. Friends and associates may be important to the extent that they contribute to potential image enhancement associated with belonging to a prestigious social network. High self-monitors may be susceptible to the lure of basking in the reflected glory of others who are seen as important, accomplished, or otherwise celebrated (Cialdini, 1989). Affiliating with others of high status is an effective means of acquiring reputational capital and power for all actors in organizations (Kilduff & Krackhardt, 1994) and may be particularly appealing to high self-monitors.

The relationships of high self-monitors also tend to be activity based. That is, high self-monitors tend to choose friends and associates based on others' relative fit to the activity at hand (Snyder, 1987). In the realm of leisure activities, high self-monitors would tend to choose tennis or golf partners based on their ability level. In work relationships, help or advice would tend to be sought from those individuals considered to have superior expertise in the domain of interest.

Those who are relatively low on self-monitoring fulfill different motives through their relationships. Low self-monitors may eschew overt impression management, preferring to display attitudes and behaviors that communicate what they consider to be their genuine selves. Low self-monitors cultivate relationships based on perceived similarities in values, beliefs, and interests. Thus, it is not surprising that low self-monitors have more homogeneous social networks than high self-monitors (Gangestad & Snyder, 2000).

Low self-monitors tend to adopt a partner-based approach to relationships. They strive to maximize the fit between themselves and their friends and associates; relationships are seen as partnerships built around the mutual appreciation of shared values, ideals, or activities (Snyder, 1987). Low self-monitors, relative to high self-monitors, demonstrate greater levels of commitment to their personal (Snyder & Simpson, 1984) and work relationships (Day et al., 2002), express less intent to leave their current jobs (Jenkins, 1993), and tend to remain with current employers longer (Kilduff & Day, 1994). These noted differences between high and low self-monitors have distinct implications for the respective types of social networks that are created and maintained, as well as for the respective kinds of social capital that are constructed.

A recent review and reappraisal of the research literature on self-monitoring noted a wide range of external criteria that directly tap a central dimension measured by Snyder's Self-Monitoring Scale (Gangestad & Snyder, 2000; Snyder & Gangestad, 1986). The categories of effects most strongly associated with the central dimension of self-monitoring were (1) variation in the predisposition to engage in impression management (behavioral variability, sensitivity to expectations, interpersonal orientation, and being impressed with physical attractiveness); (2) skills needed for effective image cultivation and projection (expressive control and nonverbal decoding skills); and (3) the relationship between private beliefs and public actions (attitude-behavior relations and attitude accessibility).

At its core, however, Gangestad and Snyder (2000) speculate that self-monitoring personality "relates to status-oriented impression management motives" (p. 547). That is, high self-monitors may strive to cultivate public images that create the appearance of social status, and therefore their social networks may serve as a primary means for status enhancement. Low self-monitors are also concerned about their public images, but may be primarily focused on their reputations as "genuine and sincere people who act on their beliefs" (p. 547). Their social networks may reflect this motive, specifically in the types of connections that are made with others. A brief review of the basic aspects of social networks in organizations follows to provide a better understanding of the dispositional effects on these systems and their relevance to important individual and organizational outcomes.

Social Networks in Organizations

In considering the role of individual differences in the construction and maintenance of work relationships, it is important to keep in mind that relationships do not exist in a vacuum; they are connected to other individuals and other relationships (Agnew et al., 2001; Bott, 1957). For this reason, every relationship represents a system (Reis et al., 2000). These relational systems can take on different appearances and can yield vastly different resources; however, not all configurations of networked relationships are equally helpful to an individual or an organization (Mehra, Kilduff, & Brass, 2001).

Social networks have been used as a primary method for measuring the social capital of individuals and organizations. In essence, social capital refers to relational resources that are embedded in the ties between individuals (Coleman, 1988). The structural, relational, and cognitive dimensions of social capital have been theoretically linked to the facilitation, combination, and exchange of resources within organizations (Nahapiet & Ghoshal, 1998). Subsequent empirical work has demonstrated positive relations between social capital and individual and group performance (Mehra et al., 2001; Sparrowe, Liden, Wayne, & Kraimer, 2001), individual career success (Seibert et al., 2001), innovation and value creation (Tsai & Ghoshal, 1998), and the aggregate leadership capacity (Day, 2001) in organizations. Overall, theory and research suggest that social networks are critical to understanding why some individuals and organizations outperform others.

A social network is defined as a set of nodes (individuals) and connections (relationships or ties) between nodes (Brass & Krackhardt,

1999). The absence of a connection between individuals can be just as informative as the existence of a connection. The important construct of a structural hole (Burt, 1992) in social networks is based on the lack of ties between certain actors. Furthermore, a relationship (or lack thereof) could be an advantage or a disadvantage to an individual. Forming a large network may be of less importance than one's position within the network. A critical feature in building social capital is network centrality; related to this concept is the strength of connections or ties with others in the network. Both of these components, as well as the advantageous likelihood of occupying a structural hole, can be influenced by individual self-monitoring orientation.

Centrality

The concept of betweenness centrality has been shown to predict the most powerful actors in a network (Brass, 1984; Krackhardt, 1990), as well as the success of individuals and groups (Sparrowe et al., 2001). It is also a key component of social capital and effective leadership in organizations (Brass & Krackhardt, 1999). Centrality refers to how central an individual is relative to others in a network. An individual who connects with those who are otherwise unconnected is considered to have high betweenness centrality and thus occupies a structurally advantageous position in the network. In more formal terms, betweenness centrality measures the frequency with which an individual falls between other pairs of network actors on the shortest (geodesic) paths connecting them (Freeman, 1979).

Recent research demonstrated that high self-monitors were more likely to have greater network centrality than low self-monitors and that high self-monitoring and central network positions contributed independently to predicting individual work performance (Mehra et al., 2001). One means of gaining a position of centrality in a network is to make lots of connections (create a large network); however, this is not a very efficient strategy. Creating and maintaining network ties requires a substantial investment in terms of time and energy. High self-monitors, in their eagerness to please others and create good impressions, may tend to agree to be part of many project teams, thereby imperiling their overall work performance. Low self-monitors may be better able to refuse tasks that are not directly connected with their own interests (Mehra et al., 2001). There are several network strategy variations that can help individuals more optimally use their connections.

Structural Holes

It has been argued that there has been "no more important advance in the social network literature within the past decade" than Burt's (1992) structural hole theory (Krackhardt, 1999, pp. 183–184). This theory develops the concept of betweenness centrality to a guiding principle for many different network situations. Ties that bridge to unconnected parts of the network may enable an actor to obtain unique information, negotiate better agreements, and generally be more powerful than an actor whose ties do not provide such a bridging role. Burt refers to this bridge or separation between nonredundant contacts as a structural hole. An individual who has two friends who themselves are not friends spans across a structural hole, brokering information and resources between two people who may be indifferent or even hostile to each other.

According to the structural hole perspective, actors can leverage their investments in social relations by establishing connections to a diverse set of actors (preferably actors unconnected to each other) rather than establishing all of their relationships with members of one cohesive group. The likelihood of gaining diverse information and other valuable resources may, it is suggested, increase in direct proportion to the extent that an actor manages network connections to avoid redundancy and increase heterogeneity. Research on the structural hole concept has suggested that individuals who span across structural holes tend to get faster promotions in corporations (Podolny & Baron, 1997); however, there is also evidence that spending time mediating between disconnected individuals in an organization's work flow network can negatively affect performance appraisals (Mehra et al., 2001). Spending time trying to work with groups that have no need to coordinate may not be helpful to one's career. Furthermore, businesspeople who spanned across the social network in a community of independent entrepreneurs tended to experience lower firm performance and survival (Oh, Kilduff, & Brass, 2002), suggesting that time spent mediating the conflicts of others may be better spent minding one's own store. The current enthusiasm for the structural hole concept must be balanced by an awareness of the opportunity costs inherent in mediating relationships across social divides.

Tie Strength

Structural hole theory is an elaboration and extension of earlier influential work on strong and weak ties. As a reminder, a tie is any connection (relationship) between any two individuals in a social system. Ties can vary in terms of their relative strength, with strong ties indicating greater emotional intensity, frequency, importance, or reciprocity than weak ties (Granovetter, 1973). Another way to think about strong ties is as friendships, whereas weak ties are more like acquaintances (Brass & Krackhardt, 1999). Research has shown that high self-monitors tend to demonstrate lower overall commitment to their social and work relationships than low self-monitors (Day et al., 2002; Snyder, Gangestad, & Simpson, 1983; Snyder & Simpson, 1984). Thus, it would be expected that high self-monitors would be more willing than low self-monitors to break strong tie relationships, to suffer less from strong tie disruptions, and to be less embedded in networks of constraining strong tie groups such as Simmelian ties—those in which two people are reciprocally and strongly tied to each other, and each is reciprocally and strongly tied to a third party in common (Krackhardt, 1999; Krackhardt & Kilduff, in press).

A defining feature of strong ties is that they tend to be characterized by trust and mutual reciprocation. Strong ties provide for more credible and timely information than weak ties and also provide social and emotional support. Thus, an advantage of strong ties is that they build social capital in the form of loyalty, trust, mutual respect, and emotional attachment, which provide a solid foundation for social influence. Strong ties have also been shown to be advantageous in the transfer of complex knowledge across organization units (Hansen, 1999). A disadvantage of strong ties is that they require a good deal of emotional energy to maintain; they require considerable investment in terms of an individual's commitment to the tie. Strong ties also may be difficult to break and prevent access to new opportunities (Brass, 2001). As a result, strong ties might impede flexible and adaptive responses when an environment changes quickly. Recent research has shown, however, that in a community of Korean immigrant entrepreneurs, high self-monitoring business owners (compared to their low self-monitoring colleagues) were more likely to span across structural holes within the community and were faster to reach outside the community to build bonds with important role players (such as bankers) in the host community (Oh et al., 2002). Strong bonds of family and ethnicity were therefore less likely to constrain high self-monitors (relative to low self-monitors) from pursuing network connections.

Weak ties were not considered to be of much importance until Granovetter's classic work (1973) on the "strength of weak ties." His original research question examined how people find jobs, with the expectation that strong ties were likely to provide instrumental contacts that led to identifying viable job opportunities (Granovetter, 1974). In other words, close friends and family members would be most influential in providing successful job leads. Surprisingly, Granovetter found instead that it was the friends of friends (or friends of acquaintances) who tended to provide the most helpful job information. The most important people in providing information were not immediate friends and family but rather people in different occupations from the contact who had passed along information obtained through others who might not have been immediate friends with the source. Specifically, the short (fewer than two intermediaries), weak links provided the most useful job information.

One reason for the strength of weak ties resides in the quality of information that is transferred. People who are closest to us and constitute strong ties have many overlapping contacts and thus share much of the same information. Information received from a strong tie is likely to be stale in that it was already received from someone else (Scott, 2000). Fresh, or nonredundant, information is therefore most likely to come from distant parts of the network. Weak ties are advantageous in terms of bridging otherwise unconnected groups and providing new information and entrepreneurial opportunities. A disadvantage is that there is a relatively weak motivation to maintain the tie or provide other kinds of resources such as loyalty or emotional support.

Weak ties are not the same as structural holes. According to Burt (1992), the strength of the tie is not as important as whether the tie bridges unconnected parts of the network. Regardless of their strength, bridging ties are less constraining on an individual than nonbridging ties. The fewer constraints that are imposed on an individual, the greater are the potential network opportunities. In addition, bridging with strong (as compared with weak) ties is preferred whenever possible because it provides for more leverage or influence in a social system. This provides a potential advantage for low self-monitors, because they are thought to be more likely to develop strong ties than high self-monitors. Low self-monitors also tend to have more homogeneous networks (connections with similar others), which reduce the likelihood of bridging to dissimilar others that creates structural holes (Popielarz, 1999). Nonetheless, with their tendency to form strong bonds of solidarity with family, friends, and similar others, low self-monitors may have powerful resources available in times of crisis compared to high self-monitors.

Negative Ties and Multiplexity

Before elaborating more on the relationship between self-monitoring personality and social networks, two additional types of ties need to be mentioned because of their relevance.

There is little in the published literature on negative ties (Labianca, Brass, & Gray, 1998, is a notable exception); nevertheless, this type of tie is worth considering because of the known role of negative affect on individual cognition and behavior. Negative ties describe relationships in which one person has a negative affective judgment of another in the network; thus, negative ties can be considered to be at the opposite end of the affective continuum from strong and weak ties (Brass, 2001). These are aversive relationships such that one (or more) of the actors is motivated to avoid the other. Low self-monitors are likely to surround themselves with strong, positive relationships, whereas high self-monitors may find themselves mediating between individuals who dislike each other.

High self-monitors, relative to low self-monitors, are also likely to find themselves dealing with negatively connected relations (see the review in Brass, 1992). These situations occur when two people are competing for the same relationship with a third person. The classic example of two people with a negatively connected relation is that of two suitors for the same marriage partner: the success of one suitor spells the failure of the other. The focal individual in the middle of two negatively connected people has the (sometimes) difficult task of choosing between them for a lunch date, a business contract, or some other competitive outcome. High self-monitors, with their tendency to bridge across unconnected groups, are more likely than low self-monitors to face the stress of competing demands for their time and other resources. Whereas the low-self-monitoring strategy is likely to focus on bringing people together, the high self-monitor may be forced to choose between favoring one party or the other.

The second additional type of tie to consider is the multiplex tie. This describes relationships in which actors are connected in more than one type of association. For example, someone might be a work associate, a neighbor, and a friend. Although proximity is likely to be a strong predictor of multiplexity (Brass, 2001), the partner-based orientation of low self-monitors is also likely to contribute to multiplex ties being created. Low self-monitors tend to affiliate with others who are similar to them, regardless of the social context, and they may prefer to form multiple relations with the same people rather than seek out specialist partners for different activities.

Social Capital of Network Configurations

Social capital refers to relational resources embedded in the ties between individuals (Coleman, 1988; Nahapiet & Ghoshal, 1998), which research has shown to enhance value creation in organizations (Tsai & Ghoshal, 1998). Furthermore, different types of network connections are associated with different forms of social capital. Attempting to manage too many ties can consume valuable resources (time) and can also have dysfunctional effects if the expectations of others are not met. This is a particular risk with having too many strong ties (Brass & Krackhardt, 1999), because a strong tie requires a greater mutual commitment than a weak tie. The most appropriate network strategy is therefore likely to be contingent on the surrounding network structure of possible connections. Prescriptive advice on how to develop an optimal network with regard to the networks of others in a social system has been largely overlooked in the literature (Carley, 1999). The question of whether there are advantages and disadvantages of high self-monitors connecting with other highs, low self-monitors with other lows, or highs and lows connecting is worth considering.

High Self-Monitor to High Self-Monitor

In general, the research literature has supported the superiority of high self-monitors over low self-monitors in obtaining desirable organizational rewards such as more promotions (Kilduff & Day, 1994), better performance ratings (Day et al., 2002), and more advantageous positions in social networks (Mehra et al., 2001). Thus, it would appear that connections between high self-monitors would lead to the most structurally advantageous network configurations. These types of configurations would tend to provide connections between central network actors and therefore be the source of novel, divergent, and nonredundant information (Brass & Krackhardt, 1999); however, the connections that are formed would tend to be low-commitment ties. This would be a natural function of the overall lower commitment of high self-monitors to their social (Snyder & Simpson, 1984) and work (Day et al., 2002) relationships. Whereas low-commitment ties might be adequate for accessing a wider variety of informational resources, they may be less likely to yield high trust or commitment. In addition, the physical and mental well-being effects that are associated with social relationships (see Reis et al., 2000, for a review) are likely to be attenuated if the nature of the relationship is one of low commitment.

High self-monitors tend to be in the minority in most social settings, forming only about 40 percent of the overall population (Gangestad & Snyder, 1985; Kilduff, 1992). Given their motivation to seek the limelight (status enhancement), high self-monitors may be relatively scarce in many organizational settings involving production and back-room tasks and relatively overrepresented in settings involving boundary-spanning activities (compare Caldwell & O'Reilly, 1982) and upper-echelon work (Day et al., 2002; Kilduff & Day, 1994). Thus, the chances of finding network connections between high self-monitors is likely to be a function of the particular organizational setting and the proportions of high self-monitors in that setting. However, high self-monitors, relative to low self-monitors, are likely to reach across spatial and geographical boundaries in search of specific friendship opportunities (Snyder et al., 1983). Therefore, it may be important in organizational settings to consider the possibility that the network relations of high self-monitors may spill outside the departmental or organizational boundaries that may enclose low self-monitors.

Low Self-Monitor to Low Self-Monitor

In contrast to the status enhancement motives of high self-monitors, low self-monitors are motivated primarily by the desire to build close social relationships of mutual trust (Gangestad & Snyder, 2000). This type of strong tie also builds loyalty, respect, and emotional commitments, which are requisite commodities for effective leadership development (Day, 2000). Strong ties also may serve as a source of resilience in crisis situations (Krackhardt & Stern, 1988). It is not that low self-monitors are completely unconcerned with impression management or public opinion. They may be acutely concerned with holding reputations as genuine and sincere people who act on their beliefs (Gangestad & Snyder, 2000). Nonetheless, the generally lower levels of ability to manage impressions effectively may result in a misperception of the behavior and motives of low self-monitors (Turnley & Bolino, 2001).

When low self-monitors build ties with others of a similar disposition, there are potential risks in addition to the advantages associated with enhanced trust and commitment. One disadvantage has to do with informational resources. Because of their relatively homogeneous social worlds (Mehra et al., 2001), low self-monitors will have more difficulty obtaining fresh, nonredundant information from their networks. A second disadvantage is that low self-monitors are more constrained by their social ties because these ties are more difficult to break, which may prevent access to new opportunities (Brass, 2001; Oh et al., 2002). This could pose a serious disadvantage in rapidly changing environments that require forming and reforming new networks in adapting to emergent challenges.

High Self-Monitor to Low Self-Monitor

There may be unique advantages for both high and low self-monitors who affiliate. High self-monitors who build network connections with low self-monitors may be able to benefit from resources that are more likely to be found in the relationships between low self-monitors. High self-monitors tend to look to others for cues as to the attitudes and behaviors that are normatively appropriate. Low self-monitors, by contrast, look within themselves for the attitudes and behaviors that express their true selves. High self-monitors therefore are more likely to be influenced by others in their attitudes and behaviors than are low self-monitors (Kilduff, 1992). The high self-monitors may gain from low self-monitors' information concerning the range of opinions and behaviors that are possible in a particular social situation. Low self-monitors may look to the high self-monitors for help in negotiating across boundaries between individuals or groups holding divergent views. Considerable research shows that high self-monitors tend to emerge as leaders in leaderless groups (Zaccaro, Foti, & Kenny, 1991) and tend to resolve conflicts through collaboration and compromise (Baron, 1989). Low self-monitors may be able to influence many more people outside their own tightly knit groups by first influencing a high self-monitor who is in a boundary-spanning position. Conversely, a low self-monitor would benefit from the nonredundant information that a high self-monitor would likely bring to the network.

A risk in connecting a high and a low self-monitor is that a potential negative tie (that is, a relationship in which one person has a negative affective judgment of another person; Brass, 2001) will form. A risk to high self-monitors is that they will come across as disingenuous because of potential inconsistencies in their opinions and behavior. Appearing disingenuous or insincere is likely to be objectionable to low self-monitors and may contribute to a lack of respect. Low self-monitors may appear dogmatic and inflexible to high self-monitors. High self-monitors who value meeting others' expectations and fitting in with prevailing social norms may end up disliking low self-monitors, who tend to express deeply held opinions even when they are not normatively appropriate. Nonetheless, there are reasons that network ties between high and low self-monitors may be advantageous to both parties. Unfortunately, there are structural (in addition to the psychological) constraints that discourage this type of connection.

Homophily and Constraints on Heterogeneous Network Ties

There is a well-established tendency for individuals to associate with others who are similar to them in one or more ways, which sociologists term *homophily* (Lazarsfeld & Merton, 1954). For this reason, ties between dissimilar people are less likely than ties between those who are similar. Support, information, access, and influence are therefore most likely to be from people who are similar to an actor. This is not always a desirable outcome because of the likelihood of receiving redundant information from similar others (Scott, 2000). A more desirable network configuration would include a portfolio of ties to dissimilar others, which are likely to provide access to different resources and information than completely homophilous ties. Recently, organizational constraints on network formation have been considered, especially constraints on heterophily, or ties between people who are dissimilar (Popielarz, 1999). This literature might help to provide insight on and motivation to address organizational constraints on network heterophily.

The principal structural constraint on heterophily is organizational homogeneity (Popielarz, 1999). The more homogeneous the organization is, the greater is the likelihood of homophilous ties. This is because organizations provide the contact opportunities necessary to make connections with others. Whereas most of the research and theory associated with network homophily has been directed at demographic characteristics such as race and sex, there is reason to suspect that organizations also pose an inadvertent constraint in terms of personality. Such constraints on personality-based heterophily can have deleterious effects for individuals and organizations. Specifically, research evidence suggests that organizations are relatively homogeneous in terms of the personality attributes of their managers, and personalities become more homogeneous as one advances to higher management levels.

Homogeneity Within Organizations

A fundamental tenet of the attraction-selection-attrition (ASA) model of organizational behavior is that people self-select into and out of organizations. Furthermore, a key factor influencing a person's decision to join and remain with an organization is the fit between his or her personality and the modal personality of the organization (Schneider, 1987; Schneider, Goldstein, & Smith, 1995). A test of this basic ASA principle using a sample of approximately thirteen thousand managers from 142 companies across a broad sampling of U.S. industries revealed the hypothesized ASA effect for organizational membership on the personality characteristics of managers (Schneider, Smith, Taylor, & Fleenor, 1998). An implication of this finding is that organizational members have contact with others who are more like themselves in terms of their personality attributes than in the society at large. Organizational constraints that tend to perpetuate homophily are the result of the dispositionally driven choices people make with regard to which organizations to join and remain with.

Homogeneity in Upper Levels

A question of great interest to researchers as well as laypeople is why certain people win out in workplace contests. Clearly, ability and merit should be important factors; however, individual personality has also been shown to shape the fates of organizational contestants. Research has demonstrated that high self-monitors have superior job performance to low self-monitors (Mehra et al., 2001), especially when performance is measured through supervisory ratings (Day et al., 2002), and receive more promotions early in their career (Kilduff & Day, 1994). Extending such findings across organizational hierarchies suggests that high self-monitors should be overrepresented in middle- and upper-management positions. Because progression into middle management has been argued to be mainly a function of likeability and perceived ability to work with senior management (Hogan, Curphy, & Hogan, 1994), high self-monitors may have a competitive advantage in promotional tournaments. As a result, they may be disproportionately represented in the upper echelons of organizations.

This conclusion corresponds with findings from a large insurance company in which employees with higher-level jobs (management) were typically high self-monitors and those with lower-level jobs (clerical, technical, and support staff) tended to be low self-monitors (Sypher & Sypher, 1983). This overrepresentation of high self-monitors in management positions may occur because of the pragmatic facility with which high self-monitors are able to adjust their attitudes and behaviors to the prevailing norms and cultures of specific organizations and positions. Whereas low self-monitors may prefer to stay in organizations or positions that allow them to express their true selves, high self-monitors may seek out new opportunities to demonstrate their skills and abilities in impression management, conflict mediation, and boundary spanning. Whereas the low self-monitors define themselves by their inner beliefs and values, the high self-monitors define themselves by the prestigious roles they play in well-defined social situations. The ASA model therefore may apply more to low self-monitors than to high self-monitors as far as fit between individual and organizational values is concerned. High self-monitors are likely to be more concerned with fit between their desire for well-defined and prestigious positions and the organizational availability of such opportunities. Whereas low self-monitors are likely to be constrained by homophily pressures, high self-monitors are likely to pursue heterophilous connections.

To the extent that hierarchical position signals status in a particular organization, we might expect to find high self-monitors, relative to low self-monitors, seeking out those of higher formal position as friends. However, status in organizations is likely to be defined both informally and formally. Ever since the Hawthorne studies, organizational researchers have been aware of the emergence of informal leaders who lack official recognition but wield influence among the workforce. High self-monitors, with their keenly adjusted social skills, are more likely than low self-monitors to detect the actual distribution of status in the organization and to cluster around the rising stars. In addition, high self-monitors (relative to lows) are likely to be better at winning the attention of high-status others through ingratiation behaviors, broadcasting their ties to high-status others through judicious name dropping (that is, basking in reflected glory), and using their contacts with high-status others for career advancement within and across companies.

Conclusion

The personality compositions of teams and the differences in relationship content and context for different personality types are relatively unexplored topics. Despite the so-called greening of relationship science across many fields in psychology (Berscheid, 1999), there is a tendency to neglect the broader environments of relationships. If a goal of relationship scholars is to seek laws governing individuals' interactions with each other, we must consider dispositional as well as the structural influences in surrounding environments. Just as recent research has led to the acknowledgment that romantic relationships do not exist in a vacuum (Agnew et al., 2001), a similar understanding is needed regarding work relationships. Because of the fundamental importance of relationships in the social capital of individuals and organizations, this is an issue of critical importance to researchers and practitioners interested in work-related behavior.

A primary goal of this chapter was to build theoretically on previous work, demonstrating that dispositional differences influence the structural advantage that some individuals have in organizations through choices that shape their interpersonal environments. Another purpose was to expound on the reasons that a consideration of network configurations is important. One's structural position in a network is of interest, but previous work has tended to overlook the dispositional motives of others with whom network connections are sought. By widening the lens to consider the self-monitoring orientation of both members of a network dyad, we hope that a better understanding is gained of some of the challenges associated with building networks that enhance the social capital of individuals and organizations.

References

Agnew, C. R., Loving, T. J., & Drigotas, S. M. (2001). Substituting the forest for the trees: Social networks and the prediction of romantic relationship state and fate. *Journal of Personality and Social Psychology, 81,* 1042–1057.

Baron, R. A. (1989). Personality and organizational conflict: Effects of the Type A behavior pattern and self-monitoring. *Organizational Behavior and Human Decisions Processes, 44,* 196–281.

Berscheid, E. (1999). The greening of relationship science. *American Psychologist, 54,* 260–266.

Blau, P. M. (1974). *Exchange and power in social life.* New York: Random House.

Bott, E. (1957). *Family and social network.* London: Tavistock.

Brass, D. J. (1984). Being in the right place: A structural analysis of individual influence in an organization. *Administrative Science Quarterly, 29,* 518–539.

Brass, D. J. (1992). Power in organizations: A social network perspective. In G. Moore & J. A. Whitt (Eds.), *Research in politics and society* (pp. 295–323). Greenwich, CT: JAI.

Brass, D. J. (2001). Social capital and organizational leadership. In S. J. Zaccaro & R. J. Klimoski (Eds.), *The nature of organizational leadership* (pp. 132–152). San Francisco: Jossey-Bass.

Brass, D. J., & Krackhardt, D. (1999). The social capital of twenty-first century leaders. In J. G. Hunt, G. E. Dodge, & L. Wong (Eds.), *Out-of-the-box leadership: Transforming the twenty-first-century army and other top-performing organizations* (pp. 179–194). Greenwich, CT: JAI Press.

Burt, R. S. (1992). *Structural holes: The social structure of competition.* Cambridge, MA: Harvard University Press.

Caldwell, D. F., & O'Reilly, C. A., III. (1982). Boundary spanning and individual performance: The impact of self-monitoring. *Journal of Applied Psychology, 67,* 124–127.

Carley, K. M. (1999). On the evolution of social and organizational networks. *Research in the Sociology of Organizations, 16,* 3–30.

Cialdini, R. B. (1989). Indirect tactics of image management: Beyond basking. In R. A. Giacalone & P. Rosenfeld (Eds.), *Impression management in the organization* (pp. 45–56). Mahwah, NJ: Erlbaum.

Coleman, J. S. (1988). Social capital in the creation of human capital. *American Journal of Sociology, 94,* S95–S120.

Coleman, J. S. (1990). *Foundations of social theory.* Boston: Harvard Business School Press.

Day, D. V. (2000). Leadership development: A review in context. *Leadership Quarterly, 11,* 581–613.

Day, D. V. (2001, Apr.). *Understanding systems forces for sustainable leadership capacity.* Paper presented at the Sixteenth Annual Conference of the Society for Industrial and Organizational Psychology, San Diego, CA.

Day, D. V., Schleicher, D. J., Unckless, A. L., & Hiller, N. J. (2002). Self-monitoring personality at work: A meta-analytic investigation of construct validity. *Journal of Applied Psychology, 87*(2), 390–401.

Festinger, L. (1954). A theory of social comparison processes. *Human Relations, 7,* 117–140.

Freeman, L. C. (1979). Centrality in social networks: Conceptual clarification. *Social Networks, 1,* 215–239.

Gabarro, J. J. (1987). The development of working relationships. In J. W. Lorsch (Ed.), *Handbook of organizational behavior* (pp. 172–189). Upper Saddle River, NJ: Prentice Hall.

Gangestad, S. W., & Snyder, M. (1985). "To carve nature at its joints": On the existence of discrete classes in personality. *Psychological Review, 92,* 317–349.

Gangestad, S. W., & Snyder, M. (2000). Self-monitoring: Appraisal and reappraisal. *Psychological Bulletin, 126,* 530–555.

Graen, G. B., & Scandura, T. A. (1987). Toward a psychology of dyadic organizing. *Research in Organizational Behavior, 9,* 175–208.

Granovetter, M. S. (1973). The strength of weak ties. *American Journal of Sociology, 78,* 1360–1380.

Granovetter, M. S. (1974). *Getting a job.* Cambridge, MA: Harvard University Press.

Hansen, M. T. (1999). The search-transfer problem: The role of weak ties in sharing knowledge across organization subunits. *Administrative Science Quarterly, 44,* 82–111.

Hogan, R., Curphy, G. J., & Hogan, J. (1994). What we know about leadership: Effectiveness and personality. *American Psychologist, 49,* 493–504.

Jenkins, J. M. (1993). Self-monitoring and turnover: The impact of personality on intent to leave. *Journal of Organizational Behavior, 14,* 83–91.

Kilduff, M. (1992). The friendship network as a decision-making resource: Dispositional moderators of social influences on organization choice. *Journal of Personality and Social Psychology, 62,* 168–180.

Kilduff, M., & Day, D. V. (1994). Do chameleons get ahead? The effects of self-monitoring on managerial careers. *Academy of Management Journal, 37,* 1047–1060.

Kilduff, M., & Krackhardt, D. (1994). Bringing the individual back in: A structural analysis of the internal market for reputation in organizations. *Academy of Management Journal, 37,* 87–108.

Krackhardt, D. (1990). Assessing the political landscape: Structure, cognition, and power in organizations. *Administrative Science Quarterly, 35,* 342–369.

Krackhardt, D. (1999). The ties that torture: Simmelian tie analysis in organizations. *Research in the Sociology of Organizations, 16,* 183–210.

Krackhardt, D., & Kilduff, M. (in press). Structure, culture and Simmelian ties in entrepreneurial firms. *Social Networks.*

Krackhardt, D., & Stern, R. N. (1988). Informal networks and organizational crises: An experimental simulation. *Social Psychology Quarterly, 51,* 123–140.

Labianca, G., Brass, D. J., & Gray, B. (1998). Social networks and perceptions of intergroup conflict: The impact of negative relationships and third parties. *Academy of Management Journal, 41,* 55–67.

Lazarsfeld, P. F., & Merton, R. K. (1954). Friendship as a social process: A substantive and methodological analysis. In M. Berger, T. Abel, & C. H. Page (Eds.), *Freedom and control in modern society* (pp. 18–66). New York: Van Nostrand.

Mehra, A., Kilduff, M., & Brass, D. J. (2001). The social networks of high and low self-monitors: Implications for workplace performance. *Administrative Science Quarterly, 46,* 121–146.

Nahapiet, J., & Ghoshal, S. (1998). Social capital, intellectual capital, and the organizational advantage. *Academy of Management Review, 23,* 242–266.

Oh, H., Kilduff, M., & Brass. D. J. (2002). *Social personality and social capital: Implications for firm performance.* Unpublished manuscript.

Podolny, J. M., & Baron, J. N. (1997). Resources and relationships: Social networks and mobility in the workplace. *American Sociological Review, 62,* 673–693.

Popielarz, P. A. (1999). Organizational constraints on personal network formation. *Research in the Sociology of Organizations, 16,* 263–281.

Reis, H. T., Collins, W. A., & Berscheid, E. (2000). The relationship context of human behavior and development. *Psychological Bulletin, 126,* 844–872.

Schachter, S. (1959). *The psychology of affiliation: Experimental studies of the sources of gregariousness.* Stanford, CA: Stanford University Press.

Schleicher, D. J., & Day, D. V. (2002). *Establishing a nomological network for self-monitoring personality: A meta-analysis.* Unpublished manuscript.

Schneider, B. (1987). The people make the place. *Personnel Psychology, 40,* 437–453.

Schneider, B., Goldstein, H. W., & Smith, B. D. (1995). The ASA framework: An update. *Personnel Psychology, 48,* 747–773.

Schneider, B., Smith, B. D., Taylor, S., & Fleenor, J. (1998). Personality and organizations: A test of the homogeneity of personality hypothesis. *Journal of Applied Psychology, 83,* 462–470.

Scott, J. (2000). *Social network analysis: A handbook* (2nd ed.). Thousand Oaks, CA: Sage.

Seibert, S. E., Kraimer, M. L., & Liden, R. C. (2001). A social capital theory of career success. *Academy of Management Journal, 44,* 219–237.

Snyder, M. (1974). The self-monitoring of expressive behavior. *Journal of Personality and Social Psychology, 30,* 526–537.

Snyder, M. (1987). *Public appearances, private realities: The psychology of self-monitoring.* New York: Freeman.

Snyder, M., & Copeland, J. (1989). Self-monitoring processes in organizational settings. In R. A. Giacolone & P. Rosenfeld (Eds.), *Impression management in the organization* (pp. 7–19). Mahwah, NJ: Erlbaum.

Snyder, M., & Gangestad, S. W. (1986). On the nature of self-monitoring: Matters of assessment, matters of validity. *Journal of Personality and Social Psychology, 51,* 125–139.

Snyder, M., Gangestad, S., & Simpson, J. A. (1983). Choosing friends as activity partners: The role of self-monitoring. *Journal of Personality and Social Psychology, 45,* 1061–1072.

Snyder, M., & Ickes, W. (1985). Personality and social behavior. In G. Lindzey & E. Aronson (Eds.), *Handbook of social psychology* (3rd ed., Vol. 3, pp. 883–947). New York: Random House.

Snyder, M., & Simpson, J. A. (1984). Self-monitoring and dating relationships. *Journal of Personality and Social Psychology, 47,* 1281–1291.

Sparrowe, R. T., Liden, R. C., Wayne, S. J., & Kraimer, M. L. (2001). Social networks and the performance of individuals and groups. *Academy of Management Journal, 44,* 316–325.

Sypher, B. D., & Sypher, H. H. (1983). Self-monitoring and perceptions of communication ability in an organizational setting. *Personality and Social Psychology Bulletin, 9,* 297–304.

Thibaut, J. W., & Kelley, H. H. (1959). *The social psychology of groups.* New York: Wiley.

Tsai, W., & Ghoshal, S. (1998). Social capital and value creation: The role of intrafirm networks. *Academy of Management Journal, 41,* 464–476.

Turnley, W. H., & Bolino, M. C. (2001). Achieving desired images while avoiding undesired images: Exploring the role of self-monitoring in impression management. *Journal of Applied Psychology, 86,* 351–360.

Zaccaro, S. J., Foti, R. J., & Kenny, D. A. (1991). Self-monitoring and trait-based variance in leadership: An investigation of leader flexibility across multiple group situations. *Journal of Applied Psychology, 76,* 308–315.

CHAPTER 9

Understanding the Dynamic Learner

Linking Personality Traits, Learning Situations, and Individual Behavior

J. Kevin Ford
Frederick L. Oswald

> Under whatever disciplinary flag, . . . someone will always ask how individuals are different from each other, how behavior changes, how people perceive, think, and plan, and how people experience reality, and even what might be going on in the regions of the mind usually hidden from view [Funder, 2001, p. 216].

The term *dynamic learner* conjures up images of an active, continuously productive person who develops over time in knowledge, skill, and motivation with the goal of accomplishing some set of desired learning outcomes. Learners and those who design new learning environments in organizations may be energized about and dedicated to the concept of the dynamic learner (and its associated buzzwords), yet it is important to understand the realistic boundaries for the individual learning process, as well as for learning environments that can be created. There exists a continuum in that no learner is completely adaptable to whatever learning situation presents itself, nor can a particular learning situation be well suited to all learners. To understand the middle ground on this continuum is to understand the learning process more fully. We must examine both the constancy and stability residing in the individual, as well as the dynamic qualities that arise from the process of the individual learner in interacting with the learning situation.

Two trends emphasize a need to understand the dynamic learning process better. The first is in self-managed learning, where potentially the learner has flexibility in choosing how, when, or even whether to explore different learning environments and various aspects within them (Brown & Ford, 2002; Warr & Bunce, 1995). The second trend is in computer-adapted learning, where there can be great latitude in tailoring the learning environment based on a learner's characteristics and responses while learning. These two trends, taken together, imply a much larger role for the personality of the learner to influence the learning situation, because much of personality relates to motivational characteristics: the direction, frequency, and intensity with which learning activities are carried out. This chapter presents a synthesis of the research literature and our thoughts on how personality traits relate to the processes and outcomes of learning and what the implications are for designing better learning environments.

The ideas we present are somewhat speculative in nature because the research literature combining personality with learning processes and outcomes is rather sparse. In personnel selection, Hough and Schneider (1996) note that the role of personality has been "phoenixlike," historically held in disrepute but currently quite well established. By contrast, Mount and Barrick (1998) point out that when it comes to learning in organizations, "there remains a relative void in the literature regarding the relationship between personality dimensions and training outcomes" (p. 852). Although the amount of research conducted on personality and learning is small compared to the work on personnel selection, it is building toward a critical mass and deserves review. This research gap should be addressed because in the light of various training environments and training design considerations, it is theoretically and practically useful to examine which broad personality dispositions or traits may be more effective in predicting individuals' standing on key criterion constructs related to learning processes, such as motivation to learn, attentional focus and self-regulation (Ford &

Kraiger, 1995), and learning outcomes such as knowledge and skill acquisition and training transfer (Kraiger, Ford, & Salas, 1993).

Approaches to studying personality effects applied to training or learning contexts have already led to some advances in our understanding of individual differences, learning processes, and learning outcomes. The recent push toward self-directed learning and blended instruction, integrating traditional and more self-directed learning activities (Bassi & Van Buren, 1999), will increase our need to understand how personality influences the choices that individuals make. Such decisions include how much effort to place into the program, how much and what type of training content to focus on, and how many practice exercises to complete in the training in which they decide to pursue and engage.

It is clear that the intent and goals of effective learning experiences such as those in training are to change how learners perceive, think, plan, and behave. What is not as clear is the context in which these changes occur: for whom, how, and when.

Personality and Research on Learning in the Workplace

Traditionally, personality theory has been dominated by three models that span the person-based and situation-based continuum: the trait model, the interactionism model, and the situational model (see Endler & Magnusson, 1976). The *trait model* views individuals as varying on a number of stable dimensions within the person. Traits are seen as the prime determinants of behavior: they predict important behaviors over time and across a variety of types of situations. At the other extreme, the *situational model* focuses on the stimuli in the situation as major determinants of behavior. Differences in situations are seen as producing differences in behavior within an individual as well as across individuals. The *interactionism model* takes a middle ground between the trait and situational model, stressing that behavior is a function of the continuous interaction between the person and the situation. Individuals are not passive to situations but can actively choose which situations to perform in; conversely, situations can have different effects on different types of individuals. In outlining these three models, Endler and Magnusson made clear that no one is advocating entirely extreme roles of traits or situations; either extreme is too deterministic. Instead, researchers must adopt a stance or "useful fiction" that rests somewhere along this continuum, making choices about the relative importance to place on person- and situation-based factors given the phenomena under study and the theoretical motivations and practical implications of the research approach.

Examining research on training and learning shows that each of these three traditional approaches to personality is represented. These approaches to training research are clearly interrelated, yet can be meaningfully reviewed from each of these different perspectives.

Traits and Learning

The research on traits and learning has focused on issues of the readiness of the trainee to take advantage of the learning experiences, as well as the influence of basic personality characteristics on knowledge and skill acquisition. Research has also focused on the influence of situational and person characteristics on learning processes and outcomes.

Trainee Readiness

In the past forty years of research on training, the primary individual differences of interest have fallen under the broad factors of intelligence and experience. These two factors are directly related to issues of trainee readiness, that is, whether individuals have the aptitude (Duke & Ree, 1996; Ree, Carretta, & Teachout, 1995) or background experiences necessary to be successful in the training program. For example, Robertson and Downs (1989) report on twenty years of research that found it is possible to predict training success across a large number of jobs (for example, carpentry, welding, and forklift operation) by having individuals learn about and perform a sample of the tasks to be learned in training.

More relevant to our chapter, trainee readiness does not include just ability and skill components. For example, Tubiana and Ben-Shakhar (1982) found that a host of personality and motivational factors contributed to trainee readiness. Sociability, activeness, responsibility, independence, promptness, and motivation to serve in a combat unit added to the prediction of training success over and above success predicted by intelligence, education, and language scores.

Personality

Training research focusing on personality has sought to understand the stable individual differences that have an impact on motivation to learn and subsequent knowledge and skill acquisition (Noe, 1986). A number of researchers have provided evidence supporting a positive relationship between trainee motivation to learn and scores on learning measures (Mathieu, Tannenbaum, & Salas, 1992; Noe & Schmitt, 1986). Such research has also found that factors such as demographics (age, education), work-related attitudes (job involvement, career planning, organizational commitment), and personality or trait factors (locus of control, anxiety, goal orientation) have an impact on learning processes and outcomes (see the review by Mathieu & Martineau, 1997).

A recent meta-analytic integrative review by Colquitt, LePine, and Noe (2000) linked trainee characteristics to motivation to learn and learning measures. These researchers accumulated evidence across results from over one hundred studies, revealing a number of important relationships. Regarding personality traits, the meta-analysis contained enough data from individual studies to report on three traits from the Big Five: locus of control, trait anxiety, and conscientiousness. Results showed a strong relationship between locus of control and motivation to learn: those with an internal locus of control showed higher motivation levels on average than those with an external locus of control. In addition, trainee trait anxiety was related to motivation, with highly anxious trainees tending to be less motivated to learn and less self-efficacious. An individual's level of conscientiousness was indirectly related to the motivation to learn through its effect on pretraining self-efficacy. Motivation to learn was positively related to knowledge and skill acquisition, reactions of the trainees to the training program, and transfer of training indexes.

These meta-analytic findings support the notion that personality traits such as conscientiousness can affect learning outcomes through their influence on motivation to learn. Yet it is clear from the limited information that the meta-analysis could gather across studies that more research is needed. Only a small subset of the personality domain has been incorporated into training studies. Colquitt et al. (2000) note that traits such as cognitive playfulness, positive and negative affectivity, need for dominance, and competitiveness have been examined in only one or two studies. Also, the meta-analysis could not examine aptitude-treatment interaction

(ATI) effects. There are too few studies on ATI effects in the training literature and an absence of a taxonomy of learning situations on which to build a cumulative review.

Situations and Creating Learning States

Despite this lack of a taxonomy, the meta-analytic results of Colquitt et al. (2000) did show that measures of other situational characteristics, such as level of supervisory support, peer support, and a positive work climate, were positively related to measures of individual motivation to learn, learning, and training transfer. The assumption behind this correlational research is that climate factors such as support create a stronger situational press than less supportive supervisors and that this support tends to lead to more effective training and work behaviors. Correlational research cannot rule out the converse explanation: those who more effectively apply trained skills to the job tend to experience or perceive greater supervisory and peer support.

Two sets of studies speak to strategies for enhancing learning states and creating "strong situations" that minimize the effects of individual differences on learning outcomes. One set of studies has focused on employee choice. Baldwin, Magjuka, and Loher (1991) found that giving individuals a choice about what training to attend can create a positive learning state—if individuals obtain their first choice, that is. Similarly, Hicks and Klimoski (1987) found that trainees given a choice of attending a training program tended to report higher levels of motivation, were more positive about the program, and received higher test scores during training than those not given a choice. These studies on individual choice and outcomes of choice indicate that justice perceptions may bear important relationships with the structure of the training environment, and much recent research in personnel selection on justice may have some bearing on this (compare Bauer, Maertz, Dolan, & Campion, 1998; Ryan & Ployhart, 2000).

A second set of experimental studies has focused on positively framing the training situation for the trainee. Martocchio (1992) attempted to create a learning state by framing microcomputer training as an opportunity for career advancement rather than as a punishment for past mistakes. He found that the career opportunity frame of reference generally led to higher self-efficacy going into the program and ultimately to better learning. Quiñones (1995) examined different effects of framing training program assignments on learning outcomes. Assignments to a training program were described as remedial or advanced. Results indicated that the framing had an impact on attributions for past performance as well as fairness perceptions, motivation to learn, and learning outcomes. Quiñones notes that context really does matter and advocates designing interventions focusing on contextual factors that increase motivation to learn across participants rather than necessarily tailoring motivational interventions to individual trainees. Very few studies have investigated the effects of various types of strong situational presses prior to or during the training experience itself.

Person-by-Situation Effects

In a review of the training field over thirty years ago, Campbell (1971) noted that one area of promise was the focus on person-by-situation effects, which take both individual differences and learning situations into account. In particular, he directed attention to the problem of how to adapt the instructional process to individual differences as an alternative to research examining trait effects on learning outcomes directly, without examining the training content and process. Campbell's approach is quite sensible because traits are more proximal to learning behaviors and the learning process that instruction entails, and they are more distal from the outcomes that the learning situation demands of the individual.

According to Cronbach (1957, 1967), individual differences and learning can relate to one another by tailoring a set of instructional goals, methods, and materials to the individual or to homogeneous groups of individuals. Typically, this sort of research has sought to investigate the effects of matching alternative modes of instruction to different characteristics of the individual so that each person uses the most appropriate learning procedure. In this context, *aptitude* is defined as any stable characteristic that resides within the individual, interacts with learning situations, and correlates with learning outcomes. Defined in this way, aptitudes are broad in scope and include cognitive, motivational, and affective factors such as cognitive abilities (the *g* factors and its components), prior knowledge and experience (physics knowledge), personality variables (trait anxiety), and motivational factors (achievement motivation).

In the educational literature, several major aptitudes have been pointed out that relate to the learning environment in schools. Regarding cognitive ability, high-ability students tend to do better in low-structure environments (discovery learning), and low-ability students tend to perform better in high-structured learning environments (Snow, 1990; Swanson, O'Connor, & Cooney, 1990). Regarding personality constructs, students low in anxiety tend to perform better with heuristic instruction (low structure) than with algorithmic instruction (high structure). Personality also has been found to relate to the educational learning environment: extraverted and moderately anxious students seem to benefit most in cooperative (versus competitive) learning situations (Hall, Dansereau, & Skaggs, 1990). In settings more related to work training, Savage, Williges, and Williges (1982) used motor and information-processing tests to develop empirical prediction models for assigning students to one of two training conditions based on predicted training time for each type of training. Making training assignments based on these individual differences resulted in a 47 percent savings in training time compared to random assignment and a 53 percent savings compared to a mismatched assignment.

As Campbell and Kuncel (2002) recently noted, all core training issues are framed by the ATI parameters and the criterion of interest. Identifying the parameters and capitalizing on them by modifying the training environment requires a firm understanding of types of contexts in which the learner might be placed. Unfortunately, as we previously lamented, we have limited understanding of the effects of varieties of learning and learning environments, but the literature we have reviewed thus far has pointed to several broad and consistent themes on both the individual and situational sides of the equation.

Beyond Broad Traits: Linking the Person, Situation, and Behavior

Traditional research on workplace learning has taken a fairly limited approach to understanding personality and its effects on learning outcomes. More specifically, trait and outcome measures have tended to reflect stability in the person and situation, respectively. Increasingly, however, learners are becoming active participants in their own learning process, which leads to a more serious need to expand research in understanding learning situations and person-learning situation interactions. Recent research in personality psychology has offered some insights and methodologies relevant to this type of learning research.

In his review of personality research, Funder (2001) notes that the goal of personality theory has to be focused on increasing our understanding of the interconnections among person, situation, and behavior. In particular, knowing about a person and his or her situation should allow for predicting what he or she will do in that situation—or that understanding the person and knowing the behavior exhibited should then tell us something about the situation the person is in. New perspectives have sought to locate the person within context, examine traits and behavioral variation, and understand the link between traits and psychological states and processes. These new perspectives have much to offer to researchers interested in expanding the domain of research on personality, learning processes, and learning outcomes.

In personality research, much effort in the 1980s and 1990s was focused on developing a consistent and coherent set of personality constructs for organizational research, particularly in personnel selection. As Hough and Schneider noted (1996), the development of personality and performance taxonomies has proven useful in finding clearer relationships between personality traits and important criterion elements that had been previously obscured. Assessment tools to operationalize these constructs have been well developed (for example, see Ozer & Reise, 1994), and the average or traited response of a person has been found to be useful in predicting or explaining both training outcomes and job performance (Barrick & Mount, 1991).

Although traits are important in reflecting an individual's consistent or typical behavior across situations, recent research efforts have begun to expand our understanding of personality as a more dynamic characteristic of a person. Similarly, there has been greater recognition that situations may contain different relevant psychological characteristics for different individuals.

Personality Traits in Context

Relevant to the previous point, Mischel and his colleagues have launched a long-term research program focusing on why dispositions lead to behavioral regularities (Mischel & Shoda, 1998; Mischel, Shoda, & Mendoza-Denton, 2002). They contend that research needs to analyze traits in a way that allows for understanding how individuals interact with situations to produce stable situation-behavior patterns (see Murtha, Kanfer, & Ackerman, 1996). This new perspective leads to refining what is meant by a person-by-situation interaction, what is considered stability, and what is considered a change in dispositions or the dynamic individual processes that underlie interactions between persons and situations. As Mischel and Shoda (1998) note, "This view is that the personality system is active and indeed proactive, not just reactive—a system that anticipates, influences, rearranges, and changes situations as well as reacts to them. Thus the personality system and the behavior it generates selects, modifies, and shapes the environment in reciprocal transactions" (p. 239).

This perspective highlights that clearly explicating cause-and-effect relationships demands taking a more dynamic interactive approach. Mischel and Shoda (1998) promote an approach that focuses on how an individual's stable personality can be expressed as a pattern of both consistency and variation in the flow of a person's behavior. These researchers have data supporting recurrent patterns of behavior that can be high for a trait in some situations and low in other situations. As an example in organizations, an employee may display agreeableness when being teased by a supervisor but aggressiveness when being teased by a peer. Mischel and Shoda would call an individual's pattern of trait-situation interactions such as this one a *behavioral signature*.

In addition, Shoda (1999) notes that situations can be thought of as similar to or different from one another along two dimensions that are similar to what have been discussed in the training literature: the physical fidelity of the situation (school setting versus home setting) or the psychological fidelity of the situation. Shoda notes that the underlying "psychologically active ingredients" may be consistent across situations in some respects but not others. For instance, a particular school environment and work environment may be similar in evoking individuals' achievement motivation but different in evoking extraversion. This suggests that learners may seek out the psychological fidelity in a learning situation to help them determine how to react or behave. The learner can then draw from experience in similar situations that evoke the same feelings of psychological fidelity. This notion is yet another reason for further research on taxonomies of situational characteristics and their psychological underpinnings (see Hattrup & Jackson, 1996).

Taking a dynamic, active learning perspective on individuals and situations captures the reality of the learning context better. An active learning perspective requires considering how people with a certain level of personality characteristic respond to particular learning situations, as well as adapt to changing learning situations. Figure 9.1 provides three graphs for the frequency of a particular type of behavior exhibited by learners for three different learning situations, given differences in a personality characteristic p across learners. Let us say that the behavior is feedback-seeking behavior, the personality characteristic is conscientiousness, and the three situations are such that $S1$ represents one-one-one training, $S2$ represents group training, and $S3$ represents computer-based training. The figure illustrates that learners with a particular level of conscientiousness show differences in the frequency of feedback seeking depending on the learning situation. The vertical arrow

Figure 9.1. Variability in Behavior: Focus on the Situation.

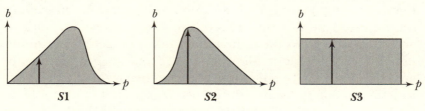

$S1$ = Situation 1 (one-on-one training)
$S2$ = Situation 2 (group training)
$S3$ = Situation 3 (computer-based training)
p = Personality characteristic across learners
b = Frequency of learning behavior across learners

represents individuals with the same level of conscientiousness, yet the amount of feedback seeking across the three different situations varies for these types of individuals, with more feedback seeking in group settings than in one-on-one or computer-based training. What is important to note is that each of the three graphs in Figure 9.1, if taken separately, depicts a typical individual-differences approach to training research (whether the level of conscientiousness predicts a learning behavior or outcome in a particular situation), but across graphs, one sees conceptually the influence of different situations and the more complex interactions of the person, the situation, and learning.

Personality Traits and Behavioral Variability

Another line of research has focused on personality as density distributions. Fleeson (2001), like Mischel and his colleagues, contends that individuals actively react to situations and that the same individual will behave differently across these different situational contexts over time. Consequently, the individual's behavior can be conceived of as forming a distribution that can be partially explained by personality constructs. More specifically, he contends that within-person variability is actually predictable as an individual difference in reactions across different types of situations.

In a recent study, Fleeson (2001) examined within-person variability and stability of the Big Five personality relevant behavior. He conducted three experience-sampling studies in which undergraduate students described how they were acting and feeling at five scheduled times per day for about three weeks. Results supported the notion that there is high within-person variability: individuals self-reported a wide range of levels of personality characteristics across situations. At the same time, their average or central tendencies were highly stable over time. He also showed that the amount of variability in the distribution of behavior (skew and kurtosis) is a stable individual-difference construct. For example, he found that the amount of within-person variability in the Big Five personality construct of Extraversion reflected individual differences in a person's reactions to situational contexts high on extraversion-relevant cues (time of day and number of others present). Some Big Five dimensions showed more variability across situations, such as Extraversion, more than others, such as Conscientiousness.

This type of personality research highlights a process approach that links traits with behaviors that express the trait. The behavioral manifestations may reflect a temporary state that the person is in relevant to the typical modal trait like behavior one would expect. Consequently, while there is stability in personality, behaviors can be thought of as trait-relevant states that are short term, continuous, and concrete ways of acting, feeling, and thinking at a particular time and place. The goal in a learning context, then, is to maintain states within individuals that lead to expressing learning-relevant behavior. In transferring the training knowledge to the workplace, maintaining these states outside the learning situation may be just as important as providing the opportunities and incentives to express the behaviors learned.

As applied to learning, Figure 9.2 illustrates variability with each of the three graphs showing how particular learners tend to vary in the frequency of a particular learning behavior across situations that vary in their personality-related content. Here we have three learners ($L1$, $L2$, and $L3$), and in this case the abscissa represents a continuum of a particular situational characteristic s within a learning situation or parts thereof (amount of structure, amount of priming for an internal or external locus of control). Each learner shows different frequencies of a particular type of learning behavior, where situations with the highest frequencies of behavior have the most situational press for that particular individual.

Figure 9.2. Variability in Behavior: Focus on the Learner.

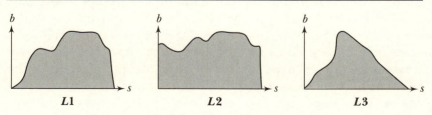

$L1$, $L2$, $L3$ = Learner 1, Learner 2, Learner 3

s = Situational characteristic across situations

b = Average frequency of learning behavior
within a learner

Taken together, Figures 9.1 and 9.2 illustrate a generalizability theory approach toward partitioning measured behaviors into different sources of variance; the graphs would be more of an exploratory supplement to generalizability theory statistics. Even a conceptual understanding that situations may vary in their personality-relevant characteristics—even when those characteristics cannot be empirically measured—implies that data should be collected on individuals across different learning situations if it is important for "the situation" to be understood as a potentially important source of variance with potential main effects and interactive effects on learning outcomes. Furthermore, this would be an empirical policy-capturing approach to creating classes of situations with similar features.

Personality Traits and Psychological States

Another line of research has focused on the differences and interrelatedness of traits and states. This research makes little distinction between personality and motivation; both are seen as influencing the direction, frequency, and intensity of behaviors. In addition, personality and motivation can be considered at the traits and state levels that influence behaviors through proximal and distal mechanisms (Kanfer, 1992). Individuals can have multiple traits that interact within particular settings to create various individual differences in states that have complex effects on thought, emotions, and actions (see Snow, 1990).

One example of this approach has been the work of Kanfer and her colleagues (Kanfer, 1990; Kanfer, Ackerman, & Heggestad, 1996; Kanfer & Heggestad, 1997) on a person-centered framework for the study of work motivation, achievement, and performance. The person-centered approach is based on the principle of the continuous and reciprocal influence of person characteristics and situational factors. These investigators note that to take such an interactionist perspective requires a clear conceptualization of the relevant person characteristics that affect work motivation processes. They identified two key motivationally relevant traits of achievement and anxiety. To understand the motivational processes, they employ a self-regulatory perspective to understanding the interrelationships of individual differences in motivational traits and subsequent psychological states. More specifically, Kanfer and Heggestad (1997) contend that self-regulatory processes are affected by cognitive, motivational, and affective states of the person that are linked in complex ways back to more stable individual differences in personality and motivational traits.

From a cognitive perspective, research has focused on metacognition—the planning, monitoring, and evaluating of one's own thought processes. Research has shown that individuals who are more aware of their cognitive processes (what strategies they are using, how they are allocating their attention, how well they are succeeding on a task, what they need to do to correct ineffective strategies) and are more effective at monitoring and evaluating their strategies concurrently with performing complex tasks are more likely to be successful (Ford, Smith, Weissbein, Gully, & Salas, 1998; Pintrich & DeGroot, 1990; Volet, 1991). From an affective perspective, researchers have highlighted the need to understand actions that individuals take that allow for emotional control. Emotional control is viewed as central to minimizing anxiety, fear of failure, and other distractions so as to maintain concentration on a task (Kanfer & Heggestad, 1997). Research has shown that interventions to reduce anxiety and fear of failure lead to more effective learning (compare Barrios & Shigetomi, 1979; Kanfer et al., 1996). Individuals with good motivation-control skills are viewed as having high levels of mastery orientation as well as desiring high levels of achievement. Research shows that individuals with high levels of motivational control are better at self-generating goals and finding ways to challenge themselves to improve their performance even if the task does not demand it (Dweck & Leggett, 1988).

The implication for these emerging research directions is clear. Prediction-type questions relating personality traits to learning outcomes are not enough. We agree with Ozer and Reise (1994) that a model of traits without understanding process reflects only a meager portion of the psychology of learning. We now have conceptual frameworks that have begun to better link more stable and underlying characteristics like motivation to approach and avoid situations to process questions such as what cognitive, behavioral, and affective type responses are changing as an individual experiences a learning event (state mastery goal orientation) and how these responses can be modified or changed. We need additional training research to understand how cognitive, affective, and behavioral learning responses result from the complex interaction of various person traits and psychological states that the learner exhibits across various types of learning contexts.

Advancing Research on Personality and Learning

All three perspectives—traits within context, traits and behavioral variability, and traits and psychological states—focus attention on taking the interrelationships among people, situations, and behaviors more seriously. These new perspectives for understanding personality highlight the opportunities for advancing our thinking about the learner within a learning situation.

Overall, research is needed that moves beyond the focus on the modal or average level of a personality trait for an individual as a predictor of learning outcomes. In this way, we can begin to match the dynamic process of learning with a more dynamic understanding of the person. This requires us to begin with the assumption that individuals with a particular trait do not always behave the same way in all situations, and to some extent the variation in behavior implies within-person variability around the average level of a personality trait. This highlights that although traits may have stability, training designers and trainers themselves can have influence over the variability around that average level, creating situations that push individuals out of their average trait zone.

Three questions are key for advancing research and practice on training and learning: What interventions can help create effective learning states and processes? When are aptitude-treatment interactions important to consider? and How do individuals matter given strong learning situations?

What Interventions Help Create Effective Learning States and Learning Processes?

It is clear that to understand the person within situation, we need a better understanding of situations that learners face. The situational context of learning that has been most studied in the training literature has been workplace climate and management support for learning. Goldstein and Ford (2002) discuss how workplace climate needs to be part of the initial organizational analysis during the needs assessment phase. In addition, climate has been found to affect motivational and training transfer outcomes (Baldwin & Ford, 1988; Colquitt et al., 2000).

Much less attention has been paid in the industrial/organizational psychology literature to what situations are embedded in the pretraining and delivery of training and how they affect learning states, motivation to learn, self-regulatory strategies, and ultimately knowledge and skill acquisition. Based on this understanding, we can begin to develop interventions to create more effective learning states.

Research in educational psychology is beginning to show that certain student learning contexts matter in terms of affecting motivation to learn and learning activities. One focus of the research deals with classroom practices that positively affect intrinsic motivation (Brophy, 1998). For example, Guthrie, Wigfield, and Von Secker (2000) designed an instructional environment for reading that included multiple pathways for affecting student intrinsic motivation. They found that regardless of individual differences, an instructional context that emphasized learning goals, real-world interaction (hands-on activities), competence support (instruction on strategies to use), and autonomy support (self-directed learning and collaboration) led to higher motivation and greater strategy use than a traditional classroom instruction that addressed the same content. Thus, the incorporation of effective learning and design principles can create learning states that are beneficial for all learners (Noe & Colquitt, 2002).

Research also indicates that many trait variables that training research has shown are important to pretraining motivation also have state variable analogues. These learning states provide a point of leverage for trainers in developing pretraining motivation. Several examples of variables that have been treated as both traits and states include locus of control, anxiety, and goal orientation (Chen, Gully, Whiteman, & Kilcullen, 2000; Fisher, 1998; Rotter, 1966; Spielberger, 1966, 1977; Weiner, 1983, 1985). For example, Chen et al. found that statelike individual difference factors such as goal orientation and state anxiety mediated the relationships between traitlike individual differences and learning performance. The fact that these variables can be viewed as states implies that they can be modifiable or created in ways beneficial to the motivation of the learner. As another example, Button, Mathieu, and Zajac (1996) contend that goal orientation is a stable trait but can be manipulated by a strong situation. Although a personality trait may be the dominant manner in which an individual prefers to learn, it is clear that learning states can also be induced by characteristics within the learning situation. It is an open question as to how to create a state that has an impact on learning prior to the person's reverting back to his or her natural tendencies, strategies, and interpretations associated with his or her dominant trait orientation (Elliot, 1999).

A recent study by Weissbein and Ford (2002) shows one approach to an intervention to affect learning states and subsequently learning outcomes. They focused directly on creating learning states regardless of the person's stable traits. For example, it is difficult to change a person's locus of control. Instead, they argue for the need to develop an intervention to affect trainee attributions or state level of locus of control. This argument is consistent with the work of Mischel, Fleeson, and others who have focused on situations, variance in personality, and behavioral signatures. In particular for this study, they showed videotapes of former trainees that attributed success in an assertiveness training program as based on persistence, effort, and strategy. The goal of this attributional retraining was to change any unproductive attribution patterns that encourage helplessness, such as attributing failure to stable and uncontrollable factors (lack of ability), into constructive attributions, such as attributing success in training to unstable and controllable factors (effort). Trainees were exposed to the attributional retraining prior to attending a training program on assertiveness. Results indicated that the intervention had an impact on learning states. These learning states were related to pretraining motivation, over and above the impact of the trait measure of locus of control, and this relationship was mediated by the attributional learning states. Motivation to learn was found to have an effect on learning in the assertiveness training program and led to better performance in the transfer setting in which the trainees conducted a salary negotiation task. Thus, even a relatively brief intervention prior to beginning the training session was found to induce beneficial attributional patterns and discouraged maladaptive attributional patterns.

This research direction shows that learning states can be created that have important impacts on self-regulatory processes and learning outcomes. Research from the clinical and social psychology literatures on affecting states should be considered for ideas on other types of interventions that have relevance for learning situations. For example, Fosterling (1985) discusses a number of other types of attribution retraining approaches such as the use of persuasion. Barrios and Shigetomi (1979) have identified five types of programs for anxiety management. Such interventions have the potential to provide trainers and training designers with a number of strategies for improving learning.

When Are ATIs Important to Consider?

ATIs are of interest because they imply that to some extent, learning experiences such as training can be optimized across specific groups of individuals. In other words, one training intervention may benefit some individuals more than others in terms of their standing on a learning outcome; in turn, those who do not benefit from this intervention will benefit from another one (or from some variation of it). Campbell and Kuncel (2002) stress that there are always relevant individual differences and always differences in training programs that make ATI relevant to any training effort. Yet there has been scant attention to examining ATIs in organizational learning situations.

Recent research has begun to reexamine the usefulness of ATIs in workplace training situations. Gully, Payne, Koles, and Whitman (2002) examined the effectiveness of error training for trainees with different levels of ability and personality traits such as openness to experience and conscientiousness. They found that the effectiveness of the training was dependent on both ability and personality traits. For example, individuals more open to experience benefited more from error-encouragement training than less open individuals did. Schmidt and Ford (2002) examined the interactive effects of goal orientation and metacognitive instruction on learning outcomes within a Web-based training environment. They found, consistent with expectations, that the metacognitive intervention (prompting learners to self-reflect) resulted in lower levels of metacognitive activity and learning for those with a high level of performance-avoidance orientation as opposed to those with low levels of performance avoidance.

These types of studies show that ATIs can be important for understanding motivational and learning outcomes. We contend that the next logical step is to begin to examine when ATIs are important enough to have practical significance. Figures 9.3 and 9.4 qualify the conditions when designing training interventions tailored to ATIs might be useful and when doing so might be less so. The gray boxes reflect the range of scores on pre- and posttraining measures, and the white dots reflect particular individuals' scores. Figure 9.3 exemplifies the strong situation where training is very effective for all involved. This may happen frequently when the training outcome is somewhat narrow, for instance, some sort of knowledge acquisition in a domain relatively unknown prior to training (training computer programmers to learn a procedure in a particular computer programming language). Here, despite possible individual differences in preference for the structure of training, trainee anxiety, and so on, all who were trained achieved mastery.

Figure 9.4 is perhaps a more interesting example, combining possible ATIs shown in scores on pretraining and posttraining measures. The rank order of individuals on scores differs from pretraining to posttraining measures (that is, some ATIs are present). The point here is that the mastery level established on the training outcome informs the extent that designing training to ATIs matters. An extreme case is where any increase on the learning outcome, no matter how slight, is valuable to the organization. In

Figure 9.3. Illustration of a Strong Situation.

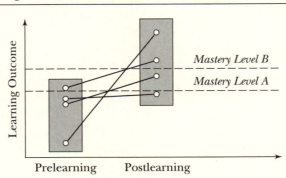

that case, the cost of training tailored to ATIs must be balanced with the benefit realized (realizing that the cost and the benefits may not entirely expressible in dollar amounts). A more practical case is where a mastery level on the training outcome is set, and individuals must achieve a posttraining score above that level. Scores beyond that level may be of value to the organization, but the explicit training goal is for trainees to obtain a score at or above the mastery level. In this case, where the mastery level is set is a key influence on whether training interventions should address ATIs that may be present. Consider, for instance, mastery level A. All individuals are below that level pretraining, but most are above that level posttraining. In this case, the training goal is met despite ATIs that may be present. Tailoring training to ATIs here may not be so important (although such tailoring may still make reaching the training goals easier or reactions to training more favorable, say, for those who prefer less structured training). Contrast this situation with one where the mastery level is set at mastery level B. Here, approximately half the trainees achieve the mastery level and half do not, so training specific to ATIs might be more valuable. ATI training may entail a supplement for some of the individuals in a training course, or it may imply different training experiences for different sets of individuals. Of course, finding the ATIs has been and will continue to be a challenge. What is also needed to link research and practice, though, is a greater appreciation of the circumstances under which finding ATIs is important.

Figure 9.4. Influence of Learning Mastery Level on Defining a Strong or Weak Situation.

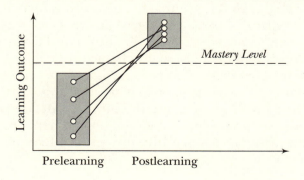

How Do Individuals Matter Given Strong Learning Situations?

Research on situational interventions to affect psychological states and person-treatment interactions must also be balanced with continued work on understanding when and how individuals matter in learning contexts. This calls for more complex examination of stable individual characteristics and the multiple ways in which people progress through learning situations. In addition, it calls for longitudinal research to study how an individual progresses through various learning situations.

Dweck (1986) identified two very different goal orientations that people can have toward learning activities. Mastery-oriented individuals believe that their efforts can lead to improved learning and retention. Individuals with a mastery orientation view ability as malleable. They focus on developing new skills, attempt to understand their tasks, and define their success in terms of challenging self-referenced standards. In contrast, performance-oriented individuals believe that ability is demonstrated by performing better than others, even during training events. Moreover, they define success in terms of normative-based standards. Thus, mastery and performance orientations represent fundamentally different ideas of success and different reasons for engaging in learning (Ames, 1992). Much of the research on goal orientation has focused on demonstrating the adaptive nature of mastery over performance goals.

Elliot and his colleagues have expanded on our understanding of achievement striving, emphasizing that approach and avoidance goals are critical to understanding achievement in learning and performance situations (see Elliot, 1999; Elliot & Church, 1997; Elliot & McGregor, 2001). Approach motivation is seen as directed toward a positive or desirable event, while avoidance motivation is directed against a negative or undesirable event. They have linked these concepts with the personality characteristics of mastery and performance goal orientations to form a four-factor model of achievement goals: mastery approach, mastery avoid, performance approach, and performance avoid. Elliot and McGregor (2001) found evidence in support of the four achievement goal types as empirically distinguishable, with differential effects on learning processes such as deep processing of material, study strategies, and anxiety levels. In addition, Elliot and Thrash (2002) present a more integrative perspective of personality, approach-avoid motivations, and goal orientation. They present evidence that personality characteristics such as extraversion and positive emotionality load on the approach dimension, while neuroticism and negative emotionality load on the avoid dimension.

From a training or learning perspective, a key issue is how much of an influence one can have on achievement goals. The framework of Elliot and colleagues suggests that the basic temperaments or underlying motivational pushes of approach and avoid are probably fairly well ingrained by adulthood. This leads to a question as to the extent to which organizations can create motivational states that are contrary to an individual's natural and personality-driven tendencies. Although the answer to this is yet unclear, some recent research provides a window into the possibility of directing attention to affecting mastery- and performance-oriented states of the learner in particular learning situations. For example, Kozlowski, Gully, Smith, Nason, and Brown (1995) instructed participants in a mastery goal condition to focus on learning the components of a task, trying out new skills, and exploring new strategies. Individuals in the performance goal condition were instructed to achieve a difficult and specific outcome goal. Results indicated that compared to trainees with performance goals, trainees with mastery goals tended to be more self-confident, gained more knowledge from training, and were more likely to generalize skills from the training task to a new and more complex transfer task.

Recent work in the educational field has gone beyond studying the simple additive effects of goal-orientation traits on behavior to focus on the multiple traits and multiple pathways that link traits to achievement-related outcomes. Increasing our understanding of these traits and pathways is critical to developing appropriate interventions to aid learning.

A multiple goal perspective (for example, see Wentzel, 1991, 1992) takes more of a developmental or process perspective to achievement motivation and learning. An assumption of this approach is that mastery goals may lead to different learning processes and different outcomes than do performance goal orientations. These different pathways and outcomes provide a more complex picture of the learner than the somewhat static view of a mastery goal orientation as being "better" than a performance goal orientation in terms of motivation, strategy use, and performance outcomes. For example, in some situations, performance goals may be adaptive—or at least not maladaptive. There may be learning objectives that are not intrinsically motivating to most individuals, even to those who tend to be mastery oriented in other situations, where individuals with a high performance goal orientation may strive to perform well. Or in some dynamic situations, staying with a mastery goal rather than moving to more of a performance goal over time may not be beneficial to continued improvement. From a multiple pathways perspective, performance-oriented learners may feel less interest and have more anxiety and more trouble dealing with failure, employ different strategies to deal with failure than a mastery-oriented person would, and yet still reach the same level of outcomes. This calls for going beyond between-subjects designs to consider examining multiple goals for individuals and their interactions across different settings or situations.

Recent studies have found support for taking a multiple goal perspective. For example, Pintrich (2000) examined goal orientation and changes in motivation, affect, strategy use, and performance across three waves of data collected from 150 eighth and ninth graders in math classes. In general, he found that the process measures such as self-efficacy, task value, and positive affect declined over time. More central to a perspective of multiple goals, he found that performance approach goals, when coupled with mastery goals, were just as adaptive as mastery goals alone. He also found that the two types of goal orientation had differential relationships over time to psychological processes such as positive affect, the use of self-handicapping strategies, and perceived task value.

Riveiro, Cabanach, and Arias (2001) conducted a study of 595 college students. They examined relationships between goal orientation and the use of various types of cognitive, self-regulatory, and motivational strategies. They found that from a multiple-goals perspective, students who developed the most positive self-regulatory strategies were those who not only were concerned about mastery but also had a desire to avoid being judged negatively by others. This outcome highlights the importance of engaging learners in both the learning goals and self-regulation in achieving those goals in order to "manage their learning and make it more flexible so they can achieve whatever seems most appropriate in each situation" (p. 570).

As a final example, Harackiewicz, Barron, Carter, Lehto, and Elliot (1997) examined the short- and long-term consequences of student achievement goals during college. Consistent with a multiple-goal perspective, both mastery and performance goals had positive and complementary effects on different measures of academic success. In particular, they found that mastery goals in the short run predicted interest in an introduction to psychology course, and in the long run they predicted the number of subsequent psychology courses students enrolled in. Performance goals predicted both short- and long-term academic performance.

These three studies show the need to consider multiple goals within training research. The studies also are consistent with calls by Snow (1992) to understand how constructs work together in the light of learning outcomes, as opposed to studying a number of learning and motivational constructs in isolation from one another. In particular, the multiple-goal idea implies that a single intervention to induce a mastery orientation may not always be appropriate or realistic. Instead, we need a better understanding about motivational traits such as goal orientation and a focus on what combination of interventions may be needed to create an effective and longer-lasting learning state.

The idea of multiple pathways can certainly be applied to other personality traits that have relevance for learning beyond goal orientation. For example, training research indicates that high internal locus-of-control individuals tend to be more motivated to learn and learn more than those low on internal locus of control or high on external locus of control. Research is needed that goes beyond these simple effects to address the question of when or under what conditions external locus of control is adaptive rather than maladaptive. In addition, investigators can begin to examine the multiple pathways that lead some externals to positive learning outcomes.

Finally, prior to recommending appropriate interventions to create a learning state such as state mastery orientation, investigators might want to focus more attention on affecting learning processes. For example, efforts could be directed toward having learners use particular study strategies or be devoted to developing skills in planning, monitoring, and evaluating their own learning. Trainees could be asked to set challenging learning goals, visualize possible courses of action, reflect on how much they have learned, and consider whether alternative learning strategies might be more effective. These efforts are more proximal to the desired learning outcomes. What is interesting is the extent to which different personality characteristics affect and are affected by interventions to improve the learning processes of the learner.

Conclusion

Most of the research on traits, situations, and aptitude treatment interactions has been conducted in traditional classroom settings. We have highlighted key advances that need to be made in training research. In meeting this research agenda, it should be noted that there is a trend toward a decrease in instructor-led classroom instruction and an increase in the use of emerging learning technologies such as distance learning, CD-ROM and multimedia instruction, Web-based training, intelligent tutoring systems, and virtual reality training (Goldstein & Ford, 2002). For example, a survey from the American Society of Training and Development suggests that classroom instruction will decline from over 80 percent of all instruction in 1996 to less than 60 percent by 2002 (Bassi & Van Buren, 1998).

The changes in learning technologies also have clear implications for training research. First, the emerging learning technologies allow for a more individualized approach to instruction. For example, Web-based and CD-ROM courses provide a number of hyperlinks that allow individuals to choose how much breadth and depth to go into in the topics in the course. Thus, the learning is more in control of the student's own learning pace, as well as the content to attend to. Second, techniques such as intelligent tutoring systems hold the promise of a learning process that can be individualized or customized to meet the training needs of each learner better. Third, individuals have more choice over when to engage in a learning activity. For example, they may choose when to attend a distance-learning program. Perhaps more important, with courses on CD-ROM or the Web, they can choose to work on a learning activity for a period of time and decide when to stop and return to it later. Finally, most traditional instruction can provide only a minimal amount of time for skilled practice because the practice time must be shared across all members in the course. The promise and potential of virtual reality training is that individuals have more options regarding how much practice they aspire to obtain and how many different scenarios or situations they practice.

Increasing learner control and customization of training provide opportunities for researchers to advance training theory of individual differences and learning while examining issues within relevant and interesting training contexts. Which traits are relevant to study in learner-controlled contexts might vary somewhat from those that have traditionally been examined, although it is an important coincidence that self-efficacy and need for structure are a major aptitude and treatment, respectively, that have gained a foothold in ATI research and at the same time are important characteristics that influence the implementation of new training technologies. The types of individuals who might learn more in a customized training approach over a normative training approach needs to be studied more carefully, so that the cost-benefit analysis of implementing new training technologies can be made more explicit. More generally, we assert a real need for research on creating learning situations, examining relevant aptitude treatment interactions, and studying multiple traits and multiple pathways across traditional and more innovative learning contexts.

References

Ames, C. (1992). Classrooms: Goals, structures, and student motivation. *Journal of Educational Psychology, 84,* 261–271.

Baldwin, T. T., & Ford, J. K. (1988). Transfer of training: A review and directions for future research. *Personnel Psychology, 41,* 63–105.

Baldwin, T. T., Magjuka, R. J., & Loher, B. T. (1991). The perils of participation: Effects of choice of training on trainee motivation and learning. *Personnel Psychology, 44,* 51–65.

Barrick, M. R., & Mount, M. K. (1991). The Big Five personality dimensions and job performance: A meta-analysis. *Personnel Psychology, 44,* 1–26.

Barrios, B. A., & Shigetomi, C. C. (1979). Coping-skills training for the management of anxiety: A critical review. *Behavior Therapy, 10,* 491–522.

Bassi, L. J., & Van Buren, M. E. (1998). The 1998 ASTD state of the industry report. *Training and Development, 52,* 21–43.

Bassi, L. J., & Van Buren, M. E. (1999). Sharpening the leading edge. *Training and Development Magazine, 53,* 7–21. [http://www.astd.org/virtual_community/research/].

Bauer, T. N., Maertz, C. P., Dolan, M. R., & Campion, M. A. (1998). Longitudinal assessment of applicant reactions to employment testing and test outcome feedback. *Journal of Applied Psychology, 83,* 892–903.

Brophy, J. (1998). *Motivating students to learn.* New York: McGraw-Hill.

Brown, K. G., & Ford, J. K. (2002). Using computer technology in training: Building an infrastructure for active learning. In K. Kraiger (Ed.), *Creating, implementing, and managing effective training and development* (pp. 192–233). San Francisco: Jossey-Bass.

Button, S. B., Mathieu, J. E., & Zajac, D. (1996). Goal orientation in organizational research: A conceptual and empirical foundation. *Organizational Behavior and Human Decision Processes, 67,* 26–48.

Campbell, J. P. (1971). Personnel training and development. *Annual Review of Psychology, 22,* 565–602.

Campbell, J. P., & Kuncel, N. R. (2002). Individual and team training. In N. Anderson, D. S. Ones, H. K. Sinangil, & C. Viswesvaran (Eds.), *Handbook of industrial, work, and organizational psychology* (pp. 278–312). Thousand Oaks, CA: Sage.

Chen, G., Gully, S. M., Whiteman, J. A., & Kilcullen, R. N. (2000). Examination of relationships among trait-like individual differences, state-like individual differences, and learning performance. *Journal of Applied Psychology, 85,* 835–847.

Colquitt, J. A., LePine, J. A., & Noe, R. A. (2000). Toward an integrative theory of training motivation: A meta-analytic path analysis of 20 years of research. *Journal of Applied Psychology, 85,* 678–707.

Cronbach, L. J. (1957). The two disciplines of scientific psychology. *American Psychologist, 12,* 671–684.

Cronbach, L. J. (1967). How can instruction be adapted to individual differences? In R. M. Gagné (Ed.), *Learning and individual differences* (pp. 123–144). Columbus, OH: Merrill.

Duke, A. P., & Ree, M. J. (1996). Better candidates fly fewer training hours: Another time testing pays off. *International Journal of Selection and Assessment, 4,* 115–121.

Dweck, C. S. (1986). Motivational processes affecting learning. *American Psychologist, 41,* 1040–1046.

Dweck, C. S., & Leggett, E. L. (1988). A social-cognitive approach to motivation and personality. *Psychological Review, 95,* 256–273.

Elliot, A. J. (1999). Approach and avoidance motivation and achievement goals. *Educational Psychologist, 34,* 169–189.

Elliot, A. J., & Church, M. A. (1997). A hierarchical model of approach and avoidance achievement motivation. *Journal of Personality and Social Psychology, 72,* 218–232.

Elliot, A. J., & McGregor, H. A. (2001). A 2 × 2 achievement goal framework. *Journal of Personality and Social Psychology, 80,* 501–519.

Elliot, A. J., & Thrash, T. M. (2002). Approach-avoidance motivation in personality: Approach and avoid temperaments and goals. *Journal of Personality and Social Psychology, 82,* 804–818.

Endler, N. S., & Magnusson, D. (Eds.). (1976). *Interactional psychology and personality.* New York: Wiley.

Fisher, S. L. (1998). *The role of goal orientation in a self-regulation framework.* Unpublished doctoral dissertation, Michigan State University.

Fleeson, W. (2001). Toward a structure- and process-integrated view of personality: Traits as density distributions of states. *Journal of Personality and Social Psychology, 80,* 1011–1027.

Ford, J. K., & Kraiger, K. (1995). The application of cognitive constructs and principles to the instructional systems model of training: Implications for needs assessment, design, and transfer. In C. L. Cooper & I. T. Robertson (Eds.), *International review of industrial and organizational psychology* (Vol. 10, pp. 1–48). New York: Wiley.

Ford, J. K., Smith, E. M., Weissbein, D. A., Gully, S. M., & Salas, E. (1998). Relationships of goal orientation, metacognitive activity, and practice strategies with learning outcomes and transfer. *Journal of Applied Psychology, 83,* 218–233.

Fosterling, F. (1985). Attributional retraining: A review. *Psychological Bulletin, 98,* 495–512.

Funder, D. C. (2001). Personality. *Annual Review of Psychology, 52,* 197–221.

Goldstein, I. L., & Ford, J. K. (2002). *Training in organizations* (4th ed.). Belmont, CA: Wadsworth.

Gully, S. M., Payne, S. C., Koles, K. L., & Whitman, J. (2002). The impact of error training and individual differences on training outcomes: An attribute-treatment interaction perspective. *Journal of Applied Psychology, 87,* 143–155.

Guthrie, J. T., Wigfield, A., & Von Secker, C. (2000). Effects of integrated instruction on motivation and strategy use in reading. *Journal of Educational Psychology, 92,* 331–341.

Hall, R. H., Dansereau, D. F., & Skaggs, L. P. (1990). The cooperative learner. *Learning and Individual Differences, 2,* 327–336.

Harackiewicz, J. M., Barron, K. E., Carter, S. M., Lehto, A. T., & Elliot, A. J.

(1997). Predictors and consequences of achievement goals in the college classroom: Maintaining interest and making the grade. *Journal of Personality and Social Psychology, 73,* 1284–1295.

Hattrup, K., & Jackson, S. E. (1996). Learning about individual differences by taking situations seriously. In K. R. Murphy (Ed.), *Individual differences and behavior in organizations* (pp. 507–547). San Francisco: Jossey-Bass.

Hicks, W. D., & Klimoski, R. J. (1987). Entry into training programs and its effects on training outcomes: A field experiment. *Academy of Management Journal, 30,* 542–552.

Hough, L. M., & Schneider, R. J. (1996). Personality traits, taxonomies, and applications in organizations. In K. R. Murphy (Ed.), *Individual differences and behavior in organizations* (pp. 31–88). San Francisco: Jossey-Bass.

Kanfer, R. (1990). Motivation and individual differences in learning: An integration of developmental, differential and cognitive perspectives. *Learning and Individual Differences, 2,* 221–239.

Kanfer, R. (1992). Work motivation: New directions in theory and research. In C. L. Cooper & I. T. Robertson (Eds.), *International review of industrial and organizational psychology* (Vol. 7, pp. 1–53). New York: Wiley.

Kanfer, R., Ackerman, P. L., & Heggestad, E. D. (1996). Motivational skills and self regulation for learning: A trait perspective. *Learning and Individual Differences, 8,* 185–209.

Kanfer, R., & Heggestad, E. D. (1997). Motivational traits and skills: A person-centered approach to work motivation. *Research in Organizational Behavior, 19,* 1–56.

Kozlowski, S.W.J., Gully, S. M., Smith, E. A., Nason, E. R., & Brown, K. G. (1995, Aug.). *Sequenced mastery training and advance organizers: Effects on learning, self efficacy, performance and generalization.* Symposium conducted at the Tenth Annual Conference of the Society for Industrial and Organizational Psychology, Orlando, FL.

Kraiger, K., Ford, J. K., & Salas, E. (1993). Application of cognitive, skill-based, and affective theories of learning outcomes to new methods of training evaluation. *Journal of Applied Psychology, 78,* 311–328.

Martocchio, J. J. (1992). Microcomputer usage as an opportunity: The influence of context in employee training. *Personnel Psychology, 45,* 529–552.

Mathieu, J. E., & Martineau, J. W. (1997). Individual and situational influences in training motivation. In J. K. Ford, S.W.J. Kozlowski, K. Kraiger, E. Salas, & M. Teachout (Eds.), *Improving training effectiveness in work organizations* (pp. 193–222). Mahwah, NJ: Erlbaum.

Mathieu, J. E., Tannenbaum, S. I., & Salas, E. (1992). Influences of individual and situational characteristics on measures of training effectiveness. *Academy of Management Journal, 35,* 828–847.

Mischel, W., & Shoda, Y. (1998). Reconciling processing dynamics and personality dispositions. *Annual Review of Psychology, 49,* 229–258.

Mischel, W., Shoda, Y., & Mendoza-Denton, R. (2002). Situation-behavior profiles as a locus of consistency in personality. *Current Directions in Psychological Science, 11,* 50–54.

Mount, M. K., & Barrick, M. R. (1998). Five reasons why the "Big Five" article has been frequently cited. *Personnel Psychology, 51,* 849–857.

Murtha, T. C., Kanfer, R., & Ackerman, P. L. (1996). Towards an interactionist taxonomy of personality and situations: An integrative situational-dispositional representation of personality traits. *Journal of Personality and Social Psychology, 71,* 193–207.

Noe, R. A. (1986). Trainee attributes and attitudes: Neglected influences of training effectiveness. *Academy of Management Review, 11,* 736–749.

Noe, R. A., & Colquitt, J. A. (2002). Planning for training impact: Principles of training effectiveness. In K. Kraiger (Ed.), *Creating, implementing, and managing effective training and development* (pp. 53–79). San Francisco: Jossey-Bass.

Noe, R. A., & Schmitt, N. (1986). The influence of trainee attitudes on training effectiveness: Test of a model. *Personnel Psychology, 39,* 497–523.

Ozer, D. J., & Reise, S. P. (1994). Personality assessment. *Annual Review of Psychology, 45,* 357–388.

Pintrich, P. R. (2000). Multiple goals, multiple pathways: The role of goal orientation in learning and achievement. *Journal of Educational Psychology, 92,* 544–555.

Pintrich, P. R., & DeGroot, E. V. (1990). Motivational and self-regulated learning components of classroom academic performance. *Journal of Educational Psychology, 82,* 33–40.

Quiñones, M. A. (1995). Pretraining context effects: Training assignment as feedback. *Journal of Applied Psychology, 80,* 226–238.

Ree, M. J., Carretta, T. R., & Teachout, M. S. (1995). Role of ability and prior knowledge in complex training performance. *Journal of Applied Psychology, 80,* 721–730.

Riveiro, J.M.S., Cabanach, R. G., & Arias, A. V. (2001). Multiple-goal pursuit and its relation to cognitive, self regulatory, and motivational strategies. *British Journal of Educational Psychology, 71,* 561–572.

Robertson, I. T., & Downs, S. (1989). Work sample tests of trainability: A meta-analysis. *Journal of Applied Psychology, 74,* 402–410.

Rotter, J. B. (1966). Generalized expectancies for internal versus external control of reinforcement. *Psychological Monographs, 609,* 1–69.

Ryan, A. M., & Ployhart, R. E. (2000). Applicants' perceptions of selection procedures and decisions: A critical review and agenda for the future. *Journal of Management, 26,* 565–606.

Savage, R. E., Williges, B. H., & Williges, R. C. (1982). Empirical prediction models for training-group assignment. *Human Factors, 24,* 417–426.

Schmidt, A., & Ford, J. K. (2002). *The role of goal orientations on metacognitive activity and learning outcomes.* Paper presented at the Seventeenth Annual Meeting of the Society for Industrial and Organizational Psychology, Toronto, Ontario.

Shoda, Y. (1999). Behavioral expressions of a personality system. In D. Cervone & Y. Shoda (Eds.), *The coherence of personality* (pp. 155–181). New York: Guilford Press.

Snow, R. E. (1990). New approaches to cognitive and conative assessment in education. *International Journal of Educational Research, 14,* 455–473.

Snow, R. E. (1992). Aptitude theory: Yesterday, today, and tomorrow. *Educational Psychologist, 27,* 5–32.

Spielberger, C. D. (1966). Theory and research on anxiety. In C. D. Spielberger (Ed.), *Anxiety and behavior* (pp. 3–37). Orlando, FL: Academic Press.

Spielberger, C. D. (1977). State-trait anxiety and interactional psychology. In D. Magnusson & N. S. Endler (Eds.), *Personality at the crossroads: Current issues in interactional psychology* (pp. 173–183). Mahwah, NJ: Erlbaum.

Swanson, H. L., O'Connor, J. E., & Cooney, J. B. (1990). An information processing analysis of expert and novice teachers' problem solving. *American Educational Research Journal, 27,* 533–566.

Tubiana, J. H., & Ben-Shakhar, G. (1982). An objective group questionnaire as a substitute for a personal interview in the prediction of success in military training in Israel. *Personnel Psychology, 35,* 349–357.

Volet, S. E. (1991). Modeling and coaching of relevant metacognitive strategies for enhancing university students' learning. *Learning and Instruction, 1,* 319–336.

Warr, P., & Bunce, D. (1995). Trainee characteristics and the outcomes of open learning. *Personnel Psychology, 48,* 347–375.

Weiner, B. (1983). Some methodological pitfalls in attribution research. *Journal of Educational Psychology, 75,* 530–543.

Weiner, B. (1985). Improving the performance of college freshmen with attributional techniques. *Journal of Personality and Social Psychology, 42,* 367–376.

Weissbein, D. A., & Ford, J. K. (2002, Apr.). *Improving training effectiveness through motivation: Creating a learning state intervention.* Paper presented at the Seventeenth Annual Conference for the Society for Industrial and Organizational Psychology, Toronto, Ontario.

Wentzel, K. R. (1991). Social and academic goals at school: Motivation and achievement in context. In M. L. Maher & P. R. Pintrich (Eds.), *Advances in motivation and achievement* (Vol. 7, pp. 185–212). Greenwich, CT: JAI Press.

Wentzel, K. R. (1992). Motivation and achievement in adolescence: A multiple goals perspective. In D. Schunk & J. Meece (Eds.), *Student perceptions in the classroom: Causes and consequences* (pp. 243–264). Mahwah, NJ: Erlbaum.

CHAPTER 10

Focusing on Personality in Person-Organization Fit Research
Unaddressed Issues

Ann Marie Ryan
Amy Kristof-Brown

Kristof-Brown (2000) noted that one can distinguish person-job (PJ) fit, or the match between an applicant's knowledge, skills, and abilities and the job requirements, and person-organization (PO) fit, that is, the match between the person and broader organizational attributes. One of the primary foci of person-environment fit research has been person-vocation (PV) fit (Holland, 1985), or the match between an individual's attributes and preferences and his or her occupation. Furthermore, researchers have recently begun to explore what could be labeled person-group (PG) fit (Barrick, Stewart, Neubert, & Mount, 1998; Kristof-Brown & Stevens, 2001; Chapter Seven, this volume), or the fit between a person and members of his or her immediate work group. In all of these types of fit—PO, PJ, PV, and PG fit—personality may play a role. Furthermore, there are relationships between these (with a poor PV fit, one may also experience poor PJ fit; poor PJ or PG fit might negatively influence perceptions of PO fit), although research has supported their distinctiveness (Kristof-Brown, 2000; Lauver & Kristof-Brown, 2002; Saks & Ashforth, 1997). We focus our chapter solely on PO fit because research on PJ and PV fit and personality is more extensive, PG fit is discussed in Chapter Seven in this volume, and the role of personality in PO fit assessment is less understood.

Our goal in this chapter is not to review the literature on PO fit. Indeed, several comprehensive reviews already exist (Judge & Kristof-Brown, in press; Kristof, 1996; Werbel & Gilliland, 1999). Considerable research has demonstrated that perceptions of PO fit relate to important individual and organizational outcomes (for example, satisfaction, organizational commitment, extra-role behaviors, organizational attraction, hiring decisions, turnover; Cable & Judge, 1997; Judge & Cable, 1997; Lauver & Kristof-Brown, 2002; Kristof-Brown, 2000; Verquer, Beehr, & Wagner, 2001). Instead, we discuss four pertinent issues regarding the role of personality in PO fit.

- Does PO fit on personality even matter?
- When is good PO fit on personality bad, and when is bad PO fit on personality good for individuals and organizations?
- How accurate are personality PO fit perceptions?
- How does fit relate to adaptability?

Does PO Fit on Personality Matter?

When choosing her first academic job from several good offers, Carolyn was most concerned about working in a department that truly valued and rewarded research activity. After two years at "Level 1 U," she began to question her fit as she became more concerned with collegiality than publishing. Without much thought, she accepted a job at Friendly U, where her new colleagues were all agreeable but not particularly conscientious. She realized that although she had felt things were amiss at Level 1 U, she did not experience as much daily frustration there as she now was at Friendly U.

When researchers ask people what PO fit means to them, they provide a wide range of answers. Bretz, Rynes, and Gerhart (1993) and Rynes and Gerhart (1990) reported that recruiters consider such diverse characteristics as grade point average, attractiveness, job-related course work, work experience, articulateness, cognitive ability, cooperative attitude, focus, work ethic, self-confidence, goal orientation, and interpersonal skills in their assessments of fit. Despite this broad array, Kristof (1996) noted that the most frequent operationalization of PO fit in research has been values congruence, or the match between the values of the individual and the organization (Bretz et al., 1993; Cable & Judge, 1996; Cable & Parsons, 2001; Chatman, 1991; Judge & Cable, 1997; Meglino, Ravlin, & Adkins, 1989; O'Reilly & Chatman, 1986; O'Reilly, Chatman, & Caldwell, 1991; Posner, Kouzes, & Schmidt, 1985; Schneider, Goldstein, & Smith, 1995).

In a follow-up investigation, Kristof-Brown (2000) asked recruiters to identify specific characteristics they used to assess PO fit in a set of common job applicants and had independent coders categorize these characteristics as (1) knowledge, skills, and abilities, (2) personality traits, (3) values, or (4) other things. Results indicated that 100 percent of the recruiters mentioned at least one personality trait as indicative of PO fit, whereas only 65 percent mentioned values. These results suggest that personality represents an important but understudied component of PO fit.

Our purpose is not to suggest that personality-based fit is more important than values-based fit, or vice versa. Instead, we hope to clarify the conditions in which each basis of fit is likely to maximize prediction of individual and organizational outcomes. To address this issue, it is necessary to clarify the relation of personality and values. This is not an easy task, as the terms have sometimes been used interchangeably. For example, Campbell (1963) included values and personality, along with habits, attitudes, and beliefs, in a list of acquired behavioral dispositions. Furthermore, studies comparing the two often find support for strong, positive relationships between particular personality traits and specific values. For example, people high on the Five-Factor Model (FFM) trait of openness to experience have been found to consistently hold the values of a "world of beauty" and being "broadminded" and "imaginative" (Dollinger, Leong, & Ulicni, 1996). Extraverts have been found to value comfort and excitement, and people high on neuroticism to value independence and freedom from conflict (Furnham, 1984). Judge and Cable (1997) found that FFM traits predicted organizational culture preferences or values, although they noted that the relations between the two were small.

Despite incidences of corresponding values and personality traits, examining the definitions of these two sets of constructs carefully suggests that they differ in meaningful ways. Values are defined as enduring beliefs about modes of conduct that are personally preferable (Rokeach, 1973). Value attainment has been described as comparing one's life activities to some predetermined standard of success (Hochwarter, Perrewe, Ferris, & Brymer, 1999). They are "what people believe to be important" and what goals they wish to pursue (Schwartz, 1994; Schwartz & Sagiv, 1995). Alternatively, personality traits are "what people are like," or their pervasive tendencies to show consistent patterns of thoughts, feelings, and actions (Herringer, 1998; McCrae & Costa, 1990). Thus, values are fundamentally aspirational or goal oriented, dealing with what a person wants to achieve, whereas personality is more descriptive, concerning how a person prefers to act or strive to achieve their goals.

A second distinction between values and personality is that although both are considered stable, traits are considered to be definably stable, with substantial internal or genetic causes (see Conley, 1984a; Dollinger et al., 1996; Rowe, 1987). Alternatively, values are susceptible to a variety of learned influences including self-confrontation, changes in society, and the influences of new environments (Cable & Parsons, 2001; Dollinger et al., 1996; Judge & Cable, 1997). Rohan (2000), in a review of the values construct, notes that an individual's value system is a way to order which requirements or desires are more or less important to "best possible living." She notes that value priorities will change in response to changes in circumstances as the definition of "best possible living" changes (for example, people tend to become more conservative in values when they become parents).

In the light of these differences, there are several reasons to expect that PO fit based on personality should be at least as influential as fit based on values. First, because values are less stable than personality, fit between a person's and an organization's values might be more susceptible to change over time than fit based on personality. For example, a person who feels achievement is an important value might decide as she ages that interpersonal warmth is more important and change her assessment of PO fit with a given organization. In addition, there are numerous examples in the literature of people's values becoming more congruent with their organization and occupations over time (Hall, Schneider, & Nygren,

1975; Mortimer & Lorence, 1979), although Kraimer (1997) notes that the extent of this change is likely to depend on the strength of initial beliefs. Because an individual's personality is expected to be more stable over time and situations, a PO fit assessment based on personality (I am a conscientious individual, and this is a conscientious organization) should not be expected to change dramatically over time.

A second reason that PO fit based on personality should be as influential as that based on values is that personality is proximal to behavior. Personality defines how a person prefers to behave, whereas values define what a person hopes to achieve. It is reasonable to assume that the former is more closely related to behavioral intentions (and, subsequently, to behaviors) than the latter. Moreover, values are notably equifinal. That is, there are many behaviors that could be used to attain them. Thus, simply knowing someone's values offers little information on the specific behaviors they will use in a particular situation.

A third reason is the relative observability of personality and values. Judge and Cable (1997) note that values may be less observable than personality, and therefore judgments of fit by others (recruiters) may be more likely to be made on personality traits than on the less observable values. Kristof-Brown's results (2000) support this notion.

Based on these considerations of stability, proximity, and visibility, personality-based PO fit should have at least as strong an influence on individuals' attitudes and behaviors than would values-based fit. However, a recent meta-analysis of the PO fit literature suggests that this is not true. In a meta-analysis of fifteen studies, Verquer et al. (2001) found that value congruence had stronger relations with outcomes than did other types of congruence, including personality. When compared with studies assessing fit as goal congruence, personality-climate match, and congruence with core principles and characteristics, value congruence studies showed a slightly larger mean correlation with satisfaction ($r = .24$ versus $r = .22$), organizational commitment ($r = .32$ versus $r = .21$), and intention to quit ($r = -.38$ versus $r = -.15$). While these results combined other types of fit with personality congruence studies, the results suggest that findings in the personality PO fit domain may be weak.

To understand this finding, we believe it is useful to look more closely at how fit is conceptualized and measured in studies of value-based versus personality-based PO fit. In particular, it is important to consider how the "O" is operationalized. In values-based studies, PO fit is typically assessed as the similarity or congruence between an individual's values and those of the organization. It is generally accepted that organizational cultures are characterized by values (Schein, 1992). These can be measured in a variety of ways, such as by examining written statements of espoused values (mission statements, for example) or asking members of the top management team to report the organization's values. When an individual's personal values are matched against company values measured in any of these ways, the type of fit being assessed is supplementary fit (Muchinsky & Monahan, 1987); that is, fit is demonstrated by similarity between individual and organizational characteristics.

Unlike studies of values, which tend to use the congruence approach, a recent review by Judge and Kristof-Brown (in press) reveals that personality fit has been operationalized in as many as six different ways. Of these, most studies of personality-based PO fit can be separated into two general types of fit assessments. The first is similar to value congruence research, in which supplementary fit is inferred if the individual's personality is similar to the organization's personality. One concern with this approach is that although it is widely accepted that organizations have values, the idea of ascribing traits to organizations is more often considered anthropomorphizing (Chatman, 1989). Slaughter et al. (2001) conducted a series of studies to demonstrate that individuals can ascribe human personality traits to organizations. However, they found that there is not a completely commensurate set of traits that is ideal for describing individuals and organizations (that is, some traits relevant for describing individuals are not readily adapted or often used to describe organizations). Because of these challenges, some researchers have resorted to assessing organizational personality as the aggregate of the personality traits of incumbent employees.

Results of studies using this approach to assessing personality-based PO fit have been equivocal at best. Day and Bedeian (1995) examined whether the relationship between an individual's FFM traits and those of current employees predicted important individual-level outcomes in a medical center setting. Although they found a positive relationship between similarity on agreeableness and job performance, their results indicated a negative relationship between conscientiousness congruence and organizational tenure, and no relationship between extraversion similarity and any work-related outcome. Similarly, in a study of 476 managers and professionals working in a large government agency, Tischler (1996) found no evidence of a significant relationship between individuals' similarity to the modal organizational personality type on the Myers-Briggs Type Indicator with either salary increases or number of promotions over time. Finally, in a study of training performance of flight attendants, Ferris, Youngblood, and Yates (1985) found no support for a relationship between newcomer-incumbent personality congruence and withdrawal behaviors, with congruence assessed as the correlation between the employee's 16PF (Cattell, 1970) profile and the profile of an average successful incumbent.

The second way personality-based PO fit is typically assessed is by testing for an interaction between an individual's traits and "objective" organizational characteristics, like reward system or size. Using this approach, commensurate measurement between individual traits and organizational characteristics is not necessary. Unlike studies of personality congruence that evaluate supplementary fit, these studies appear to be assessing complementary fit, in which the environment meets the needs or preferences of the individual (Muchinsky & Monahan, 1987). Thus, the basis for what constitutes a fit is very different in these types of studies. In addition, these studies emphasize fit on specific personality traits, whereas most of the congruence studies assess similarity of individual and organizational personality profiles. Because profile correlations conceal the individual contribution of the specific traits (Edwards, 1993), it is difficult to determine whether there are important fit relationships that are being concealed in the overall profile.

In contrast to the personality congruence studies, results of studies using the interaction approach have successfully demonstrated significant effects of personality-based PO fit. Turban and Keon (1993) found that job seekers' personality characteristics of self-esteem and need for achievement moderated the impact of organizational characteristics such as centralization, size, and reward structure on organizational attraction. Similarly, Bretz and colleagues (Bretz, Ash, & Dreher, 1989; Bretz & Judge, 1994) reported that personality traits including locus of control and risk aversion moderated the relationship between human resource systems and job seekers' attraction to organizations. Cable and Judge (1994) extended these findings with a policy-capturing study that demonstrated that interactions between personality traits (materialism, locus of control, individualism/collectivism, self-efficacy, and risk aversion) and compensation system attributes predicted job choice. Turban, Lau, Ngo, Chow, and Si (2001) found that prospective labor market entrants' risk aversion and need for pay moderated the relationship between type of ownership (wholly owned foreign enterprise versus international joint venture) and organizational attractiveness, probability of seeking an interview, and probability of accepting a job offer. Taken as a whole, these results support the importance of a fit between a wide array of individual personality traits and organizational characteristics.

Reviewing the personality-based PO fit literature reveals a number of important implications. First, there are several reasons to support the notion that examining personality-based PO fit is meaningful. Personality is stable over time and proximal to behaviors, and certain traits are relatively easy to observe. Therefore, the personality fit between a person and an organization is unlikely to change much over time, should influence behavior as well as attitudes, and may be easy for recruiters to assess. Having said that, the empirical evidence suggests that how personality-based PO fit is conceptualized and measured matters a great deal. Specifically, it is a useful predictor when assessed as the complementary fit between individuals and objective organizational characteristics, such as compensation system, centralization, or ownership form. In these instances, the organization is meeting the individual's needs or preferences and therefore providing something that the individual desires. However, when PO fit is measured as the congruence between individuals' personalities and those of others in the organization, it is not typically a useful predictor. This is perhaps not surprising when one considers that the individual interacts with only a small percentage of the total workforce in an organization.

We believe it is more likely that an individual will be influenced by personality compatibility with those in his or her immediate work group. This implies that if fit is to be assessed as personality congruence rather than as an interaction, it may be more influential when assessed as PG rather than PO fit. Constructs at adjacent levels of analysis (person and group) should be more strongly related than those that are more distal (person and organization; Simon, 1973).

Referring back to our example at the beginning of this section, Carolyn was initially unhappy with her position because of a poor PO fit on values. Her values regarding collegiality were not congruent with those of others in her organization. After moving to a new university that shared her value for collegiality, she was struck by the lack of fit in terms of conscientiousness with the others in her department. Because she interacts with these individuals on a daily or at least weekly basis, this lack of fit on personality was negatively affecting her attitudes about her work and coworkers. Both types of misfit (PO misfit on values and PG misfit on personality) resulted in negative consequences for Carolyn.

We believe that an important next step in fit research is to investigate the relative impact of these various types of fit. Kristof-Brown, Jansen, and Colbert (2002) have conducted preliminary research in this area, using a policy-capturing design to demonstrate that PJ, PG, and PO fit each has important independent effects on satisfaction. Their results also showed that people with different amounts and types of work experience weight each type of fit differently and that most individuals use complex strategies for combining their perceptions of these multiple types of fit. Additional research demonstrating when, and for whom, a particular type of fit will be most influential is needed.

In addition, research on personality-based PG fit is clearly necessary. In one of the only studies on PG fit, using separate samples of M.B.A. project teams and long-standing manufacturing teams, Kristof-Brown, Barrick, and Stevens (2001) demonstrated that members' attraction to their teams was highest when their level of extraversion was different from that of their team members. Their results show a complementary fit relationship for the trait of extraversion. Additional personality traits should be investigated to understand more fully how fit on personality operates within teams.

One issue for this research to consider is how best to operationalize the personality of the team or organization. Kristof-Brown et al. (2001) assessed the team's extraversion by using the average of team members minus the person whose fit was being assessed. However, results by Barrick et al. (1998) suggest additional ways in which team personality may be modeled. They described three methods of operationalizing team personality composition: mean score for the group, variability (variance, proportion of members possessing a particular trait), and minimum and maximum scores on a trait. Whether these methods could be applied to the assessment of PG or even PO fit with any meaning is another question worth pursuing.

One final issue is that the question of whether personality-based PO fit matters may be too simplistic. Given our knowledge of the usefulness of certain personality traits as predictors of performance, we could ask whether any organization cares about fit on conscientiousness and emotional stability; instead, firms want to hire individuals high on these traits regardless of the current levels in the workforce. However, PO fit on these two traits will still matter for outcomes such as satisfaction, as the highly conscientious individual will be less satisfied when there is low fit. Thus, it is overly simplistic to talk about PO fit on personality affecting outcomes. We must consider what traits we are talking about and what outcomes we are hoping to predict. We expand on this more fully in the next section.

When Good PO Fit Is Bad and Bad PO Fit Is Good

Juan recalls his short tenure at XYZ Inc. as an unpleasant time but a valuable experience. Juan naturally strives to get along with others, so he was surprised to find himself in a workplace where criticism, backbiting, and overt hostility were the substance of interpersonal interactions. Juan was glad to leave XYZ, though he notes that he learned a lot about dealing with difficult coworkers. He says that now he can more quickly spot what the difficulties will be in working with a particular client and has developed strategies for more effectively handling disagreeable clients.

Schneider, Smith, and Goldstein (2000) argued that traditional PE fit theory argues for positive, individual-level outcomes (higher job satisfaction, lower turnover, greater commitment) from good fit, but that the attraction-selection-attrition (ASA) model suggests negative, organizational-level outcomes from good fit (for example, inability to adapt, less innovation, groupthink). They note that this occurs because the ASA model suggests that organizations will tend toward homogeneity of personality. Schneider and colleagues argue that in general, good fit leads to personality homogeneity and poor organizational health. Thus, the current wisdom is that personality-based PO fit is good for the person and short-term individual affective outcomes, but bad for the organization and long-term performance outcomes.

In this section, we discuss this dark side of personality-based PO fit and when it is likely to occur. Building on some comments of Schneider et al. (2000), we discuss when good PO fit can be bad and, expanding on that, argue that bad PO fit can sometimes result in good consequences. We reiterate that our focus is on PO fit in terms of personality. Schnedier et al. noted that good fit on goals might always be good, but good fit on personality characteristics sometimes might not be.

When discussing the potential dark side of personality fit, it is important to remember the distinctions that we drew in the first section of this chapter. When personality-based PO fit is conceptualized as complementary fit, such that individuals' needs are met by an objective organizational characteristic (compensation system or type of ownership), it is difficult to anticipate negative consequences for individuals. It is possible, of course, that an individual's personality may change in such a way that the organizational characteristic no longer meets his or her needs. However, personality is inherently stable and is therefore unlikely to shift dramatically over time. Conley (1984b) demonstrated that self-opinion traits (self-esteem) are more variable than other types of personality traits, so there is the potential for a person's self-esteem to change over time, thereby changing the level of PO fit. Even in this situation, however, the resulting negative consequences are more likely due to a worsening of PO fit than to negative effects of good fit.

Even if it is unlikely that good complementary personality-based PO fit would have negative consequences for individuals, it is possible that poor complementary fit may offer some individual-level benefits. When there is a poor fit between an individual's personality and organizational characteristics, turnover is only one option. For example, a risk-averse individual who is working in an organization where a large portion of pay is at risk may put more effort into performing well so that his or her pay will be more secure. A person with a high need for achievement working in a flat organization may learn to value lateral moves rather than just promotions. A different but also favorable consequence is that the perception of misfit may lead the individual to become more self-aware and seek other employment options, where his or her needs would be better fulfilled. Research has indicated that many people have inaccurate self-views (see Mabe & West, 1982, for a review), and inconsistent information can lead to questioning one's self-perceptions (Dilto & Lopez, 1992). Thus, misfit may afford an opportunity for development.

When personality-based PO fit is assessed as the congruence between individuals and other members of the organization (supplementary fit), somewhat different outcomes may be expected. The PO fit literature generally discusses congruence (on values or personality) as having only positive consequences for the individual. While we would agree with this in terms of affective outcomes (satisfaction), it may be that good fit can have negative consequences for individual productivity depending on the type of performance required and the personality traits being considered. If performance involves problem solving or decision making, good fit may suppress content-related conflict, which is necessary for high-quality decisions (Chatman, 1989). Therefore, when performance requires creativity or problem solving, poor PO personality fit may offer an advantage. The type of personality trait also is likely to determine the relationship between fit and productivity. For example, an individual low in conscientiousness in an environment with little emphasis on organization and details may be quite satisfied, but his or her lack of persistence is likely to lead to a lowered level of productivity than someone who was a misfit because of higher conscientiousness. This example highlights the fact that the main effects for personality on performance should not be ignored when considering the effects of personality-based PO fit on outcomes.

Furthermore, we propose that the lack of personality congruence with others in the organization could offer potential advantages for people. In the PV fit area, Holland's theory suggests a developmental value to bad fit (Holland, 1985), with individuals learning and adjusting from bad fit experiences (spending a summer working in a psychiatric hospital, for example, may convince an individual to pursue other fields of psychology). As we suggested previously, the person who works in an organization that does not allow for expression of his or her true personality can learn a lot about himself or herself from the experience, as well as a lot to bring to future job situations. The person may decide to learn new behaviors or gain new skills to fit into the company better. This may stimulate an overall increase in adaptability that would benefit the person regardless of his or her organizational circumstances—as in the case of the skills that Juan in our scenario was able to garner from his poor-fit situation. The literature on executive development often points to the need for challenging or stretch opportunities as ways for individuals to grow as leaders (Hall & Mirvis, 1995).

Moos (1987) argues that we should help people select environments that promote personal maturation, not just maximize congruence. For example, it might be good to suggest to a person low in conscientiousness to work with a group of highly conscientious individuals. The strong environment might force this person to attend to things against his or her natural proclivities. Finally, it is possible that by having a different personality from others in the organization, an individual might draw attention to himself or herself in a favorable way. For instance, the extraverted engineer may receive greater accolades and promotions than his or her introverted counterparts because of willingness to self-promote and call attention to past accomplishments. Kristof-Brown et al. (2001) presented evidence from two independent samples that being different from other team members on extraversion leads individuals to view their team as more cohesive and subsequently to contribute more fully to the performance of the team.

An interesting question is whether particular types of individuals might seek organizations where there is less than perfect congruence for reasons of self-enhancement. Pervin (1992) argued that people prefer similarity where they value part of themselves but not where a nonvalued part of the self is involved. He argued that in the latter case, individuals would desire environments seen as taking them in the direction toward which they aspire. Thus, a nonconscientious individual who would like to be more conscientious should prefer an environment that is conscientious. Others have noted that those with a positive self-image prefer environments like their self-image and those with a negative self-image select environments least like their self-image (Keon, Latack, & Wanous, 1982). Thus, low-self-esteem individuals may actually seek out poor fit.

Touting the developmental value of poor personality-based PO fit can be stretched only so far. Personality is stable in adulthood, so we should not expect individuals to change their dispositions after a bad-fit experience. What can be changed is the ability to adapt (see the next section) and ways of coping with an incompatible environment. As Schneider et al. (2000) have also pointed out, not only does the environment act on the person but the person acts on the environment. While someone may be unlikely to change his or her personality because of poor fit, it is possible that the person might attempt to change the environment, with the consequences of such a change depending largely on the nature of the personality characteristic. For example, positive consequences would likely result for an organization from a poor-fitting conscientious individual who raises standards of performance, whereas negative results might be expected for a company with a poor-fitting supervisor high in neuroticism who has a negative effect on the work of others. Moreover, the amount of change will likely depend on the power of the individual, with upper-level managers having a greater impact on the work environment than frontline employees. We encourage researchers to explore more thoroughly the factors that influence an individual's decision to influence the work environment in situations of poor fit.

In none of these cases are we suggesting that the individual will be more satisfied when there is a poor fit. Instead, we propose that poor fit is likely to lead to some kind of discomfort, which in turn *might* lead to development, self-awareness, better performance, or attention from others. The caveat is that the degree of misfit cannot be so extreme as to make the person withdraw or seek other employment.

Shifting the focus from the individual to the organization, we ask, "When is good PO fit bad for the organization?" Schneider et al. (2000) do qualify the assertion that good fit is bad for the organization by noting that it may be bad for certain groups in the organization (top management teams), but that homogeneity for other groups (line workers with little decision-making latitude) may not be so problematic. They also note that good fit may be more problematic in situations such as crises, where a diversity of viewpoints is important. A similar argument can be made with regard to situations requiring innovation. Chatman (1989) argued that high levels of fit could lead to reduced innovation in organizations. Walsh and Holland's review of the PV literature (1992) found negative outcomes of fit for problem solving and decision making, which would be in line with this prediction for PO fit. Thus, good PO fit of members has been suggested as bad for decision-making purposes or in decision-making contexts.

We think that this proposition may need refinement for personality traits that involve adaptability, flexibility, or openness to change. Because these traits deal specifically with the ability to change, excessive levels of these traits are unlikely to lead to stultification or strategic myopia. Indeed, the opposite effect would be expected: the organization would become highly responsive to the environment. Given the rapid nature of change in today's businesses, it is difficult to see how increased responsiveness could have negative consequences for the company. As Schneider et al. (2000) noted, good fit *can* be bad if homogeneity leads to groupthink, but it seems unlikely that homogeneity on personality characteristics dealing with flexibility would create that problem.

In summary, a determination of whether personality PO fit is a good thing should consider the type of fit (congruence/supplementary versus complementary), the specific traits that are being assessed, and the outcomes (affect, performance) to be addressed. Because complementary fit implies that needs are being filled, it is unlikely to generate negative consequences for individuals or organizations in performance or affect. In terms of personality congruence, however, good PO fit may result in positive individual attitudes but not have benefits for productivity, depending on the traits under examination. Moreover, bad fit of either type might result in positive individual consequences for both performance and affect when it leads to growth and development. For organizations, we agree with Schneider and colleagues that good supplementary fit will generally lead to negative consequences in productivity. However, we suggest the caveat that when the trait has to do with flexibility, openness, or adaptability, good fit might actually improve organizational responsiveness and result in positive consequences for the company. Additional research is clearly needed on the individual and organizational-level consequences of good and bad personality fit, with particular attention to traits that represent flexibility and responsiveness and the specific outcomes of concern.

Accuracy of Fit Perceptions

Fiona was delighted with the offer from Acme Corporation. Of all the places she interviewed at, this was the one she really resonated with, where she thought she would fit best. The people she had met, as well as the organization's literature, conveyed a sense of sophisticated, worldly, witty people—just what Fiona longed to be.

After just a short time on the job, however, Fiona was surprised at how misguided her thinking had been. She hardly got a word in at meetings because she was less assertive than her colleagues, so her boss felt she was "not contributing much." She found the wittiness translated into an office where barbs and snipes were used as put-downs. Her lack of experience and frugal lifestyle left her with little to contribute to nonwork discussions about travel abroad and the hottest restaurant in town. How could she have so misjudged her fit with this workplace?

This scenario raises the question, "How accurate are people's fit self-assessments?" Given that relationships have been found between PO fit perceptions and outcomes (turnover, job offer acceptance), it seems plausible to argue that perceptions are at least somewhat accurate. However, studies comparing subjective fit to objective or actual fit indicate a relatively low correlation (Cable & Judge, 1997; Kristof-Brown & Stevens, 2001). Some have argued that fit perceptions are often inaccurate (Cable, Aiman-Smith, Mulvey, & Edwards, 2000; Saks & Ashforth, 1997), particularly when individuals have little information on which to form impressions (job seekers early in the search process).

We would argue that the distinction between complementary and supplementary fit might be important to understanding the accuracy of self-perceptions. Supplementary fit perceptions based on personality may often be inaccurate. Job seekers may lack "organization personality" information. Web sites, brochures, and recruiting activities may not convey much or even accurate information on which to judge personality congruence, even if they contain direct statements of values. The source and accuracy of the information conveyed in recruiting should influence the accuracy of supplementary fit assessments. The realistic job preview (RJP) literature clearly attests to how the nature of information influences expectations (see Phillips, 1998, for a meta-analysis); one would expect that realistic organizational previews that provide information related to personality congruence would be helpful.

Alternatively, complementary fit assessments should be more accurate because they are based on objective organizational characteristics and self-assessments of personality. Thus, the differences already noted in findings of studies examining supplementary and complementary fit based on personality may be reflective of the accuracy with which one can assess the "O" side of the fit equation in these instances.

A second issue with regard to the accuracy of fit assessments is the extent to which individuals are able and willing to change those assessments given feedback regarding objective fit. Dineen, Ash, and Noe (2001) pursued the behavioral plasticity hypothesis with regard to self-esteem and fit, which would suggest that those with low self-esteem would be more affected by fit feedback when forming impressions of attraction than high self-esteem individuals who are less behaviorally malleable. They found that high self-esteem individuals were more likely to follow their objective fit regardless of whether they were given feedback regarding high or low fit with the organization; individuals with low self-esteem deviated from their objective fit when told they did not fit. They did not find a similar effect for conscientiousness. Thus, personality traits may influence how individuals respond to information about fit and the extent to which they can adjust fit assessments. Stated another way, are there certain types of individuals who misjudge fit more often than others? Could these be individuals with less accurate self-assessments? Or are these individuals who look in terms of aspirations (what one would like to be) rather than what is and seek an environment that will affect the self? We expect that certain individual differences are related to the accuracy of fit assessments (self-esteem) just as they are related to the accuracy of self-assessments (Mabe & West, 1982).

It is also important to understand whether organizational representatives can accurately assess personality-based PO fit. Cable and Judge (1997) found that interviewers' assessments of applicants' values and PO fit were fairly inaccurate (there was a fairly small relation between actual and perceived values congruence). However, recruiters often rely on personality assessments in making fit judgments (Kristof-Brown, 2000). A considerable literature shows that strangers or acquaintances can assess certain personality traits with some accuracy after brief exposure to people (Albright, Kenny, & Malloy, 1988; Borkenau & Liebler, 1993; Colvin & Funder, 1991; Funder & Colvin, 1988; Gangestad, Simpson, DiGeronimo, & Biek, 1992). In work with recruiters, Barrick, Patton, and Haughland (2000) found moderate correlations between interviewer assessments of personality traits and self-reports; however, they found that interviewers were more accurate in assessing Extraversion than Emotional Stability and Conscientiousness. One question would be what the relative roles of various traits are in recruiter fit assessments. Reliance on traits that have a social component, and are thus more likely to be evident during interpersonal interactions, should have better predictive validity for fit assessments than reliance on less accurately evaluated traits. However, it is interesting to note that in terms of overall performance, the less observable traits of Conscientiousness and Emotional Stability are better predictors (Barrick & Mount, 1991).

In summary, we suggest that personality-based fit assessments that are complementary may be more accurate than those that are supplementary (evaluations of personality congruence). We further note that there are likely individual differences in the ability to self-assess fit accurately. Finally, recruiter assessments of personality congruence may possess some degree of accuracy for certain traits.

Adaptability and Fit

Lauren believes that we all should make the best of our situation, whatever it is. Al believes, "to thine own self be true." Both are organized and efficient workers who avoid missing deadlines, pay attention to details, and willingly pitch in to help others. At eAcme, a growing Internet startup, Lauren initially found the lack of planning, the last-minute calls to work all night to meet a deadline, and the many slip-ups to be somewhat of a shock. However, she applied her philosophy and learned to work within the environment, maintaining organization in what she did, but not letting the poor planning of others cause her stress (it served as a source of amusing stories over dinner with her husband). Al, in contrast, feels perpetually frustrated at work and resents having to "mop up" the problems of others. He feels an urgent need to find a new job. What leads Lauren to be able to adapt to a poor fit and Al not to?

Muchinsky and Monahan (1987) noted that whether a good fit today will be a good fit tomorrow depends on the stability of the variables on which matches are made. We have already noted that personality is viewed as stable in adulthood; however, today's organizational environments have been characterized as more fluid than ever before, with the only constant being change (Howard, 1995; Offerman & Gowing, 1990). Organizations are seeking adaptable people so that they might be responsive to organizational change (LePine, Colquitt, & Erez, 2000). Thus, the final research area that we address is the relationship of adaptability to personality-based PO fit.

We see a wealth of research opportunities related to the emphasis in hiring practices on seeking both adaptability and fit. First, if an organization selects adaptable individuals, how important is initial fit? Would adaptable individuals simply adapt to whatever organizational environment is present? Second, in organizations where most employees have good personality-based supplementary PO fit, there will be little need to adapt in terms of internal organizational environments because of the homogeneity. But will the organization necessarily fail to adapt to the external environment and fail (as Schneider, 2001, suggests) if all of these good-fitting employees are also high in adaptability? Third, does adaptability lead one to change oneself to increase PO fit, assess environments as having good fit regardless of their characteristics, or develop effective strategies for coping with poor fit? In terms of our scenario, why is Lauren able to adapt and Al is not?

Morrison and Hall (2001) present a model of adaptability that may prove useful for this discussion. They propose that adaptability consists of adaptive competence (the ability to change) and adaptive motivation (the willingness to change). Perhaps those high in adaptive competence may not need good fit to be successful; they can change to fit the situation. Those low in adaptive motivation may need good fit to be satisfied; they are unwilling to change to secure PO fit.

Besides understanding the relationship of adaptability and personality-based PO fit, we also need research on how to enhance both adaptation and PO fit. The topic of adjustment and PE fit is a long-standing one (Caplan & VanHarrison, 1993), with an interest on who generates the ways to cope with poor fit, that is, the individual or an imposed intervention. For example, an organization might increase fit through interventions that aid self-selection, such as RJPs (Wanous, 1992), and interventions that aid adaptation, such as orientation programs (Cable & Parsons, 2001; Klein & Weaver, 2000). However, Cable and Parsons (2001) found that firms using random, variable tactics of socialization might be decreasing values congruence, suggesting that poorly planned or poorly implemented interventions can leave individuals without the tools needed to adapt or to a worsening of fit. Further research on socialization that examines how poor fit can be decreased or adjusted to is needed.

There is a need to integrate research on the effects of personality on adaptation with that on personality-based PO fit. For example, LePine et al. (2000) found that Openness to Experience was positively related to decision-making performance after change, and the dependability facets of Conscientiousness were negatively related to adaptation. This might be interpreted as suggesting that individuals low in openness or high in dependability may be less able to cope with poor-fit situations than others. Alternatively, it may be that in this particular context (a decision-making task), there is low fit on these traits, but they do not affect adaptation to poor fit situations in general. Furthermore, as LePine et al. point out, adaptability in task performance or to planned changes may relate to different traits than adaptability in contextual behaviors or to shifting organizational missions. Thus, the role of personality congruence in adaptation may be contingent on the nature of the adaptation.

In summary, we need to investigate how adaptive competence and adaptive motivation relate to adjustment to poor-fit situations and responsiveness to organizational interventions to enhance fit. We need to discover whether the role of personality traits in adaptation to change is related to personality congruence (supplementary fit).

Conclusion

We have raised four issues of relevance to understanding the role of personality in PO fit assessments. First, we considered the question of whether personality-based PO fit even matters. Because of the stability, proximity, and visibility of personality, we argue strongly that PO fit on personality does matter, but that it depends on the specific type of fit that is being assessed. Our review of the literature suggests that when personality-based PO fit is measured as complementary fit rather than personality congruence, stronger results are found.

The second question we addressed was when good PO fit on personality has negative consequences and when bad PO fit might actually benefit individuals and organizations. In particular, we described the positive outcomes of bad fit when it leads to growth and development and when good fit exists on characteristics that involve flexibility and adaptability.

Third, we considered the accuracy of personality-based PO fit perceptions and concluded that again it depends on whether complementary or supplementary fit is being considered and the specific traits involved. Complementary fit should be more accurately assessed because it tends to be based on personal needs and objective organizational characteristics, whereas supplementary fit is more contingent on accurate assessments of others' personalities. More visible personality traits (those that involve a social component) should lead to more accurate fit assessments by recruiters, coworkers, and other observers. Moreover, we suggest that individuals may systematically differ in the extent to which they accurately perceive fit and are willing to change themselves or the environment in order to increase fit.

Finally, we discussed what we see as a fruitful area for future research: the link between personality-based PO fit and adaptability. Although we do not claim to answer the four questions we set out at the beginning of the chapter, we hope that by raising them and discussing the issues that are relevant to their resolution, we will inspire further research on personality-based PO fit.

References

Albright, L., Kenny, D. A., & Malloy, T. E. (1988). Consensus in personality judgments at zero acquaintance. *Journal of Personality and Social Psychology, 55,* 387–395.

Barrick, M. R., & Mount, M. K. (1991). The Big Five personality dimensions and job performance: A meta-analysis. *Personnel Psychology, 44,* 1–26.

Barrick, M. R., Patton, G. K., & Haughland, S. N. (2000). Accuracy of interviewer judgments of job applicant personality traits. *Personnel Psychology, 53,* 925–951.

Barrick, M. R., Stewart, G. L., Neubert, M. J., & Mount, M. K. (1998). Relating member ability and personality to work-team processes and team effectiveness. *Journal of Applied Psychology, 78,* 111–118.

Borkenau, P., & Liebler, A. (1993). Convergence of stranger ratings of personality and intelligence with self-ratings, partner ratings, and measured intelligence. *Journal of Personality and Social Psychology, 65,* 546–553.

Bretz, R. D., Ash, R. A., & Dreher, G. F. (1989). Do the people make the place? An examination of the attraction-selection-attrition hypothesis. *Personnel Psychology, 42,* 561–581.

Bretz, R. D., & Judge, T. A. (1994). The role of human resource systems in job applicant decision processes. *Journal of Management, 20,* 531–551.

Bretz, R. D., Rynes, S. L., & Gerhart, B. (1993). Recruiter perceptions of applicant fit: Implications for individual career preparation and job search behavior. *Journal of Vocational behavior, 43,* 310–327.

Cable, D. M., Aiman-Smith, L., Mulvey, P., & Edwards, J. R. (2000). The sources and accuracy of job seekers' organizational culture beliefs. *Academy of Management Journal, 43,* 1076–1085.

Cable, D., & Judge, T. A. (1994). Pay preferences and job search decisions: A person-organization fit perspective. *Personnel Psychology, 47,* 317–348.

Cable, D. M., & Judge, T. A. (1996). Person-organization fit, job choice decisions, and organizational entry. *Organizational Behavior and Human Decision Processes, 67,* 294–311.

Cable, D. M., & Judge, T. A. (1997). Interviewers' perceptions of person-organization fit and organizational selection decisions. *Journal of Applied Psychology, 82,* 546–561.

Cable, D. M., & Parsons, C. K. (2001). Socialization tactics and person-organization fit. *Personnel Psychology, 54,* 1–24.

Campbell, D. T. (1963). Social attitudes and other acquired behavioral dispositions. In S. Koch (Ed.), *Psychology: The study of a science* (Vol. 6, pp. 94–172). New York: McGraw-Hill.

Caplan, R. D., & VanHarrison, R. (1993). Person-environment fit theory: Some history, recent developments, and future directions. *Journal of Social Issues, 49,* 253–275.

Cattell, R. B. (1970). The profile similarity coefficient, *rp,* in vocational guidance and diagnostic classification. *Journal of Educational Psychology, 39,* 131–142.

Chatman, J. A. (1989). Improving interactional organizational research: A model of person-organization fit. *Academy of Management Review, 14,* 333–349.

Chatman, J. A. (1991). Matching people and organizations: Selection and socialization in public accounting firms. *Administrative Science Quarterly, 36,* 459–484.

Colvin, C. R., & Funder, D. C. (1991). Predicting personality and behavior: A boundary on the acquaintanceship effect. *Journal of Personality and Social Psychology, 60,* 884–894.

Conley, J. J. (1984a). Longitudinal consistency of adult personality: Self-reported psychological characteristics across 45 years. *Journal of Personality and Social Psychology, 47,* 1325–1333.

Conley, J. J. (1984b). The hierarchy of consistency: A review and model of longitudinal findings on adult individual differences in intelligence, personality and self-opinion. *Personality and Individual Differences, 5,* 11–25.

Day, D. V., & Bedeian, A. G. (1995). Personality similarity and work-related outcomes among African American nursing personnel: A test of the supplementary model of person-environment congruence. *Journal of Vocational Behavior, 46,* 55–70.

Dilto, P. H., & Lopez, D. F. (1992). Motivated skepticism: Use of differential decision criteria for preferred and nonpreferred conclusions. *Journal of Personality and Social Psychology, 63,* 568–584.

Dineen, B. R., Ash, S. R., & Noe, R. A. (2001, Apr.). *A web of applicant attraction and self-selection: Person-organization fit in the context of web-based recruitment.* Paper presented at the Annual Meetings of the Society for Industrial and Organizational Psychology, San Diego, CA.

Dollinger, S. J., Leong, F.T.L., & Ulicni, S. K. (1996). On traits and values: With special reference to openness to experience. *Journal of Research in personality, 30,* 23–41.

Edwards, J. R. (1993). Problems with the use of profile similarity indices in the study of congruence in organizational research. *Personnel Psychology, 46,* 641–665.

Ferris, G. R., Youngblood, S. A., & Yates, V. L. (1985). Personality, training performance, and withdrawal: A test of the person-group fit hypothesis for organizational newcomers. *Journal of Vocational Behavior, 27,* 377–388.

Funder, D. C., & Colvin, C. R. (1988). Friends and strangers: Acquaintanceship, agreement and accuracy of personality judgment. *Journal of Personality and Social Psychology, 55,* 149–158.

Furnham, A. (1984). Personality and values. *Personality and Individual Differences, 5,* 483–485.

Gangestad, S. W., Simpson, J. A., DiGeronimo, K., & Biek, B. (1992). Differential accuracy in person perception across traits: Examination of a functional hypothesis. *Journal of Personality and Social Psychology, 62,* 688–698.

Hall, D. T., & Mirvis, P. H. (1995). Careers as lifelong learning. In A. Howard (Ed.), *The changing nature of work* (pp. 323–362). San Francisco: Jossey-Bass.

Hall, D. T., Schneider, B., & Nygren, H. T. (1975). Personal factors in organizational identification. *Administrative Science Quarterly, 15,* 176–190.

Herringer, L. G. (1998). Relating values and personality traits. *Psychological Reports, 83,* 953–954.

Hochwarter, W. A., Perrewe, P. L., Ferris, G. R., & Brymer, R. A. (1999). Job satisfaction and performance: The moderating effects of value attainment and affective disposition. *Journal of Vocational Behavior, 54,* 296–313.

Holland, J. L. (1985). *Making vocational choices: A theory of vocational personalities and work environments* (2nd ed.). Upper Saddle River, NJ: Prentice Hall.

Howard, A. (1995). A framework for work change. In A. Howard (Ed.), *The changing nature of work* (pp. 3–44). San Francisco: Jossey-Bass.

Judge, T. A., & Cable, D. M. (1997). Applicant personality, organizational culture, and organization attraction. *Personnel Psychology, 50,* 359–394.

Judge, T. A., & Kristof-Brown, A. L. (in press). Personality, interactional psychology, and person-organization fit. In B. Schneider & B. Smith (Eds.), *Personality and organizations.* Mahwah, NJ: Erlbaum.

Keon, T. L., Latack, J. C., & Wanous, J. P. (1982). Image congruence and the treatment of difference scores in organizational choice research. *Human Relations, 35,* 155–166.

Klein, H. J., & Weaver, N. A. (2000). The effectiveness of an organizational-level orientation training program in the socialization of new hires. *Personnel Psychology, 53,* 47–66.

Kraimer, M. L. (1997). Organizational goals and values: A socialization model. *Human Resource Management Review, 7,* 425–447.

Kristof, A. L. (1996). Person-organization fit: An integrative review of its conceptualizations, measurement, and implications. *Personnel Psychology, 49,* 1–49.

Kristof-Brown, A. L. (2000). Perceived applicant fit: Distinguishing between recruiters' perceptions of person-job and person-organization fit. *Personnel Psychology, 53,* 643–671.

Kristof-Brown, A. L., Barrick, M., & Stevens, C. K. (2001). *A test of competing models of person-group fit on extraversion.* Paper presented at the Annual Academy of Management Meeting, Washington, DC.

Kristof-Brown, A. L., Jansen, K. J., & Colbert, A. E. (2002). A policy-capturing study of the simultaneous effects of fit with jobs, groups, and organizations. *Journal of Applied Psychology, 87,* 985–993.

Kristof-Brown, A. L., & Stevens, C. K. (2001). Goal congruence in project teams: Does the fit between members' personal mastery and performance goals matter? *Journal of Applied Psychology, 86,* 1083–1095.

Lauver, K. J., & Kristof-Brown, A. L. (2002). Distinguishing between employees' perceptions of person-job and person-organization fit. *Journal of Vocational Behavior, 59,* 454–470.

LePine, J. A., Colquitt, J. A., & Erez, A. (2000). Adaptability to changing task contexts: Effects of general cognitive ability, conscientiousness, and openness to experience. *Personnel Psychology, 53,* 563–594.

Mabe, P. A., & West, S. G. (1982). Validity of self-evaluation of ability: A review of and a metanalysis. *Journal of Applied Psychology, 67,* 280–296.

McCrae, R. R., & Costa, P. T. (1990). *Personality in adulthood.* New York: Guilford Press.

Meglino, B. M., Ravlin, E. C., & Adkins, C. L. (1989). A work values approach to corporate culture: A field test of the value congruence process and its relationship to individual outcomes. *Journal of Applied Psychology, 74,* 424–432.

Moos, R. H. (1987). Person-environment congruence in work, school, and health care settings. *Journal of Vocational Behavior, 31,* 231–247.

Morrison, R. F., & Hall, D. T. (2001). *Individual adaptability and its antecedents.* Paper presented at the Annual Conference of the Society for Industrial and Organizational Psychology, San Diego, CA.

Mortimer, J. T., & Lorence, J. (1979). Work experience and occupational value socialization. *American Journal of Sociology, 84,* 1361–1385.

Muchinsky, P. M., & Monahan, C. J. (1987). What is person-environment congruence? Supplementary versus complementary models of fit. *Journal of Vocational Behavior, 31,* 268–277.

Offermann, L. R., & Gowing, M. K. (1990). Organizations of the future. *American Psychologist, 45,* 95–108.

O'Reilly, C. A., & Chatman, J. A. (1986). Organization commitment and psychological attachment: The effects of compliance, identification, and internalization on prosocial behavior. *Journal of Applied Psychology, 71,* 492–499.

O'Reilly, C. A., Chatman, J. A., & Caldwell, D. F. (1991). People and organizational culture: A profile comparison approach to assessing person-organization fit. *Academy of Management Journal, 34,* 487–516.

Pervin, L. A. (1992). Transversing the individual-environment landscape: A personal odyssey. In W. B. Walsh, K. H. Craik, & R. H. Price (Eds.), *Person-environment psychology* (pp. 71–87). Mahwah, NJ: Erlbaum.

Phillips, J. M. (1998). Effects of realistic job previews on multiple organizational outcomes: A meta-analysis. *Academy of Management Journal, 41,* 673–690.

Posner, B. Z., Kouzes, J. M., & Schmidt, W. H. (1985). Shared values make a difference: An empirical test of corporate culture. *Human Resource Management, 24,* 293–309.

Rohan, M. J. (2000). A rose by any name? The values construct. *Personality and Social Psychology Review, 4,* 255–277.

Rokeach, M. (1973). *The nature of human values.* New York: Free Press.

Rowe, D. (1987). Resolving the person-situation debate: Invitation to an interdisciplinary dialogue. *American Psychologist, 42,* 218–227.

Rynes, S. L., & Gerhart, B. (1990). Interviewer assessments of applicant "fit": An exploratory investigation. *Personnel Psychology, 43,* 13–35.

Saks, A. M., & Ashforth, B. (1997). A longitudinal investigation of the relationships between job information sources, applicant perceptions of fit, and work outcomes. *Personnel Psychology, 50,* 395–426.

Schein, E. (1992). *Organizational culture and leadership.* San Francisco: Jossey-Bass.

Schneider, B. (2001). *E = f(P, B) + e: Evolution of the ASA Model.* Paper presented at the Annual Conference of the Society for Industrial and Organizational Psychology, San Diego, CA.

Schneider, B., Goldstein, H. W., & Smith, D. B. (1995). The ASA framework: An update. *Personnel Psychology, 48,* 747–773.

Schneider, B., Smith, D. B., & Goldstein, H. W. (2000). Attraction-selection-attrition: Toward a person-environment psychology of organizations. In W. B. Walsh, K. H. Craik, & R. H. Price (Eds.), *Person-environment psychology: New directions and perspectives* (pp. 61–85). Mahwah, NJ: Erlbaum.

Schwartz, S. H. (1994). Are there universal aspects in the structure and contents of human values? *Journal of Social Issues, 50,* 19–45.

Schwartz, S. H., & Sagiv, L. (1995). Identifying culture-specifics in the content and structure of values. *Journal of cross-cultural psychology, 26,* 92–116.

Simon, H. A. (1973). The organization of complex systems. In H. H. Patee (Ed.), *Hierarchy theory* (pp. 1–27). New York: Braziller.

Slaughter, J. E., Zickar, M. J., Highhouse, S., Mohr, D. C., Steinbrenner, D.,

& O'Connor, J. (2001, Apr.). *Personality trait inferences about organizations: Development of a measure and tests of the congruence hypothesis.* Paper presented at the Annual Conference of the Society for Industrial and Organizational Psychology, San Diego, CA.

Tischler, L. (1996). Comparing person-organization personality fit to work success. *Journal of Psychological Type, 38,* 34–43.

Turban, D. B., & Keon, T. L. (1993). Organizational attractiveness: An interactionist perspective. *Journal of Applied Psychology, 78,* 184–193.

Turban, D. B., Lau, C., Ngo, H., Chow, I.H.S., & Si, S. X. (2001). Organizational attractiveness of firms in the People's Republic of China: A person-organization fit perspective. *Journal of Applied Psychology, 86,* 194–206.

Verquer, M. L., Beehr, T. A., & Wagner, S. (2001, Apr.). *Narrative and meta-analytical reviews of person-organization fit research: Conceptual and measurement issues and relationships with work attitudes.* Paper presented at the Annual Conference of the Society for Industrial and Organizational Psychology, San Diego, CA.

Walsh, B. W., & Holland, J. L. (1992). A theory of personality types and work environments. In B. W. Walsh, K. H. Craik, & R. H. Price (Eds.), *Person-environment psychology: Models and perspectives* (pp. 35–69). Mahwah, NJ: Erlbaum.

Wanous, J. P. (1992). *Organizational entry.* Reading, MA: Addison-Wesley.

Werbel, J. D., & Gilliland, S. W. (1999). Person-environment fit in the selection process. In G. R. Ferris (Ed.), *Research in personnel and human resource management* (Vol. 17, pp. 209–243). Greenwich, CT: JAI Press.

CHAPTER 11

Emerging Trends and Needs in Personality Research and Practice
Beyond Main Effects

Leaetta M. Hough

Changes in world economies and their workforces continue to change the world of work, and thus the practice and science of industrial/ organizational (I/O) psychology. Movement from an industrial economy to a service and information economy, globalization, digitization, workforce diversity, and the increasingly rapid rate of change have created work settings that require different competencies and different models for understanding and explaining behavior. I/O psychologists have responded, and personality constructs and theories have provided the content for advances in I/O thinking (Hough, 2001).

Brief History

During a dark ages period from about 1965 to 1985, the accepted wisdom was that personality variables explained little, if any, variance in outcomes of interest to I/O psychologists. Personality variables played virtually no role in our field's models and theories of performance.

Then during the 1990s, personality variables experienced a renaissance with a phoenix-like rise to prominence. Research surged.

Meta-analyses that grouped personality measures into constructs, such as the Five-Factor Model (FFM) of personality, allowed previously obscured relationships between personality constructs and criteria to emerge. Personality variables were related to criteria of interest. They accounted for significant variance above and beyond cognitive variables and experience; personality variables were shown to have main effects. A renaissance occurred in the research and use of personality variables in the workplace.

Project A, the major research project in our field during the 1980s, provided incontrovertible evidence of the importance of personality variables for understanding and predicting behavior at work (see Campbell & Knapp, 2001, for a description of the project and many of its findings). Project A had a number of seminal findings:

- When validity coefficients from previous validity studies are summarized according to personality constructs and criterion constructs, meaningful relationships emerge (Hough, Eaton, Dunnette, Kamp, & McCloy, 1990).
- Different personality constructs predict different work performance criteria (Hough et al., 1990).
- Socially desirable responding can be detected; more important, it affects criterion-related validity minimally, if at all (Hough et al., 1990).
- Cognitive ability tests predict some performance criteria better than personality scales (for example, "can do" criteria), whereas personality scales predict other criteria better than cognitive ability tests ("will do" criteria; McHenry, Hough, Toquam, Hanson, & Ashworth, 1990).
- Accuracy of prediction increases when personality variables are combined with cognitive ability measures (McHenry et al., 1990).
- When personality variables are added to models of the determinants of supervisory ratings of performance, variance explained increases significantly (Borman, White, Pulakos, & Oppler, 1991).

These findings fueled interest in personality variables during the 1990s.

Barrick and Mount's meta-analysis (1991) of the criterion-related validities of the Big Five personality variables for predicting performance criteria provided the next critically important set of findings that focused I/O attention on the relevance of personality variables for predicting performance at work. Indeed, this meta-analysis became the most cited *Personnel Psychology* article in the 1990s (Hollenbeck, 1998). The Project A findings, the Barrick and Mount meta-analysis, and earlier research by such eminent personality psychologists as Paul Costa, Lew Goldberg, Harrison Gough, Robert Hogan, Douglas Jackson, Robert McCrae, and Auke Tellegen provided a solid foundation for the renaissance of personality variables in I/O in the 1990s.

Change in Models of Work Performance

The nature of work and work performance has changed dramatically (Howard, 1995; Ilgen & Pulakos, 1999). Virtually all aspects of work and many worker requirements have changed. Much more than ever before, work is team based, service and information oriented, and digital. Organizations and teams are flatter, even virtual. The job description, reflecting a stable description of the job incumbent's duties and responsibilities, is no longer a ubiquitous phenomenon. Stable job descriptions still exist in many settings, but most work settings today require flexibility and quick response to rapidly changing business conditions. Our theories and models needed, and still need, a different set of variables.

Early Models of Performance

Hunter (1983) meta-analytically investigated the relationships among three variables: cognitive ability, job knowledge, and performance (measured with work samples and supervisory ratings). Path analyses supported a causal model in which cognitive ability is indirectly related to supervisory ratings of performance through its direct effects on job knowledge and work sample performance (both directly related to supervisory ratings of performance). Job knowledge is directly related to both work sample performance and supervisory ratings of performance. Hunter (1983) recognized that other factors "account for a very large part of the variation in ratings" (p. 265).

Guion (1983) critiqued Hunter's model (1983), concluding that "although Hunter has found some validity for ratings, he has not found much" (p. 269). Guion suggested that the model should be enlarged to include characteristics of ratees (appearance, annoyance syndrome, frequency of communication with a supervisor, and interpersonal skill), characteristics of raters (bigotry, cognitive complexity, and leadership roles), and context variables (level of peer performance, quality of equipment and material, and incentives).

Nonetheless, the next major addition to the causal model was job experience (opportunity to learn). Schmidt, Hunter, and Outerbridge (1986) added this variable to their causal model of the determinants of performance, finding it had a role similar to cognitive ability: an indirect effect on supervisory ratings of job performance through its direct effect on both job knowledge and work sample performance.

Later Models of Performance

Although personality constructs were not among the variables in Hunter's model (1983), Guion's enlarged model (1983), or Schmidt et al.'s expanded model (1986), they now play prominent roles in theories and models of the determinants of work performance.

Broad Models

Using Project A data, Borman et al. (1991) partially confirmed Hunter's model (1983), but accounted for more than twice the variance in ratings with a model that added achievement orientation, dependability, awards, and disciplinary actions (for problem behavior). In this expanded model, achievement orientation and dependability had both a direct influence on supervisory ratings and an indirect influence through their substantial effects on awards and disciplinary actions, respectively. The analyses demonstrated the importance of personality constructs as determinants of supervisory ratings of performance and highlighted the role of dependability in the acquisition of job knowledge.

Additional personality variables were included in the Borman, White, and Dorsey (1995) model. They identified four personality factors—dependability, friendly, obnoxious, and show-off—and examined their effects, as well as the effects of cognitive ability, job knowledge, technical proficiency, and performance ratings, on supervisory and peer ratings. Dependability influenced performance as it had in the Borman et al. (1991) study. Friendly (or agreeableness) did not influence overall performance ratings provided by either supervisors or peers, whereas obnoxious influenced (negatively) peer ratings of overall performance but not supervisor ratings, and show-off influenced peer ratings of overall performance (positive correlation, acting perhaps as suppressor variable) but not supervisor ratings. With the inclusion of the three personality variables—dependability, show-off (a compound variable consisting of high Extraversion and low Agreeableness according to Hough & Ones, 2001), and obnoxious—variance accounted for in supervisor ratings of overall job performance was approximately twice that accounted for by the Hunter (1983) model and more than two and a half times for peer ratings.

The Borman et al. models (1991, 1995) are certainly improvements over the Hunter (1983) and Schmidt et al. (1986) models. Nonetheless, even the Borman et al. models are hampered by the kinds of jobs studied, use of overall job performance as the outcome variable (albeit a carefully developed criterion), and inadequate theory. The Borman et al. (1995) study examined determinants of supervisory and peer ratings of overall job performance of soldiers in five military jobs: infantrymen, armor crew members, radio teletype operators, light wheel vehicle mechanics, and medical specialists. (The Borman et al., 1991, study also included only soldiers in military jobs.) Borman et al. studied the determinants of the performance as measured by raters, hence the thought that ratee agreeableness might be relevant.

However, a good theory about the determinants of overall performance in military jobs is not likely to include ratee agreeableness as a determinant. Meta-analytic evidence existing at the time indicated that across jobs, agreeableness is not related to overall job performance (Barrick & Mount, 1991; Hough, 1992; Hough et al., 1990), and even more important for military jobs, agreeableness is not related to combat effectiveness but rugged individualism is

(Hough, 1992). Rather than demonstrating that agreeableness is not a determinant of performance, the Borman et al. (1995) study demonstrates that ratee agreeableness is not a factor in influencing subjective ratings of overall performance made by peers or supervisors of several military jobs. If, instead of military jobs, civilian jobs involving significant customer contact had been studied, agreeableness might have been a causal factor in determining overall performance (Frei & McDaniel, 1998; Hurtz & Donovan, 2000; Mount, Barrick, & Stewart, 1998). If instead of overall performance, teamwork had been the outcome variable, ratee agreeableness might have been a causal factor in determining soldier performance (Hough, 1992; Mount et al., 1998; Neuman & Wright, 1999), especially since it was a garrisoned force. Our theories, and hence our models, need to be more specific yet more integrative in terms of causal and outcome variables.

More Specific Models

Theories with more specific independent, dependent, and intervening variables, type and form of the relationships, and situational variables that moderate or define the limits of generalizability are needed. A step in the right direction is Motowidlo, Borman, and Schmit's framework (1997) for a theory of individual differences in task and contextual performance. Although they do not specify the precise variables and relationships, they do describe in general the kinds of variables and their roles in determining two types of performance. Similarly, Robertson and Callinan (1998) provide a framework for a theory of specific determinants of performance that incorporates genetic and perceptual factors as well. These frameworks provide useful guides to future theory building and research.

New Directions: Dependent Variables

We make many choices when building models and conducting research. An especially important set of choices involves the outcome variables, that is, the dependent or criterion variables in our models. The relationships between personality variables and a wide variety of criteria have been examined. Most of our research and hence knowledge relates to individual-level performance variables, although research with teams has focused our attention on group-level performance variables as well. In addition, our theories and models need to be sensitive to change in performance over time (the dynamic criteria), hence changes in relationships between variables over time (Hough & Oswald, 2000), as well as differences that may be due to other characteristics of criteria, such as typical versus maximum performance.

Individual-Level Performance Variables

Although research examining the determinants of overall job performance is extremely important, the array of other criterion variables relevant to the world of work is enormous. In addition to overall job performance, personality variables have main effects on a variety of other important outcome variables. Examples are counterproductive behavior, contextual performance, task performance, educational and training outcomes, career success, life satisfaction, job satisfaction, accidents, stress, decision making under stress, goal setting, conflict attributions, workplace aggression, evading capture by the enemy, leadership, embracing and adapting to change, entrepreneurial risk taking, innovation and creativity, job search behavior, job offers, tenure, work-family balance, and volunteerism. Meta-analyses have been performed in several of these areas. Hough and Furnham (2003) provide a list of meta-analytic findings summarized according to personality construct and criterion construct. Taken together, the results demonstrate the importance of matching predictor constructs with criterion constructs, the importance of a variety of personality variables other than the Big Five, and useful levels of criterion-related validity of personality variables for many important workplace criteria in both military and civilian settings.

With the increasingly rapid rate of change in the workplace, the importance of other criteria such as initiating, embracing, and adapting to change, change leadership, decision making in rapidly evolving situations, and innovation is greater today than yesterday, and their importance will not diminish anytime soon. The changing world of work requires that criterion constructs such as these become part of our models.

Besides criteria such as overall job performance, our models need to include other broad, individual-level criteria such as work adjustment, training, and career success. In addition, our performance models need to incorporate specific individual-level performance criteria.

Group-Level Performance Variables

Research with teams has advanced our thinking about the importance of and differential prediction of group-level outcomes, but we have barely skimmed the surface. Jackson (1992) identified six types of team effectiveness outcomes: creative decision making, problem solving, task execution, internal group processes, group stability, and external liaison. Cohen and Bailey (1997) categorized team effectiveness criteria into somewhat different categories: performance, attitudinal, and behavioral outcomes. In their summaries, Jackson (1992) and Cohen and Bailey (1997) reviewed previous research, concluding that criterion type moderated the relationship between predictor variables and team effectiveness. Perhaps a hierarchical (or nested) taxonomy that integrates both sets of group-level criteria (Jackson's and Cohen and Bailey's) would be useful.

A test of a multilevel model found that group-level processes affect group-level creativity; they moderate the relationship between aggregated individual creativity (group-level predictor) and group-level creativity (Taggar, 2002). Emerging evidence also suggests that individual- and group-level personality characteristics predict different individual- and group-level performance variables and have different types and forms of relationships with group-level performance variables as compared with individual-level performance variables. These complex findings are described in somewhat more detail later in this chapter.

Dynamic Criteria

Our models need to reflect the changing nature of within-individual job performance over time, hence change in the relative contributions of the determinants of performance. Using a latent growth curve framework, Ployhart and Hakel (1998) examined personality predictors of interindividual differences in latent intraindividual sales performance. Self-assessed empathy was moderately and positively related to initial performance and rate of performance improvement and negatively related to performance decrements (absolute r ranged from .15 to .21), whereas self-assessed persuasiveness was positively related to initial performance, rate of improvement, and performance decrement (r ranged from .10 to .15). Although complex, the findings are sensible. Empathic salespeople relate to and understand their clients' needs, whereas use of persuasive tactics ultimately alienates clients. In this study, although the predictor-criterion relationships did not appear to change over time, performance did, demonstrating the importance of incorporating links between predictors and temporal performance variability in our models of performance.

Typical Versus Maximum Performance Criteria

Another important characteristic of performance criteria is whether they are maximum or typical performance indicators. According to Sackett, Zedeck, and Fogli (1988), three characteristics distinguish maximum from typical performance measures: short time duration of performance, evaluative context, and acceptance of the challenge to perform maximally. Not surprisingly, personality variables relate differently to criteria that are categorized as maximum or typical based on these three characteristics. Openness to Experience, for example, is most predictive of maximum transformational leadership performance criteria, whereas Emotional Stability is most predictive of typical transformational leadership criteria, with Extraversion predictive of both (Ployhart, Lim, & Chan, 2001).

Most personality scales are regarded as measures of typical behavior and as such might be expected to correlate with measures of typical rather than maximum performance criteria. The Ployhart et al. (2001) study indicates that is an overly simplistic expectation. Speculating on other possible examples, the predictors of decision-making quality (typical performance criterion) versus decision-making quality under stress or in rapidly changing circumstances (maximum performance criterion) may differ. Emotional Stability (reaction to stress) may predict quality of decision making under duress but not under normal circumstances. Our models should incorporate the distinction between maximum and typical performance criteria.

New Directions: Independent Variables

Another important set of choices we make when building models and conducting research is the independent variables we include. Compound variables, newly important Big Five variables such as Openness to Experience, variables more specific than Big Five variables, non–Big Five variables (such as interest and emotion), group-level personality variables, and situational variables (such as type of task/team/job, fit, and culture) have received some attention. They deserve more.

Compound Personality (Predictor) Variables

Compound variables, defined by Hough and Schneider (1996) as a combination of basic personality traits that do not necessarily co-vary, have rapidly become a new frontier of personality research. There are a number of examples of insights gained about important work-related outcomes and the role of compound variables in those outcomes:

- Fox and Spector (1999) in their study of work frustration and aggression
- Penner and his colleagues (Penner & Finkelstein, 1998; Penner, Fritzsche, Craiger, & Freifeld, 1995; Penner, Midili, & Kegglemeyer, 1997) in their study of prosocial personality
- Bateman, Crant, Seibert, and Kraimer (Bateman & Crant, 1993; Crant, 1995; Seibert, Crant, & Kraimer, 1999; Seibert, Kraimer, & Crant, 2001) in their study of the proactive personality variable
- Judge and his colleagues (Erez & Judge, 2001; Judge & Bono, 2001a, 2001b; Judge, Locke, Durham, & Kluger, 1998) in their study of core self-evaluations
- Leach (2002) in his study of soldiers who evade capture by the enemy
- Ones, Viswesvaran, and Schmidt (1993) in their meta-analysis of integrity scales

- Frei and McDaniel (1998) in their meta-analysis of customer service scales
- Ones and Viswesvaran (2001) in their study of criterion-focused occupational scales
- Ones, Hough, and Viswesvaran (1998) in their meta-analysis of managerial potential scales
- R. Schneider and his colleagues (R. Schneider, Ackerman, & Kanfer, 1996; R. Schneider, Roberts, & Heggestad, 2002) in their study of social competence
- Sternberg and his colleagues (Kihlstrom & Cantor, 2000; Sternberg, 1985) in their study of social intelligence
- Goleman (1995, 1998) and Salovey and Mayer and their colleagues (Salovey & Mayer, 1990; Mayer & Salovey, 1993, 1997; Mayer, Salovey, & Caruso, 2000) in the area of emotional intelligence

One of the risks of the proliferation of compound variables is the return to the chaotic situation of the dark ages in which we lacked an understanding of the taxonomic structure of personality variables and, hence, the relationships among personality variables. We do not want to return to the "good old daze" (Hough, 1997, p. 233). We can avoid such chaos if we do our homework researching the nomological nets of our compound variables to understand their relationships to more basic personality variables. For example, do the compound variables proactive personality and core self-evaluation consist of the same basic personality variables? Similarly, do the compound variables social competence, social intelligence, and emotional intelligence consist of the same basic personality variables? The research examining the nomological net of integrity tests and customer service scales is instructive. These two compound variables consist of the same Big Five factors but in different concentrations (Ones & Viswesvaran, 1996, 1998).

More research on the nomological nets of compound variables is needed. We need to form compound variables with an understanding of their construct validity—their nomological nets—so that we can form new compound variables to predict behavior in work settings that represent unique configurations of work requirements and situations (Hough, 2001; Hough & Furnham, 2003). Hough and Ones (2001) provide a structure for categorizing, examining, and understanding compound variables using the

Big Five factors and their facets. This structure can help integrate our research with compound variables into bodies of knowledge, thereby enhancing understanding of personality variables and their many roles in work settings. A "back to the future" scenario must be avoided.

Openness to Experience (Big Five Predictor Variable)

This variable will play an increasingly important role in explaining behavior in a world of work characterized by diversity and rapid change. However, as currently defined, it is too amorphous and heterogeneous. The conceptual underpinning of the Openness to Experience factor includes components such as culture, inquiring intellect, intellectance (intelligent, perceptive, knowledgeable, analytical), absorption (capacity for absorbed and self-altering attention), regression in service of the ego, emotional sensitivity, aesthetic interests, liberalism, independence, independent judgment, intellectual flexibility, emotional flexibility, depth and intensity of attention, scope of awareness, tender-mindedness, imagination, sensation seeking, rebelliousness, nonconforming, unusual thought processes, and preference for complexity (McCrae & Costa, 1997a). An example of the confusion surrounding the Openness construct is present even in the gold standard of Big Five personality inventories, the Revised NEO Personality Inventory (NEO PI-R; Costa & McCrae, 1992). The NEO facet excitement seeking, thought by some to be a part of Openness, is instead a part of the NEO Extraversion scale. In the NEO PI-R, Openness consists of six facets— fantasy, aesthetics, feelings, actions, ideas, and values—with a subscale to measure each.

Although Openness to Experience is the most controversial and debatable of the five Big Five factors (Digman, 1990), it is an important construct. However, it is too heterogeneous for communicating findings effectively. Many of the components and facets correlate differently with criteria; many undoubtedly play different types of roles in explaining behavior. A theme of openness is apparent in several of the components of Openness; nonetheless, some of the components are likely to warrant status as separate constructs. Our models of performance will improve when the nomological nets (construct validity) of the components of Openness to Experience have been better explicated.

Non–Big Five Predictor Variables

Personality variables that are more specific than Big Five factors or simply not included in the Big Five are also important. An example of insights gained about important outcome variables and the role of a specific personality variable not a part of the Big Five is work by Stewart and Roth (2001) in their meta-analysis of risk propensity of entrepreneurs. Risk propensity is greater for entrepreneurs than managers; even larger differences exist between venture- or growth-focused entrepreneurs and family income-focused entrepreneurs. A provocative study by Douglas and Martinko (2001) found that trait anger, attribution style, negative affectivity, attitudes toward revenge, self-control, and previous exposure to aggressive cultures (several non–Big Five personality variables) accounted for 62 percent of the variance in self-reported workplace aggression. (For a list of other variables not well represented in the Big Five, see Hough and Furnham, 2003.)

Entire domains of variables are not well represented in the Big Five and need to be incorporated into our taxonomy of personality variables and theories about performance. In this section, two such domains—interests and emotions—are described and their importance portrayed.

Interests

Research with Holland's hexagon model (1985) of personality types (RIASEC, that is, Realistic, Investigative, Artistic, Social, Enterprising, Conventional), their overlap with the Big Five factors of personality, and their usefulness in predicting important work criteria has been growing among I/O psychologists. Although the Big Five is the favored personality taxonomy of many I/O psychologists for examining relationships between personality variables and individual work performance, Holland's RIASEC types play important roles in theories of team performance (Muchinsky, 1999) and, hence, group-level work performance.

Researchers examining the overlap between Holland's six personality types and the Big Five factors have come to different conclusions. Larson and Borgen (2002) concluded that only three Holland themes—Artistic, Enterprising, and Investigative—are consistently related to Big Five factors. Ackerman and Heggestad (1997), however, in their summary of relations between personality and interest variables, concluded that three of the Big Five—Conscientiousness, Extraversion, and Openness to Experience—correlate moderately with Holland's interest themes, and all of the RIASEC themes are represented, at least at the facet level, in the Big Five. A meta-analysis to determine more precisely the overlap between personality and interest variables would be informative.

However, even if much of the variance in Holland's RIASEC personality types is shown to overlap with Big Five factors, research that has examined the criterion-related validity of Holland interest and Big Five personality variables indicates that they predict different types of work-related outcomes. De Fruyt and Mervielde (1999) found that the Holland RIASEC personality types and the Big Five personality factors differed in their validity for predicting employment status (employed versus unemployed) and nature of employment (type of job). RIASEC types were clearly superior in explaining the type of work in which participants were employed (realistic, artistic), whereas Extraversion and Conscientiousness (Big Five factors) were superior in predicting employment status, such as employed or unemployed. If Hough's nomological-web clustering approach (Hough & Ones, 2001) were used to investigate the taxonomic structure of the two sets of variables, an expanded taxonomy of personality variables would undoubtedly emerge to account for the different nomological nets of these variables.

Emotion and Affect

Emotionality, emotional expressivity, emotional regulation, and affectivity variables are important for understanding work behavior. Research on the subject has burgeoned. Theories (Weiss & Cropanzano, 1996), books (Ashkanasy, Hartel, & Zerbe, 2000; Lewis & Haviland-Jones, 2000; Lord, Klimoski, & Kanfer, 2002), journals (*Emotion*), special issues of journals, and hundreds of articles on the subject exist. Emotionality and affectivity play a role in models related to satisfaction (Judge & Hulin, 1993), leadership (Glomb & Hulin, 1997), organizational citizenship behavior and workplace deviance (Lee & Allen, 2002), workplace violence (Glomb, Steel, & Arvey, 2002), counterproductive behavior (Iverson & Deery, 2001), voluntary work behavior (Spector & Fox, 2002), happiness (Diener, 2000), and burnout (Brotheridge & Grandey, 2002; T. Wright & Cropanzano, 1998), to name just a few. (See Chapter Five, this volume, for more information about personality and affect.)

The differences among emotion, affect, mood, and personality traits need to be clarified. Lord and Kanfer (2002), for example, argue that emotions are different from mood, although affect, which they consider to be a more general term than *emotion,* can be either a mood or an emotion. Plutchik (1997) argues that emotion and personality variables are part of the same domain. Averill (1997) believes that emotions are characterized by three prototypic features—passivity (beyond personal control, almost), intentionality (focused), and subjectivity (inner experiences)—and are organized by researchers categorically (and often hierarchically, using terms such as *sadness, pain, fear,* and *anxiety* at the generic level) or dimensionally with two bipolar dimensions repeatedly used: evaluation (negative-positive) and activation (aroused-unaroused). He argues that personality traits play a prominent role in emotion and are at a higher (broader) level than emotions in the hierarchy of behavior. In spite of the already excellent thinking in this area, more research is needed to clarify the relationships among variables in this (enlarged) domain.

Group-Level Personality Predictor Variables

The results of the few studies that have examined the relationships of group-level personality variables with individual- and group-level criteria are provocative. Fascinating results are emerging. For example, (1) dyad (group) levels of Extraversion and Conscientiousness correlate with relationship conflict, (2) although dyad levels of Conscientiousness correlate with relationship conflict, differences between dyad members in levels of Conscientiousness do not, and (3) Agreeableness and Openness correlate with relationship conflict at the individual level, although the strongest effects are at the dyad level (Bono, Boles, Judge, & Lauver, 2002). In another study, teams higher in Conscientiousness, Agreeableness, Extraversion, and Emotional Stability received higher ratings on team (group level) performance, and teams higher on Extraversion and Emotional Stability received higher ratings on team (group level) viability (Barrick, Stewart, Neubert, & Mount, 1998). Using a conjunctive task, Neuman and Wright (1999) found that group-level Agreeableness and Conscientiousness predicted objective and subjective indicators of group-level (team) performance. Group-level Conscientiousness has both main and interaction effects on outcome variables (LePine, Hollenbeck, Ilgen, & Hedlund, 1997). In addition, type of task may moderate the relationships. For example, group-level Extraversion appears to be related curvilinearly to team performance on creative problem-solving tasks (Barry & Stewart, 1997) and linearly to team performance on compensatory tasks (Barrick et al., 1998). Although the complexities of the relationships are almost overwhelming, they must be reflected in our models of performance.

The research in this area highlights the importance of conducting a mission analysis (akin to job analysis at the individual level) that takes into account required group-level (team) competencies, group-level criterion variables, type and form of the relationships, and situational variables. Studies in this area also highlight the difficulties of operationalizing group-level predictor variables.

Situational Variables

Hattrup and Jackson's plea (1996) for learning about individual differences by taking situations seriously has been taken seriously. The once extreme positions of early situationism and trait psychology are today blended; even Mischel has modified his position (Mischel, Shoda, & Mendoza-Denton, 2002). The importance of both individual differences (especially personality variables) and situations is now recognized, and it is nowhere more apparent than in the study of teams—their composition and their effectiveness. Situations can interact with individual differences in personality, differentially eliciting cooperative and competitive behavior (Graziano, Hair, & Finch, 1997). Situations can mediate and moderate the effects of personality variables on outcome variables. The growing awareness that an individual's fit with the environment affects work adjustment is a clear recognition of the importance of situations.

The following variables incorporate the situation into their definition or measurement: type of task, type of team, type of job, culture, research setting, and fit. (See Chapter Ten, this volume, for a discussion of fit between the individual and the organization.) Each of these "situations" can interact with independent variables in our models to affect dependent variables. These situations also act as moderator and mediator variables as well.

Type of Task

Steiner (1972) developed a set of task types (additive, compensatory, conjunctive, and disjunctive) that potentially moderates results and is thus helpful in organizing research findings. If another task type—creative—were added to Steiner's set, the differences in the Barrick et al. (1998) and Barry and Stewart (1997) results would be confirming rather than seemingly conflicting. Specifically, Barrick et al. (1998), working with manufacturing teams (primarily compensatory tasks), found that Conscientiousness (as well as Agreeableness, Extraversion, and Emotional Stability) predicted team performance. Barry and Stewart (1997), working with teams involved in creative problem-solving tasks, found that Conscientiousness did not predict team performance. Given the finding that dependability (one facet of Conscientiousness) correlates negatively with criteria involving creative tasks (Hough, 1992), these results, when organized according to a revised Steiner taxonomy, demonstrate that task type moderates the relationship between predictor (personality) variables and team effectiveness. We need additional research on the taxonomic structure of tasks to better define the boundaries beyond which our results do not generalize.

Type of Team

Cohen and Bailey (1997) reviewed research on teams conducted between 1990 and 1996, concluding that type of team (work teams, parallel teams, project teams, and management teams) moderated relationships between independent and dependent variables. Other classifications of teams exist (Gibson & Kirkman, 1999; Klimoski & Jones, 1995). Perhaps instead of types of teams, we need a set of independent variables on which teams vary that can be used to profile team situations. Such a set of variables would be helpful in increasing the precision of our theories and models.

Type of Job or Job Characteristic

In addition to more team-based work settings, also more common are customer service jobs requiring interpersonal skill and autonomous work settings, all of which have been shown to moderate relationships between personality variables and performance. For example, degree of interpersonal interaction is a job characteristic that moderates relations between personality characteristics and performance (Frei & McDaniel, 1998; MacLane, 1996; Mount et al., 1998). Another example of a job characteristic that can moderate relationships between personality characteristics and performance is autonomy. In managerial jobs, degree of job autonomy moderates the validity of Conscientiousness, Extraversion, and Agreeableness (Barrick & Mount, 1993). Conscientiousness and Extraversion are more highly positively correlated with performance in high-autonomy jobs than in low-autonomy jobs; Agreeableness is more highly negatively correlated with performance in high-autonomy jobs than in low-autonomy jobs. This study highlights the importance of situations and their impact on both the type (moderator) and direction (positive versus negative) of relationships in our models.

Researchers conducting meta-analyses often summarize validities within job (manager, police officer, sales job), and often validities are found to differ depending on the job. However, the number of jobs in any economy is enormous, and in today's economy, many are changing. Building separate theories about the determinants of performance for each job is unhelpful to the science and practice of I/O psychology. Theory building requires better strategies to define situations.

Some researchers have used Holland's RIASEC model as a taxonomic structure for classifying work environments and educational specialty. When criterion-related validities of personality variables are examined within the six job types, validities differ, indicating the importance of type of job as a moderator variable (Fritzsche, McIntire, & Yost (2002; Hogan, Hogan, & Roberts, 1996). Hough and Furnham (2003), however, provide a caution to this interpretation. They suggest that if, instead of overall job performance, specific performance constructs were the criteria, the apparent moderating effects of the RIASEC job types would disappear.

Fit

Instead of conceptualizing the work environment as a moderator variable, many researchers have conceptualized its role in terms of fit between the individual and the environment. "Fit" indexes thus involve measurement of both the individual and the situation, resulting in a variable indicating degree of congruence between the two in terms of some set of variables. When fit concepts are part of a model, interest and cognitive ability variables are often included (Dawis & Lofquist, 1984; Gottfredson, 1986). Personality variables are now playing a more important role. De Fruyt (2002), for example, concluded that when RIASEC person-environment fit indexes include Big Five personality variables, predictive validity increases. (See Chapter Ten, this volume, for a thorough discussion of fit.)

The concept of fit is not new; it is fundamental in vocational counseling and personnel psychology (Dawis and Lofquist's theory of work adjustment [1984], Holland's theory of vocational choice [1985], Gottfredson's occupational aptitude patterns map [1986]), as well as in organizational psychology (B. Schneider's attraction—selection—attrition cycle [1987]). Nonetheless, more careful and complete integration of congruence and fit concepts in our models is needed. For example, the emphasis on classifying jobs into types or categories in some theories is unwise. Taxonomies of jobs (job types or job families) require a stable environment, an essentially unchanging work environment. Given the changing nature of the world of work, any model we build that incorporates job types is akin to building a sandcastle. Such models are destined to be temporary, unable to stand the test of time. Instead, our models should incorporate individual difference variables and work difference variables, not person types or job types. Fit indexes should be based on profile or pattern analyses, not type analyses.

Culture

The world of work is multinational and multicultural. Culture moderates, mediates, and interacts with personality in complex ways to affect performance, and this added complexity of cultural plurality must be reflected in our performance models. Its importance is demonstrated in a study of the different influences of personality variables on life satisfaction in two individualistic and three collectivistic cultures (Schimmack, Radhakrishnan, Oishi, Dzokoto, & Ahadi, 2002). Research on the determinants of expatriate performance is another example where the importance of culture (for example, adjusting to an environment other than one's own) is acknowledged. Culture is important in ways other than adjusting to it. Leadership, for example, is affected by culture (House, Wright, & Aditya, 1997).

Incorporating culture into our performance models requires that we describe culture on a set of dimensions. A good taxonomy of cultural variables is required. House et al. (1997) reviewed cross-cultural differences and concluded that Hofstede's four constructs (power distance, uncertainty avoidance, individualism versus collectivism, and masculinity versus femininity; 1980) were the most useful for describing and differentiating cultures. Recently, Hofstede and his colleagues (Hofstede et al., 1998) proposed many more constructs. Triandis and Suh (2002) suggested a hierarchical structure consisting of four—complexity, tightness, collectivism, and individualism—at the highest level, with subdimensions, such as vertical and horizontal, within the broader dimensions of collectivism and individualism. These cultural variables need to be incorporated into our models of performance if we expect to understand the conditions under which our models are accurate portraits of the determinants of performance.

An important issue when studying personality and culture is the structure of personality across cultures. Proponents of the Big Five argue for the universal nature of the five factors, citing as evidence similarity of factor structures of Big Five personality questionnaires administered in different cultures and languages (McCrae & Costa, 1997b). Recently, however, Big Five researchers have acknowledged that the fit is better in some countries than in others and recommend that more attention be given to middle-level personality constructs (Saucier & Goldberg, 2001), a point of view I have long advocated.

Research Setting

Student settings are often used to test our theories with the hope that the results will generalize to work settings. Recent findings reiterate the importance of ensuring that our findings do generalize to work or applied settings. For example, evidence of the fakeability of personality inventories is clear, and the magnitude of distortion in directed faking studies is significant (Ones, Viswesvaran, & Reiss, 1996). However, in actual applicant settings, intentional distortion is less significant, and although criterion-related validities are significantly lower in directed faking studies, validities are higher in applicant settings, indeed similar to the level of validity obtained in incumbent settings (Hough, 1998a). Another example of the tenuous nature of generalizing from student settings to work (business) settings is research on the personality correlates of leadership behavior. In business settings, conscientiousness correlated .05 (corrected) with leadership, whereas in student settings, conscientiousness correlated .36, corrected (Judge, Bono, Ilies, & Werner, 2002). Research setting is a potential moderator variable that our meta-analyses should routinely incorporate into the coding scheme and analyses.

New Directions: Types of Relationships and Roles for Personality Variables

Although many, if not most, of our models portray personality variables as having main effects, personality variables have moderator, mediator, suppressor, and interaction effects as well. Moreover, the direction (positive, negative) and form (linear, curvilinear, configural) vary depending on a variety of variables. For example, research on the determinants of team performance indicates that a relationship between a personality variable and an outcome variable may be curvilinear in one situation and linear in another, as in creative problem-solving tasks versus compensatory tasks (Barry & Stewart, 1997; Barrick et al., 1998). Moreover, interpersonal interaction can affect outcomes. For example, personality characteristics of team members can interact with those of the leader to determine team performance (LePine et al., 1997). Team-based and customer service work settings are interpersonal in nature and are thus dynamic within short episodes of interactions as well as over time. The form and type of relationships between personality variables and outcome measures are thus also likely to change over time. These are but a few examples of the complex nature of the type, form, and direction of relationships of personality variables with other variables in our models.

Other New Directions

Our research and model building are changing in other ways as well. For example, researchers are examining and proposing different personality theories and taxonomies. Researchers have gained new insights about the measurement of personality variables, and new methods have emerged. In addition, the social, demographic, and legal environment has changed, with personality variables playing a prominent role.

Other Personality Theories and Taxonomies

Much of the I/O research investigating the role of personality in affecting workplace behavior is based on a hierarchical model of trait variables, specifically, the FFM (often referred to as the Big Five) identified through analysis of lexical terms (language). (For a review of the advantages and disadvantages of this model of personality from an I/O perspective as well as other hierarchical models, see R. Schneider & Hough, 1995; Hough & Schneider, 1996; and Chapter One, this volume.)

Many other models of the structure of personality variables exist. One of the more recent approaches to developing a taxonomy of personality variables is Hough's nomological-web clustering approach (Hough & Ones, 2001). Hough and Ones call for research and refinement of the initial set of constructs, arguing that once I/O has an understanding of the nomological webs of personality variables, compound variables can be synthesized to predict behavior in a rapidly changing work world with unique configurations of criterion (performance) constructs. Other structural models integrate emotion and personality (Plutchik, 1997) and interpersonal behavior (Wiggins, 1980) into a circumplex structure. The field of personality psychology has many theories of personality as well. Already, our models incorporate motivational forces as part of our definition of personality, forces that activate and energize behavior. Our models of performance will benefit from greater use of some of these other personality theories. (See Hogan, Johnson, & Briggs, 1997, and Roberts & Hogan, 2001, for an in-depth review of personality theories and their relevance to I/O.)

Measurement Methods

With the surge in research with personality variables has come a renewed interest in improving our measurement strategies, understanding the threats to the accuracy of our measurement, and developing entirely new ways of measuring personality variables. A focus on the content of the individual item (referred to as item frame of reference) and bandwidth issues reflects interest in improving the validity of self- or other-report measures of personality. A focus on the cross-cultural applicability of our measures reflects the reality of globalization and its impact on our measures and generalizability of our models. Different sets of instructions to test takers are now recognized as a way to affect validity and decrease intentional distortion. New content, new constructs, and new modes of measurement have emerged.

Item Frame of Reference

A growing body of evidence indicates that specifying the context or situation portrayed in items moderates validity. Responses to complete sentences that provide context yield higher criterion-related validities than adjectives (Cellar, Miller, Doverspike, & Klawsky, 1996). Items that provide context by describing the situation yield higher criterion-related validities, lower error variances, and more accurate differentiation among groups than items that ask about feelings or behavior in general (Schmit, Ryan, Stierwalt, & Powell, 1995; Robie, Schmit, Ryan, & Zickar, 2000; J. Wright, Lindgren, & Zakriski, 2001). These results provide support for Murtha, Kanfer, and Ackerman's suggested interactionist taxonomy of personality and situations (1996), as well as J. Wright and Mischel's "conditional" approach to personality measurement (1987). Our models will provide more accurate predictions when the situation is considered during scale development.

Bandwidth

The nature of the controversy concerning narrow versus broad bandwidth measures has changed. The answer to the question, "Which is better, broad or narrow measures?" is, "It depends on the nature of the criterion." Criterion-related validities are higher when a construct-oriented approach is used to match predictors to criteria, including bandwidth considerations, whereby narrow predictor constructs are matched with narrow criterion constructs and broad predictor constructs are matched with broad criterion constructs (Hough & Furnham, 2003). This is an important conclusion that can help guide theory building and research.

Cross-Cultural Issues

When personality measures are developed in one language, translated, and used cross-culturally, construct equivalence is critically important. Most of the research addresses the extent to which the factor structure of the personality inventory replicates in different languages and cultures. A review of the evidence indicates that for most of the well-known inventories, the same or similar structures are found cross-culturally; however, relatively little evidence exists regarding the generalizability of criterion-related validities of personality variables across cultures (Paunonen & Ashton, 1998). (For a review of the many issues involved in cross-cultural measurement, see Church, 2001.)

Instructions to Test Takers

Studies of the effects of intentional distortion on validity often involve instructions to test takers, for example, "Respond honestly" or "Respond in a way to maximize your chances of being hired as a salesperson." Many think that the motivation to portray oneself favorably on a self-report personality inventory in an applicant setting results in lower validity (criterion-related and construct validity) of personality scales, an example of the situation moderating validity. The situation does moderate validity, but not in a way often thought.

When validities of personality scales are examined according to applicant versus incumbent versus directed faking settings, validity is approximately the same in applicant (motivated) and incumbent (honest) settings, but dramatically lower when test takers are instructed to fake, that is, directed faking studies (Hough, 1998a; Hough & Furnham, 2003). Another example of instructions to test takers that affects responses (reduces the amount of distortion) is informing or warning test takers that distorted responses can be detected and that consequences exist for such distortion (Dwight & Donovan, 1998). Another type of instruction to test takers that can affect responses is informing people of the characteristic being measured (Kleinmann, Kuptsch, & Köler, 1996). Our models need to be sensitive to instructions to test takers as an independent variable that can affect dependent variables.

New, Promising Methods

Several approaches to measuring personality characteristics have emerged in terms of content measured and mode of measurement (see Hough & Furnham, 2003). Subjective methods other than self-report (for example, others' reports, descriptions, and observations) are more common, as are objective methods such as conditional reasoning, a strategy pioneered by James (1998) for measuring personality characteristics based on the logic an individual uses to justify behavior. Although genetic testing (mouth swabs for DNA) is infrequently used, it may become more common. In the United States, however, legislative actions, Equal Employment Opportunity Commission guidelines for interpreting the Americans with Disability Act, and case law may preclude its use. Similarly, technology (digitization) has changed the mode of testing, making new constructs possible, as well as new modes of measuring existing constructs (for example, response latency to measure extraversion). Testing using virtual reality has yet to come to fruition, but it will. Of course, new constructs and modes of measuring them bring new concerns about construct validity, equivalence, intended and unintended consequences, and new, unforeseen issues.

Multilevel Perspective

A multilevel perspective is one of the most important recent trends in our field. It represents a paradigm shift from a focus on just the individual or just the organization (or a subunit such as a team or work group) to a perspective that incorporates multiple levels of analysis. The multilevel personnel selection framework that B. Schneider and his colleagues (B. Schneider, Smith, & Sipe, 2000; Ployhart & Schneider, 2002) propose exemplifies this approach to theory building. New ways of thinking about work—tasks; required knowledge, skills, and abilities (predictor constructs, including personality variables); and performance constructs—as well as validation models are required. The research and trends already described for group-level performance variables and group-level personality predictor variables are especially relevant to multilevel research and theories.

Another study highlights the importance of using a multilevel approach to conceptualize, measure, and analyze variables and data. Griffin (2001) hypothesized and found different effects when different levels of analyses were used to examine the effects of stable personality characteristics and work characteristics on worker reactions. Specifically, between-group variance in worker reaction outcomes increased when emotional stability and extraversion were included, with group-level variables explaining more variance in worker reactions when dispositions were included, whereas studies using only individual-level analyses indicate a decrease in the relationship between work characteristics and worker reactions when stable personality variables are included. In addition to all the factors described throughout this chapter, the usefulness, accuracy, and validity of our theories also depend on level of analysis. Our theories need to reflect the multitude and complexity of world of work outcomes and their multiple determinants.

Social and Legal Implications

With increased ethnic diversity within national workforces and globalization of markets comes a desire for greater representation of all ethnic groups in all areas of employment (equality in personnel selection ratios across jobs). Two streams of research indicate that merit systems (as opposed to forced equality or quota systems) can be used to advance this important social and business goal. First, the evidence is persuasive that overall validity increases when personality and cognitive measures are used in combination (Schmidt & Hunter, 1998). Second, summaries of mean score differences between ethnic groups indicate that most ethnic groups score similarly on most personality variables (Hough, 1998b; Hough, Oswald, & Ployhart, 2001) whereas on measures of cognitive ability, significant mean score differences exist.

One obvious strategy for obtaining more equal selection ratios is to include both personality and cognitive ability measures in selection systems. However, even when a typical cognitive ability measure is equally weighted with a personality variable on which all ethnic groups score similarly, the reduction in the composite mean score difference between whites and, for example, African Americans will be less than the expected half (Sackett & Ellingson, 1997). Moreover, on some facets of the Big Five, small mean score differences do exist, with whites scoring lower than some minority groups on some facets and higher on other facets. For example, whites score approximately .12 standard deviations lower than African Americans on surgency but approximately .31 standard deviations higher on affiliation, both of which are facets of Extraversion.

Employment law cases now include arguments about the use of alternative predictors such as personality variables (for example, *United States of America* v. *City of Garland, TX,* 2002). Employers increasingly are expected to include personality variables in their personnel selection systems.

Conclusion

We make many choices when building models and conducting research. Examples are choice of independent (antecedent, predictor) variables, dependent (criterion) variables, intervening (mediator) variables, individual- versus group-level outcome variables, situations (tasks, jobs, culture) within and across which relationships are hypothesized, and type of hypothesized relationships or effects (linear, curvilinear, configural, moderator, interaction). Given the complexity of the measurement of the constructs, relations between variables, direction, shape, and type of relationships, it is not surprising that during the dark ages between approximately 1965 and 1985, I/O psychologists (with the exception of a few such as Ghiselli, 1966) accorded personality variables a minor, if any, role in theories of the determinants of work-related behavior. Research during the 1980s and 1990s demonstrated the important main effects of personality variables in determining behavior and performance. Now, evidence for the many roles of personality variables in determining behavior and performance is persuasive.

Besides a need for more complex models, we must examine and develop additional taxonomic structures of personality, criterion, and situational variables, structures that incorporate more variables than the Big Five in the personality domain and more variables than overall, task, and contextual performance as dependent variables. We need to develop an adequate taxonomy of situational variables. We need to incorporate other theories of personality into our models of the determinants of performance. We need models that recognize that variables and relationships are dynamic, changing over time. Our models of performance must include multilevel measures of independent and dependent variables and address relationships between variables at multiple levels. The complexity is enormous. Unless our theories and models reflect this complexity, the variance our theories and models explain will be minimal.

References

Ackerman, P. L., & Heggestad, E. D. (1997). Intelligence, personality, and interests: Evidence for overlapping traits. *Psychological Bulletin, 121,* 219–245.

Ashkanasy, N. M., Hartel, C.E.J., & Zerbe, W. J. (Eds.). (2000). *Emotions in the workplace: Research, theory, and practice.* Westport, CT: Quorum Books.

Averill, J. R. (1997). The emotions: An integrative approach. In R. Hogan, J. Johnson, & S. Briggs (Eds.), *Handbook of personality psychology* (pp. 513–541). Orlando, FL: Academic Press.

Barrick, M. R., & Mount, M. K. (1991). The Big Five personality dimensions and job performance: A meta-analysis. *Personnel Psychology, 44,* 1–26.

Barrick, M. R., & Mount, M. K. (1993). Autonomy as a moderator of the relationships between the Big Five personality dimensions and job performance. *Journal of Applied Psychology, 78,* 111–118.

Barrick, M. R., Stewart, G. L., Neubert, M. J., & Mount, M. K. (1998). Relating member ability and personality to work-team processes and team effectiveness. *Journal of Applied Psychology, 83,* 377–391.

Barry, B., & Stewart, G. L. (1997). Composition, process, and performance in self-managed groups: The role of personality. *Journal of Applied Psychology, 82,* 62–78.

Bateman, T. S., & Crant, J. M. (1993). The proactive component of organizational behavior: A measure and correlates. *Journal of Organizational Behavior, 14,* 103–118.

Bono, J. E., Boles, T. L., Judge, T. A., & Lauver, K. J. (2002). The role of personality in task and relationship conflict. *Journal of Personality, 70,* 311–344.

Borman, W. C., White, L. A., & Dorsey, D. W. (1995). Effects of ratee task performance and interpersonal factors on supervisor and peer performance ratings. *Journal of Applied Psychology, 80,* 168–177.

Borman, W. C., White, L. A., Pulakos, E. D., & Oppler, S. H. (1991). Models of supervisory job performance ratings. *Journal of Applied Psychology, 76,* 863–872.

Brotheridge, C. M., & Grandey, A. A. (2002). Emotional labor and burnout: Comparing two perspectives of "people work." *Journal of Vocational Behavior, 60,* 17–39.

Campbell, J. P., & Knapp, D. J. (Eds.). (2001). *Exploring the limits in personnel selection and classification.* Mahwah, NJ: Erlbaum.

Cellar, D. F., Miller, M. L., Doverspike, D. D., & Klawsky, J. D. (1996). Comparison of factor structures and criterion-related validity coefficients for two measures of personality based on the Five Factor Model. *Journal of Applied Psychology, 81,* 694–704.

Church, A. T. (2001). Personality measurement in cross-cultural perspective. *Journal of Personality, 69,* 979–1006.

Cohen, S. G., & Bailey, D. E. (1997). What makes teams work: Group effectiveness research from the shop floor to the executive suite. *Journal of Management, 23,* 239–290.

Costa, P. T., Jr., & McCrae, R. R. (1992). *Revised NEO Personality Inventory (NEO PI-R) and NEO Five-Factor Inventory (NEO-FFI): Professional manual.* Odessa, FL: Psychological Assessment Resources.

Crant, J. M. (1995). The proactive personality scale and objective job performance among real estate agents. *Journal of Applied Psychology, 80,* 532–537.

Dawis, R. V., & Lofquist, L. H. (1984). *A psychological theory of work adjustment: An individual difference model and its applications.* Minneapolis: University of Minnesota.

De Fruyt, F. (2002). A person-centered approach to P-E fit questions using a multiple-trait model. *Journal of Vocational Behavior, 60,* 73–90.

De Fruyt, F., & Mervielde, I. (1999). RIASEC types and Big Five traits as predictors of employment status and nature of employment. *Personnel Psychology, 52,* 701–727.

Diener, E. (2000). Subjective well-being: The science of happiness and a proposal for a national index. *American Psychologist, 55,* 34–43.

Digman, J. M. (1990). Personality structure: Emergence of the Five-Factor Model. *Annual Review of Psychology, 41,* 417–440.

Douglas, S. C., & Martinko, M. J. (2001). Exploring the role of individual differences in the prediction of workplace aggression. *Journal of Applied Psychology, 86,* 547–559.

Dwight, S. A., & Donovan, J. J. (1998). *Warning: Proceed with caution when warning applicants not to dissimulate (revised).* Paper presented at the Thirteenth Annual Meeting of the Society for Industrial and Organizational Psychology, Dallas, TX.

Erez, A., & Judge, T. A. (2001). Relationship of core self-evaluations to goal setting, motivation, and performance. *Journal of Applied Psychology, 86,* 1270–1279.

Fox, S., & Spector, P. E. (1999). A model of work frustration-aggression. *Journal of Organizational Behavior, 20,* 915–931.

Frei, R. L., & McDaniel, M. A. (1998). Validity of customer service measures in personnel selection: A review of criterion and construct evidence. *Human Performance, 11,* 1–27.

Fritzsche, B. A., McIntire, S. A., & Yost, A. P. (2002). Holland type as a moderator of personality-performance predictions. *Journal of Vocational Behavior, 60,* 422–436.

Ghiselli, E. E. (1966). *The validity of occupational aptitude tests.* New York: Wiley.

Gibson, C. B., & Kirkman, B. L. (1999). Our past, present, and future in teams: The role of human resource professions in managing team performance. In A. I. Kraut & A. K. Korman (Eds.), *Evolving practices in human resource management: Responses to a changing world of work* (pp. 90–117). San Francisco: Jossey-Bass.

Glomb, T. M., & Hulin, C. L. (1997). Anger and gender effects in observed supervisor-subordinate dyadic interactions. *Organizational Behavior and Human Decision Processes, 72,* 281–307.

Glomb, T. M., Steel, P.D.G., & Arvey, R. D. (2002). Office sneers, snipes, and stab wounds: Antecedents, consequences, and implications of workplace violence and aggression. In R. G. Lord, R. J. Klimoski, & R. Kanfer (Eds.), *Emotions in the workplace* (pp. 227–259). San Francisco: Jossey-Bass.

Goleman, D. (1995). *Emotional intelligence: Why it can matter more than IQ.* New York: Bantam Books.

Goleman, D. (1998). *Working with emotional intelligence.* New York: Bantam Books.

Gottfredson, L. S. (1986). Occupational aptitude patterns map: Development and implications for a theory of job aptitude requirements [Monograph]. *Journal of Vocational Behavior, 29,* 254–291.

Graziano, W. G., Hair, E. C., & Finch, J. F. (1997). Competitiveness mediates the link between personality and group performance. *Journal of Personality and Social Psychology, 73,* 1394–1408.

Griffin, M. A. (2001). Dispositions and work reactions: A multilevel approach. *Journal of Applied Psychology, 86,* 1142–1151.

Guion, R. M. (1983). Comments on Hunter. In F. Landy, S. Zedeck, & J. Cleveland (Eds.), *Performance measurement and theory* (pp. 267–275). Mahwah, NJ: Erlbaum.

Hattrup, K., & Jackson, S. E. (1996). Learning about individual differences by taking situations seriously. In K. R. Murphy (Ed.), *Individual differences and behavior in organizations* (pp. 507–541). San Francisco: Jossey-Bass.

Hofstede, G. (1980). *Cultures consequences: International differences in work-related values.* Thousand Oaks, CA: Sage.

Hofstede, G., Arrindell, W. A., Best, D. L., De Mooij, M., Hoppe, M. H., et al. (1998). *Masculinity and femininity: The taboo dimension of national cultures.* Thousand Oaks, CA: Sage.

Hogan, R. T., Hogan, J., & Roberts, B. W. (1996). Personality measurement and employment decisions. *American Psychologist, 51,* 469–477.

Hogan, R. T., Johnson, J., & Briggs, S. (Eds.). (1997). *The handbook of personality psychology.* Orlando, FL: Academic Press.

Holland, J. (1985). *Making vocational choices: A theory of vocational personalities and work environments.* Upper Saddle River, NJ: Prentice Hall.

Hollenbeck, J. R. (1998). *Personnel Psychology*'s citation leading articles: The first five decades. *Personnel Psychology, 51*(4), [introduction].

Hough, L. M. (1992). The "Big Five" personality variables—construct confusion: Description versus prediction. *Human Performance, 5,* 139–155.

Hough, L. M. (1997). The millennium for personality psychology: New horizons or good old daze. *Applied Psychology: An International Review, 47,* 233–261.

Hough, L. M. (1998a). Effects of intentional distortion in personality measurement and evaluation of suggested palliatives. *Human Performance, 11,* 209–244.

Hough, L. M. (1998b). Personality at work: Issues and evidence. In M. Hakel (Ed.), *Beyond multiple choice: Evaluating alternatives to traditional testing for selection* (pp. 131–166). Mahwah, NJ: Erlbaum.

Hough, L. M. (2001). I/Owes its advances to personality. In B. W. Roberts & R. T. Hogan (Eds.), *Personality psychology in the workplace* (pp. 19–44). Washington, DC: American Psychological Association.

Hough, L. M., Eaton, N. L., Dunnette, M. D., Kamp, J. D., & McCloy, R. A. (1990). Criterion-related validities of personality constructs and the effect of response distortion on those validities [Monograph]. *Journal of Applied Psychology, 75,* 581–595.

Hough, L. M., & Furnham, A. (2003). Importance and use of personality variables in work settings. In W. C. Borman, D. R. Ilgen, & R. J. Klimoski (Eds.), *Comprehensive handbook of psychology: Vol. 12. Industrial/organizational psychology* (pp. 131–169). New York: Wiley.

Hough, L. M., & Ones, D. S. (2001). The structure, measurement, validity, and use of personality variables in industrial, work, and organizational psychology. In N. Anderson, D. S. Ones, H. K. Sinangil, & C. Viswesvaran (Eds.), *Handbook of industrial, work and organizational psychology* (Vol. 1, pp. 233–377). Thousand Oaks, CA: Sage.

Hough, L. M., & Oswald, F. L. (2000). Personnel selection: Looking toward the future—remembering the past. *Annual Review of Psychology, 51,* 631–664.

Hough, L. M., Oswald, F. L., & Ployhart, R. E. (2001). Determinants, detection, and amelioration of adverse impact in personnel selection procedures: Issues, evidence, and lessons learned. *International Journal of Selection and Assessment, 9,* 152–194.

Hough, L. M., & Schneider, R. J. (1996). Personality traits, taxonomies, and applications in organizations. In K. R. Murphy (Ed.), *Individual differences and behavior in organizations* (pp. 31–88). San Francisco: Jossey-Bass.

House, R. J., Wright, N. S., & Aditya, R. N. (1997). Cross-cultural research on organizational leadership: A critical analysis and a proposed theory.

In P. C. Earley & M. Erez (Eds.), *New perspectives on international industrial/organizational psychology* (pp. 535–625). San Francisco: New Lexington Press.

Howard, A. (Ed.). (1995). *The changing nature of work*. San Francisco: Jossey-Bass.

Hunter, J. E. (1983). A causal analysis of cognitive ability, job knowledge, job performance, and supervisor ratings. In F. Landy, S. Zedeck, & J. Cleveland (Eds.), *Performance measurement and theory* (pp. 257–266). Mahwah, NJ: Erlbaum.

Hurtz, G. M., & Donovan, J. J. (2000). Personality and job performance: The Big Five revisited. *Journal of Applied Psychology, 85,* 869–879.

Ilgen, D. R., & Pulakos, E. D. (Eds.). (1999). *The changing nature of performance*. San Francisco: Jossey-Bass.

Iverson, R. D., & Deery, S. (2001). Understanding the "personological" basis of employee withdrawal: The influence of affective disposition on employee tardiness, early departure, and absenteeism. *Journal of Applied Psychology, 86,* 856–866.

Jackson, S. E. (1992). Consequences of group composition for the interpersonal dynamics of strategic issue processing. In P. Shrivastava, A. Huff, & J. Dutton (Eds.), *Advances in strategic management* (Vol. 8, pp. 345–382). Greenwich, CT: JAI Press.

James, L. R. (1998). Measurement of personality via conditional reasoning. *Organizational Research Methods, 1,* 131–163.

Judge, T. A., & Bono, J. E. (2001a). A rose by any other name: Are self-esteem, generalized self-efficacy, neuroticism, and locus of control indicators of a common construct? In B. W. Roberts & R. T. Hogan (Eds.), *Personality psychology in the workplace* (pp. 93–118). Washington, DC: American Psychological Association.

Judge, T. A., & Bono, J. E. (2001b). Relationship of core self-evaluation traits—self-esteem, generalized self-efficacy, locus of control, and emotional stability—with job satisfaction and job performance: A meta-analysis. *Journal of Applied Psychology, 86,* 80–92.

Judge, T. A., Bono, J. E., Ilies, R., & Werner, M. (2002). Personality and leadership: A qualitative and quantitative review. *Journal of Applied Psychology, 87,* 765–780.

Judge, T. A., & Hulin, C. L. (1993). Satisfaction as a reflection of disposition: A multiple source causal analysis. *Organizational Behavior and Human Decision Processes, 56,* 388–421.

Judge, T. A., Locke, E. A., Durham, C. C., & Kluger, A. N. (1998). Dispositional effects on job and life satisfaction: The role core evaluations. *Journal of Applied Psychology, 83,* 17–34.

Kihlstrom, J. F., & Cantor, N. (2000). Social intelligence. In R. J. Sternberg (Ed.), *Handbook of intelligence* (pp. 359–379). Cambridge: Cambridge University Press.

Kleinmann, M., Kuptsch, C., & Köler, O. (1996). Transparency: A necessary requirement for the construct validity of assessment centers. *Applied Psychology: An International Review, 45,* 67–84.

Klimoski, R., & Jones, R. G. (1995). Staffing for effective group decision making: Key issues in matching people and teams. In R. Guzzo & E. Salas (Eds.), *Team effectiveness and decision making in organizations* (pp. 291–332). San Francisco: Jossey-Bass.

Larson, L. M., & Borgen, F. H. (2002). Convergence of vocational interests and personality: Examples in an adolescent gifted sample. *Journal of Vocational Behavior, 60,* 91–112.

Leach, J. (2002). Personality profiles of potential prisoners of war and evaders. *Military Psychology, 14,* 73–81.

Lee, K., & Allen, N. J. (2002). Organizational citizenship behavior and workplace deviance: The role of affect and cognitions. *Journal of Applied Psychology, 87,* 131–142.

LePine, J. A., Hollenbeck, J. R., Ilgen, D. R., & Hedlund, J. (1997). Effects of individual differences on the performance of hierarchical decision-making teams: Much more than g. *Journal of Applied Psychology, 82,* 803–811.

Lewis, M., & Haviland-Jones, J. M. (Eds.). (2000). *Handbook of emotions* (2nd ed.). New York: Guilford.

Lord, R. G., & Kanfer, R. (2002). Emotions and organizational behavior. In R. G. Lord, R. J. Klimoski, & R. Kanfer (Eds.), *Emotions in the workplace* (pp. 5–19). San Francisco: Jossey-Bass.

Lord, R. G., Klimoski, R. J., & Kanfer, R. (Eds.). (2002). *Emotions in the workplace.* San Francisco: Jossey-Bass.

MacLane, C. N. (1996). *Relationship of biodata validities and social demands of jobs.* Paper presented at the Eleventh Annual Conference of the Society for Industrial and Organizational Psychology, San Diego, CA.

Mayer, J. D., & Salovey, P. (1993). The intelligence of emotional intelligence. *Intelligence, 17,* 433–442.

Mayer, J. D., & Salovey, P. (1997). What is emotional intelligence? In P. Salovey & D. J. Sluyter (Eds.), *Emotional development and emotional intelligence* (pp. 3–31). New York: Basic Books.

Mayer, J. D., Salovey, P., & Caruso, D. (2000). Models of emotional intelligence. In R. J. Sternberg (Ed.), *Handbook of intelligence* (pp. 396–420). Cambridge: Cambridge University Press.

McCrae, R. R., & Costa, P. T., Jr. (1997a). Conceptions and correlates of openness to experience. In R. Hogan, J. Johnson, & S. Briggs (Eds.),

Handbook of personality psychology (pp. 825–847). Orlando, FL: Academic Press.

McCrae, R. R., & Costa, P. T., Jr. (1997b). Personality trait structure as a human universal. *American Psychologist, 52,* 509–516.

McHenry, J. J., Hough, L. M., Toquam, J. L., Hanson, M. A., & Ashworth, S. (1990). Project A validity results: The relationship between predictor and criterion domains. *Personnel Psychology, 43,* 335–354.

Mischel, W., Shoda, Y., & Mendoza-Denton, R. (2002). Situation-behavior profiles as a locus of consistency in personality. *Current Directions in Psychological Science, 11,* 50–54.

Motowidlo, S. J., Borman, W. C., & Schmit, M. J. (1997). A theory of individual differences in task and contextual performance. *Human Performance, 10,* 71–83.

Mount, M. K., Barrick, M. R., & Stewart, G. L. (1998). Five-Factor Model of personality and performance in jobs involving interpersonal interactions. *Human Performance, 11,* 145–165.

Muchinsky, P. M. (1999). Applications of Holland's theory in industrial and organizational settings. *Journal of Vocational Behavior, 55,* 127–135.

Murtha, T. C., Kanfer, R., & Ackerman, P. L. (1996). Toward an interactionist taxonomy of personality and situations: An integrative situation–dispositional representation of personality traits. *Journal of Personality and Social Psychology, 71,* 913–207.

Neuman, G. A., & Wright, J. (1999). Team effectiveness: Beyond skills and cognitive ability. *Journal of Applied Psychology, 84,* 376–389.

Ones, D. S., Hough, L. M., & Viswesvaran, C. (1998, Apr.). *Validity and adverse impact of personality-based managerial potential scales.* Symposium conducted at the Thirteenth Annual Convention of the Society for Industrial and Organizational Psychology, Dallas, TX.

Ones, D. S., & Viswesvaran, C. (1996, Apr.). *What do pre-employment customer service scales measure? Explorations in construct validity and implications for personnel selection.* Paper presented at the Eleventh Annual Conference of the Society for Industrial and Organizational Psychology, San Diego, CA.

Ones, D. S., & Viswesvaran, C. (1998). Integrity testing in organizations. In R. W. Griffin, A. O'Leary-Kelly, & J. M. Collins (Eds.), *Dysfunctional behavior in organizations: Vol. 2. Nonviolent behaviors in organizations* (pp. 243–276). Greenwich, CT: JAI Press.

Ones, D. S., & Viswesvaran, C. (2001). Personality at work: Criterion-focused occupational personality scales used in personnel selection. In B. W. Roberts & R. T. Hogan (Eds.), *Personality psychology in the workplace* (pp. 63–92). Washington, DC: American Psychological Association.

Ones, D. S., Viswesvaran, C., & Reiss, A. D. (1996). Role of social desirability in personality testing for personnel selection: The red herring. *Journal of Applied Psychology, 81,* 660–679.

Ones, D. S., Viswesvaran, C., & Schmidt, F. L. (1993). Comprehensive meta-analysis of integrity test validities: Findings and implications for personnel selection and theories of job performance [Monograph]. *Journal of Applied Psychology, 78,* 679–703.

Paunonen, S. V., & Ashton, M. C. (1998). The structured assessment of personality across cultures. *Journal of Cross-Cultural Psychology, 29,* 150–170.

Penner, L. A., & Finkelstein, M. A. (1998). Dispositional and structural determinants of volunteerism. *Journal of Personality and Social Psychology, 74,* 525–537.

Penner, L. A., Fritzsche, B. A., Craiger, J. P., & Freifeld, T. S. (1995). Measuring the prosocial personality. In J. N. Butcher & C. D. Spielberger (Eds.), *Advances in personality assessment* (Vol. 10, pp. 147–163). Mahwah, NJ: Erlbaum.

Penner, L. A., Midili, A. R., & Kegglemeyer, J. (1997). Beyond job attitudes: A personality and social psychology perspective on the causes of organizational citizenship behavior. *Human Performance, 10,* 111–131.

Ployhardt, R., & Hakel, M. D. (1998). The substantive nature of performance variability: Predicting interindividual differences in intraindividual performance. *Personnel Psychology, 51,* 859–901.

Ployhart, R. E., Lim, B., & Chan, K. (2001). Exploring relations between typical and maximum performance ratings and the Five Factor Model of personality. *Personnel Psychology, 54,* 809–843.

Ployhart, R. E., & Schneider, B. (2002). A multilevel perspective on personnel selection: Implications for selection system design, assessment, and construct validation. In F. Yammarino & F. Dansereau (Eds.), *Research in multi-level issues* (Vol. 1, pp. 95–140). New York: Elsevier.

Plutchik, R. (1997). The circumplex as a general model of the structure of emotions and personality. In R. Plutchik & H. R. Conte (Eds.), *Circumplex models of personality and emotions* (pp. 17–45). Washington, DC: American Psychological Association.

Roberts, B. W., & Hogan, R. T. (Eds.). (2001). *Personality psychology in the workplace.* Washington, DC: American Psychological Association.

Robertson, I., & Callinan, M. (1998). Personality and work behaviour. *European Journal of Work and Organizational Psychology, 7,* 321–340.

Robie, C., Schmit, M. J., Ryan, A. M., & Zickar, M. J. (2000). Effects of item context specificity on the measurement equivalence of a personality inventory. *Organizational Research Methods, 3,* 348–365. Errata: (2001). *Organizational Research Methods, 4,* 84–87.

Sackett, P. R., & Ellingson, J. E. (1997). The effects of forming multi-predictor composites on group differences and adverse impact. *Personnel Psychology, 50,* 707–721.

Sackett, P. R., Zedeck, S., & Fogli, L. (1988). Relations between measures of typical and maximum job performance. *Journal of Applied Psychology, 73,* 482–486.

Salovey, P., & Mayer, J. D. (1990). Emotional intelligence. *Imagination, Cognition and Personality, 9,* 185–211.

Saucier, G., & Goldberg, L. R. (2001). Lexical studies of indigenous personality factors: Premises, products, and prospects. *Journal of Personality, 69,* 847–879.

Schimmack, U., Radhakrishnan, P., Oishi, S., Dzokoto, V., & Ahadi, S. (2002). Culture, personality, and subjective well-being: Integrating process models of life satisfaction. *Journal of Personality and Social Psychology, 82,* 582–593.

Schmidt, F. L., & Hunter, J. E. (1998). The validity and utility of selection methods in personnel psychology: Practical and theoretical implications of 85 years of research findings. *Psychological Bulletin, 124,* 262–274.

Schmidt, F. L., Hunter, J. E., & Outerbridge, A. N. (1986). Impact of job experience and ability on job knowledge, work samples performance, and supervisory ratings of job performance. *Journal of Applied Psychology, 71,* 432–439.

Schmit, M. J., Ryan, A. M., Stierwalt, S. L., & Powell, A. B. (1995). Frame-of-reference effects on personality scale scores and criterion-related validity. *Journal of Applied Psychology, 80,* 607–620.

Schneider, B. (1987). The people make the place. *Personnel Psychology, 40,* 437–454.

Schneider, B., Smith, D. B., & Sipe, W. P. (2000). Personnel selection psychology: Multilevel considerations. In K. J. Klein & S.W.J. Kozlowski (Eds.), *Multilevel theory, research and methods in organizations: Foundations, extensions, and new directions* (pp. 91–120). San Francisco: Jossey-Bass.

Schneider, R. J., Ackerman, P. L., & Kanfer, R. (1996). To "act wisely in human relations": Exploring the dimensions of social competence. *Personality and Individual Differences, 21,* 469–481.

Schneider, R. J., & Hough, L. M. (1995). Personality and industrial/organizational psychology. In C. L. Cooper & I. T. Robertson (Eds.), *International review of industrial and organizational psychology* (pp. 75–129). New York: Wiley.

Schneider, R. J., Roberts, R. D., & Heggestad, E. D. (2002). *Exploring the structure and construct validity of a self-report social competence inventory.* Symposium conducted at the Seventeenth Annual Conference of the Society for Industrial and Organizational Psychology, Toronto, Canada.

Seibert, S. E., Crant, J. M., & Kraimer, M. L. (1999). Proactive personality and career success. *Journal of Applied Psychology, 84,* 416–427.

Seibert, S. E., Kraimer, M. L., & Crant, J. M. (2001). What do proactive people do? A longitudinal model linking proactive personality and career success. *Personnel Psychology, 54,* 845–874.

Spector, P. E., & Fox, S. (2002). An emotion-centered model of voluntary work behavior: Some parallels between counterproductive work behavior (CWB) and organizational citizenship behavior (OCB). *Human Resources Management Review, 12,* 269–292.

Steiner, I. D. (1972). *Group process and productivity.* Orlando, FL: Academic Press.

Sternberg, R. J. (1985). *Beyond IQ: A triarchic theory of human intelligence.* Cambridge: Cambridge University Press.

Stewart, W. H., Jr., & Roth, P. L. (2001). Risk propensity differences between entrepreneurs and managers: A meta-analytic review. *Journal of Applied Psychology, 86,* 145–153.

Taggar, S. (2002). Individual creativity and group ability to utilize individual creative resources: A multilevel model. *Academy of Management Journal, 24,* 315–330.

Triandis, H. C., & Suh, E. M. (2002). Cultural influences on personality. *Annual Review of Psychology, 53,* 133–160.

United States of America v. City of Garland, TX. (2002). Civil Action No. 3:98-CV0307-L (N.D. Tex.).

Weiss, H. M., & Cropanzano, R. (1996). Affective events theory: A theoretical discussion of the structure, causes and consequences of affective experiences at work. In B. M. Staw & L. L. Cummings (Eds.), *Research in organizational behavior* (Vol. 18, pp. 1–74). Greenwich, CT: JAI Press.

Wiggins, J. S. (1980). Circumplex models of interpersonal behavior. In L. Wheeler (Ed.), *Review of personality and social psychology* (Vol. 1, pp. 265–294). Thousand Oaks, CA: Sage.

Wright, J. C., Lindgren, K. P., & Zakriski, A. L. (2001). Syndromal versus contextualized personality assessment: Differentiating environmental and dispositional determinants of boys' aggression. *Journal of Personality and Social Psychology, 81,* 1176–1189.

Wright, J. C., & Mischel, W. (1987). A conditional approach to dispositional constructs: The local predictability of social behavior. *Journal of Personality and Social Psychology, 53,* 1159–1177.

Wright, T. A., & Cropanzano, R. (1998). Emotional exhaustion as a predictor of job performance and voluntary turnover. *Journal of Applied Psychology, 83,* 486–493.

CHAPTER 12

Research Themes for the Future

Michael K. Mount
Murray R. Barrick
Ann Marie Ryan

If we were to choose one overarching theme that has consistently re-curred throughout this book, it is that understanding personality-related phenomena in the workplace is a very complex undertak-ing, perhaps more so than previous research has acknowledged. Most authors agree that a great deal of progress has been made in understanding the relationship of personality to work outcomes. Greater understanding of the structure of personality, coupled with meta-analytic methods for cumulating results across studies, were major reasons for these advances. The approach used in studies by Barrick and Mount (1991), Hough (1992), and Hough, Eaton, Dunnette, Kamp, and McCloy (1990), whereby the Big Five per-sonality factors (or some close variant) were related to performance criteria for different jobs, was a useful starting point. Perhaps the most important contribution of these studies is that they legitimized the study of personality and its relationship to performance. That is, after a period of about twenty-five years when personality re-search was largely absent from the industrial/organizational (I/O) psychology literature, it was once again acceptable to investigate personality-performance relationships.

However, in some respects, these studies may have oversimpli-fied the nature of the relationship between personality and performance. This may be explained partially by the fact that at that time, we were just beginning to demonstrate that personality matters at work. Thus, the overall theme that emerges in these chapters is that although we have made considerable progress, there is much left to be accomplished. Further advancements require that more complex questions and methodologies be incorporated into studies. In Chapter Eleven, Hough makes these points quite forcefully. Overall, each of the chapters provides stimulating and thought-provoking ways that we can further understand the relationship of personality to work-related criteria.

At least five other major themes resurface throughout this book. One that appears in several chapters is that researchers must give careful consideration to the meaning and relevance of specific personality traits. This construct-oriented approach to studying personality underscores the importance of assessing appropriate traits for the questions being addressed. Second, researchers need to account for mediating influences when studying relationships between personality and work-related outcomes. Third, and relatedly, researchers need to account for the moderating influences of situational factors when studying relationships between personality and outcomes. Fourth, researchers must specify with greater precision the criteria of interest. To this end, it is clear that in order for us to advance, we must develop an accepted taxonomy of performance that delineates levels and content of criterion constructs. This theme recognizes the way the lack of a classification scheme for personality traits hindered personality research more than a decade ago. Finally, researchers need to examine personality and its role with models that consider multiple levels of analysis.

Relevant Personality Constructs at the Appropriate Level

The importance of studying personality at the appropriate construct level was discussed in several chapters throughout the book (Saucier and Goldberg, Lucas and Diener, Day and Kilduff, Ryan and Kristof-Brown, and Hough in Chapters One, Two, Eight, Ten, and Eleven, respectively), albeit in somewhat different ways. Chapter One by Saucier and Goldberg was intentionally unique because it discusses progress pertaining to personality attributes and how they can best be organized and structured. The purpose in inviting these authors to contribute to this volume was to provide the I/O community of researchers with a summary of research on the structure of personality from the perspective of two leading scholars from the broader field of personality psychology. They point out that Allport (1937) reviewed definitions of the concept of personality and catalogued over fifty distinct meanings for the term. This is not a trivial issue; definitions force researchers to make explicit their assumptions, and they also influence which criterion variables will be selected. After reflecting on these comments, we were struck by how seldom researchers studying the role of personality in the workplace explicitly define personality (we count ourselves among the guilty!). The de facto approach seems to be that personality is defined as whatever constructs are measured by the inventory the researcher has chosen to use.

An important contribution of Saucier and Goldberg is that while the Big Five factor solution is robust, other factor structures emerge that may also be useful. For example, one-, two-, three-, seven-, and nine-factor solutions have also been derived. Support for the Big Five model is strong in terms of social importance, breadth, stability, cross-observer agreement, and generality across peer and self-rating data. But the Big Five compares less favorably to alternative models on criteria such as causal clarity, correspondence to main lines of biological influence, predictive validity, generalizability across cultures and languages, association with theory, and comprehensiveness.

Saucier and Goldberg also discuss a vexing problem for our field: the relative advantages of subdividing the broader factors into more specific subcomponents (facets). The problem with this approach is the difficulty in achieving consensus about how many facets there are and what they measure. An advantage of measuring subcomponents pertains to the potential gain in predictive validity, which comes from tapping into many specific sources of variance. In general, however, it appears that the more specific the level of constructs is, the more potential confusion is engendered for researchers.

The challenge for I/O psychologists becomes one of determining which structural model of personality is best for predicting work outcomes. A question we need to address is whether we have become overly reliant on the Big Five model when framing research questions. Ultimately, the appropriate personality structure or set of traits to examine depends on the intended purpose of the researcher. For example, in some situations, a one- or two-factor model of personality may be appropriate. Saucier and Goldberg note that one-factor solutions consistently yield an unrotated factor labeled Evaluation, with desirable traits at one end and undesirable traits at the other. If this factor reflects a general evaluative (desirable versus undesirable) component, it may be useful to examine how scores on this scale predict general overall performance compared to specific performance. Scullen, Mount, and Goff (2000) have shown that performance ratings capture both a general and a specific performance component associated with the particular attribute being rated. The evaluative personality factor may be a better predictor of the general performance component than of the specific performance components.

Similarly, two-factor solutions constantly yield personality traits related to positively valued dynamic qualities associated with individual ascendancy and socialization. These two factors have been alternatively labeled Agency and Communion (Bakan, 1966), Getting Ahead and Getting Along (Hogan, 1983), and Factors Beta and Alpha (Digman, 1997). Digman (1997) showed that Factor Alpha consists of the Five-Factor Model (FFM) factors of Conscientiousness, Emotional Stability, and Agreeableness, whereas Factor Beta consisted of the FFM factors of Extraversion and Openness to Experience. It may well be that the second higher-order construct, Factor Alpha, depicts a "functional personality" at work (Mount & Barrick, 1995), and emerging evidence suggests that this may be a valid predictor of overall performance across numerous occupational groups. For example, a second-order meta-analysis by Barrick, Mount, and Judge (2001) revealed that at least two of the components of Factor Alpha, Conscientiousness and Emotional Stability, predict performance across jobs. Further evidence is provided by research on employee reliability, which found that integrity test validities were generalizable ($\rho = .41$) and that these measures consisted of Conscientiousness, Emotional Stability, and Agreeableness (Ones, Viswesvaran, & Schmidt, 1993). In addition, Customer Service Orientation has been found to consist of these same three personality traits, and this composite measure again has moderately large (ρ = .50) and generalizable validity (Frei & McDaniel, 1998).

Taken together, this research illustrates there may be a functional personality at work. Those who are planful, dependable, and achievement oriented (Conscientious), as well as calm, not depressed, and confident (Emotional Stability), and those who are kind, courteous, and trusting (Agreeable) are likely to be better performers. And again, it may well be that these validities are primarily due to the underlying relationship with the common, overall performance component rather than specific performance facets.

One other example of the type of question that may focus on a higher-order structure than the Big Five has to do with the relationship between two major individual difference paradigms: personality traits and vocational interests. Prior research has shown that the RIASEC vocational interest types (Holland, 1985) can be explained by higher-order factors, similar to Factors Beta and Alpha found in the Big Five. For example, Hogan (Hogan, 1983; Hogan & Blake, 1999) argues the RIASEC vocational interest types consist of two higher-order dimensions, which he labels Conformity and Sociability. In many respects, the definitions of these two dimensions correspond closely with those provided previously for Factors Alpha and Beta. Consequently, analyses of vocational interests and personality traits at the higher-order level may show that the personality factors of Alpha and Beta have counterparts in vocational interest. Thus, when the construct that personality is being compared to is broadly defined, as are interests in the RIASEC model, the personality constructs need to be equally broad to enhance understanding. In the case of understanding structural relations between personality and vocational interests, it may be best to use a higher-order model of personality than the Big Five.

Conversely, as a number of chapters emphasize (Saucier and Goldberg in Chapter One, Johnson in Chapter Four, and Hough in Chapter Eleven), it is likely to be appropriate and even necessary to use a lower-level model of personality than the Big Five when the goal is to enhance understanding about the relationship between personality and specific performance facets rather than to predict overall performance. That is, to examine how personality relates to specific performance components, there is likely to be value in assessing equally specific personality traits. The same might also be said of other outcomes discussed in this book (affect, counterproductivity, team processes, social relations, and learning in, respectively, Chapters Five through Nine) in that greater specificity in the criterion may warrant greater specificity in the personality construct. Indeed, Day and Kilduff (in Chapter Eight) eschew the Big Five and focus on the role of self-monitoring in dyadic relations. However, the field will be advanced more quickly if there were a widely accepted classification scheme for facets of personality available for researchers to use fully.

The importance of studying personality-related phenomena at the appropriate construct level is also illustrated in Chapter Two pertaining to relationships between worker happiness and productivity. Lucas and Diener recommend that researchers who are interested in studying subjective feelings of well-being and happiness focus on one or more of four separable components of happiness at work. The first two components are positive affect and negative affect, which refer to a person's affective well-being. The third and fourth components refer to cognitive judgments about one's satisfaction with one's life and satisfaction with one's job. This distinction is important because a single worker could be simultaneously high on positive affect, average on negative affect, low on life satisfaction, and average on job satisfaction. Lucas and Diener contend, as do several other authors (Barrick, Mitchell, and Stewart in Chapter Three; Johnson in Chapter Four; Cullen and Sackett in Chapter Six; Ford and Oswald in Chapter Nine; and Hough in Chapter Eleven), that challenges in understanding these relationships are increased given the multiple ways that productivity is defined, ranging from objective measures (including worker output, efficiency, turnover, and absenteeism) to subjective ratings of performance, potential, counterproductivity, and citizenship. Thus, in order to understand worker happiness, it is critical that the individual difference measure matches the criterion of interest.

Mediators and Moderators of Personality

The second and third themes that emerge across several chapters are that we must account more fully for the mediating influences of motivational processes and the moderating influences of situational factors if we are to understand how personality relates to workplace behavior and affect. These two themes, discussed by Barrick et al. (Chapter Three), Johnson (Chapter Four), Cullen and Sackett (Chapter Six), Stewart (Chapter Seven), Ford and Oswald (Chapter Nine), and Hough (Chapter Eleven), present new sets of challenges for researchers. For example, Barrick et al. propose that cognitive-motivational work intentions must be accounted for as an explanatory mechanism for why personality traits are associated with high levels of work performance. They focus on the role of three motivational components or personal strivings, which they define as specific means of attaining desired end states. Accomplishment striving is cognitively accessible as representing intentions to exert effort and work hard, communion striving refers to getting along with others, and status striving refers to gaining power and refers to getting ahead of others. These three cognitive-motivational intentions or strivings are proposed as a core set of higher-order goals that regulate behavior at work. Consequently, an important contribution of this chapter is that it provides a theoretical model for understanding how cognitive-motivational intentions link personality and outcomes.

Johnson (Chapter Four) also discusses the need to understand mediating variables through which personality influences performance. He illustrates how different personality variables influence different components of motivation, which in turn influence different components of performance. An important contribution of this chapter is the discussion of three components of motivation: motives, proactive cognitive processes, and on-line cognitive processes. Motives include variables such as job attitudes (for example, organizational citizenship behaviors, job satisfaction, and organization commitment), as well as the three cognitive-motivational intentions discussed by Barrick et al. Proactive processes include motivational constructs such as self-efficacy, expectancy, and goal setting. On-line cognitive processes refer to the translation of intention to action. Johnson's view is that a complete understanding of motivation requires consideration of all three categories of motivation. The common theme of the chapters by Barrick et al. and Johnson is that self-regulatory processes represented by motivation are important mediators of relations between personality and performance, and previous research has inadequately accounted for their effects. As Johnson states, self-regulatory processes are important for several reasons. They are strongly related to personality, they help explain how people overcome habits, and they account for situations where those with similar ability, knowledge, goals, and desires differ in their performance levels.

Other chapters also suggest mediational links between personality and criteria of interest. For example, Cullen and Sackett (Chapter Six) discuss how a motivational variable (a motive to comply with norms) might be a mediator between personality and counterproductive work behaviors, but they also discuss attitudinal and affective constructs as potential mediators of these relations. The complexity of their model reflects the complexity of the influence of personality on work behavior.

In proposing and examining mediational processes in these models, we think Weiss and Kurek's admonishment in Chapter Five is important to consider: a productive analysis will tie together existing constructs (for example, well-accepted personality traits and well-accepted motivational constructs) rather than create new individual difference measures. Furthermore, we note the ongoing discussion in the self-regulatory literature of considering motivational individual differences, such as goal orientation, as traits or as states. Models that explain personality as operating through motivational processes will eventually need to clarify whether the influence is on motivational traits or motivational states.

The theme that situations must be more fully accounted for as moderators of the personality-motivation and personality-performance relationships is present in a number of chapters as well. In the Barrick et al. model in Chapter Three, situational influences moderate the relationship between the three cognitive-motivational intentions and personality-performance relationships. Examples include whether the job involves cooperative or competitive demands and the degree of autonomy in the job. In the Johnson model in Chapter Four, situational moderators that can influence the magnitude of personality-performance relationships include situational strength, occupation, time on the job, and autonomy. Hough's discussion in Chapter Eleven focuses on the effects of situations such as type of task, type of team, type of job, culture, research setting, and fit. Regardless of the specific type of situation, the theme across these chapters is that situational factors are important because they influence both which traits will be expressed and how they will be expressed.

To determine which set of personality traits and behavioral criteria is particularly important in a specific job, it is apparent today that we need to consider the situation thoroughly. Although job analysts have long assessed situational attributes of the job, many of the authors in this book call for a different approach. For example, Ford and Oswald (Chapter Nine) discuss the role of the types of contexts in which the learner is placed. Thus, training researchers need to consider such situational characteristics as level of supervisory and peer support, the role of a positive work climate, and the strength of the situation (referred to as situational press). However, they also emphasize the dynamic nature of the situation in recognizing that people can choose whether to attend training or what type of training to attend. They also propose a new perspective on the viability of accounting for person-by-situation effects. Furthermore, in Chapter Seven, Stewart demonstrates that one can also consider a work group as a dynamic context, in that members of the group exert change on the situation over time. The chapters in this book highlight the necessity of thinking about a person's traits and their effects within contexts that are not static and that can even be changed because a person with those traits is in situations that are rapidly changing. That is, the situation influences a person's behavior, but people also influence situations.

Given the importance of the situation for understanding the role of personality on work-related outcomes, how can we characterize situational variables to obtain consistency across studies? In Chapter Three, Barrick et al. approach the development of a taxonomy of situational features by focusing on one key aspect of work: the social setting. They argue that people spend considerable time in social situations, and how effectively we navigate these settings has considerable impact on our success and well-being. Furthermore, personality traits are likely to be important predictors of how we function in social settings (Barrick, Stewart, Neubert, & Mount, 1998). Based on this reasoning, there seems to be considerable value in examining whether the person's "personality" interacts with how work is coordinated and controlled, when predicting behavior. Another approach, advocated by Hough in Chapter Eleven, suggests that Holland's RIASEC (Realistic, Investigative, Artistic, Social, Enterprising, Conventional) model may be a meaningful way to describe the "psychological" characteristics of a work setting. Such an approach underscores the importance of the attributes of the people in the situation. Both Chapters Three and Eleven suggest a different perspective on assessing the situation than traditional job-analytic approaches that focus on the importance of the things people do on the job. Many other chapters in this book contain expanded thinking about the situation or propose novel ways to assess contextual influences.

Specification of Criteria

A fourth theme that runs throughout nearly all of the chapters in this book is the need for greater explication of the criterion that researchers are interested in predicting. I/O psychologists are interested in personality because it predicts what we feel and do (that is, our behavior) at work. To deepen our understanding of personality at work, researchers must adopt a behavioral focus. Ironically, although we are now giving more thought to which specific personality traits are relevant in a work setting, there is considerably less theoretical or empirical work focused on which behaviors we are interested in predicting with personality constructs and why. The authors in this book have implicitly and explicitly recognized this criterion problem and thus have developed a number of propositions about ways in which personality traits are likely to affect how people perform and what activities involve them. More important, a careful reading of this book would help identify the basic kinds of behaviors and what ways are useful for assessing them. Thus, many of these behaviors are likely to be fundamental components of any behavioral taxonomy at work. Although we do not propose such a taxonomy here, the chapters in this book review many of the important components that such a model would have to consider.

Job performance is obviously an important indicator of the value of an employee's behavior because it indicates the overall value of his or her contributions to the organization. Furthermore, selection decisions tend to rely on a composite measure of individual performance. For this reason, a measure of overall performance dominates many of the models discussed here, such as those by Barrick et al. (Chapter Three) and Johnson (Chapter Four). However, as these authors and others make clear, overall performance is not the only important outcome or set of behaviors. For instance, Lucas and Diener (Chapter Two) focus on worker happiness, Weiss and Kurek (Chapter Five) highlight affective experiences, Cullen and Sackett (Chapter Six) illustrate the importance of counterproductive workplace behavior, and Ford and Oswald (Chapter Nine) discuss the learning and training performance of the dynamic learner.

This book also goes beyond these innovative ways of thinking about more traditional outcomes by examining a number of other criteria that are also worthy of consideration. For example, Ryan and Kristof-Brown (Chapter Ten) emphasize the nature and importance of the fit between individuals and the job, group, or organization, while Stewart (Chapter Seven) focuses on the fundamental role of personality in work team outcomes. Day and Kilduff (Chapter Eight) also underscore the importance of social networks and encourage researchers to examine the individual's skill in monitoring and managing relationships in groups and organizations. Johnson (Chapter Four) and Hough (Chapter Eleven) identify other fundamentally important behavioral variables at work, including career success, job and life satisfaction, safety, conflict attributions, workplace aggression, leadership, adaptive performance, and adaptability to change.

In short, development and evaluation of models emphasizing behavioral criteria will provide an essential step toward a greater scientific understanding about how personality influences success at work. We believe that valid measurement of behaviors that lead to or detract from important organizational outcomes will significantly enhance the contributions that personality research can make to the broader field of psychology. Furthermore, clearly identifying and defining the outcomes we are trying to predict should enable us to make better selection decisions. For example, Cullen and Sackett (Chapter Six) explicate the covariance structure of counterproductive work behaviors and their relations to organizational citizenship behaviors and contextual performance; knowing how specific outcomes we are interested in relate to one another will enable a clearer understanding of personality's influence.

Another way to think about outcomes is to evaluate the role of personality using two critical questions: "Are you able to do it?" and "Are you happy doing it?" Research on personality in work settings tends to focus on the former question (satisfactoriness) rather than the latter (satisfaction). Thus, today we have greater understanding of how personality relates to satisfactoriness or performance at work. And yet it is also important to consider how personality affects life and job satisfaction and other affective constructs, as Lucas and Diener (Chapter Two) and Weiss and Kurek (Chapter Five) attest. Recent meta-analyses illustrate that personality traits, particularly Emotional Stability, Extraversion, and Conscientiousness, are important predictors of job satisfaction (Judge, Heller, & Mount, 2002) and different facets of subjective well-being (DeNeve & Cooper, 1998). Similarly, in this book, Lucas and Diener (Chapter Two) review findings related to worker happiness and productivity. To illustrate this further, they show that happy workers have many benefits when interacting with the world, but the impact of these individual differences on worker productivity depends on the nature of the tasks the workers perform. Happy workers may be more talkative and friendly, but whether this affects work outcomes depends on the nature of the tasks performed. Another recent meta-analysis (Barrick, Mount, & Gupta, in press) reveals that although personality traits (the FFM) share some common variance with interests (the RIASEC), the two sets of dispositional measures are not as highly correlated as we might expect. This finding underscores the need to examine the unique effects of personality on satisfaction and other affective variables.

Lucas and Diener (Chapter Two), Weiss and Kurek (Chapter Five), and Hough (Chapter Eleven) discuss a number of different ways researchers might approach the question regarding the nature of the relationship between personality and satisfaction or affect. Weiss and Kurek's emphasis on striving to understand the process through which personality influences the generation of emotional change, as well as the consequence of these behavioral and emotional changes, is particularly promising and is likely to lead to a number of fruitful scientific inquiries. As researchers, we need to recognize that only when there is a high degree of correspondence achieved on both of these dimensions—that is, we are both happy and effective at work—will we maximize benefits for both individuals and organizations. For these reasons, satisfaction and affect, in addition to satisfactoriness, are important issues for future research to address.

Personality in Multilevel Theories

A final theme that is apparent across a number of chapters in this book is recognition of the increasing examination of the role of personality in organizational life across multiple levels of analysis. Explicit examples can be found in Stewart's chapter (Chapter Seven) on the multilevel role of personality in teams, Hough's discussion of group-level personality predictor variables in Chapter Eleven, Day and Kilduff's discussion in Chapter Eight of self-monitoring and dyadic work relationships, and Ryan and Kristof-Brown's discussion in Chapter Ten of organizational personality in person-organization fit research. But multiple levels of analysis also enter into the models presented in many other chapters (Lucas and Diener in Chapter Two, Barrick et al. in Chapter Three, Johnson in Chapter Four, Cullen and Sackett in Chapter Six, and Ford and Oswald in Chapter Nine), as many of the situational antecedents and other moderators proposed in their models are group-level or organizational-level characteristics of environments. Thus, this book makes clear that the traditional focus on the individual level, which permeates research on personality and work, is being supplanted with a richer understanding of personality and work that incorporates multilevel theorizing.

What are the implications of incorporating multiple levels into our theories and research on personality and work? Kozlowski and Klein (2000) noted, "Virtually all organizational phenomena are embedded in a higher-level context, which often has either direct or moderating effects on lower-level processes and outcomes. Relevant contextual features and effects from the higher level should be incorporated into theoretical models" (p. 15). This principle is applied in a number of the models presented in this book. Lucas and Diener (Chapter Two) mention the nature of the job as a moderator of the happy worker–productive worker hypothesis, Barrick et al. (Chapter Three) discuss cooperative and competitive demands, Johnson (Chapter Four) mentions situational moderators of individual motives to individual performance links, Cullen and Sackett (Chapter Six) mention organizational events, Stewart (Chapter Seven) discusses the team setting as a moderator between individual traits and individual performance, Day and Kilduff (Chapter Eight) discuss features of networks, Ford and Oswald (Chapter Nine) consider learning situations, and Ryan and Kristof-Brown (Chapter Ten) relate how organizational features result in individual complementary fit assessments. It is clear that no formulation of the effects of personality in work settings, even on individual-level outcome variables (such as learning, counterproductivity, or performance), should leave out a consideration of the influence of the higher-level context. As we have already noted, researchers in the area of personality and work must avoid simplistic theorizing and embrace models that contain concepts at multiple levels.

Another principle of multilevel theory building stated by Kozlowski and Klein (2000) is that "conceptualization of emergent phenomena at higher levels should specify, theoretically, the nature and form of these bottom-up emergent processes" (p. 18). In the area of personality and work, one example of these processes occurs when assessing the personality of a team or an organization. Ryan and Kristof-Brown (Chapter Ten) noted the problems of conceptualizing the "personality of the organization," and Hough (Chapter Eleven) mentions the difficulty of operationalizing higher-level predictors such as dyadic levels of extraversion. Day and Kilduff (Chapter Eight) provide an illustration of how one might examine the role of personality in the formation and maintenance of dyadic relations in their chapter on self-monitoring and social networks. Stewart (Chapter Seven) also tackles this difficult task and provides a detailed discussion of team-level personality and a genetic analogy to describe the possible nature of the processes by which a team-level trait might be formed. In order for our understanding of the attraction-selection-attrition model, social network formation, and team composition effects to advance, such conceptualization is critical.

Multilevel theories generally recognize the concept of bond strength (Simon, 1973)—that relationships across levels are greater for more proximal levels. As Ryan and Kristof-Brown (Chapter Ten) note, it may be more fruitful to pursue the notion of personality fit at the team or group level than at the organizational level because more proximal levels are being connected. Stewart (Chapter Seven) illustrates this by providing a good rationale for cross-level linkages between personality and performance at the individual and group levels. Similarly, Day and Kilduff (Chapter Eight) discuss the complexity of considerations at the dyadic level that underlies social network analysis. It may thus be more fruitful to focus research resources toward understanding the role of personality in predicting dyadic or group-level phenomena than organizational-level outcomes.

Multilevel theories must also consider how effects are manifested over time (Kozlowski & Klein, 2000). The effects of individual personality on dyadic, group-level, and organizational outcomes are not likely to occur quickly. For example, a change in the personality composition of a team may not have immediate effects on team coordination, productivity, or other group-level outcomes but may have considerable long-term effects on these same variables. One implication for many of the issues presented in this book is that future research must examine the role of personality over long time periods. For example, research in groups or organizations must allow sufficient time to pass so that the effects of personality are allowed to emerge. This may mean that the study of personality and dyadic or group-level or organizational-level phenomena necessitates longitudinal or time-series designs.

Kozlowski and Klein (2000) noted the importance of a sampling strategy that allows for between-unit variability at all relevant levels of the model if one wishes to test a multilevel theory adequately. Thus, assessing the role of team personality or organizational personality requires sampling to ensure variability across the range of personality combinations that one would expect at that level. Furthermore, it suggests that sampling for variability in situational determinants of personality (such as cooperative or competitive demands) is also of importance.

In conclusion, several of the chapters in this book recognize that we must expand our theories of personality and work outcomes to be truly multilevel theories. This will include operationalizing concepts at multiple levels, specifying emergent processes, and hypothesizing cross-level relationships. In short, future research on personality and work must take a multilevel focus.

Applications

Although much of what is presented in this book is based on applied research in the workplace, there is not a specific chapter on practical applications of research on personality in organizations. We believe that issues related to application such as cross-cultural equivalency of measures, socially desirable responding, applicant perceptions of personality inventories, and the like are certainly important, but our focus here is on understanding the role of personality in work-related behaviors and affective responses to work rather than on how personality can or should be assessed for work-related applications. Nevertheless, we believe that this book does speak volumes about considerations in assessing personality for personnel decision making and organizational intervention purposes.

One example is in the area of employee selection. Recent research has highlighted the utility of personality in predicting valued outcomes in organizations (for example, less counterproductive behavior, higher quality and quantity of performance, and lower likelihood to withdraw), as well as obtaining more diverse hiring (that is, low disparate impact). Although this book does not have a chapter dedicated to selection issues, many, if not all, of the chapters address the implications that personality has for the practice of hiring.

For example, Barrick et al. (Chapter Three) note that higher performance can be obtained across all jobs if one hires employees who are highly conscientious and emotionally stable, but whether other personality traits (Extraversion, Agreeableness, and Openness to Experience) result in higher performance depends on whether these traits are relevant to the actual job activities. Hough (Chapter Eleven) illustrates that although Openness to Experience has not been found to be relevant to performance at work, facets of Openness are likely to be relevant to outcomes related to the increasing diversity and rapid change of the workplace.

Also, several chapters imply a fundamentally different approach to selection than that typically conducted. For example, the chapter on fit (Chapter Ten, by Ryan & Kristof-Brown) emphasizes the idea that whom an organization hires may depend on who is currently in the job, group, or organization. Similarly, Stewart's discussion of teams in Chapter Seven recognizes that the role of personality is more complex in such situations because the effect obtained from personality traits may be dependent on the personality of other employees in the work environment. Consequently, a team composed entirely of extraverted members is likely to be less effective than a team composed of members varying on extraversion (some extraverted and some introverted members). As a field, we have not thought these implications through sufficiently, and these chapters provide guidance regarding ways to proceed in examining these novel yet critical selection issues. We think similar analyses of the content of the book would provide insights for other applications where personality must be assessed in the workplace.

Conclusion

The overarching theme of this book is that future theoretical and empirical work investigating the role of personality at work requires a complex analysis of the person, the situation, and behaviors. To reflect this complexity fully, researchers will have to incorporate one or more of the themes discussed in this chapter. A critical theme is that future research must take a construct-oriented perspective of the personality trait and give careful consideration to the appropriate hierarchical level. A second theme necessary to advance research is to explain the mechanism through which distal personality traits affect performance outcomes at work. As suggested here, motivational processes are likely to serve as important mediators of these relationships. Third, the context within which these variables are related will play a crucial role in determining the magnitude of the relationship, particularly for those traits (such as Extraversion, Agreeableness, and Openness to Experience) that have consistently been found to have contingent relationships with performance. Fourth, researchers must attend more thoughtfully and systematically to the criterion of interest. Fifth, we need to give careful consideration to the appropriate level of analysis of many of these variables, including the situation and motivational processes. It is difficult to find an example of research on personality and work that would not be enhanced by incorporating one or more of these themes. Consequently, to advance the field significantly beyond our present understanding, future studies must address one or more of these themes in a complex way.

References

Allport, G. W. (1937). *Personality: A psychological interpretation.* New York: Holt.

Bakan, D. (1966). *The duality of human existence: Isolation and communion in Western man.* Boston: Beacon Press.

Barrick, M. R., & Mount, M. R. (1991). The Big Five personality dimensions and job performance. *Personnel Psychology, 44,* 1–26.

Barrick, M. R., Mount, M. K., & Gupta, R. (in press). Meta-analysis of the relationship between the Five-Factor Model of personality and Holland's occupational types. *Personnel Psychology.*

Barrick, M. R., Mount, M. K., & Judge, T. A. (2001). The FFM personality dimensions and job performance: Meta-analysis of meta-analyses. *International Journal of Selection and Assessment, 9,* 9–30.

Barrick, M. R., Stewart, G. L., Neubert, M., & Mount, M. K. (1998). Relating member ability and personality to work team processes and team effectiveness. *Journal of Applied Psychology, 83,* 377–391.

DeNeve, K. M., & Cooper, H. (1998). The happy personality: A meta-analysis of 137 personality traits and subjective well-being. *Psychological Bulletin, 124,* 197–229.

Digman, J. M. (1997). Higher-order factors of the Big Five. *Journal of Personality and Social Psychology, 73,* 1246–1256.

Frei, R. L., & McDaniel, M. A. (1998). Validity of customer service measures in personnel selection: A review of criterion and construct evidence. *Human Performance, 11,* 1–27.

Hogan, R. (1983). Socioanalytic theory of personality. In M. M. Page (Ed.), *1982 Nebraska symposium on motivation: Personality—Current theory and research* (pp. 55–89). Lincoln: University of Nebraska Press.

Hogan, R., & Blake, R. (1999). John Holland's vocational typology and personality theory. *Journal of Vocational Behavior, 55,* 41–56.

Holland, J. L. (1985). *Manual for the self-directed search.* Odessa, FL: Psychological Assessment Resources.

Hough, L. M. (1992). The "Big Five" personality variables–construct confusion: Description versus prediction. *Human Performance, 5,* 139–155.

Hough, L. M., Eaton, N. K., Dunnette, M. D., Kamp, J. D., & McCloy, R. A. (1990). Criterion-related validities of personality constructs and the effect of response distortion on those validities. *Journal of Applied Psychology, 75,* 581–595.

Judge, T. A., Heller, D., & Mount, M. K. (2001). Five-Factor Model of personality and job satisfaction: A meta-analysis. *Journal of Applied Psychology, 87,* 530–541.

Kozlowski, S.W.J., & Klein, K. J. (2000). A multilevel approach to theory and research in organizations: Contextual, temporal, and emergent processes. In K. J. Klein & S.W.J. Kozlowski (Eds.), *Multilevel theory, research, and methods in organizations: foundations, extensions, and new directions* (pp. 3–90). San Francisco: Jossey-Bass.

Mount, M. K., & Barrick, M. R. (1995). The Big Five personality dimensions: Implications for research and practice in human resource management. *Research in Personnel and Human Resources Management, 13,* 153–200.

Ones D. S., Viswesvaran C., & Schmidt F. L. (1993). Comprehensive meta-analysis of integrity test validities—findings and implications for personnel-selection and theories of job-performance. *Journal of Applied Psychology, 78,* 679–703.

Scullen, S. E., Mount, M. K., & Goff, M. (2000). Understanding the latent structure of job performance. *Journal of Applied Psychology, 85,* 956–970.

Simon, H. A. (1973). The organization of complex systems. In H. H. Pattee (Ed.), *Hierarchy theory* (pp. 1–27). New York: Braziller.

Name Index

Kasser, T., 65
Katigbak, M. S., 7
Kay, P., 6, 15
Keefe, D. E., 141
Kegelmeyer, J., 103, 298
Kelley, H. H., 207
Kelloway, E. K., 153
Keltner, D., 37
Kemeny, M. E., 43
Kenny, D. A., 220, 279
Kenrick, D. T., 69, 186, 194
Keon, T. L., 268, 275
Kernan, M. C., 105
Kerr, N., 37
Ketelaar, T., 137, 167
Kets de Vries, M.F.R., 189
Kiers, H., 158
Kiesler, D. J., 16
Kihlstrom, J. F., 299
Kiker, D. S., 99
Kilcullen, R. N., 245
Kilduff, M., 205, 209, 210, 211, 214,
    218, 220, 222
Killen, P. J., 162
Kim, Y., 65
King, L. A., 36, 37
Kinney, D. K., 46
Kirby, L. D., 134, 139, 140
Kirkman, B. L., 305
Kitayama, S., 70
Klawsky, J. D., 311
Klein, H. J., 105, 281
Klein, K. J., 188, 193, 198, 338, 339, 340
Kleinmann, M., 312
Klimoski, R., 234, 302, 305
Kluger, A. N., 298
Knapp, D. J., 290
Kohler, S. S., 45
Köler, O., 312
Koles, K. L., 247
Konovsky, M. A., 166
Kouzes, J. M., 264
Kozlowski, S.W.J., 188, 193, 198, 251,
    338, 339, 340
Krackhardt, D., 206, 209, 211, 212,
    213, 214, 217, 218, 219
Kraiger, K., 231

Kraimer, M. L., 205, 211, 266, 298
Kramer, G. P., 47
Kristof, A. L., 263, 264
Kristof-Brown, A. L., 262, 263, 264,
    266, 267, 270, 274, 277, 279
Kuhl, J., 102, 105, 106
Kuhlman, D. M., 158
Kulik, C. T., 64, 169
Kuncel, N. R., 236, 247
Kuptsch, C., 312
Kurek, K. E., 121, 129, 137
Kwun, S. K., 128

L

Labianca, G., 216
Laczo, R., 152
Lance, C. E., 99
Landy, F. J., 30
LaRocco, J. M., 169
Larsen, R. J., 131, 135, 137, 140, 141,
    143, 167
Larson, L. M., 301
Latack, J. C., 275
Latham, G. P., 65
Lau, C., 269
Lauver, K. J., 262, 263, 303
Lazarsfeld, P. F., 221
Lazarus, R. S., 134, 173
Le, B., 129
Leach, J., 298
Ledford, G. E., Jr., 32
Lee, C., 73
Lee, K., 7, 9, 302
Leggett, E. L., 139, 243
Lehto, A. T., 253
Leiter, M. P., 172
Leong, F.T.I., 264
LePine, J. A., 90, 97, 185, 186, 200,
    233, 280, 281, 304, 309
Leslie, J. B., 93
Levin, I., 127, 128, 170
Levinson, D. J., 197
Lewis, M., 302
Liden, R. C., 205, 211
Liebler, A., 279
Lim, B., 297
Lindgren, K. P., 311

Subject Index

A

Abridged Big Five-Dimensional Circumplex (AB5C model), 17

Absenteeism, and worker happiness, 39, 44–45, 52

Accomplishment Striving: and Conscientiousness and Emotional Stability, 67–68, 76, 78; defined, 66; as psychological motive, 104

Adaptability: and person-organization (PO) fit, 279–282; relationship between personality variables and, 96–97

Adaptive performance, 91, 93, 95

Affect: approaches for linking personality to, 130–133; as component of worker happiness, 31–32; disconnect between personality and, 125–126; momentary variability of, 122–125; as predictor variable, 302–303; process of generating, 133–135; research on personality and, 126–130; as state, 122. *See also* Negative affect; Positive affect

Affective dispositions, 32

Agreeableness: and context, 73–74; cooperation's relationship to, 71–72; facets of, 86; and personal striving, 68, 74; relationship between job performance and, 60, 63, 64, 68, 71–72, 73–74, 84; and teams, 184, 185, 193–194

American Society of Training and Development, 254

Aptitude-treatment interaction (ATI): and motivation to learn, 233–234; when to consider, 247–249

Attitudes: job, relationship between personality variables and, 103; toward counterproductive workplace behaviors (CWBs), 159–164

Attraction-selection-attrition (ASA) model of organizational behavior, 221–222

Autonomy: effect on job performance by teams, 186–187, 197; effect on personality-performance link, 72–73

B

Behavioral signatures, 238

Big Five factor structure. *See* Five-Factor Model (FFM)

Big Five personality traits: facets of, 14, 16, 86–87, 189; and Holland's RIASEC personality types, 301–302; of individual team members, 184–186; and job performance by teams, 184–186, 189–191, 193–195; and learning, 233, 240; listed, 7, 60, 86–87; person-organization (PO) fit and, 267–268, 279, 281; as predictor variables, 300; as predictors of counterproductive workplace behaviors (CWBs), 153–154; relationship between cognitive processes and, 104–106;

NEO-PI-R. *See* Revised NEO Personality Inventory (NEO-PI-R)

O

Openness to Experience: facets of, 87; importance of, as predictor variable, 300; relationship between job performance and, 60, 63, 64, 84; and teams, 184

Organizational citizenship behaviors (OCBs): and counterproductive workplace behaviors (CWBs), 152–153; distinction between contextual performance and, 89; motives for engaging in, 103–104

Organizational events, perception of, and counterproductive workplace behaviors (CWBs), 168–175

P

Perceived injustice, individual perceptions of, and counterproductive workplace behaviors (CWBs), 169–175

Performance: adaptive, 91, 93, 95; citizenship, 89–91, 93, 94–95, 96; contextual, 89; managerial, 92; task, 89, 93, 94, 96. *See also* Job performance; Personality-performance link

Performance variables: group-level, 296; individual-level, 295–296

Person-by-situation effects, on learning, 235–236

Person-organization (PO) fit: accuracy of self-perceptions of, 277–279, 282; adaptability and, 279–282; defined, 262; good and bad, 271–277, 282; methods of assessing, 267–269; relevance of, 263–271, 282

Personal strivings: effect on personality-performance relationships, 67–68, 74, 76; toward goals, 64–66

Personality: and affect, 126–133; defined, 1–2, 328; mediators and

moderators of, 331–335; models of effects of, in teams, 198–201; as moderator between organizational events and counterproductive workplace behaviors (CWBs), 168–175; in multilevel theories, 313–314, 338–340

Personality models: criteria for comparative evaluation of, 20–21; dominant, 231–232; employed in personnel selection, 314–315, 341–342; lexical approach to, 5–13; subcomponents (facets) in, 13–20, 86–87, 328; taxonomic approach to, 3–4; variable selection for, 2–6; varying number of factors in, 7–13, 328–330. *See also* Personality variables

Personality traits: attitudes toward CWBs determined by, 159–164; and context, 69–74; counterproductive workplace behaviors (CWBs) determined by, 157–159; distal, relationship between job performance and, 64–66; group-level, 188–198, 303–304; of individual team members, 184–188; learning and, 232–234, 238–244; moods linked to, 165–167; non–Big Five, as predictor variables, 301–303; and personal strivings, 67–68; as predictors of counterproductive workplace behaviors (CWBs), 153–157; of teams, 188–198, 303–304. *See also* Big Five personality traits; Personality variables

Personality variables: future research on, 309–314; history of, 289–291; measuring, 310–313; in models of job performance, 292–294; multilevel perspective on, 313–314; in personnel selection systems, 314–315, 341–342; as predictor variables, 298–304; relationship between adaptability and, 96–97;